The Politics of Gender in Colonial Korea

ASIA PACIFIC MODERN

Takashi Fujitani, Series Editor

The Politics of Gender in Colonial Korea

Education, Labor, and Health,
1910–1945

Theodore Jun Yoo

UNIVERSITY OF CALIFORNIA PRESS

Berkeley   Los Angeles   London

University of California Press, one of the most distinguished
university presses in the United States, enriches lives around
the world by advancing scholarship in the humanities, social
sciences, and natural sciences. Its activities are supported by
the UC Press Foundation and by philanthropic contributions
from individuals and institutions. For more information, visit
www.ucpress.edu.

University of California Press
Berkeley and Los Angeles, California

University of California Press, Ltd.
London, England

Library of Congress Cataloging-in-Publication Data

Yoo, Theodore Jun, 1972–
    The politics of gender in colonial Korea : education,
    labor, and health, 1910–1945 / Theodore Jun Yoo.
        p.   cm.—(Asia Pacific modern : 3)
    Includes bibliographical references and index.
    ISBN 978-0-520-25288-2 (cloth : alk. paper)
        1. Women—Korea—Social conditions—20th
    century.   2. Korea—History—Japanese occupation,
    1910–1945.   3. Sex role—Korea—History—20th
    century.   I. Title.
    HQ1765.5.Y644   2008
    305.48'895700904—dc22   2007040017

Manufactured in the United States of America

17   16   15   14   13   12   11   10   09   08
10   9   8   7   6   5   4   3   2   1

This book is printed on New Leaf EcoBook 50, a 100%
recycled fiber of which 50% is de-inked post-consumer
waste, processed chlorine-free. EcoBook 50 is acid-free
and meets the minimum requirements of ANSI/ASTM
D5634-01 (*Permanence of Paper*). ♾

CONTENTS

ILLUSTRATIONS

ACKNOWLEDGMENTS

To my parents, Min Chul Yoo and Suk Za Yoo, "amesegënallo" for your love, encouragement, and support. To my sister ChaeRan Freeze and brother-in-law Gregory Freeze, "A sheynem dank!" I would not have been able to complete this book without your support and daily encouragement.

I would like to express my sincere thanks to my mentors at Chicago, Professors Bruce Cumings, Prasenjit Duara, and Tetsuo Najita, whose training and unstinting support have contributed immensely to this project. They have guided me through my intellectual peregrinations, and I will always be grateful. I also owe a particular debt of gratitude to Professor Anne Walthall for her constant encouragement and valuable advice throughout the years.

At various stages of this project, I have benefited tremendously from the assistance of friends and colleagues. I owe a special thanks to Professor Takashi Fujitani for taking an interest in my work and for his thoughtful, perceptive reading of the entire manuscript and valuable recommendations for revisions. During the revision process, Professor Tani Barlow offered detailed comments on several chapters. Many others have contributed ideas and encouragement; they include Nancy Abelmann, Hyaeweol Choi, Kyeong-hee Choi, Henry Em, Chong-myong Im, Joy Kim, Suzy Kim, Sho Konishi, Tong Lam, Namhee Lee, Michael

McMillan, Louise McReynolds, Robert Oppenheimer, Andre Schmid, Jun Uchida, and Sakurai Yuki. I am particularly grateful to Kathy Ragsdale, who edited and polished the text. I also owe a special thanks to Jinsook Park, Michael Han, and Maiko Kawanishi for looking over my romanization.

I would like to also thank Professors Chang Pil-hwa, Cho Hyoung, Jin-sook Park, and Sin Yong-suk in Korea for their support and taking extra time out during their busy schedules to meet with me. I am also grateful to the Korean Women's Institute and Center for Women's Studies in Asia at Ewha Womans University for providing me with an institutional affiliation. I would also like to thank Ahn Tae-yoon, Han Seung-hee, Kim Chung-hui, Lee Euna, Noh Song-suk, Won Mi-hye, Yoo Seung-hye, and Yoon Hye-rin for their hospitality and friendship. I am especially grateful to Yi Hui-sun for helping me photocopy hundreds of articles. Thanks to Eizaburo Okuizumi at the University of Chicago, Seunghi Paek and Sumiko Ando at Harvard-Yenching, and Michiko Kitsmiller at the Library of Congress for helping me locate materials.

I would like to extend my thanks to all my colleagues in the history department at the University of Hawai'i at Mānoa for their generosity and encouragement. I wish to especially thank Professors Jerry Bentley, Margot Henriksen, Peter Hoffenberg, Karen Jolly, and Herbert Ziegler for introducing me to world history. The experience of teaching world history has enriched my perspective on Korean history and has helped me to place my work into a broader, comparative context. Many thanks to Gwen Agina, Susan Abe, Margaret Hattori, and Linda Miyashiro for helping me out with administrative duties.

I had the opportunity to present earlier versions of chapters at several workshops and conferences. For their many suggestions, I thank the participants at the Association of Asian Studies Conference, Sin Fronteras: Women's Histories, Global Conversations, Thirteenth Berkshire Conference on the History of Women, Posco International Symposium on Korean Studies, East Asian Studies Talk Series at the University of Texas Austin, and Korean Studies Colloquium Series at the University of Michigan.

Financial assistance for my research was generously provided by the Northeast Asia Council of the Association for Asian Studies, the University of Hawai'i Summer Research Fund, the University of Hawai'i Department of History Idus Newby Award, the Bernadotte E. Schmidt Grant of the American Historical Association, the Fulbright-Hays Doctoral Dissertation Research Abroad Program Grant, the Center for East Asian Studies Dissertation Grant at the University of Chicago, the Asada Eiji Travel Grant, the Harvard-Yenching Travel Grant, and the William Rainey Harper Dissertation Writing Grant.

I have been extremely fortunate to have a wonderful editor at the University of California Press. I want to thank Reed Malcolm for taking on this project and seeing it through the end. I owe special thanks to Kalicia Piviroti, Mary Severance, and Elizabeth Berg for their painstaking copyediting. Two anonymous readers for the Press provided me with well-informed, detailed, and thoughtful comments. Whatever flaws and interpretations remain in my work are of my own doing.

An earlier version of chapter 2 appeared in my article "The 'New Woman' and the Politics of Love, Marriage, and Divorce, in Colonial Korea." I gratefully acknowledge *Gender and History* to permission to reproduce it in revised form.

Finally, I would like to thank Ms. Lee Ok-jung. Um Sang-mi, Paek Jae-hui, Lee Hee-ae, and all of my friends at Magdalena's House. I am eternally grateful to you all!

Introduction

> What did change the concept of "women" by furnishing it
> with a new terrain was not so much class, which multiplied
> the old ambiguities as it refurbished them, but "the social.". . .
> [T]he concerns of the social are familial standards—health,
> education, hygiene, fertility, demography, chastity and
> fecundity—and the heart of the family is inexorably the
> woman.
>
> Denise Riley, "Am I That Name?"

On 5 August 1926, the *Tonga ilbo* reported a double suicide on the *Tokuju Maru*, a daily liner that ferried students, honeymooners, immigrants, workers, and raw materials from Shimonoseki to Pusan. Eyewitnesses claimed that a "middle-aged man" and his female companion, both clad in Western clothing, embraced each other and plunged into the choppy waters as the ferry approached the Taema (Tsushima) Islands. They had officially registered as Kim Su-san and Yun Su-sŏn for the trip, but the public would soon learn their true identities. The former was an aspiring playwright, Kim U-jin (1897–1926), who had graduated with an English degree from Waseda University, hailed from a wealthy family in Mokp'o, and was married with one child.

The more familiar figure was his lover, Yun Sim-dŏk (1897–1926), the first Korean female recipient of a Government-General scholarship to study music in Tokyo. She was a popular vocalist who had recently signed an exclusive contract with Nitto Records. After a humble upbringing in a Christian family in P'yŏngyang, Yun's mercurial rise to fame began in 1915, when she embraced the opportunity to study in Japan. After three years of language study at the Aoyama Academy, Yun transferred to the Tokyo Music School in April 1918 with the aspiration of becoming a soprano with a repertoire centered on Western music. The accolades and packed auditoriums were to no avail; when Yun returned to Korea in 1923, she suffered a blow to her personal reputation that almost ruined her career. Under family pressure, she attempted to borrow money from a Seoul magnate, Yi Yong-mun, to finance her brother's education. Malicious rumors that she had prostituted herself for the money drove Yun from Korea to Harbin, Manchuria, where she volunteered her musical talents to further the work of Pastor Bae Hyŏng-sik. After six months of self-exile, Yun returned to Japan in July 1926 in the hope of rejuvenating her singing career. She recorded twenty-six new songs, including her crowning piece, "Sa ŭi ch'anmi" (The glorification of death).

Yun's recording of "The Glorification of Death," an adaptation of Josef Ivanovich's "Wave of the Danube," was released just three days before the suicide, making the event all the more dramatic. Sales of her record skyrocketed, as the public clamored for details of her death. Several advertising companies cashed in on the tragedy by comparing it to the double suicide of the Japanese novelist Arishima Takeo (1878–1923) and his companion, the reporter Hatano Akiko, in 1923. To some contemporary observers, Yun and her partner were "doomed lovers" from the start, caught up in their own vanities and unwilling to accept their failures. That they chose death not in the service of the Korean nation but for "shallow and superficial" reasons sparked intense public criticism of their misguided idealism and glorification of death.[1] On the one hand, her death was seen as a direct consequence of Japan's colonial project, which had allowed her to succeed in her musical career only to end in a meaningless death. On the other hand, the public was also critical of her selfish choices, especially her choice to pursue her own personal whims rather than use her talents to serve the Korean nation.

This study examines the new terrain traversed by Korean women during the colonial period (1910–45) and the impact of the Japanese colonial experiment on the daily lives and identities of these women. It argues that Korean women's encounter with modernity was profoundly mediated by the context of colonialism. As women left their traditional spheres to occupy new spaces created by modernity in schools, factories, hospitals, and other sites, they increasingly confronted the pervasive control of the colonial state, which sought to mold them into pliant and industrious subjects. At the core of this book is the interplay between Korean women and the intrusive colonial apparatus that sought to impose its own brand of modernity on their ideas, relationships, social behavior, and bodies. Though some conformed to the dictates of colonial hegemony, others took pains to distinguish between what was modern (i.e., Western outfits) and thus legitimate, and what was Japanese and thus illegitimate. Some viewed Japanese policies as synonymous with progress and an improvement in the quality of their lives. Still others took advantage of the new spaces and possibilities that had been created by colonial modernity to redefine their own identities, roles, and status in society. Some even attempted to induce far-reaching reforms.

Several factors contributed to the distinct encounters of Korean women with colonial modernity. First, as Miriam Silverberg has observed, colonial modernity "was not some coherent system that could be imported with marginal adaptations." Rather, these dual, interrelated forces of change—"colonialism" and "modernity"—were constantly "shifting, contradictory, and deeply ideological." As we will see, individuals found numerous opportunities to exploit the inherent inconsistencies so as to subvert and resist the assimilationist goals of the colonial state.

Second, unlike other colonized territories around the globe, the Japanese could not carve a new country out of a five-hundred-year-old kingdom with well-defined geographical, linguistic, cultural, and ethnic boundaries. Japan's conciliatory cultural policy, which allowed greater cultural expression in the aftermath of the March First Movement (1919), led to the destabilization of accepted identities, gender arrangements, and culture. During the *bunka seiji* (cultural rule, 1919–31) period, a vibrant print industry with burgeoning newspapers, magazines, and literature offered forums for nationwide debates about nationality, modernity, and gender relations. References to the "new" were ubiquitous. Neologisms like "new women," *sinhŭng* (up-and-coming), "new family," "the modern girl and boy," *rump'en* (lumpen), "speed," and "youth movements" filled the headlines.[3]

As we will see, competing visions of Korean womanhood dominated these discussions as the public engaged the "woman question" with unprecedented enthusiasm. The emergence of new female categories unhinged traditional understandings of women's status and role in society. At one end of this modern space were women like Yun Sim-dŏk, who represented an exciting new world in which talent, education, and productivity (rather than class or gender) served as markers of success. Distinguished by their new knowledge, cultural finesse, Western dress, and activism—all integral elements of their "modern" identity—the "new women" demanded that their voices be included in the reform agenda of the nation. At the other end were Korea's rural women, who experienced firsthand the accelerated pace of industrialization and urbanization that accompanied Japanese colonization. As a result of mass migration from the countryside to urban centers and the entry of Korean women into the paid workforce, there was a sharp discrepancy between the ideal of the Korean woman working at home and the reality of women's growing participation in the labor force over the thirty-five years of colonial rule. The transformation of peasants into modern industrial workers was but one of many changes in colonial Korea. Although rural and migrant voices found few expressions in print, they nonetheless challenged society to reconsider the roles of women who struggled to balance work and family.

Finally, Korean women had to contend with modern mechanisms of control instituted by the Japanese state, which did not necessarily seek to promote modernity but certainly wanted to reinforce imperial hegemony and power. The Government-General, wary of creating a power vacuum, enforced *budan seiji* (martial rule) in 1910 to prepare the populace for large-scale social and political engineering. It centralized power by replacing the old bureaucracy, comprising largely the *yangban* class (scholar-officials), with a large contingent of Japanese bureaucrats, civil servants, and clerks.[4] Furthermore, it engaged Koreans as supervisors, managers, and overseers in factories, schools, and health facilities to enforce colonial policies. The pragmatic strategy of divide and rule, exemplified by pitting Korean male managers against subordinate female workers, proved critical to colonial policy.

Colonial authorities also resorted to modern forms of surveillance that Michel Foucault terms "bio-power."[5] On one level, the colonial state took great interest in the regulation of birth, sexuality, illness, and health. In part, this was achieved by the utilization of specialists (from economists to anthropologists, demographers to medical doctors) to conduct studies about the life processes of the Korean people. For the first time, surveys and studies of Korean early marriage, adolescent pregnancy, genetic illnesses, and other topics proliferated in both private and state sectors. Yet colonial prescriptions for managing the Korean social body often put Japanese national interests ahead of modern practice (e.g., promotion of population growth over modern birth control), much to the detriment of women's health and well-being.

By enhancing the legibility of society—that is, reducing a complex reality to categories—the colonial authorities sought to bring about extensive utopian changes to people's everyday lives.[6] At a micro level, breaking down all aspects of human life into quantifiable units through censuses, sanitary reports, maps, and so forth created a new politics of representation, generating an uneven relationship between the state and its citizenry. By simplifying the country (especially the rural areas) for better administration, it fulfilled its primary goal: to ensure that the subject population—"its health, resources, productivity, and regularities"— would become objects of governance.[7]

On another level, bio-power involved the discipline of the body through continual surveillance and control. As in Europe, these techniques of power pervaded the Korean social body, especially in key institutions like the family, schools, factories, and hospitals.[8] For example, in urban factories, the time-card machine and the assembly line became mechanisms by which to "instruct and validate the rules" while merging workers' individuality into the system.[9] By training the body to accept the rules as norms, the colonial state created what Michel Foucault has described as "a policy of coercions that act on the body," which ultimately sought to produce "subjected and practiced bodies, 'docile' bodies."[10]

HISTORIOGRAPHY

In his introduction to Michel de Certeau's *The Writing of History*, Tom Conley observes that historians work within the limits imposed upon them by their disciplines.[11] For de Certeau, the writing of history is a selective process in which the historian decides what is worthy of discourse, thus privileging certain documents over others.[12] Historical events, after all, represent an individual's "own mental projects," which bear "strong ideological and political imprints." Because of these limitations, it has become incumbent on historians to scrutinize what they have "deemed trivial or worth forgetting" in a more critical light.[13] This task is particularly important for Korean history, which has been shaped by strong ideological and political agendas.

This study builds on a recent direction in Korean historiography that scrutinizes those privileged narratives and stories. Until recently, Korean historiography was dominated by studies on the colonial period, the occupation of Korea by the United States, the partition of the peninsula, and the subsequent military regimes. Though colonialism inspired Korea's first women's movement—women's clubs and political groups that advocated equal education and reform—it was not until the late 1960s that women became a legitimate subject of study.

The emergence of Korean women's history coincided with Park Chung-hee's economic development plans, designed to transform Korea into an export-oriented economy—a process characterized by draconian labor policies and harsh exploitation of workers. The plight of female factory workers, who bore the brunt of these measures, prompted women scholars to search for a usable past through which to make sense of the present. Pak Yong-ok later lamented the painful birth of the new historical field, which suffered from a dearth of primary sources on women that had contributed to their second-class status in the historiography.[14]

Despite a difficult beginning, scholars from two prominent women's universities—Sookmyung Women's University and Ewha Womans University—began to subvert rigid disciplinary structures by organizing seminars and gathering materials to reclaim the female past. On 1 September 1960, Sookmyung Women's University established the Research Institute of Asian Women (Asea yŏsŏng munje yŏn'guso) and launched a study group that would publish their original research. The resulting collections of essays were the first attempt to examine Korean history—from the enlightenment to the colonial period—from a woman's perspective.[15]

In 1967, a group of prominent scholars from Ewha Womans University reached another milestone when they formed the Committee for the Compilation of the History of Korean Women (Han'guk yŏsŏngsa p'yŏnch'an wiwŏnhoe) to produce a comprehensive history of Korean women.[16] The project, which commemorated Kim Hwal-lan's fifty years of service to Ewha Womans University, had a lasting impact on subsequent generations of women scholars.[17] The three-volume *History of Korean Women* (1972), which was later translated into English (1977), broke new ground by delving back as far as the premodern Three Kingdoms period (57 B.C.E.–668 C.E.). Using the tools of social history, scholars such as Ch'oe Suk-kyŏng (premodern), Yi Hyo-jae (enlightenment period), Kim Yŏng-dŏk (literature), Yi T'ae-yŏng (law), Chŏng Se-hwa (education), Ha Hyŏn-gang (religion), and Yu Hŭi-gyŏng (clothing) documented the everyday lives of ordinary women—their family and social practices, dress codes, rituals, religion, and so forth. Despite a few gaps, the collection is still by far the most comprehensive survey of Korean women's history.

Despite major gains in historical research and the development of women's studies programs in Korea,[18] the nascent field of Korean women's history still confronted two related challenges. The first was methodological: should women's history be integrated into mainstream historiography or remain separate to highlight the differences in men's and women's experience? Moreover, the feminist aim of transforming women into historical subjects and the principal actors of the narrative risked essentializing one sex.[19] The second dilemma was institutional: although these studies on women were groundbreaking, they were still ignored by the male historical establishment and mainstream historiography. As feminist scholars acknowledged, their ideas had been articulated exclusively within a circle of women, without any interaction with their male counterparts. The aim of these early scholars was to highlight the neglected experiences of women; however, in the process they had created a historical framework neither within nor in opposition to the structures their male counterparts had imposed. As a result, the mainstream historical establishment was content to view feminist scholarship as relevant only to women scholars. Even as women's history gained legitimacy, it remained relegated to the margins.

One solution to the problem of separateness was the "history from below" approach, which offered historians a way to integrate women into the general historical narrative. The Korean version of history from below was the *minjung* approach, which gained popularity in conjunction with Park Chung-hee's initiation of the "Big Push" program and his draconian *yusin* (revitalization) system in the early 1970s.[20] In contrast to international pundits who praised the miracle of Korea's economic modernization and evolution toward liberal democracy, *minjung* history offered a counternarrative that highlighted the regime's harsh exploitation of workers, especially women.[21] The inclusive category of *minjung* pluralized the object of historical inquiry by transforming oppressed social groups like peasants and women into legitimate historical subjects.

The study of the *yŏ'gong* (factory girls) toiling in the textile and garment industries, a popular research topic, not only politicized the problem of female labor but also allowed scholars to insert women into the broader working-class structure.[22] *Minjung* history relies on essentialized social categories like woman, worker, and peasant to highlight the relationships between these groups; it rarely if ever examines differences within these categories. These contemporary studies prompted historians like Yi Hyo-jae to reexamine the Japanese colonial period for precedents.[23]

Despite the appealing aspects of *minjung* history, it nonetheless poses several challenges for this study. First, the category of *minjung* has a deceptively simple definition, much like the concept of the subaltern in India.[24] An individual might share dominant features with some groups and situations, and peripheral positions with others. In a complex grid of shifting relations, as in colonial Korea, it is difficult to recover and describe the lives and views of those whose positions keep changing vis-à-vis others.[25] To be sure, one could argue that a subaltern consciousness is "subject to the cathexis of the elite" and "never fully recoverable" and also "irreducibly discursive."[26] Though it is never possible to recover everything, nonetheless a subaltern approach can be applied to ruling-class documents so that they can "be read both for what they say and their silences."[27] Owing to the paucity of sources and the near-absence of ordinary Korean women's voices, this study will attempt to analyze official documents by employing this subaltern approach.

Second, most *minjung* scholarship subsumes women's relation to men under the broad spectrum of the working class and fails to focus on gendered experiences under capitalism. Though concepts like "ideology," "state," or "class struggle" (in Marxist scholarship) have provided *minjung* scholarship with a framework, its general premise rests on the universal category of the worker, and it does not specifically distinguish women's oppression from other aspects of class oppression. It often presumes that some subjects speak on behalf of their more silent and less active counterparts. All too often, this kind of grand narrative of working-class formation has portrayed workers in colonial Korea as valiant nationalists closely tied to the struggles of independence. Despite these shortcomings, the *minjung* approach has helped broaden the historical terrain beyond the familiar "male" episodes and sources.[28]

The inclusion of Korean women's history in mainstream disciplines has also led to a more rigorous engagement with feminist theory and scholarship. In 1994, Chŏng Hyŏn-baek argued that women could not be treated as a unified category any more than men.[29] She proposed dismantling the binary analysis to favor *sŏngbyŏlsa* (gender history) over *yŏsŏngsa* (women's history), the latter defined as "a history of women worthies," or "compensatory history."[30] Deeply influenced by Scott's "gender analysis," Chŏng redirected the task of Korean women's studies from documenting women's distinct historical experiences to "deciphering the processes by which gender difference—indeed sexual difference itself— had been established, maintained, and transformed."[31]

Though Korean feminist scholarship has employed gender analysis in creative and useful ways, it has engaged less with poststructuralist theories, which I view as an important framework for examining the complexity and instability of subject identifications. As Judith Butler contends, social categories (e.g., race, class, or gender) are constructed discursively and represent "performative acts" created through linguistic or cultural oppositions, which "naturalize certain attributes and experiences." In other words, repeated performances of ritualized activity and everyday life (i.e., women preparing meals for the family) construct a system of gender differences that appear normative over time. Gender performs this work of naturalization through "stylized repetitions," inscribing them in a system of differences.[32] As this study will show, becoming gendered in Korea meant intense interaction with special formations of power, institutions, practices, and discourses that established and regulated the shape and meaning of gender. Gender was an identity that Korean women performed and actualized over time within the constraints of colonialism.

This is not, of course, the first attempt to examine the impact of colonialism on Korean women's lives. A growing feminist scholarship in

Korea has examined the lives of Korean women using many disciplinary approaches.[33] Sociological studies by Mun So-jŏng, Cho Ŭn, and others have challenged the traditional view of women as confined to the home.[34] These works have examined the impact of industrialization on everyday practices (early marriage, divorce, and so forth) and gender roles in both rural and elite families in the early twentieth century. The research of labor and social historians, such as An Yŏng-sŏn, Chŏng Chin-sŏng, Sin Yŏng-suk, and Yi Chŏng-ok, has added new knowledge about daily life, gendered division of labor, and politics in the factories. These scholars have also reconsidered the complex family relations of female workers.[35] In addition, Kang I-su's use of oral histories has contributed a new dimension by incorporating the real voices of female workers and their experiences in the factories.[36]

Scholarship by No In-hwa, Kim Yŏng-ju, and Ch'oe Suk-kyŏng has recast the traditional narratives about Korean women's education in a more critical light. In contrast to traditional historiography, they conclude that this education was not as progressive as historians have imagined.[37] In a similar vein, scholars like Kim Ŭn-ju have challenged the official histories of missionary schools, which praise Christianity for empowering Korean women and liberating them from patriarchal Confucian norms. Kim has defined missionary work and its ideals as a form of cultural colonialism whereby missionaries planted Western bourgeois values in the minds of the first generation of female students.[38] Other scholars have focused on the impact of education on women's consciousness. By examining the various groups involved in establishing schools for women, Yun Hye-wŏn's study analyzed the impact these movements had on women's consciousness during the enlightenment period, while Kim Sŏng-ŭn's study focused more broadly on the gender inequalities of colonial education and the various social problems afflicting female students.[39]

More recently, studies by literary scholars like Ch'oe Hye-sil and Kwŏn Podŭrae have provided a new understanding of women writers in the colonial period and their views of modernity. Their work has been complemented by scholars who have edited multiple volumes and contributed to the modern women's history project at Sookmyung Women's University's Research Institute of Asian Women.

Although a study conducted by the Korean Women's Research Center in 1994 found that feminist historians still believed that women's history had yet to acquire "its right of citizenship in the general historiography," recent trends suggest that this goal is being realized.[40] Recent monographs by male scholars like Kim Kyŏng-il and others (including this study) are a testament to the growing interest in women and gender studies outside of exclusively women's circles.[41]

SCOPE OF THE BOOK

This study seeks to add to this body of knowledge and to employ these new methodologies by analyzing how Korean women from different socioeconomic backgrounds experienced the tumultuous period of Japanese colonialism. In particular, it seeks to examine the formation of new gendered subjectivities in the three interlocking domains of education, labor, and health. It follows V. N. Voloshinov's mandate that women's lives should be examined in a discursive context in literary (e.g., novels) and nonliterary forms (e.g., newspapers, government statistics). By examining women as "a contested ideological category," one can decode how the state, industrialists, doctors, teachers, journalists, and contemporary writers in colonial Korea constructed particular representations, which were often filled with tensions and contradictions.[42]

Chapter 1 provides background by examining the values and structures of the Chosŏn dynasty (1392–1910) and the advent of Westernization through modern education. Instead of viewing the traditional family as simply an oppressive patriarchal structure with an abstract set of rules, this chapter examines how the family was defined and how social and cultural institutions like ancestor veneration, funerary rites, succession, inheritance, and marriage shaped gender roles during the Chosŏn dynasty. I examine the emergence of a "culture of dissent" in response to the enforcement of stricter neo-Confucian gender roles and socioeconomic and political upheavals during the Chosŏn period. This culture of dissent transformed its focus and agenda over the colonial period in accord with the changing needs of women from different classes and political backgrounds.

Chapter 1 also examines the impact of education during the Chosŏn period. The development of Western-style schools for men and women in Korea depended on the interplay of three important forces—American missionaries, the colonial government, and traditional Korean schools. The principal thesis is that during the twenty-year period (1890–1910) of active missionary work, the honeymoon with Western ideas, a small window of opportunity allowed a generation of Korean women to receive a Western-style education. If modern educational discourses and practices sought to produce certain types of schoolgirls and boys, it also elicited a fractured subjectivity, open to subversion.

Chapter 2 analyzes a small coterie of educated women who emerged in the 1920s, challenging tradition and crafting new gender roles and identities. The visibility of the "new woman" in the public sphere fueled sharp debates about this new prototypical female who rejected traditional domesticity, espoused free love, and demanded the right to divorce or remarry unconditionally. Though some scholars have argued that traditional Korea and the modern agenda of these women were incompatible, and hence the new woman was destined to fail, this chapter seeks to reconceptualize the issue. Rather than address the question of success or failure, I examine how education gave new women the tools to articulate their sense of spatial location and identity as they negotiated their own vision of Korean womanhood.

Chapter 3 explores the transition of Korean women from the home to the factories during a period of rapid industrialization when colonial authorities reorganized the labor force through an intense sexual division of labor. The *yŏgong*, or factory girl, emerged as a new social category at this time, reshaping Korean notions of work and class. This new female workforce experienced dramatic transformations in work ethics, living patterns, family relations, and worldviews. By focusing on three feminized industries, this chapter analyzes how gender shaped the politics of work and intersected with the meaning of class.

Chapter 4 focuses on labor unrest among Korean women workers and the public debate among Korean reformers and the Japanese state about how to reassert control over this unruly group. It highlights the paradoxical image of the female worker as at once a helpless victim of economic oppression and an assertive activist. Her image as victim rendered her less threatening (i.e., as a ward of the state or of bourgeois philanthropy) while her activism raised the specter of social disruption and violence. As the economic crisis of the Japanese empire intensified in the 1930s, concessions to Korean female workers declined, leading to more militant strikes that were better organized both in terms of national and socialist ideology.

Chapter 5 examines the discursive forces that competed to define Korean women's bodies and reproductive capacities within the framework of medical science. Reproducing the nation was a top priority for all modernizing countries but was even more pressing under colonial occupation. To emerge victorious and independent, Koreans needed not only numbers but strong, healthy bodies and minds to rebuild the homeland. Critical debates about the modernization of childbirth, birth control, age of marriage, and hygiene opened up a new arena of discourse on sex. I argue that while Korean and Japanese scientific experts concurred that practices like early marriage needed to be eradicated and that new reproductive knowledge and technologies had to replace primitive practices, they had different agendas. While the colonial government sought to improve the quality and quantity of its workforce in the empire, Koreans aimed to create a healthier population to assume control over an independent nation. They also resisted Japanese attempts to colonize the Korean "national body" by maintaining as much control as possible over the public discourse.

By exploring the "new terrain of the social," this study seeks to integrate Korean women's experiences during the colonial period into mainstream history and to shed light on how competing identities were constructed in relation to power.

CHAPTER ONE

Women in Chosŏn Korea

If the family of a scholar's wife lives in poverty and destitution,
there is no reason why she should not work a little if it serves
as a means of survival. . . . In so far as raising chicken and ducks,
buying and selling soy sauce, vinegar, wine, and oil . . . securing
[her] family's livelihood should not be her only reason; after all
it is one of [her] many *sugong* [manual tasks].

Yi Tŏng-mu, *Sasojŏl* (A scholar's
minor matter of etiquette), 1775

Innaech'ŏn; sa-in yŏch'ŏn
Every human being is an embodiment of heaven; serve
every human being as you would serve heaven.

Ch'oe Che-u, *Yongdam yusa*
(Hymns from Dragon Pool), 1860

In his 1895 memoir, Henry Savage-Landor describes his first encounters with Korean women upon his arrival in the capital: "I remember how astonished I was during the first few days that I was in Seoul, at the fact that every woman I came across in the streets was just on the point of opening a door and entering a house. . . . The idea suddenly dawned upon me that it was only a trick on their part to evade being seen."[1]

Under the leadership of Yi Sŏng-gye (1335–1408), the founders of the Chosŏn dynasty (1392–1910) had launched a series of social, economic, and political reforms designed to transform the kingdom into a male-dominated neo-Confucian society. Yet while the image of the secluded woman popularized by Savage-Landor symbolizes the conservative character of the dynasty, the Confucianizing of Korea was a gradual, ever-evolving process that met with resistance, especially from women who stood to lose power with the reorganization of society. Though the penetration of Confucian ideals into Korean society was most visible at the level of discourse and ceremonies, the reform of social habits and kinship structures generated intense conflict, as individuals employed diverse resources and strategies to counter the state's quest to create a uniform neo-Confucian order. By the mid-eighteenth century, a new culture of dissent had emerged in Korean society that fostered new mentalités and demands for reform.

This chapter provides a broad overview of the transformation of Korean society—the processes of reform, accommodation, and dissent—during the long Chosŏn period. First, I examine the social structures that defined class hierarchies, gender relations, and customs.[2] The emergence of a strict patriarchy during the Chosŏn dynasty, which differed significantly in organization from the preceding Koryŏ society (918–1392), was shaped largely by social elites. Despite its oppressive character, this new patriarchal structure was not immune to demands for negotiations and concessions. By analyzing the gendered nature of tensions rather than conflicts between social entities, this study seeks to emphasize the diverse, even competing, interests of women within a single family or social class.

To contextualize these changes, I then explore the development of a broader "culture of dissent" and the rise of new historical players in Chosŏn society at large. In particular, it examine two distinct moments—the first coalescing after the Imjin wars (1592, 1598) and the second emerging after the Manchu invasions (1627, 1636). These upheavals triggered intense reactions from a wide spectrum of society, prompting the elites to defend their claim to power against disenchanted groups that insisted on a complete overhaul of the existing order. These two historical moments spawned new intellectual and religious movements, as well as a series of peasant uprisings that generated major socioeconomic upheavals. This powerful culture of dissent—which included new mentalités, language, symbols, political activism, and even violence—bequeathed a complex repertoire for resistance against the Japanese colonial state.

Finally, this chapter examines a new space for women created during this period—the field of modern education—and its impact on the culture of dissent. From 1885 to 1910 a generation of Korean women received a Western-style education at American missionary schools and emerged in the 1920s as leaders, challenging tradition and crafting new gender roles and identities. Although the missionaries claimed that they would prevent Westernization of their wards, their teachings and curriculum invariably instilled American cultural and religious mores that deeply influenced Korean women. With the onset of colonization, female students often utilized Western ideas, adapted and reconfigured to suit the Korean context, to counter a colonial state that vigorously reasserted traditional roles and values, as well as a nationalist agenda that promoted a new cult of domesticity. As a result, women's education became intimately linked to broader issues about cultural authenticity and national identity.

SOCIETY, FAMILY, AND THE STATE

Families, themselves hierarchical, operated within the larger framework of social classes that defined Chosŏn society. In 1868, Ernest Oppert (1832–1903) of Prussia headed a tomb-digging expedition to Korea. His mission was to blackmail the Chosŏn court into accepting Christianity and opening its ports to trade. He observed in Korea a "strict and rigid division of the castes, which part[s] the various ranks of the population of the peninsula from each other, showing on one hand some analogy to the caste institution prevailing amongst the Hindus in India."[3] Though the hierarchical relations in Korean society appeared "rigid" to an outsider, they were governed by complex social and gender conventions. Relations in the Chosŏn period were defined by "degrees of dignity" among classes, age, male and female, and even between the sexes in the Dumontian sense.[4] The tenets of neo-Confucianism placed great emphasis on moral imperatives. As Martina Deuchler explains, "These were the relationship between sovereign and subject guided by *ŭi* (righteousness), *ch'in* (the relationship between father and son guided by parental authority), *pyŏl* (the relationship between husband and wife guided by the separation of the functions), *sŏ* (the relationship between elder and young brothers guided by the sequence of birth), and *sin* (the relationship between senior and junior guided by faithfulness)."[5]

At a domestic level, the moral imperative of duty dominated Confucian family ethics. Duty meant an understanding of where every individual stood in relation to the whole. Acceptance of personal rank signified awareness of one's place in the world. As a result, these values promoted "hierarchy without shame, a hierarchy that is self-conscious but without conscious abuse, without necessarily infringing on what it means to be human."[6]

Within the larger Chosŏn hierarchy, there were four distinct social classes: scholar-officials, collectively known as *yangban* ("civil and military branches"); *chungin*, administrators and yamen who literally lived in the middle of the cities; *sangmin* or *yangmin* (commoners), namely farmers, merchants, and craftsmen; and *ch'ŏnmin* ("base people"), who occupied the lowest rungs of the social ladder. The *yangban* were members of a hereditary class who occupied important positions in state service based on their status and the civil service examinations. Although commoners could not take the examinations, talent, which had once been a prerequisite for attaining these coveted posts, became less meaningful by the mid-seventeenth century, as powerful clans used their influence to ensure that they dominated the examination system.

The *chungin* formed the backbone of the bureaucracy as lower administrators and technical specialists in the government. To qualify for one of the eight professional occupations, the *chungin* were required to pass an examination on specified subjects, known as *chapkwa*.[7] The majority of the population was in the *sangmin* class. They assumed a disproportionate burden of taxation, performed heavy corvee labor, and supplied young men for the military. Finally, the *ch'ŏnmin* class, despite being at the bottom of the social ladder, included some important positions. Their rank and file included a variety of groups, ranging from slaves through professional mourners, shamans, servants, and *kisaeng* (female entertainers).[8] The *paekchŏng*, comprising mainly butchers, lived in segregated villages and were exempt from government conscription.

Accompanying this complex and evolving class structure, with its many implications for the prospects and activities of men, was a transformation of the family from the Koryŏ to the Chosŏn dynasty that resulted in a gradual decline in women's status and visibility in the public sphere. During the Koryŏ period, the state's endorsement of Buddhism as the state religion offered a wide range of opportunities for female activities outside the domestic sphere. Women not only joined temples and learned to read sutras but contributed to the faith as nuns. People also revered the female bodhisattvas: the Kwanŭm posal or the Avalokiteshvara (female bodhisattvas of compassion), for example, had the power to grant the petitions of couples who desired children. In addition, Korean women enjoyed many familial privileges, because Buddhism recognized the right of women to remarry and inherit property. Marriage was neither universal nor a duty imposed upon women; rather, women could choose to live alone, marry, or even have multiple husbands (although this was not common). It was customary for parents to reside with their daughters rather than their sons, as a matter of preference or convenience.[9]

The neo-Confucian vision of a rational, well-ordered society provided the Chosŏn leaders with a blueprint for reorganizing and tightening control over the family. An orderly family became synonymous with the stability of the kingdom. The stricter family hierarchy granted greater prerogatives to the male patriarch and ensured women's subservience through the *samjong chido* (three obediences): to be obedient to their fathers, husbands, and sons. The introduction of primogeniture transferred all rights of property to men, which resulted in a radical deterioration of women's social position and legal rights. As inheritance became the exclusive right of the eldest son, it was incumbent on *yangban* households to compile a *chokpo* (genealogy), which excluded women. As we will see, although the new dynasty sought to define the boundaries of family lineage and class lines, ideals often did not translate into practice. In fact, those who stood to lose power, especially women, resisted attempts to encroach on their prerogatives and rights.

THE ELITE FAMILY

As neo-Confucian scholars of the early Chosŏn dynasty embarked on their reform agenda, they castigated the "unordered" family as the root of all social chaos in Korean society. Monumental compendiums like the *Kyŏngguk taejŏn* (Grand code of the nation), Zhu Xi's *Jiali* (Family rites) and the *Liji* (Book of rites) discussed the important four rites (*sarye*) of Korean family life—capping, wedding, funeral, and ancestor veneration—as the central pillars of stability. They also described how to maintain and strengthen "class privilege in general and for the descendants in particular."[10] If properly observed, the four rites determined the relationships within the domestic sphere and stabilized the social foundation of the public realm. In other words, the peace and prosperity of a state could only be guaranteed in proportion to the purity of family ritual life.

As a result, the emergent neo-Confucian Chosŏn state sought a radical redefinition of the family through restrictive legislation intended to ensure harmony in both the domestic and political realms. One significant change was a shift from a matrilineal to a patrilineal structure of kinship and identity. In Koryŏ, it was customary for the newlywed couple to live with the bride's family. This uxorilocal arrangement offered numerous advantages for women, not the least of which was economic: they could safeguard their portion of the inheritance, which they shared equally with their male siblings. Even if the wife moved to the husband's residence, she retained inheritance rights. If the husband had multiple wives (a custom of the royal house that was emulated by aristocrats and some commoners), they usually resided with their natal families, which impacted marital power relations in favor of the woman. In such "plural marriages," all wives and their children enjoyed equal status, perhaps with the exception of the *ch'ŏp*—a servant who served primarily as a sexual partner but lacked the status of wife.[11]

The triumph of the patrilineal line naturally eroded rights and privileges that women had enjoyed during the Koryŏ period. Whereas a woman's inheritance, which she received as a dowry upon her marriage or upon the death of her parents, had been independent of her marriage, now it became part of "an inalienable conjugal fund" and reverted to her husband and his descent group. This deprivation of economic assets no doubt had an impact on power relations within the marriage, precluding the dissolution of the union without financial ruin. In fact, it became nearly impossible for a married woman to sue for divorce or remarry, because after she entered a new descent group she had no way of separating herself from it.[12]

The power of the patrilineal line was nowhere as apparent as in the changing residential arrangements. Zhu Xi's *Jiali*, a detailed description of a Confucian wedding ceremony, introduced new elements to the rituals, including the *ch'in-yŏng*, in which the bridegroom brought the bride into his home. But as complaints from Korean officials reveal, the attempt to impose new residential patterns on married couples met with stiff resistance. In a harsh critique of the tenacious hold of uxorilocal marriages on Korean society, one key reformer, Chŏng To-jŏn (1337–98), argued: "Since the groom moves into the bride's home, the wife unknowingly depends on her parents' love and cannot but hold her husband in light regard. Her arrogance thus grows with each day; in the end there will be quarreling between husband and wife, whereby the rights of the family decline."[13] In other words, it was difficult to impose the "proper" power relations in a family that catered to the wife's whims and desires. Only when the "natural" hierarchy of marriage became the norm could there be order in state and society. To ensure the subordination of women, the Confucian legislators emphasized the final act of the wedding ceremony—the *sinhaeng* or *ugwi*, when the bride officially entered her husband's household and took her place in the inner quarters (*anch'ae*). Her husband's family now took precedence over her own.

According to the *Jiali*, the appropriate marriage age for a *yangban* male was between sixteen and thirty, while girls were to be between fourteen and twenty.[14] To preserve some aspects of Koryŏ dynasty custom, the bridegroom went to the bride's home for the marriage ceremony (*pan ch'in-yŏng*) and stayed there the first night.[15] People with the same family name and ancestral home (i.e., geographical origin) could not marry, and those who disobeyed received sixty strokes and were forced to divorce.[16]

Though marriage was an important institution for forging alliances between two families and an important rite of passage for an individual man or woman, the stated purpose of marriage was to "bring forth male offspring." Because the lineage was rooted in patrilineal descent, this was "society's means of survival."[17] The *Jiali* states that "the ceremony of marriage is intended to be a bond of love between two surnames, with a view, in its retrospective character, to secure the continuance of the family line."[18] In other words, "Marriage was to guarantee uninterrupted continuation of the descent group in two directions, taking the living as the starting point—toward the dead and toward the unborn."[19]

Since the arduous burden of sustaining the prestige and honor of a household by safeguarding the lineage fell primarily on the shoulders of the eldest son, producing a son was paramount for sustaining the lineage. Thus, "when a boy was born, they would lay him on a bed, clothe him with good garments, and give him a precious stone to play with, while [when] a girl-child was born, they would lay her on the floor, clothe her with a diaper only, and let her play with pieces of tiles."[20]

If a householder did not produce an heir, the family had several options. They could bring in a concubine, seek a divorce, engage a *ssibaji* (surrogate mother), marry in a son-in-law, or adopt a son.[21] Children were classified according to their mother's social status if their parents were from different social classes. This had a detrimental impact on illegitimate sons born of women other than legal wives. Furthermore, a man of a higher class could marry a woman from a lower class but not vice versa. If a commoner woman, for example, married a slave, she lost her commoner status. While some commoners continued to practice marrying in a son-in-law, by the late Chosŏn period the *yangban* household had taken up agnatic adoption. This practice sought to eliminate women as heirs by placing a premium on primogeniture. Adoption, however, differed from many other societies in that the average age of the adopted son was between twenty and thirty years; infants were rarely adopted. All adoptions had to be approved by the proper authorities, and by 1555 an illegal adoption could lead to arrest.[22]

In contrast to the Koryŏ period, women's freedom of movement became severely restricted as Confucian moralists imposed a strict division of the sexes, allegedly to prevent adultery and other sexual improprieties. Starting in the early fifteenth century, the state forbade women from visiting Buddhist temples (except to perform ritual ceremonies for deceased parents), shaman houses, and even the mountains with a women's temple group. Depriving women of such expressions of solidarity through popular religion and ritual may have served as a way to deprive women of any semblance of spiritual power. Unmarried daughters of *yangban* families were to remain confined to the domestic sphere as they prepared for their future roles as wives and mothers. While these restrictions were gradually extended to commoner women, these women still had greater access to the outside world because of their work in the fields and marketplace. Their ability to move beyond the inner rooms facilitated their transition to the new economic changes in colonial Korea but also put them at odds with reformers who sought to modernize them according to their own visions of womanhood.

MARRIAGE PRACTICES
AMONG COMMONER FAMILIES

Despite the paucity of documents on commoners, available sources suggest that during the first half of the Chosŏn dynasty, the lower strata of society adhered to marriage practices of the Koryŏ dynasty. Interclass marriages were frequent among commoners. For example, a slave woman could marry a commoner, or a commoner man could marry a servant. In either case, the children from the union would inherit commoner status. However, as the Chosŏn state sought to enforce its rigid social hierarchy, new legal codes mandated that bride and groom hail from the same social group. In families of mixed descent, children inherited the social status of the mother regardless of the higher status of the father.[23]

During the Chosŏn period, a matrilocal arrangement was prevalent, in which the commoner man lived with the wife's parents. In part, this arrangement resulted from the inability of single men to afford the *kyŏlnap* (betrothal price) at the time of wedding. According to a study by Chŏng Sŏng-hŭi, the average *kyŏlnap* was equivalent to the market price of a cow. The groom could pay this sum in cash to the bride's family. If he could not afford to pay the whole sum, the bride's family sometimes accepted payment equivalent to the cost of a pig, but this arrangement did not come without a price for the groom, who faced social ostracism and derision for the rest of his life.

Rather than delay marriage and suffer the social stigma of bachelorhood—a single man was described as living "like a beast"—most commoner men preferred to pay the *kyŏlnap* through the institution of *pongsahon*, service to the bride's family as a hired hand for a designated period of time. One option was going to work at the bride's home as a *mŏsŭm sŏbang* (farmhand husband). In most cases, the man would have to work for approximately three years. More often than not, the *mŏsŭm* was allowed to begin a family while rendering his services to the bride's family. For poor families with several daughters, the labor of a groom (*taeril sawi*) for three years proved economically beneficial. In addition to the matrilocal arrangement, commoners also adhered to *ilbu ilch'ŏ* (one husband, one wife), or monogamous relationships.

For the indigent, marriage was not even an option. Poor tenant farmers who barely eked out a living, for instance, often resorted to selling their daughters to *yangban* households as concubines or *kogong* (hired farmhands). *Sirhak* scholar Chŏng Yag-yong's (1762–1836) epic poem "Sogyŏng ege sijip kan yŏja" [The girl married off to a blind man] was inspired by the sale of a young girl to a forty-eight-year-old blind fortune-teller.[24]

One option for poor commoner men was to marry a female slave (*yangch'ŏn kyŏlhon*) owned by a member of the *yangban* class—unions that the elites encouraged for the sake of increasing their property. Chosŏn law unequivocally gave masters sole ownership rights over the children of female slaves. Slaves, who occupied the lowest position in this rigid social hierarchy as *ch'ŏnmin*, were divided into two categories: *kongnobi* (state-owned) and *sanobi* (privately owned). The latter were subdivided into *solgŏ nobi* (service slaves) and *oegŏ nobi* (outside resident slaves). Han Yŏng-guk's study of household records in the Ulsan area during the seventeenth century shows that marriage rates among *oegŏ nobi* were three or four times higher than those of *solgŏ nobi*. Han notes that roughly half of the male *oegŏ nobi* were married to the master's adopted daughters and a third were married to private slaves; the rest were married to maidservants and government servants. However, for female slaves the choices were broader: approximately a third married private male slaves, and the rest chose servants, soldiers, marines, and commoners. Among the *solgŏ nobi*, the fate of many young girls depended on the whims of the owner. Because of the frequency of rape, a large number of female *solgŏ nobi* bore illegitimate children and were forced to raise them.

Marital rates among slaves differed considerably by gender. According to Han Yŏng-guk's 1609 survey of 136 households in the Ulsan area, out of a total of 572 slaves (314 female, 258 male), 144 slaves (94 female and 50 male) were registered as married.[25] The disproportionate number of female slave marriages can be explained largely by their broader options for marital partners. Male slaves were limited to marrying women in the same household. This was naturally to the master's advantage; for example, when a *no* (male slave) married a *bi* (female slave) from the same household, their child legally belonged to the master. If a male slave married a female slave from a different household, however, there were harsh consequences; in the most extreme case, the master punished him by death. To prevent these kinds of relationships, owners allowed their male slaves to marry adopted women from their own household.

Yi Yŏng-hun's survey of slave families in the Kyŏngbuk area during the late fifteenth and sixteenth centuries shows that the average slave family included three or four members. After giving birth to her own child, a married female slave often rendered services to the master as a wet nurse. In return, she received preferential treatment over other slaves, especially if she also raised her master's children. It was not unusual for a married slave to bear the illegitimate child of her master or his son. The social stigma attached to these offspring was severe, and their very existence raised thorny moral and legal questions during the latter decades of the Chosŏn period.[26]

Even as cultural ideals of the family (*kajok*) propagated by Confucian ideologues gained widespread acceptance, they did not necessarily translate into practice, especially when economic realities made that impossible. By the latter half of the Chosŏn period, moreover, the contradictions between social status, wealth, and cultural ideals were becoming apparent. For instance, a wealthy peasant family (who did not have elite social standing) might celebrate an elaborate wedding according to Confucian norms, while a poor *yangban* family with limited economic resources could not provide a proper dowry for their daughter. In fact, during the mid-nineteenth century, prosperous peasants began to emulate elite practices such as *pan ch'in-yŏng* and mourning. Quite apart from issues of wealth, Confucian cultural ideals would also collide with traditional gender norms and ideas about women that were firmly rooted in popular culture and social practices.

CONFUCIANISM AND ITS DISSENTERS

In spite of the new dynasty's efforts to restrict their activities, Korean women retained residual forms of power, often through subversive means. At the heart of the Confucian image of woman were contradictions that could be exploited: a woman was to be submissive yet strong, modest yet responsible.[27] Though female power could not fully dislodge the Confucian patriarchal system, women were not entirely without recourse. As Michelle Zimbalist Rosaldo observes about women in oppressive conditions, they could "exert important pressures on the social life of the group" regardless of whether their "influence [was] acknowledged or not."[28]

To an outsider's eye, Korean women suffered from strict regulations and surveillance over their physical mobility, dress, and social interactions. As one Western observer wrote: "Women of the Far East are kept so secluded and are not allowed that free intercourse with their fellowmen that is accorded to women in the West"; the higher her social status, "the more complete is her seclusion."[29] And as one descended down the social ladder, "all restrictive laws and all inequalities between the sexes are toned down, so that when we reach the lowest classes, we find that the relations are much the same as in our land."[30]

In contrast to *yangban* women, lower-class women could cross gender boundaries into the public sphere (the fields, marketplace, and so forth) more easily as a result of their work, which facilitated interaction with men and with other women. They could converse with men at their leisure, and even go out unveiled, whereas *yangban* women were "very punctilious as to the observances of their severe rules."[31] The American educator William Griffis contrasted the social isolation of *yangban* women with the greater freedom of peasant women, who performed manual labor in the fields rather than hiding behind their veils after dusk. However, he conceded that this freedom from seclusion was hardly a privilege, for in "going to the market, the [peasant] women carry the heavier load."[32]

1. A *yangban* woman in her *chang-ot* (hood).

Observers also commented on the relaxed, even immodest, style of commoner women's dress as a sign of greater personal freedom. Following a trip to Korea, the Prussian evangelist Charles Gutzlaff (1803–51) remarked that village women wore less restrictive, modest attire and plaited hair, which distinguished them from the nobility.[33] Homer Hulbert observed that women of the lower classes, to his shock and dismay, even "exposed their breasts."[34] He went so far as to declare that slave women were "the freest women in the country since they are not bound by the laws of the custom which holds the women of the upper class with a never-ending grip. They go where they please without regard to being seen by men, wearing no cover over their faces as do the other women."[35]

Though women of various social classes clearly enjoyed different degrees of personal freedom, they all suffered from the cultural taboo and restrictions on widow remarriage, as well as the common practice of child marriage, especially prevalent among commoners, which posed serious problems for family reformers during the colonial period.

Yet a *yangban* woman was not wholly unable to escape the restrictions of Confucianism, as Western observers believed. There were some concessions that provided a venue for socialization with other women and protection from the arbitrary and unilateral power of a husband. There were designated times during the evening when women were permitted to leave their homes. Louise Miln reported in the nineteenth century that "after the curfew rings, it is illegal for a Korean man to leave his own house; then it becomes legal for Korean women to slip out and take the air and gossip freely."[36] Henry Savage-Landor also noted those times when women could leave their domestic sphere for an outside realm of female sociability: "Men are confined to the house from about an hour after sunset and until lately were severely punished both with imprisonment and flogging if found walking about the streets during 'women's hours.' The gentler sex was and is therefore allowed to parade the streets, and go and pay calls on their parents and lady friends, until a very late hour of the night, without fear of being disturbed by the male portion of the community."[37] Laws banning their social mobility during the day, spelled out in the *Kyŏngguk taejŏn*, punished women who visited temples and mountains with one hundred lashes but could be breached during these "women's hours." Laws establishing norms of social conduct for women also were not as rigid as they appeared. This was true even for the *ch'ilgŏ chiak* (the "seven evils" rules), which could serve as a pretext for their husbands to divorce them. These seven evils were inability to bear a son, disobedience to parents-in-law, adultery, displays of jealousy, chronic illness, theft, and garrulity.

The severity of the seven evils rules was attenuated by a high bar of corroboration and verification; it was far easier for a man to accuse his wife of violating a rule than it was to prove that she had done so. Furthermore, there were protective clauses, such as the *sambulgŏ* (three reasons not to be let go), that could be employed by a wife to annul a divorce filed by a husband. A wife could either claim that she had no place to go, prove that she had served the three-year mourning period after the death of her husband's parents, or demonstrate to the court that she was the source of the household's wealth. A wife could also divorce her husband on the grounds that he had forced her to commit adultery, sold her to another man to become his wife, committed incestuous acts with his mother-in-law, or struck her parents or grandparents.[38]

Among commoners, there was far greater license and divorce was exceedingly easy and common, because there were no laws that punished women for promiscuity or infidelity.[39] The *kisaeng* (female entertainers), for example, were literate in various arts, music, literature, dancing, and even calligraphy, and had the most freedom of access to public events. As Louise Miln observed, "There are one or two advantages in being a woman in Korea. There are very few crimes for which a Korean woman can be punished. Her husband is answerable for her conduct, and must suffer in her stead if she breaks any ordinary law." Another advantage of being a woman in Korea was that she "has very largely the selection of her own daughters-in-law, and if the daughter-in-law proves unsatisfactory, she has only herself to blame."[40]

Despite the outward rigidity of Korean patriarchy, the otherwise unbending *samjong chido* (three rules for women)—that is, to cultivate obedience to one's father before marriage, to one's husband during marriage, and to one's son after the death of a husband—were softened by the intimate mother-son relationship, which became a unique feature of Korean family life. In fact, Cho Haejong suggests, "Korean society might be an ideal case for studying the relationship between mother power and woman power and the mechanism by which a rigid male dominant system can be maintained alongside an overwhelming mother power."[41]

This power was not merely affective but practical as well, especially after the death of a husband or father-in-law, when an energetic mother could assume control over matters related to marriage and inheritance.

No husband was permitted to meddle in the household affairs of his wife, whose responsibilities included the management of the family, the preparation for regular ancestral rites, and the education of her children.

Women from both the elite and commoner classes took very seriously their responsibility to prepare children for the complex world of Confucian adulthood. In Chosŏn society, self-improvement began at home under the care of the mother, who provided a moral foundation through proper child rearing and character building. At a more practical level, elite women who successfully reared their sons (to pass the national exam) and daughters (to marry them off to a wealthy family) could legitimize an elevation in status and power as they aged.

Foreign contemporaries could not help admiring the power wielded by Korean wives in everyday life. In the words of Horace Underwood, one of the first American missionaries in Korea, "I beheld a justly irate wife dragging home her drunken husband from the salon; and firmly grasping this, I have seen more than one indignant female administering that corporal punishment which her lord and master no doubt richly deserved." If the Korean wife "stands and serves her husband while he eats, labors while he smokes," when it comes to family affairs, "she take[s] the helm (that is to say, the top-knot) in hand, and puts the ship about."[42] Angus Hamilton (a fellow missionary) concurred that "it is impossible not [to] admire the activity and energy of the Korean woman. Despite the contempt with which she is treated, she is the great economic factor in the household and in the life of the nation."[43] Another missionary added: "Many a time while passing along the street, we have been amused to note that while a husband was calling his wife all the names he could think of, he actually ended up attaching to the verb an ending indicative of his unbounded respect for the partner of his bosom. There is still one more fact indicating the position of women: While foreigners are expected to talk 'low' or 'impolite' talk to their male servants, the women, seamstresses and nurses who are in their employ expect to be addressed in polite terms, and object if spoken to in any other way."[44]

Little wonder that the idealized images of the *hyŏnmo yangch'ŏ* (wise mother and good wife) became an integral aspect of Korean culture, "softening the edges of an otherwise strict patriarchy."[45]

Another powerful female figure who maintained a strong influence over Korean daily life was the shaman or *mudang*. In the earlier Koryŏ period, shamanism had coexisted, without any significant conflict, with Buddhism and Confucianism. However, the new gendered priorities of the neo-Confucian state clashed head-on with the philosophy of shamanism. First, the "superstitious" elements of shamanism—the notion that all objects, animate and inanimate, possessed spirits that needed to be appeased—were incongruous with the "rational" ideas of neo-Confucianism. For instance, instead of shamanism's constant interaction with the spirits of the dead (whether as communion or appeasement), death was final, inevitable, and natural in the neo-Confucian belief. To be sure, the custom of venerating ancestors was still upheld, but this practice did not entail contact with dead spirits.

Perhaps more important, the power of the female *mudang* as the mediator of the spirit world or as a healer posed a threat to the neo-Confucian gender hierarchy, in which women were deprived of key leadership roles. Despite efforts by Confucian reformers to destroy the influence of these female leaders, they could not prevent Koreans, even the kings who were "exemplar Confucian monarchs," from seeking the women's intervention. For example, during the *kiuje* (ceremony to pray for rain), Kings T'aejong, Sejong, and Sŏngjong all, in their time, called on shamans to offer prayers during droughts. In many respects, shamanism represented the feminine in the world of religion, in contrast to Confucianism, which stressed male prerogatives. Even Buddhism, which in earlier periods had allowed women access to rituals, did not allow them to serve as high priests in the same capacity as the *mudang*. Not only did the *mudang* have the power to "report from out there" by manifesting spirits in their bodies, but they occupied a female space that was alien to the spirit of neo-Confucianism.[46]

Korean women retained residual forms of power during the Chosŏn period, even as state and society sought to negate their influence. In particular, the "wise mother, good wife" and shaman came to represent archetypal figures of dissent who manipulated social relationships (i.e., mother-son or spiritual leader-follower) to exert their authority in both conventional and subversive ways. Confucian ideals did not prevent them from reinforcing their prerogatives; these strong women represented the contradictions between the "powerlessness" of their subordinate status in neo-Confucian society and the real power they wielded in everyday life. As Korea underwent significant economic transformation during the Chosŏn period, women of different classes found that the contradictions between Confucian ideals and realities grew more pronounced in the context of a changing economic and intellectual landscape.

ECONOMIC TRANSFORMATIONS AND NEW MOVEMENTS OF DISSENT

Toyotomi Hideyoshi's invasion of Korea in 1592 and 1597, which wreaked havoc and devastation in the land, generated significant socioeconomic transformations that eventually gave rise to new movements of dissent. Hard-pressed for revenues and needing to rejuvenate the ruined rural economy, Chief State Councilor Yi Wŏn-ik urged the king to consider replacing the old tribute tax system with a uniform land tax law (*taedong-pŏp*) that would levy on each household roughly one percent of its harvest (twelve *tu* of rice) for every arable *kyŏl* of land.[47] Unlike the previous tax system, which accepted only rice payments, taxes could now be paid in cotton cloth (*taedongp'o*) or coins (*taedong jŏn*), alleviating the burden on peasants. The minting of coins not only increased revenues for the state but transformed rural life, as markets and fairs appeared throughout the provinces.

As inland and coastal trade brokers (*kaekchu* and *yŏgak*) took full advantage of this new commercial economy, permanent trading towns like Kaesŏng, Miryang, and Anju appeared. Commoners could now seek new vocations in these towns, as peddlers, innkeepers, restaurateurs, moneylenders, and even small shopkeepers. Merchants who engaged in whole-sale distribution of prized commodities like cotton, ginseng, or paper became extremely wealthy. Unregulated commercial activities also affected the agrarian economy, as opportunities prompted many peasants to diversify and invest in commercial farming. The social impact of these economic changes was significant, leading to the rise of a new dissent movement that exposed the cruel realities of Korean society and demanded greater social and gender equality.

The Emergence of the Sirhak Movement

Economic growth led to the emergence of a class of nouveau-riche peasants and merchants, which disrupted the rigid traditional class system and its mores, triggering a moral and epistemological crisis. Many rural literati were appalled to find themselves no better off than the average commoner. To remedy their social decline, a coterie of disaffected intellectuals—many of whom were from the *namin* (southerners) faction—sought concrete solutions to the socioeconomic ills plaguing the dynasty, which was crippled by partisan fighting in the court. This broad and varied socio-economic movement, better known as the *sirhak* (practical studies) movement, became an important social force and a key challenge to the existing order. Though their concerns ranged from social issues such as abolishing class distinctions to the development of a sound agricultural economy run by independent farmers, *sirhak* scholars concurred on one thing: change was inevitable.

The agenda was as diverse as the group's activists. Some scholars who had sojourned in Qing China, like Pak Chi-wŏn (1737–1805) and Pak Che-ga (b. 1750), believed that solutions to Korea's domestic problems were to be found outside the country, and they looked toward Chinese models of the well-ordered society. Others, however, were more inward-looking and resorted to satirical writings in the vernacular *han'gŭl* to expose the hypocrisies of the ruling elite and address other inequalities in society, such as the evils of slavery.[48] Similarly, in his treatise *Oju yŏnmun changjŏn san'go* (Random expatiations of Oju), Yi Kyu-gyŏng (1788–1865) sought to abolish restrictions on the remarriage of widows, which he redefined as a serious societal problem rather than a personal dilemma that could be resolved through moral training.[49]

One dominant theme in *sirhak* writings was the underutilization of female labor skills and power, which the scholars argued had damaged both Korean women and society in general.[50] For example, Yi Tŏng-mu (1741–93) argued that *yangban* women needed to work in the changing commercial economy, not because the households were in dire need of cash but because of their business acumen, ability, and resourcefulness; he also pointed out the growing number of talented and literate women in the population.[51]

The need to highlight women's achievements led Pinghŏgak Yi (1759–1824), the wife of the *sirhak* scholar Sŏ Yu-bon (1762–1822), to compile the *Kyuhap ch'ongsŏ*, an encyclopedic tome that was intended to guide the lives of her daughters.[52] The entries are most notable for the strong presence of women in various commercial enterprises. Not only did Yi provide information about pioneers in these areas, but she also offered concrete recommendations on how to cultivate and sell rice, barley, tobacco, cotton, medicine, and other special products. Her description of "women's chores"—including meal preparation, liquor distillation, sewing, weaving, raising silkworms and domestic livestock, fieldwork, flower gardening, and child rearing—reflected the ever-expanding field of Korean women's work. Moreover, Yi's compilation of *yŏllyŏrok* (records of virtuous women)—role models she wanted her daughters to emulate—included not only well-known "virtuous and chaste" wives and daughters-in-law but a diverse group of talented and learned women from Korea and China ranging from female warriors to Taoist hermits.[53] For Yi, the solution to Korea's social ills was an expansion of female roles in the economic and literary spheres, accompanied by social acceptance and respect for their achievements.[54]

Another group of *sirhak* scholars looked to Christianity as a panacea for Korea's social inequalities. Treatises like *Ch'ŏnhak ch'oham* (First steps in Catholic doctrine), which filtered into Korea from China, promised that the egalitarian message of Christianity would provide an alternative to rigid neo-Confucian orthodoxy. According to Ch'oe Yŏng-kyu's study of early converts, from 1784 to 1801, 602 Koreans (480 men and 122 women) converted to Catholicism. The number of male converts decreased during the height of government persecution, between 1802 and 1846, while the number of female converts increased to 159.[55] Notably, not all female converts were from the *yangban* class; many came from the commoner or *ch'ŏnmin* (base) class. The occupations of female converts included weavers, needle workers, court ladies, day workers, attendants, and *kimch'i* peddlers. According to government records, female converts were arrested because they left their homes to go to Seoul; went out in the streets, moving from house to house; remained single; assumed the identity of a widow when they were single; congregated in worship with the opposite sex; met men in the inner room; or were baptized by foreigners.[56]

The Emergence of Ch'oe Che-u's Tonghak Movement

As harsh persecution drove Catholic converts underground, a growing number of disaffected *yangban* in the countryside started to mingle with the impoverished masses, which fueled popular discontent. Desperate to alleviate their suffering, many peasants resorted to slash-and-burn agriculture in the mountains (*hwajŏn*) but confronted a succession of natural calamities and poor harvests. This agrarian crisis culminated in a series of peasant outbursts, starting with the Hong Kyŏng-nae rebellion in P'yŏngan Province in 1811.

In response to the crisis in the countryside, a humanistic millenarian movement emerged under the leadership of the charismatic Ch'oe Che-u (1824–64), who promised to rescue farmers from poverty and transform the existing social order. In stark contrast to the male-dominated Confucian order, Ch'oe envisioned an alternative social order organized around the concept of *innaech'ŏn* (every human being is an embodiment of heaven), in which the world would be free of discrimination and suffering. Drawing on eclectic indigenous and foreign traditions, Ch'oe's egalitarian social message was aimed at two disadvantaged groups: peasants and women.[57] An illegitimate child, Ch'oe had experienced stigma and pain firsthand, sensitizing him to the plight of the downtrodden and fostering political consciousness. In his writings, he vociferously criticized such oppressive *yangban* practices as restrictions on widow remarriage and concubinage.[58]

Ch'oe's vision of a new Korean womanhood developed from his humanistic ideals. Contrary to the famous Confucian adage that blamed the intelligent and skilled woman for bringing misfortune to the household, Ch'oe deplored her subordinate and dependent status. He argued that the wife should exercise her power to be the "master of the home." Instead of taking their important work for granted, men should value women's role in the family. Likewise, he condemned ethical codes such as the *samgang oryun* (three bonds and five relations) as barriers to women's mobility and development.[59] He was dedicated to eradicating the rigid status system and set a personal example by adopting two female slaves (one as his daughter-in-law and the other as his daughter). He even taught his daughters how to read and write.[60] Ch'oe's execution in 1864 did not put an end to the movement. Despite the state's aggressive campaign to persecute all his followers, disciples such as Ch'oe Si-hyŏng (1829–98) sought to preserve their master's teaching and started an underground network of Tonghak churches. Like his mentor, Ch'oe Si-hyŏng sought to rid the world of inequality and attached great significance to the elevation of women. In the *Tonggyŏng taejŏn* (Great compendium of Eastern scripture), Ch'oe stressed the need to cultivate human affections and equality among family members. Reforming the broader structures of society meant change within individual families as women were given status equal to male family members.[61]

The desire to ameliorate the status of Korean women in Chosŏn society would find expression not only in these social movements of dissent but also in the field of education. In fact, the reform of women's education left one of the most enduring legacies of the Chosŏn period; not only were women given the opportunity to study and engage in new professions, but they also gained a new consciousness and identity as modern Korean women.

EDUCATIONAL CHANGE AND NEW
OPPORTUNITIES FOR WOMEN

During the Chosŏn dynasty, the general Korean population had little access to formal education. Only elite men in the upper echelons of society (the *yangban* class) had the privilege of attending a *sŏwŏn*, or private academy. Each county had a *hyanggyo* (county school) and almost every town had a *sŏdang* (private village school) run by some learned man. When a boy completed his training at a *sŏdang*, he transferred to the *hyanggyo*. Those who completed the *hyanggyo* proceeded to the Sŏnggyun'gwan (National Confucian Academy) in Seoul, the highest institution of learning in the country. The curriculum at all levels was limited to the Chinese classics, and the method of teaching was formal. In the village schools, the primary goal was to prepare young literati men for the civil service examinations (*kwagŏ*). Among the *yangban* class, education meant learning in the Confucian sense of the word—the gradual development of character—rather than a systematic acquisition of scientific knowledge.

For the vast majority of Korean women during the Chosŏn dynasty, *kyoyuk* (education) meant informal training in the basics of domesticity. As Reverend George Gilmore (1868–1923) observed, "They [had] no part in the educational system. While we hear now and again of educated females and such figures in fictions and tales of the peninsula, it is said in such a way as clearly to show that they are the exceptions, and are the wonder of their connections."[62] Lulu Frey (1868–1921), a missionary teacher, once suggested that Korean society kept women in ignorance because it feared their full potential:

> It is discovered later that the Korean woman's mind is quicker and more active than that of the Korean man and she is able to plan and

plot with great skill. It may be that to keep her from eclipsing man, customs arose which crushed within her the ambition to study. . . . Thus it came about that the women of this land became adept at many kinds of manual work, but confined within the stove and mud walls of the home their minds became so dull and inert and their vision as narrow as those walls.[63]

Indeed, the neo-Confucian ideology of *namhak yŏmaeng* (learned men, ignorant women), which became prevalent during the Chosŏn dynasty, held learned women in contempt. As Yi Ik (1681–1763), a scholar of *sirhak* (practical studies) and a progressive intellectual during his time, wrote: "Reading and learning are the domain [of] men. For a woman it is enough if she knows the Confucian virtues; she will bring disgrace to the family [if she knows more]."[64] Women must be limited to *Samgang haengsilto* (Illustrated guide to the three relationships): loyalty, filial piety, and chastity.

Manuals like the *Naehun* (Instructions for women), a text written by Queen Sohye in 1475, provided elite women with guidelines for decorum in the household. Seven chapters covered topics such as a woman's manner of speech, her conduct, filial piety, matrimony, marital relations, motherhood, family relations, and thrift. For example, it taught that "wives should stay inside and prepare every meal. They should devote themselves to wine brewing, cooking and cloth making and not to political affairs. No matter how talented and wise she may be, a wife should not interfere in such affairs, though she may just offer a piece of advice to the master. Always remember that a hen that crows in the early morning brings misfortune."[65] Under these strict codes, women had to abide by the *samjong chido*, or "three obediences." As discussed above, these included subservience to her parents before marriage, to her husband after marriage, and to her son after his birth. For those exceptional women who learned to read Chinese, other manuals were available, such as the *Sohak* (Little learning), *Yŏllyŏ-jŏn* (Five biographies of faithful women), *Yŏsasŏ* (Four books for women), *Tongmong sŏnsŭp* (First training for the young and ignorant), *Yŏgye* (Moral teaching for women), and *Yŏch'ik* (Rules of conduct for women).[66] Although novels like *Ch'unhyang-jŏn*

(The tale of Ch'un-hyang), *Sim Ch'ŏng-jŏn* (The tale of Sim Ch'ŏng), or *Kuunmong* (The nine cloud dream) were available, only a handful of women could read them.

As new knowledge and technology slowly penetrated the peninsula fol-lowing the Kanghwa Treaty of 1876,[67] the court sought to formulate a pol-icy to address the foreign demand for more economic openness and the infiltration of Western ideas. The court risked losing its legitimacy if it yielded to foreign pressure; more important, it feared that any concessions to foreign infiltration could lead to the colonization of the peninsula.

The retirement of the Taewŏn'gun (1829–98) and the ascension of the Kaehwa (progressive) faction marked a change from isolationism to an open-door policy. This coterie of young, liberal-minded intellectuals held a more conciliatory attitude toward modernization and sought to discredit the Taewŏn'gun's exclusionist policies. Their position was supported by King Kojong (r. 1863–1907), who convinced the court that it was imperative for Korea to break out of its isolation and embark on a course of "self-strengthening" and "enlightenment," despite vigorous resistance by conservative leaders of the government. New attitudes at the top led to several important decisions that would influence the deci-sion to import Western education.

First, the court organized several missions to Japan and China. Kim Hong-jip (1842–96), the vice-minister of rites, led the first goodwill mission to Japan in 1880. Accompanied by fifty-eight ministers, the primary goal was to revise the Kanghwa Treaty, postpone the opening of Chemulp'o (Inch'ŏn), and visit universities, regular schools, girls' schools, vocational schools, and military academies. In 1881, the state dispatched sixty-nine officials, students, and artisans to Tientsin to observe Qing mil-itary drills and methods of weapons manufacturing. But perhaps the most useful exploratory trips, in the view of Korean reformers, were to neigh-boring Japan. In October 1881, King Kojong dispatched twelve younger officials on a three-month mission under the guise of a *sinsa yuram-dan* (gentlemen's sightseeing group) to visit Japanese government offices, shipyards, regular schools, girls' schools, industries, hospitals, and prisons. Not only did the Korean delegates observe the operation of Japan's industrial and administrative infrastructure, but they also saw the social and cultural developments that had accompanied industrialization and modernization.

Delegates were particularly struck by the number of schools for both sexes. Some delegates concluded that to become a truly modern nation, Korea not only needed to consider fundamental economic reforms, but also should reassess women's roles in the family and general society. Most important, they acknowledged the social value and political utility of women's education. In their view, educated mothers would raise accomplished and learned men who would strengthen the moral and intellectual fiber of the nation.

Yi Su-jŏng, better known to his Japanese counterparts as Ri Jutei, was one of the first reformers to recognize the urgent need to create girls' schools in Korea. In September 1882, as part of the second Korean diplomatic mission to Japan, Yi went to study with Tsuda Sen, a renowned authority on agriculture and leader of the Christian movement. During his stay in Japan, he sent a letter to the American missions through Henry Loomis of the American Bible Society, urging them to consider dispatching female missionaries to Korea. "In my opinion," Yi wrote, "women missionaries would be of the first importance. The Corean [*sic*] customs are quite unlike either the Chinese or Japanese, the power of the sexes being about equal." He concluded that the task of these foreign missionaries "would be to elevate, reform, and educate the Koreans, in particular the children." He continued, "On this account, I think a girls' school is very important. Wherefore I desire that a lady missionary be sent to my country, and I, although an ignorant man, will do everything in my power to introduce and aid her in my work."[68]

Yun Ch'i-ho (1865–1945), a participant in the 1881 *sinsa yuram-dan* mission (and a member of the Independence Club in 1896), also remarked extensively on the development of schools for girls in the United States.

He observed in his journal in January 1891, during a trip to Nashville, that five in seven members of the reading population of the city were women. Moreover, at Nashville University, there were eleven males to forty-two females in the graduating class.[69] Another visit included Wythville, the "prettiest and healthiest town on the road," which boasted ten churches, two weekly and semiweekly newspapers, and the most important attraction—three or four female schools.[70] The lesson that Yi drew from his tour was that to become a truly modern nation, it was imperative for Korea to educate its girls.

How—and whether—Korea should become modern was itself unclear. Should Korea maintain its ties with China by adhering to its centuries-old institutions, customs, and educational system or should it enter into the world of nation-states and forge new political alliances and modern institutions?

With the aim of conveying their opinions, a coterie of reformers created the Independence Club under the direction of Sŏ Chae-p'il (Philip Jaisohn).[71] He obtained a generous grant of money from Yu Kil-chun, the home minister, to launch the *Tongnip sinmun* (The independent), a thrice-weekly newspaper, on 7 April 1896. In this bilingual paper (in *han'gŭl* and English), editorials stressed the need to safeguard the nation's sovereignty from foreign encroachment. However, writers also advocated promoting civil rights and expanding education for the masses, especially women. Editorials in other fledging newspapers, like the *Hwangsŏng sinmun* and the *Cheguk sinmun*, echoed similar concerns.

Sŏ Chae-p'il, who promoted women's education, explained that the debate would be fierce because traditional power hierarchies and gender relations were at stake: "The life of a woman is not that inferior to men," because "men are not enlightened" and only seek to use their physical strength to oppress women. As a result, he cautioned, "Be aware, women." Through the gradual acquisition of knowledge, women would eventually gain equal rights and be able to confront these "irrational" men.[72] To begin the process of reform, Sŏ proposed that the state make education accessible to both boys and girls:

There should be no distinction between the sexes when teaching the children of our people. It is proper to establish one school for girls whenever one school for boys is established. However, the government does not educate girls, which means that half of our national population is abandoned in the state [of ignorance] and left uneducated. How regretful this is! We grow sad seeing Korean women treated so scornfully. We are determined to fight men for [the rights of] women at the same time.[73]

Sŏ's writings echoed the ideals of the *in'naech'ŏn* philosophy of universal equality advocated by Ch'oe Che-u.[74] Some argued that the concept of universal equality in education would gradually ameliorate sexual inequality in the home. As one reformer put it:

Wives are called helpers at home. This means that wives help their husbands at home. Unfortunately, however, women are looked down upon. While fathers are treated with respect, mothers are regarded as inferior. Wives are treated as bondswomen who cook rice, wash clothes, or go on errands. How can wives be called helpers of the home?[75]

There were, of course, daunting obstacles to overcome if the king was to extend educational opportunities to all regardless of social background or gender and hence create a "civilized and enlightened" society. First, it would be necessary to convince 20 million people to discard old customs and embrace new ones. Second, the country lacked an educational infrastructure; although missionaries had established private girls' schools in the late nineteenth century, the state so far had opened only the Hansŏng Normal School to train teachers, five primary schools for boys, and a foreign language school. There were no public schools for girls. Despite its rhetoric, in reality the state gave priority to the creation of boys' schools, much to the chagrin of reformers, who complained: "The government has just started to teach children, yet girls are still neglected. How could they discriminate against girls? It is proper [to create] a school for girls whenever they establish a school for boys."[76] Likewise,

Tongnip sinmun (1896) pointed out that only one hundred out of 6 million girls attended school, which was "simply a drop in the ocean." The writer also pointed out that "the thoughtlessness and negligence" of the female population was a defining "Oriental" trait. Korea would have to emulate those countries in Europe and America where "mothers, wives, sisters, and daughters" received the same opportunities as their brothers and sons. Only then would Korea be able to overcome its backwardness.[77] In 1894, the government enacted the Kabo Reforms, which abolished the Confucian examination system and created a new Ministry of Education (Hakpu). However, in the final analysis, these reforms had little impact on women's education.[78]

The peninsula's neighbor, Japan, openly derided Korea's ill-fated attempts to modernize through public education: "No serious attempt was made to put [it] in force" because "the law has been a dead letter from the moment of its birth."[79] It was the Japanese view that without the assistance of Japan, Korea would struggle to establish a public education system for both sexes. Many writers for *Tongnip sinmun* who had spent time in Japan and the United States acknowledged this criticism and lamented the dismal state of Korean women compared to women in the West or even Japan. As one writer wrote in 1896:

> Europe [was] the pioneer of modern civilization . . . a fountainhead of reasoning power and human knowledge. Behold the woman of a civilized nation. She enjoys equal rights with man. She studies all branches of learning in schools. When she grows into womanhood marriage does not mean bondage to her. Nay, she is honored because she is not inferior to her husband in education and accomplishment.[80]

Given Korea's limited resources, one reformer argued, it must prioritize its needs, and "not a cent should be spent by the government on high schools and colleges until the people of the entire peninsula have been provided with rudimentary schools."[81] Even an uneducated mother could benefit from her child's school experiences—the first step toward the transformation of women.[82] Hence, during the 1880s and 1890s, reformers employed the notion of women's education and equal rights for every citizen (*manmin p'yŏngdŭng*) as a means of spreading enlightenment; education became the means of constructing modern nationhood.[83]

THE ADVENT OF MISSIONARIES

Protestant missionaries were keenly aware of the dismal results of Western nations' efforts to penetrate Korea's closed doors. They also had been discouraged by the 1866 execution of nine French missionaries and eight thousand Catholic converts for their attempts to enact religious change. Horace Newton Allen's (1852–1932) arrival in Seoul in 1884 to serve as the American Legation's physician proved critical in gaining the king's trust. As Allen recalled, "We arrived in Seoul, a few months before the outbreak of a bloody *emeute* wherein Western medical and surgical methods were favourably tested."[84] He saved the life of Prince Min Yŏng-ik, the queen's nephew, who was severely wounded during the bloody coup d'état staged by Kim Ok-kyun and a group of progressive leaders. Allen gained the king's confidence and was granted the right to bring other missionaries to serve as advisors to the king.

Allen received permission to open the Kwanghyewŏn, the first royal hospital, in February 1885. In his memoirs, he recalled: "The medical successes in this instance prepared the way for the opening of missionary work proper."[85] Shortly thereafter, Mary F. Scranton and Henry Appenzeller and his wife came to Korea to work at the hospital. Miss Louisa Rothweiler and Miss Annie J. Ellers joined the staff in 1887, opening the first department of gynecology at the hospital. In 1896, the North American Presbyterian Mission dispatched an additional nineteen female missionaries to work at Kwanghyewŏn hospital and Pogu yŏgwan, the first women's clinic.[86]

One missionary described the success of the Presbyterian missionaries: "The seventeen months that have elapsed have proven the greatest need of this hospital in its present form. Sixteen thousand patients have been treated in the daily dispensary clinic and 490 have been admitted to the wards, while a large number of visits to homes have been made by the physicians and their assistants."[87] Dr. Mary M. Cutler, the physician in charge of Po ku Nyo Koan (Pogu yŏgwan), was pleased at the growing number of female patients. The largest number of patients treated in one day was forty-five women, and the clinic averaged eighteen patients a day.[88] The opening of "milk stations" lured many mothers concerned about lactation to the clinics.[89] Through these kinds of philanthropic activities, missionaries began to make inroads into Korea.[90]

Missionaries nonetheless found it difficult to gain the trust of Korean women. Mary F. Scranton, the founder of the first girls' school in Korea, reflected on her experience:

> You who have come more recently can, I think, scarcely realize
> the difference between Korea of today and the country to which
> we came more than ten years ago. . . . Nothing remained, therefore,
> for us to do but to win hearts, if such a thing lay within the range
> of possibilities, and acquire the language. Both of these under the
> circumstances proved difficult. Our presence on the street in too
> close proximity to the women's apartments was often times the signal
> for the rapid closing of doors and speedy retreat behind screens, while
> children ran screaming with as much lung power as they could bring
> to bear on the occasion.[91]

The seclusion of elite women posed difficulties. Horace Allen expressed his frustration at the extreme modesty of one patient: "As illustrating this faith and the close seclusion in which women are kept, a Korean lady actually died rather than see me, though I had been called to the house and she seemed to think that if I simply looked at her she would recover. She could not bring herself to permit a strange man to look upon her and actually died rather than violate the inbred custom of her country."[92]

Experience like Allen's prompted missionaries to show more respect for Korean cultural and gender practices by segregating their Sunday schools. Services for women were scheduled during the evenings, when the minister would hang a curtain to separate himself from his female audience. In 1890, churches were built in an L-shape, allowing men and women to sit in separate wings while facing the pulpit, which was located at the apex.[93]

Confronting patriarchal family relations and such rituals as ancestor veneration (which was idolatry in the eyes of the missionaries) proved to be a Herculean task. Instead of direct confrontation with these local practices, missionaries sought to "extend God's love and grace" through philanthropy. As L. George Paik observed, "Hospitals and schools [were] termed indirect missionary work, as distinguished from direct proselytizing efforts through open preaching and religious observations."[94]

Missionaries in Korea engaged in what Jean and John Comaroff have called "didactic philanthropism." A school, for example, was not only the "door to the church"; rather, "schooling provided the model for conversion; conversion the model for schooling."[95] As one missionary reported: "One of the most powerful agencies at work in this direction is the work of Christian missions, especially Protestant Missions. Christian evangelization has always claimed general education as her handmaiden and all over the country schools have been and are being opened by Christian missionaries."[96]

Yet, although the missionaries' primary goal was proselytizing, they undeniably were successful educators as well, especially where women were concerned. As Yun Ch'i-ho wrote in 1935, "If the Christian missionaries had accomplished nothing in Korea, the introduction of female education deserves our lasting gratitude."[97]

The intended beneficiaries of the missionary efforts could not see this far into the future, of course. The most important goal for Mary Scranton was to create a desire to learn. She recalled: "It seems I must get to the mothers before I can reach the daughters."[98] By January 1887, the number of students had grown to a lucky seven. "They, the girls," Scranton recollected, were not "made over again after our foreign ways of living, dress, and surroundings, because it occasionally appears from home and even in the field that we thought to make a change in all ways." More importantly, she felt that it was their role to make "Koreans better Koreans only"; her wards needed to be "proud of Korean things" in order to recreate a "perfect Korea through Christ and his teachings."[99]

The missionaries' desire to maintain Korean culture even as they sought to change native mores and values made them intolerant of any attempt to emulate Western ways. In 1906, one missionary woman described in the *Korean Review* her first association meeting with a group of upper-class Korean women. These women had asked her to instruct them about the Bible every Sabbath evening and, during regular school days, to provide lessons in "secular studies." They also wanted the American to review their prospectus, which outlined the guidelines of their club, in order to garner her personal approval. The missionary could hardly contain her disgust at the Korean women's crude imitation of Western culture and ideals. She described the woman who had escorted her to the meeting as someone who was "evidently not one from the usual order of Korean women." Her scanty foreign clothes, "which were terribly mismatched," were absolutely unsuited for winter. The feather fan she held, a large pair of round glasses that resembled goggles (an essential trademark of the future "new woman" in the 1920s), and poorly selected jewelry—all made her look ridiculous in the eyes of her Western observer.[100]

The appalled missionary regretted her assumption that only Korean men attempted to emulate foreigners. It was a cold day when she met the members of this fledgling club. The women donned two-piece purplish Western outfits made of cotton cloth. She learned later that these women had encouraged schoolgirls "to go back and forth from school in broad daylight with no shelter apron over their heads" just to show their escape from the clutches of "Eastern superstition" and their commencement on the "road of progress." "To anyone familiar with Korean custom, such a change is appalling given the extreme care with which the daughters of even the poorest [classes] are sheltered."[101] Missionaries believed they could introduce enlightenment through new ideas, language (English), and religion without generating changes in Korean life—an erroneous assumption, as we will see.

The desire of Korean women to gain knowledge secured imperial sanction in 1885, when Queen Min (1851–95) visited Scranton's school, which she renamed the Ewha haktang (Pear blossom school).[102] This visit not only raised the public image of the school but validated female education as a worthwhile endeavor. Within a couple of years, the public agreed that the school had done "no harm" to the girls, and "the scowls changed and pleasant faces and smiles greeted us."[103]

Scranton eventually could cite many successes. In 1886, she had but one student; thirteen years later, the number of students at Ewha haktang had increased to forty-seven. She proudly reported: "[Their] average age is twelve years, with ages ranging between eight and seventeen years. English and *ŏnmun* (*han'gŭl*) are the media through which knowledge is imparted. Elementary Western branches are taught in English; certain Western studies and religious literature are studied in *ŏnmun*. English is optional and taught to perhaps one-third of the girls."[104]

The growth of Ewha haktang and the interest in female education were important for missionaries. According to the Council for Mission of Presbyterian Churches' recommendation in 1893, the conversion of women and the training of Christian girls through education were imperative because "mothers exercise so important an influence over future generations."[105] The board of Ewha haktang even placed a full-page ad in the *Hwangsŏng sinmun* to advertise their "modern" curriculum and urge parents to send their daughters to this institution:

Primary: National language, Chinese language, composition, arithmetic, drawing, geography, elementary gymnastics, English
Middle: Bible, Chinese language, moral training, geography, Korean history, arithmetic, English, physiology, hygiene, zoology, botany, drawing, cooking, bookkeeping, elementary gymnastics
High: Bible, Chinese language, algebra, geometry, trigonometry,

astronomy, physiology, psychology, educational studies, biology, chemistry, English, world geography, advanced physiology, economy, world history (modern, medieval, England, America)
Elective: Optional music[106]

Despite the goal to make "Koreans better Koreans only"—to avoid Westernizing the students—this advertisement reveals that the school exposed the girls to a new Western language (English), a history of the world that included English and American experiences, and a new moral code through the Bible. For all the missionaries' complaints about the Koreans' desire to emulate their culture, their own teachings promoted Western thought and culture.

That Koreans embraced these new schools with enthusiasm greatly encouraged missionaries like the Canadian James S. Gale (1863–1937), who had come to Korea in 1888: "A great fever for education has taken possession of the people of the peninsula. At every public gathering where education is mentioned, it touches a thousand electric buttons, and men are on their feet, wide awake, and excitement runs high. All eyes are bright when education speaks. Schools are cropping out of the soil like mushrooms."[107]

Many of these fledging schools received patronage from donors in the United States. For example, the girls' school in Kunsan received support from "the ladies of Lexington (Virginia) Presbyterian, who became interested in the school through their missionary, Mrs. Bull."[108] Patrons from various churches provided donations to cover many of the expenses for starting up a school. In other instances, local citizens pledged to provide the salary of the teacher at the An-pyŏn school in Wŏnsan.[109]

Although the earlier missionaries established Christian girls' schools in areas with a Christian constituency, by 1900 missionaries sought to expand their influence into "heathen" areas.[110] In Seoul alone, there were twenty-two day schools in 1911, "all under the control of one superintendent." Many of these schools did not have their own buildings. For example, the school in the East Gate used the basement of a church, where a graduate of Ewha haktang offered courses to seventy-eight students.[111] Although three girls graduated from the highest grade at the Sa-kang school, none of them was able to continue their education at a formal institution because of the lack of government-sponsored public girls' schools or because their parents were too poor to send them to Ewha haktang.[112]

Still, even an education cut short could be transforming. Missionary schools not only stimulated the desire to read and write; equally important, the message of Christianity, especially its fundamental ideals of equality and liberating women from oppression, hit a responsive chord among the lower classes. In an interview, Gill, "a farmer of small means and humble station" from P'yŏngyang province, praised the good schools for children and the hospitality of the missionaries toward the lower class: "I found their hospitals different from the others. These foreign doctors treated rich and poor, high and low, with equal willingness and kindness." "Among other things these missionaries preached," he observed, "they said that in the sight of God, all men are equal."[113] Missionaries often encouraged native converts to participate in programs like their Sunday schools and vacation Bible schools and to spread the gospel. In 1906, for example, 154 men and women teachers taught 3,013 students and opened forty-six schools in eleven cities and towns.[114]

Although these were not formal schools, "the new ones who [came] to church, especially the young women if they are not able to read, [were] taught the native characters."[115] More importantly, Bible schools offered a rare opportunity for women to voice their opinions about social issues. For example, after a devotional service, one Bible school debated whether women should be consulted on matters pertaining to the welfare of the household. As Myrtle Elliott Cable observed, "Both men and women took part of the debate, and the pros and cons were fully discussed. This is surely a step in the advance for womanhood in Korea."[116] Miss Lulu Frey, the fourth principal of Ewha haktang, remarked on the importance of Sunday schools for women: "[It] has grown so on the women's side that all who attend cannot get into the classroom and it is quite impossible to make my voice reach the number which now fill the main part of the

2. Students from Ewha haktang going on a field trip (1900).

church. The time has come when they must be divided into classes and given into the hands of native teachers. I have not done this before because I wanted to teach the women myself as long as I possibly could."[117]

Although these weekly informal Sunday schools did not offer any academic courses, they did allow many rural women to learn to read and write. In her 1911 assessment of Bible schools, Millie M. Albertson expressed amazement at the enthusiasm with which Korean women read the Bible, a practice that helped promote literacy: "No American school girl ever looked forward to the periodicals that would give the next chapter of a continued story with more eagerness than these women looked forward to the time when the entire Bible should be translated into the Korean language."[118]

GOING BEYOND MISSIONARY GOALS:
SECULAR INSTITUTIONS FOR GIRLS

The rapid growth in the number of Christian schools stimulated interest in the development of secular private schools for girls. A number of women's organizations, such as the Yŏja kyoyuk-hoe (Society for

Women's Education) and the Chinmyŏng puin-hoe (Chinmyŏng Women's Society), emerged during this period. Many of these fledging women's organizations sought to elevate the status of women as well as establish schools.[119]

One such organization, the Ch'anyang-hoe (Promotion Society),[120] had a membership of roughly four hundred women from the upper classes. It established the Sunsŏng Girls' School, the first secular girls' school in December 1898. Members of the Ch'anyang-hoe sought government recognition and funding. In a memorial to the king on 11 October 1898, the leaders of the organization expressed their desire to emulate enlightened countries in Europe and America, where "competent persons receive education and knowledge is disseminated." They lamented the fact that there was not a single school in Korea for women. If Korea showed equal treatment to their women and educated their girls, they declared, it would surely become a civilized and enlightened country.[121] Despite the efforts by the Ch'anyang-hoe to pressure the Ministry of Education through an imperial ordinance, conservative minister Sin Ki-sŏn and other cabinet members urged the king to reverse his decision, citing the need to focus on more important financial matters. Though the founders went ahead and established a private school, hoping for government support in the future, the school failed in 1901, and the buildings were ultimately mortgaged to a Japanese businessman.[122]

As the first attempt by a group of women to create a girls' school, the organization received its share of criticism from the press. One newspaper provided a class analysis: "The members of the Ch'anyang-hoe wear silk coats and they favor the rich by giving out membership cards to them." It accused the organization of only thinking about promoting the welfare of elite girls and declining to give cards "to members who are poor unless they pay the fees beforehand."[123] The women of the Ch'anyang-hoe put up a feisty defense:

Are there perhaps any differences between men and women in their bodies, arms and legs, or ears and eyes? Why should our women live

on what their husbands [earn] as though they were fools, confin-
ing themselves to their deep chambers for [their] entire lives and
subject[ing] themselves to regulations imposed by their husbands?
Upon [observation of other] enlightened countries, we know that
men and women are equal there and boys and girls go to school
early in their childhood, learning various skills and principles and
broadening their vision. [When they are grown up], women [get]
married to men. As long as wives reside with their husbands all
their [lives], the former are not a bit regulated by the latter but are
[extremely respected]. Their skills and principles are equal to those
possessed by their husbands. How beautiful is this! We should
establish girls' schools as in other countries by abolishing our old
custom and following the new style so that our girls can learn
various skills and principles and methods of [creating] a success in
life. We are going to establish girls' schools with the aim of making
women equal to men in the future. Interested women and men
among our compatriots are asked to register their names in our
school membership.[124]

Interestingly, the excessive optimism of Korean women about gender
equality touched a few raw nerves among missionary women, who were
more realistic about the true nature of gender relations in the West. The
woman who had been appalled at the gaudy "Western" appearance of the
new upper-class women's association expressed her dismay in the *Korean
Review* by highlighting two misconceptions on which these women had
built their aspirations and goals.[125] First, she argued that they had an "ex-
aggerated and mistaken" idea of the "woman's sphere and her ideals" in
the West. The "free and independent" Western woman whom they
sought to emulate could only be found "in novels, the plays, the police
gazettes, and on the world's great globe trotting highways." Other des-
picable "new women" were those who "talk back, who govern, make
noise, and parade on platforms."[126] She asserted that the second mis-
conception was their view of progress, liberty, and civilization. The idea
of doing anything or whatever one pleased was a notion held only by "an-

archists, socialists, and other revolutionary societies." She compared the woman's association to a "great fete in an Eastern city built upon boards and canvasses which represented a grand old forest monarch—skillfully painted and covered with paper leaves and blossoms." Inevitably, rain and floods would destroy these superficial imitations and illusions.[127]

Such sobering warnings did little to dampen the enthusiasm for Korean women's education. Between 1906 and 1909, the Ministry of Education (Hakpu) set up sixty new elementary schools and nineteen new secondary schools. Although the Ministry of Education decided in 1899 on three years of common school and two years of higher education for girls, it was only in 1908 that the government opened the Hansŏng Girls' High School, the first public institution of higher learning for girls.[128] Although there were only a handful of girls who qualified for high school, some reformers pushed for opening more government schools.

Reformers like Yun Hyo-chŏng contended that it was imperative for the state to continue to open schools of higher learning for women in order to create more compatible wives for educated husbands: "If a man who is brilliant and grounded in learning of the new marries a traditional woman skilled in washing, fetching water, cooking, and sewing, and knows nothing about managing the household or social affairs, he would lose his desire for her and seek another woman."[129] If the state invested in men's education, it should expend equal resources on women's education; an unequal state of affairs would lead to intellectual disparities and the ultimate breakdown of many marriages.

Although some conceded that women's education was important, they wanted to create a curriculum "more suitable" to women, which would teach them practical things like how to deal with "household matters, hygiene, household economy, how to raise their children and how to use the abacus."[130] But not all reformers agreed; those who were critical of the traditional *hyŏnmo yangch'ŏ* (wise mother and good wife) ideology argued that instead of "making women into machines" they should cultivate their *ch'ŏnp'um* (natural talents) and *ingyŏk* (personalities) in order to become "independent individuals." One writer, Chŏng Yŏng-t'aek, noted that educating women would only enhance the status of the family and society, as well as the nation.[131]

By the end of the Chosŏn period, it became clear that Korean women were not satisfied with the limited goals the missionaries had set out for them. While the missionaries focused establishing primary schools, Koreans recognized the importance of creating institutions of higher education so that women could continue their learning.

Literacy and education were arenas in which gender inequality was particularly evident prior to the arrival of Protestant missionaries. Aside from a handful of literati women who were indoctrinated in classical texts, the majority of Korean girls and women had no access to education. Protestant missionaries contributed much to the development of female education in Korea. They introduced women to the marvelous world of letters and provided some degree of literacy. This small taste of knowledge could not be quenched by the limited educational opportunities in Korea, so some women traveled abroad to continue their education. Such opportunities were rare, however, and most Korean women had to content themselves with the little education they received in the missionary institutions.

Even this avenue soon narrowed dramatically. As a result of a series of educational ordinances promulgated by the colonial government, many Christian schools closed down or could no longer attract Koreans because they were not recognized by the state. Despite the formal closing of these institutions, Korean women found a way to receive instruction in basic literacy through informal Bible study groups and church activities. Perhaps the most significant contributions of the missionary schools were in breaking the ground for female education and instilling a love of learning in a population that had heretofore been excluded from the world of letters.

The long Chosŏn era was a period of significant transformation for Korean women. In contrast to static images of a rigid, uniform patriarchal society that oppressed women, new studies have shown the importance of internal fissures, movements of dissent that promoted greater egalitarianism, and efforts of Korean women to overcome the restrictions on them by utilizing loopholes in Confucian laws or manipulating traditional social relations (i.e., mother-son ties). Despite the strict regulation of their conduct and social interaction, Korean women were able to soften the edges of Confucian patriarchy through their roles as mothers, wives, and spiritual leaders. On the political front, Korean women joined in social movements for change, obtaining an education in radical dissent—a legacy that they would draw on in their efforts against the Japanese occupation.

Finally, Korean women took advantage of the opportunities offered by modern education to ameliorate their status. Although their numbers were small, the first generation of students, mainly graduates of the missionary schools, emerged in the early 1920s to challenge efforts to control their knowledge and identity. Despite the pressures of the dominant Confucian cultural system, the missionaries' attempts to suppress emulation of Western styles, and the repressive measures of a colonial government seeking to reassert traditional subservience and domesticity, the "new women" rejected the boundaries set for them. They would articulate this new identity through their dress, attitudes, careers, and writings in order to negotiate a new vision for Korean womanhood.

CHAPTER TWO

The "New Woman" and the Politics of Love, Marriage, and Divorce in Colonial Korea

> It is in space, on a worldwide scale, that each idea of "value" acquires or loses its distinctiveness through confrontation with the other values and ideas that it encounters. . . . Groups, classes, or fractions of classes cannot constitute themselves, or recognize one another, as "subjects" unless they generate (or produce) a space. Ideas, representations or values which do not succeed in making their mark on space . . . will lose all pith and become mere signs. . . . Whatever is not invested in an appropriated space is stranded. . . . [S]pace's investment— the production of space—has nothing incidental about it: it is a matter of life and death.
>
> Henri Lefebvre, *The Production of Space*

On 24 June 1922, the daily *Tonga ilbo* ran a sensational story about a young woman who had attempted to disguise herself as a man to attend the Chŏngch'ŭk Training School in Sŏdaemun. The reporter suggested that her "bobbed hair" and brazen transgression of male public space were the main sources of the controversy.[1] The woman behind this affront to popular sentiments was Kang Hyang-nan, a former *kisaeng* (female entertainer) from Seoul. A tumultuous love affair with a young scholar had convinced her to leave her old profession and to pursue an education at Paehwa haktang. When her lover abruptly terminated the relationship and the funding of her studies, Kang contemplated suicide; only the intervention of one of the school's teachers persuaded her that she could "live like a man," crop her tresses, and take her rightful seat in the classroom.[2] Stories like these generated great anxiety in Korean society, especially among male nationalist reformers who argued that women represented the barometer by which to measure progress. While some argued condescendingly that Korean women were simply trying out new identities and habits, others feared that they had gone too far. These educated women, whom reformers had nurtured and upheld as symbols of modernity, civilization, and nationalism, were undermining the stability of the family, compromising sexual morality, and degrading national character.

In this chapter, I explore the changing discursive forces that competed to define Korean women's identity and role within the context of the new spaces created by education. I argue that under the guise of Westernization and progress, a small coterie of literate women seized the initiative to enhance their education, determine their own physical appearance, and contribute to the debate about changing gender roles and expectations in Korean society. With her bobbed hair, short skirts, and air of determination, the "new woman" took center stage during the 1920s, as she sought to redefine Korean female identity. Indeed, according to a study by Na Kyŏng-hŭi, more than 230 editorials on the "woman question" appeared in the *Chosŏn ilbo* and the *Tonga ilbo*—two of the most widely circulated newspapers during the colonial period, from 1920 to 1940.[3]

Lefebvre once observed that for "ideas, representations, and values" to maintain their distinctiveness, groups must carve out a particular space.[4] For the "new Korean woman," the challenge was not simply to produce that space but to defend it from nationalist reformers who sought to undermine her existence. While these reformers declared their intention to modernize women through education, the cult of domestic-

ity, and medical science, they were no more prepared to accept the educated, independent woman than were the conservative elements of society. To minimize the threat of the "new woman," nationalist reformers sought to create new ideologies of womanhood that would appeal to
her modern sensibilities while containing her within traditional gender
boundaries. At the same time, they could ill afford to leave this visible
group out of the reform process, and the construction of new gender roles
and identity would invariably involve resistance, negotiation, and compromise. To understand the emergence of and controversies surrounding the new woman, this chapter examines the specific context of colonial modernity and its impact on Korean women, the politics of beauty
and voice, and the national debates about gender roles and ideologies of
womanhood.

REFORMING KOREAN EDUCATION:
JAPANESE GOALS AND METHODS

In his memoir, *Chōsen no tabi* (Travels in Korea), councillor Hara Shōichirō
described his 1914 inspection of the Kyŏngsŏng Girls' Higher Common
School. He concluded that it would be very difficult to implement any social or economic reform in Korea without enlisting the support of Korean women. In his view, Korean women were more "self-conscious and
far easier to influence" than the men. Moreover, their strong disposition
and power in the home ensured that they would have little trouble
"influencing the men."[5]

The colonial government disdainfully dismissed the so-called advancements in female education promoted by Western missionaries. As
one report observed, "Prior to the establishment of the Residency General, nothing worthy of notice—at least in the modern sense—existed
in regard to education in Korea."[6] Despite their emphasis on "modern
pedagogy," colonial authorities viewed women's education in purely util-
itarian terms. The goal was not to further knowledge for its own sake or
to foster equal rights, but to create loyal imperial subjects who had in-

ternalized the rules and mores of the empire. Educators like Shidehara Taira firmly believed, moreover, that Japanese methods of education would "cultivate good" and promote peace for the Korean people.[7]

For the first ten years after annexation, under the *budan seiji* (martial rule) of Governor-General Terauchi Masatake (1910–16), Japanese reformers and educators thus sought to reorganize Korean education around a new pedagogy founded on moral instruction and disciplinary techniques. The promulgation of Imperial Ordinance No. 229 in August 1911 marked the first of a series of ordinances to direct the building of a new state school system.[8] It was based on the principles of the Imperial Rescript on Education (Kyōiku chokugo), which had shaped the Japanese educational system some years earlier. The goal was to inculcate "moral character and general knowledge" in the younger generation of Koreans to make them loyal subjects of imperial Japan. At the same time, it sought to "enable them to cope with the present conditions existing in the Peninsula."[9] W. Carl Rufus described the process: "The national policy of Japan in Chōsen is the complete assimilation of the Korean race. Japan approached the Gordian knot in true Alexandrine humor. In 1910, the sword had cut the political bonds that held the Koreans together, and military rule under the highly centralized Government-General of Chōsen bound them to Japan." The Japanese not only resorted to military methods; in fact, the "chief among these auxiliaries" would be the Japanese system of education for the Koreans.[10]

The first order of business was to eliminate the Hakpu (Ministry of Education) and replace it with the Naimushō (Home Affairs Department) with its "Bureau of Education." Governor-General Terauchi recommended that all schools be classified into three kinds: *futsū* (common), *jitsugyō* (industrial), and *senmon* (specialized). The system would consist of four years of primary education, followed by four years of secondary education for boys and three years of secondary education for girls. The aim of colonial schools was to impart "common knowledge and art indispensable to daily life with special attention to arousing national characteristics, the extended use of the national language, and the fostering of feminine virtues such as constancy and domesticity" in girls. Finally, it sought to "cultivate moral character and national spirit."[11]

The Fate of Missionary Schools

Japanese had recognized the Protestant missions during its annexation of Korea, but all that changed with the abortive attempt by An Myŏng-gŭn to assassinate Governor-General Terauchi at Sŏnch'ŏn on 28 December 1910. The state charged the missionaries with training and harboring nationalists involved in the Korean independence movement. The roundup of more than six hundred suspects, mainly members of the Sinminhoe (New People's Association), and the subsequent trial of the *paegoin sakkŏn* (Case of the 105 in 1912) prompted the government to launch measures to curtail missionary activities. According to Allen Clark, of the 124 put on trial, 98 professed to be Christians.[12]

Even before annexation, colonial authorities had sought to curb the number of missionary schools by promulgating the *shiritsu gakkō rei*, or private school ordinance, in 1908.[13] According to this regulation, all private schools (mission and nonreligious) had to adhere to the new government standards and obtain recognition. Each school principal had to submit to the Bureau of Education an annual report on the condition of his or her school.[14] Furthermore, the standardization of textbooks, equipment, buildings, and grounds "meant a very considerable financial expenditure" for many of the missionary schools.[15] The government charged that most of the two thousand or so private schools on the peninsula lacked adequate funds, staff, or equipment to be called educational institutions. Moreover, it noted that "instead of participating in sober educational work, some of them often meddled in political agitation against the Government, and used text-books of a seditious nature."[16] The Bureau of Education's new ordinance designated private schools as "recognized" or "designated." By 1912, all private schools were required to conform to government standards. These new regulations sought to curtail the hours spent in Bible courses and to secularize the curriculum. By the end of 1911, the number of private schools shrank to 1,700 (including 700 missionary schools) with only 39 schools receiving government recognition. A total of 461 schools closed down because of financial constraints.[17] Other schools closed down to protect their religious liberty rather than compromise a basic conviction.[18]

The standardized education system entailed a complete overhaul of the curriculum in existing schools to preclude criticism or, even worse, closure. As Lulu Frey recalled, "Children are coming to us from every direction but government regulation and more intelligent parents make it necessary that the equipment of the schools and the educational attainments of the teachers be beyond question." To retain the status of a recognized school was critical, because it provided "opportunities for the continuation of studies in government institutions of a higher grade." Those students who graduated from unrecognized or undesignated schools had to take a series of difficult examinations to be certified as a primary school teacher.[19]

The question of acquiring recognized or designated status received priority at a conference of the Mission Council in 1922. The majority of the Korean constituents favored missionary schools becoming registered schools.[20] As Hugh Cynn noted:

> As soon as people were thoroughly aroused on the subject of education, they began to be more particular concerning the kind of education they wanted. It was soon recognized that the government controlled the whole system. If one wanted an education which would lead to the Imperial University, one which would lead to a position of honor and a good salary, and having to stand difficult examinations, then he must get into the government system, or into the school which was fully recognized by the government department of education.[21]

To qualify as a recognized school demanded an increase in expenditures for such things as renovation of facilities to meet government standards and purchase of new textbooks. Though some schools were able to solicit aid from outside donors to help pay for these expenses, many private institutions had to increase tuition and add fees, as did Ewha haktang, when it sought government recognition.[22] In 1934, the *Tonga ilbo* reported that a female student at Ewha College would have to pay roughly 380 *wŏn* to cover room and board and tuition costs. However, for an extra 100 *wŏn*, she could go to Japan and study at a more prestigious university.[23] Another writer complained that schools had previously given free textbooks, notebooks, and pencils to their students but now imposed a monthly fee to cover these expenses.[24] In other words, Christian education, which had once been, for the most part, free and accessible to anyone now required a substantial expenditure and was relegated to an inferior status.

The dearth of institutions (which was compounded by the forced closing of some missionary schools) made it difficult to realize the goal of universal education for both sexes. For example, in 1919, only 84,306 (3.7 percent) of Korean children attended public primary schools.[25] The colonial government did not immediately compensate for the decrease in missionary schools, which declined from 1,317 in 1912 to 690 in 1919. In fact, there were only five public and seven recognized private high schools for Korean boys and two public and four private high schools for Korean girls.[26]

Reforms and the Colonial Project

In the aftermath of the March First demonstrations in 1919, the Japanese sought to ease colonial policies and reform the Korean educational system. For W. Carl Rufus, the independence demonstrations during the preceding year indicated that "the subject race possessed a body and a soul."[27] Saitō Makoto replaced Terauchi as governor-general, and a special committee met to discuss much-needed reforms that would serve as the basis for the promulgation of a newly revised educational ordinance in 1922. One of the main clauses in the revised ordinance specified that Koreans be "afforded equal opportunity under one and the same system as the Japanese."[28] Interestingly, Koreans were no longer automatically classified as non-native speakers but could attain full recognition as native speakers.[29] At the same time, this revised educational ordinance could be used as a means for transmitting Japanese cultural and political values.[30]

Though the colonial government did not intend to enforce compulsory education as in Japan, it insisted on some fundamental changes. The committee maintained that while Japanese and Koreans would be schooled separately, there would be much more uniformity with the system of education in Japan proper. In other words, the rules governing "the period of study, entrance qualification, subjects of study, hours of instructions per week" would be the same, the only exception being the teaching of Korean language and history.[31] Furthermore, all public-approved high schools would be renamed girls' or boys' higher common schools. Under this new ordinance, the length of primary education was extended from four to six years and secondary education from four to five years for boys and three to four years for Korean girls.

Koreans who supported the efforts of the government urged parents to seize this opportunity to send their daughters to school. One writer urged compatriots in 1924 to act like responsible parents by sending their five- or six-year-old sons and daughters to nurseries and enrolling their eight- or nine-year-old daughters in common schools instead of wasting their lives on chores like carrying siblings on their backs or fetching water. Twelve-year-old children should also be encouraged to complete their education instead of dropping out to fulfill family obligations. "You do not have to look afar," the reporter informed his readers. "Just look at the Japanese boys and girls. They all carry books and when they reach five or six years old, they are all in school."[32] Although the process was gradual, parents began to enroll their children in these common schools in the 1920s to take advantage of the promise of upward social mobility through education. The *Tonga ilbo* noted an elevenfold increase in the number of applicants to common schools and a twenty-five-fold increase in middle school applications in 1922.[33]

Another transformation in educational opportunities was sparked by a 1920 regulation that allowed Korean students greater freedom to pursue their studies abroad. That year, the number of students studying in Japan grew to one thousand, the majority in Tokyo.[34] According to the historian Jihang Pak, of those who opted to study abroad, more than 80 percent chose Japan, while the remaining 20 percent went to the United States or to Europe.[35] The *Tonga ilbo* reported a debate sponsored by the Korean Women's Educational Association at Sungdong Chapel over the best course: to develop institutions at home or to support female students who wanted to study abroad.[36]

To enhance his position, Governor-General Saitō invited a group of Koreans and missionaries for consultation and asked them to state their concerns so that he could launch his *bunka seiji* (cultural rule). The Federation Council for Protestant Evangelical Missions in Korea responded with a petition that demanded seven concessions: (1) to allow the Bible in their curriculum and other religious activities; (2) to remove restrictions on the use of the Korean language; (3) to allow more liberty in the management of schools; (4) to grant teachers and students more liberty of conscience; (5) to provide Koreans the same opportunities as their Japanese counterparts in education and more freedom in the use of textbooks; (6) to permit graduates of private schools with government permits to be eligible for all privileges accorded to graduates of government schools; and (7) to guarantee that the government would curtail excessive financial requirements on private schools.[37] Cognizant that Saitō would not agree to all these requests, the missionaries sought a compromise. In the end, mission schools were granted one concession: to teach Western languages and science to all secondary students on the condition that the Japanese language be a compulsory requirement in their schools. Religious instruction was only permitted at unaccredited private mission schools.

Although the ordinance of 1922 provided missionaries with an opportunity to continue their evangelizing, the restrictions on private schools limited their ability to engage in informal teaching methods. This prompted new Korean women's organizations, like the Young Women's Christian Association (YWCA) and the Korean Women's Educational Association, to take a more active role in educating young girls throughout the country. The YWCA did not have to adhere to government school regulations, and through prayer meetings and Bible studies, teachers taught "*han'gŭl*" and English to women in night schools and worked to improve the economic and educational conditions of women in the countryside."[38] The Korean Women's Educational Association also ran night schools, held monthly lectures, and published a journal (*Women's Times*), while preparing three hundred girls for entry into government high schools.[39] While student Cho Wŏn-suk likened her experience of studying in Seoul without her parents' knowledge to a "prisoner leaving the prison gates or a bird flying out of its cage into the skies,"[40] Kim Mirisa (1880–1955), a cofounder of the Korean Women's Educational Association, cautioned her readers that female education was still "very crude." Not only were most women restricted to the home, but they were not "able to write a letter on their own or read a newspaper."[41]

Though the government had succeeded in closing down many missionary schools, it had not yet fulfilled its pledge to establish one public primary school for every three districts (*sam myŏn il kyoje*) by 1920, one public high school in each of the thirteen provinces by 1922, and one school for every district (*il myŏn il kyoje*) by 1929. Indeed, according to the figures of a 1929 Government-General survey, there were only 1,505 common schools in Korea, of which 68 were located in the twelve cities.[42] According to Helen Kim's appraisal, this meant that there were only 1,437 schools for a rural population of 18,014,726 (95.5 percent of the total population). Moreover, the 1,437 rural schools were located not in the villages where the children lived but in the market towns. Instead of finding one school in every three districts, she found one school in every 19.7 villages, or one school for every 59.1 square miles.[43]

Perhaps the most visible change was in the educational staff and their goals. Though the majority of primary school teachers were still Korean, the majority of teachers at Korean secondary schools were now Japanese who sought to inculcate loyalty to the state and cultivate "desirable" character traits that were allegedly lacking in Koreans.[44] The curriculum made even the Korean primary school teachers part of this project:

There are 137 lessons in morals throughout the six years of common school. Out of these, fifty-eight lessons are on personality traits, such as patience, diligence, honesty, orderliness, faithfulness, and good manners. Next to the list is Emperor Worship, and duties of citizens, such as paying taxes; twenty-seven lessons are written on this subject. Eighteen lessons are on social relationships such as friendliness and greeting neighbors. Fourteen lessons are on family relationships, emphasizing particular filial piety. The remaining few lessons are distributed among topics such as health, kindliness to animals, and introduction of the school to children. The one lesson on vocation merely states that we should all have vocations and make our own living.[45]

To reinforce the educational goals of the colonial state, the lessons needed to be reinforced at home so that children could internalize the rules of citizenship. The role of the mother in instilling these values pushed the question of female education to the fore.

Teaching Modern Parenting to Imperial Female Subjects

To create loyal imperial citizens, the colonial state needed to focus specifically on the education of Korean women, who were at the heart of the family. As one family manual put it, "The mother's role in raising an infant is a very important responsibility, an investment in his future."[46]

Informal education of women, or indoctrination in the home, took the form of advice manuals and books that promised to teach Korean women how to become better mothers through the techniques of modern parenting. For instance, Kim Sang-dŏk noted that the *Mother's Reader* devoted a section to lullabies: "It is natural for a mother to sing a lullaby to children to put them to sleep. Whether in Seoul or the countryside, educated or uneducated mothers . . . love to sing songs to their children to put them to sleep. . . . Lullabies are important for a child's development (mentally/physically)." She urged Korean mothers not to sing just any old songs, but to be more selective and emulate other mothers around the world, who sing lullabies composed by Brahms and Schubert, which have "good long-term effects on children."[47]

Disguised as parenting advice, however, was a colonial agenda that sought to promote conformity and self-surveillance. Good parenting, according to these manuals, required strict control over every minute detail of a child's educational and social life. In 1936, for instance, a writer for the *Uri kajŏng* urged parents to assume greater responsibility for the development of their children at every stage. He enjoined parents of first and second graders, who were "in their prime of growth," to discuss every school lesson, ensure the company of good friends, and teach proper hygiene. Above all, they were to instill in children the importance of diligence and respect for their superiors. Parents of third and fourth graders were to assign one or two "suitable household tasks" to their children to inculcate a sense of responsibility.[48]

Paradoxically, the Korean writers who penned these manuals and journal articles often added subversive warnings to undermine the intentions of the colonial authorities. On the surface, a book might simply address how to raise children who valued industry, order, and deference to the colonial state. However, underneath the "public transcripts" (to use James Scott's term) lay hidden explanations and warnings. For instance, the writer of *Uri kajŏng* cautioned parents not to fight in front of their children. While this might be understood as a matter of decorum, it could also be a warning that the walls had eyes and ears. Even children and neighbors could reveal the "hidden transcripts" of opposition that might be let slip during a heated argument. Moreover, parents could maintain some control over the mechanisms that shaped their children at school by understanding the content of learning, controlling a child's peer group, and teaching them how to mask "hidden transcripts" through orderly conduct and appearance. In other words, knowledge was one way to resist the surveillance of the state.[49]

Another goal of the advice manuals was to teach girls the proper gender performance of domesticity and docility. One chapter in the *Uri kajŏng* urged girls to learn how to sew: "Sewing is an important virtue of girls. Even if girls from wealthy families do not want to sew with their own hands . . . [one cannot] separate sewing from girls." The rudimentary skill of sewing would teach girls not only the essentials of tailoring their own clothes but the important virtue of responsibility.[50]

Proper gender performance was also imparted through formal education. While primary education trained Korean girls to be "moral citizens" (i.e., loyal imperial subjects), secondary education aimed to create more "feminine" women. The highly gendered division of courses encouraged women to select "feminine" courses. In principle, women could enroll in "masculine" courses like ethics, national language (Japanese), Korean and Chinese literature, history, geography, mathematics, or science. However, students who chose these courses found themselves pressured to change their selection to courses like "house-keeping, sewing and handicraft," which were considered more appropriate for women.

According to one Government-General report, the new curriculum aimed to make the "education of girls as useful as possible for their practical daily life." Of course, it was identical to what was offered to girls in Japan to promote "feminine virtues and to instruct [girls] in knowledge and art that would be useful to make a livelihood, especially to cultivate their moral character and to become equipped to be good housekeepers."[51] For example, in the curriculum at Sukmyŏng Girls' Higher Common School from 1911 to 1921, knitting and sewing classes took up ten out of the thirty-one hours of instruction a week. Japanese language classes came in second with six hours of instruction per week.[52] Thus colonial education promoted a cult of domesticity not for the purpose of fostering modern middle-class womanhood in the Western sense, which included cultivation of moral sensibilities, cultural refinement, and aesthetic taste (bildung), but with the sole intent of maintaining Korean women, who were knowledgeable about "modern ideas," within the traditional constraints of domesticity.

Gender and national inequality in the establishment of schools and acceptance rates was apparent in a Government-General survey con-

ducted in May 1929. Only thirty-nine higher common private and public (secondary schools) existed in Korea, of which twenty-four were for
boys and only fifteen for girls.[53] According to Ch'oe Yŏng-su, establishing a school in Korea now "was even more difficult than catching a
cloud in the skies" and parents were less concerned about securing money
to finance their children's education than about simply "getting their child
into a school."[54] The *Tonga ilbo* lamented the 100 percent acceptance rate
of Japanese students at the primary level while Korean school children
struggled through difficult entrance examinations.[55]

Furthermore, of the sixty-six graduates of Ewha High School, only
thirty continued their studies at the university or at the Ewha Kinder-
garten Normal School.[56] "What about the remaining thirty-six?" Ada
Hall asked. "That is the question that constantly confronts us. Not one
got a position. Without a year of normal training above high school,
qualification to teach in primary is not granted."[57] Of the seventy-five
Koreans admitted to the one government normal school for girls in Korea, only five were accepted from Christian schools. In other words, by
1930, even graduates from Ewha were having difficulty entering government schools. It was becoming apparent to teachers like Ada Hall that
the future of the thirty-six women who were seeking entry into higher
education "was in industrial work" or some kind of practical job.[58]

The gains in female education were quite modest in the eyes of Korean women intellectuals. Kim Mirisa, an educator and advocate of
change, used the metaphor of a carriage in which "one of the wheels is
lagging" to describe the unequal status of women's education.[59] Indeed,
in 1920, illiteracy still remained high among women, at 93 percent.[60] Kim
I-ryŏp, the first editor of the journal *Sin yŏja* (New woman), reiterated
the need to educate all women and girls. Without education, she argued,
a woman would never be able to discover her individuality, and her life
would remain incomplete.[61] Pak Sa-jik also lamented the shortage of
schools for girls and stressed the need to educate mothers as well as wives,
even if it meant sending them to a *sŏdang* (village school).[62]

Korean women who had had the opportunity to study abroad were not content with such minimal goals and advocated the creation of better schools and opportunities for young girls. For instance, one woman who had studied medicine in Japan stated that a Western-style education had given her the opportunity to become an individual and she had come to understand what independence really meant.[63] Han So-je echoed similar sentiments when she stated that the reason she had become a physician was because she detested the idea of cadging money from a man's hand and yearned for independence.[64] Na Hye-sŏk, the first Korean woman to be recognized as an artist in the modern period, asserted that studying art provided a sense of her own individuality, and declared that she had finally become a "self-conscious human being."[65]

Others opposed the notion that the primary purpose of female education was to promote individuality and independence. Kim Hwal-lan argued that "more" education for women was not the answer. In an interview with *Sin tonga*, she argued that her education at Ewha (a Christian school) was "too academic." In fact, during her studies at Columbia University's Teachers College, Kim became convinced that only female education that "was closer to practical living" could serve women's interests in Korea.[66]

The idea of a practical education—preparing women to assume their "rightful" position in the home as mothers and wives—found the greatest support among male intellectuals like Chu Yo-sŏp. Chu argued that a "cultivated" woman (one knowledgeable in literature, language, or science) would not serve the interests of her family because she would be more inclined to pursue her own scholarly interests rather than her duties at home.[67] A fellow writer, Yi Kwang-su, concurred and stressed the need to focus the curriculum on motherhood. This was not to suggest that the state or private schools eliminate women's education altogether; rather, he suggested a curriculum that would provide formal training and guidance to future wives and mothers.[68]

Advocates of women's domestic education also opposed the imposition of Western values on Korean schools. Sharp criticism of Westernized education struck a responsive chord with Korean intellectuals as a result of growing reports of delinquency in the girls' schools, especially in the dormitories of private schools. Min T'ae-wŏn argued that the segregation of girls in schools was precisely the root of many social problems.[69] In particular, teachers and parents voiced concerns about intimate contact between girls, which might lead to lesbian tendencies and behavior.[70] Several incidents in which female students had committed suicide at schools alarmed contemporaries, who viewed them as evidence of a decline in morals.[71] Reformers proposed stricter rules at schools and an end to "the bad habit of male students sending love letters to female students to captivate their hearts."[72] Frustrated by what he saw during his visit to Tongdŏk Girls' School, one intellectual conceded that he could not prevent these girls from becoming "new women," but urged them to be "Korean new women" and not to imitate Western ways so blindly.[73] In many respects, the view of Korean intellectuals, who saw modernity as a source of moral corruption, was not that different from that of the Japanese colonial authorities, who also pushed a more traditional educational agenda. The only difference was that the Koreans desired a national alternative devoid of colonial overtones.

Whatever the position of intellectuals on female education, they all agreed that a new type of Korean woman had begun to emerge, which required supervision and control. The "new woman" rejected the gender performance set out for her by the colonial state and Korean national reformers; she wanted to write her own script by crossing gender boundaries and demanding access to knowledge restricted to men, espousing new mentalités, dress, and ideas of female emancipation.

THE EMERGENCE OF THE "NEW WOMAN": THE POLITICS OF FREEDOM AND FAMILY

Although their numbers were few, the first generation of educated women, mainly graduates of Protestant missionary schools, sought to challenge the Confucian patriarchal system and articulate their sense of spatial location through their writing, in the process negotiating a new vision for Korean women. Many had returned from sojourns in Japan and the West, where they had spent years studying and absorbing new values. Now they sought self-expression and independence in their own cities.[74]

One distinguishing feature of the "new women" was the defiant personal appearance that failed to conform to accepted gender performance. Discarding traditional dress, they donned "raised skirts exposing their knees" (as one newspaper scornfully observed), stacked heels, and cloche hats.[75] Instead of modest feminine coiffures, they flipped their bobbed hair in a manner that hinted at a subtle masculinity with an air of sexual permissiveness. They were hardly the docile and self-sacrificing women that Korean intellectuals had envisioned would lead the nation into the new era of progress and national freedom. Starting in the 1920s, a flurry of journalistic debates centered around two aspects of young women's appearance: short skirts and bobbed hair.[76]

Although a series of social reforms in 1894 sanctioned Western-style dress for men and compulsory cutting of the topknot, the state completely ignored reforms for women and expected them to adhere to traditional norms. However, Kang's shocking appearance on 24 June 1922 at the Chŏngch'ŭk Training School would change things. That a woman was seeking entry to a men's institution was one matter, but that a Korean woman would openly challenge the traditional codes of female etiquette posed a greater challenge to contemporaries. Kang's flaunting of her new *tanbal* (bobbed hair) not only defied traditional gender expectations but also represented a form of rebellion against the cultural norms imposed on Korean women.[77] After her appearance, many women, under the guise of Westernization, began to develop their own definition of ideal beauty, demonstrating that this was an area in which women could have a voice.

One of the most controversial expressions of women's rebellion proved to be in the area of hairstyles. After Kang's revelation, a series of polemic debates emerged in the newspapers and journals. Some women students who were interviewed by the press noted that since men did not allow them to bob their hair, they regarded this as a form of resistance to the status quo.[78] It was not only the students who took up the issue of bobbed hair with such passion. A group of thirteen teachers and administrators who were invited to a roundtable discussion by the Tonggwang Youth Association also expressed their views on bobbed hair, unanimously acknowledging the style's virtues. Cho Chŏng-hwan, a teacher at Ewha haktang, noted that bobbed hair was useful from the standpoint of hygiene, beauty, and economics. Cho Tong-sŏk, a teacher at Tongdŏk Girls' School, observed that bobbed hair was much more suitable for working women. Even Yamanoe Chōjirō, a Japanese superintendent of school affairs at Sukmyŏng Girls' School, agreed that there was nothing wrong with girl students bobbing their hair.[79] Female intellectuals like Kim Hwal-lan sought to justify bobbed hair by arguing that a uniform haircut for all sexes and ages was a step forward for women and the Korean nation.[80] In other words, only through a subversive confusion of gender (i.e., short hair for men and women) could the notion of equality begin to take hold.

This approving viewpoint was quite the opposite of that expressed by male intellectuals, who opposed the short hairstyles adopted by Korean women. In an article entitled "Second-Class Humans," one writer wrote a scathing critique of bobbed hair as a feeble attempt by Korean women to mimic Western ideals. He declared, "The short hair of a woman only signifies the degree to which her intelligence had shrunk."[81] Another editorial compared the new styles to a boiling pan of water—a temporary fashion that would soon dry up.[82] Another writer declared that the sight of women with bobbed hair frequenting taverns and restaurants and "displaying no shame" was an affront to morality.[83]

In a poignant cartoon published in the journal *Sin yŏsŏng*, an artist sketched a picture of a woman kneeling in front of a dresser cluttered with all kinds of makeup, holding a pair of scissors in her hands, ready to cut her long hair. The caption sarcastically read: "If a village girl goes to Seoul, instead of studying, the first thing she learns to do is to wear a short skirt, cut her front hair, wear high-heeled shoes, and write letters."[84] Clearly, contemporaries viewed the blurred distinctions between male and

3. The educator Kim Hwal-lan with her *tanbal* (bobbed hair) (1922).

female hairstyles as a disruptive phenomenon that could undermine the formation of an orderly society based on distinct gender roles.

Despite the rhetoric, Korean women fought to keep their new short and elegant haircuts. That Korean women defiantly adopted these hair trends reveals much about their independent creativity—a trait that has been overlooked. By defending and keeping their bobbed hair, Korean new women sought to assert their own ideals of what was attractive and comfortable and retained the right to define beauty, sexuality, and identity for themselves.

Some writers in the press approved the new disposition toward long hair and fake coiffures, while others derided the new styles with mocking headlines. This mixed response to women's hairstyles (as well as their attire, as we will see) reflected in part a response to Korean women's adaptation of Western values and morals, in part discomfort at their new assertiveness and self-definition.

If women's bobbed hair prompted an outcry, the casual discarding of traditional garb in favor of short skirts that "showed quite a bit of leg" represented a direct affront to traditional sensibilities. Contemporaries described the trend as a "disease" and a sign of extravagance.[85] In one editorial, a writer noted that in the past Korean women only showed their eyes, but now these new women did the opposite by provocatively revealing other parts of their bodies and "hiding only their eyes with large spectacles."[86] One artist sketched a cartoon of a girl standing on top of a sack of rice bragging to her "ignorant" father that she had paid eighteen *wŏn* for a pair of shoes.[87] Another cartoon, however, portrayed a family taking a stroll, with the husband and child wearing comfortable Western clothing while a woman in traditional garb lagged behind.[88]

The *chŏgori* (blouse) and *ch'ima* (full skirt) were the traditional accouterment of a Korean woman. Hence, advertisements in the newspapers for a Western-style two-piece outfit (blouse and skirt) or oxford shoes generated disgust among both men and women who wanted to uphold the traditional values and customs.[89] The *Tonga ilbo*, for example, printed a series of conversations between Kim Wŏn-ju (also known as Kim I-ryŏp) and Na Hye-sŏk on the virtues of Western or traditional clothing. Kim supported Western clothing on the premise that the traditional Korean *ch'ima chŏgori* was not hygienic. She argued that the girdle was too restricting to the lungs and a principal reason for women's pulmonary apicitus. Moreover, a Korean woman's back and chest were always red from the excessive binding. Kim recommended that the *chŏgori* be altered to make it more comfortable for women and that the *ch'ima* be shortened so that a woman would be able to walk without hindrance; in this way Korean women could share the good health of Western women.[90] Pang Sŭng-bin concurred that the girdle used to wrap the chest was indeed unhealthy and, regardless of its esthetically pleasing appearance, should be removed if women found it uncomfortable.[91]

Na Hye-sŏk begged to differ with Kim, arguing that to imitate Western clothing was shallow and superficial. She went to great lengths to illustrate the virtues of the *chŏgori* by showing its practicality and how it could be taken apart and sewn together at any time. Furthermore, she noted that there were a variety of materials and colors women could use

4. A cartoon published in the popular magazine *Pyŏlgŏn'gon* (1927), showing a young girl asking her father to admire her shoes, which cost as much as two sacks of rice.

to make their *ch'ima chŏgori*.[92] Whereas Na sought to show the virtues of traditional garb, another editorial took the approach of arguing that Western clothing would only make Korean women look obese.[93]

Initially, the issue of women's dress attracted little interest in the press. There were, of course, occasional articles about Western clothing, which served more as a description of novel curiosities than a polemical debate on gender divisions and cultural norms. However, by the early 1920s, with the emergence of the new woman in her suggestive garb, as well as the appearance of a growing number of advertisements for Western clothing, some contemporaries believed that it was time to respond more forcefully. While reformers cast the debate about hairstyles and clothing in national terms—glorification of Western culture at the expense of native culture reflected an underlying tension in the modernization of Korea—it is clear that they were equally if not more troubled by the disruption of gender identities and roles.

Quite apart from her provocative physical appearance, the new woman's vocal demand for liberation made her visible in the public sphere. Western literature promoting gender equality and liberation, which was now easily available in translation, helped raise the consciousness of Korean women and provided a vocabulary for protest. Henrik Ibsen's (1828–1906) play, *A Doll's House*, for instance, struck a responsive chord in many women, who identified themselves with Nora Helmer, the infantilized woman trapped in an empty life without her own identity and shackled to the "sacred" ideals of the "good wife and wise mother."[94] Nora's decision to leave the house and her husband to find new meaning in her life and a new identity inspired readers to become "Korean Noras."

Empowered by reading Ibsen's play, Na Hye-sŏk composed a poem with the same title, *Inhyŏng ŭi chip* (A doll's house), which was published in *Maeil sinbo* on 3 April 1921. She criticized the husband's authority in the Korean home and warned that if his power went unchallenged, it would create the impression that the subordination of women was acceptable. Korean women needed to "leave the house" and question the idea of marriage being "sacrosanct."[95] Another female editorial writer declared, "Women cannot be less than men."[96] The new women refused to be treated as objects to be represented and addressed by men; rather they were awakened individuals who had the right to confront men and to converse with other women about the issues that represented their interests.

In the eyes of Korean nationalists, the call for female emancipation was a highly selfish act. In the words of one editorial, "Liberation is a word to be used for all Korean people and not only women."[97] To highlight her narcissistic desires and goals, the public discourse portrayed the new woman as a sexual seductress who posed a danger to the hallowed institution of the family. She was the wedge that created a rift between traditional wives and their acculturated husbands, as illustrated in a cartoon entitled "The Appearance of a New Woman and Other Family Discords." In this caricature, the acculturated husband (dressed in his finest Western suit) looks disparagingly at his wife, who is dressed in a traditional outfit with a bundle containing her personal belongings on her head. The caption above the husband reads, "You are so unattractive. Please leave." To this the wife's responds, "Well, let's see how long you can live with your 'ideal' woman."[98] In other words, the new woman was only a passing fad who could not possibly meet the basic necessities of the family.

Interestingly, the "new man" or "modern boy" who had succumbed to the temptation of the new woman received his share of criticism as well. In a mockery of the "emasculated" male intellectual, a cartoon entitled "Makes Aged Parents Cry, Goes Abroad and Returns: A Leading Gentleman and New Lady" depicted a man and a woman with placards on their necks. The man's placard read, "Purchased doctorate, miserable, and preparing for divorce, assets worth 100,000 *wŏn*, seeking love with a pretty woman." The new woman's read, "Self-appointed artist and philosopher, experienced in love scores of times."[99] If these "decadent" Koreans were the future, social reformers argued, radical transformations needed to be made to protect the core values of Korean society and the integrity of the nation.

The new women posed a threat to male hegemony. In contrast to the past, when women remained silent in public debate, the new women protested the reformers' desire to construct new roles and identities for them. A group of outspoken Korean women boldly asserted that they were not mere objects of male policies and discourses, and sought to rectify this gender imbalance by becoming active participants in the construction of their own modernity. They sought to articulate their sense of spatial location and establish a woman's public sphere. By pushing the boundaries between the prescribed traditional woman's sphere and this new space of modernity, a coterie of educated women sought to redefine, through their writings, the nature of public and private.

One public response to the threat of the new woman was to denigrate them by portraying them in sexual terms, as promiscuous nymphomaniacs who seduced married men or as lesbian lovers. Indeed, women who crossed gender boundaries in career, education, or lifestyle risked being smeared with rumors about their sexual lives. Another response was to neutralize the new women by allowing them to voice their opinions. In response to the demands of these literate women, the *Chosŏn ilbo* decided in 1924 to promote a ladies' column, while its rival, the *Tonga ilbo*, hired a woman journalist.[100] The conceptual "space" or discourse of "femininity" created by these women served as an important part of the women's movement and of their interaction with the state. Moreover, it pushed male reformers to negotiate the vision they had for the future of Korean women.

New Ideals for Korean Women: Marriage, Love, and the Home

The emergence of the Korean new woman challenged the ideology of *hyŏnmo yangch'ŏ* (wise mother and good wife), which had traditionally defined Korean womanhood. Even male reformers acknowledged that it was unrealistic and shortsighted to expect women to embrace such a role without some accommodation to the changing cultural and socioeconomic realities. Indeed, new ideas about womanhood, family, and marriage from the West were ubiquitous. Starting in the 1920s, translations of influential books from abroad became available for public consumption. These included Margaret Sanger's *Family Limitation*, Bertrand Russell's *The Family of the Future*, essays by Alexandra Kollontai, Abe Isoo's *Sanji seigen-ron* (Discussion on birth control), Ellen Key's *Love and Marriage*, and Friedrich Engels's *Origins of the Family, Private Property and the State*.[101] The challenge for both the new women and nationalist reformers was how to adapt these ideas to the needs of Korean society. There were two conflicting agendas at stake: the new women's desire for self-definition and increased rights in marriage, and the nationalist reformers' desire to create a stronger nation through the stabilization of marriage and family.

The reform of marriage and family stood at the core of the debate among social reformers. To all appearances, the Korean family seemed to have made little progress; in fact, it had degenerated into complete disorder. Late nineteenth-century efforts to abolish early marriage, for example, had had no visible impact on the countryside.[102] One study showed that out of 128,258 women who married in 1932, 85,873 (67 percent) were under the age of nineteen and 12,575 (9.9 percent) were under seventeen.[103] But the main concern was the increasing divorce rate, especially in the cities. In Seoul alone, local courthouses reported five to six divorces a day.[104]

The new women applauded these developments and encouraged women to liberate themselves from their unhappy marriages and pursue their own happiness. One woman writer urged unhappy wives to "be bold, break free from the past, and move on to a brighter future." She argued that divorce was not "the first or last road in life" but rather a means to find one's true self.[105] Others justified divorce as the only recourse in a family system constructed to oppress women. As Kim Sŏn-ŭn put it, divorce was inevitable because "girls were being purchased and sold like a commodity." She argued that this kind of unethical marriage system, which deprived a woman of her freedom, had to be reformed or it would lead to the disintegration of the family, the bedrock of social stability.[106] Other reformers echoed her sentiments when they stated that marriages with "no spirit" or "arranged marriages" that involved the exchange of money could only lead to divorce.[107] Kim Myŏng-sun, an actress and prolific writer, entitled an article on divorce "Nae chasin wihae" (For my own self); in her view, divorce required no other justification.[108] These articles often borrowed from the ideas of Friedrich Engels, who viewed the separation for couples who lacked affection as inevitable and a "blessing for both parties and society."[109]

Conflicts arose between the new women writers and socialist writers over a solution to the family crisis. The former stressed the need for "free love," while the latter argued that one had to differentiate between the social principle of love and "materialistic love," which meant being sold as a commodity. The question of individual love could only be discussed after the success of class struggle.[110] In response, the proponents of free love challenged socialists and conservatives alike, at a roundtable discussion sponsored by the popular journal Samch'ŏlli, to address real life questions. How could a woman possibly maintain her chastity if her husband or lover was in prison or had fled the country? Should she remain chaste like a "discarded worn-out shoe"?[111] For female intellectuals like Hwang Sin-dŏk, love and fidelity were two separate things. Hwang argued that to love somebody did not necessarily mean one had to maintain one's fidelity. [112] In fiery testimony, a fifty-year-old widow explained why she had remained chaste: "The reason [that I remained faithful] was because of our society's long-established custom of morality." Lamenting the moments when she had to suppress her "instinctive sexual desire," the widow condemned the social norms that had "forcefully blocked" her pursuit of love.[113] In another provocative article, Im In-sik narrated a recent incident of a married woman who fell in love with a younger man; as a result of social pressures, she ended up committing suicide. In this case, love could not be achieved through marriage.[114]

Free love advocates were avid admirers of Ellen Key, who wrote that "real fidelity" could only come to fruition "when love and marriage became equivalent terms." Furthermore, the object of Lutheran marriage, according to Key, was not only to unite man and woman "with or without love," but also to secure "their mutual morality" and "to make them breeders of children for society." She argued that by relentlessly pursuing this idea, the church had succeeded in "damming up" an individual's "purifying sensuality," thus "developing a sense of responsibility.[115] Pang In-kŭn, who drew heavily on Key's writings, argued that all forms of the old "tyrannical and oppressive" marriage system (i.e., forced and early marriage) had to be replaced by the new ideal of love.[116] In a survey conducted by the journal *Yŏsŏng* in 1938, an overwhelming 90 percent of the graduating class of female students agreed that marriage and love were two separate ideals that should be distinguished.[117]

These idealistic visions of the free love advocates met strong opposition from conservatives, who viewed *yŏnae* (free love) as nothing more than lust and a mark of irresponsibility. One writer asked his readers if it was acceptable for Professor An Ki-yŏng to run away with a female student, Kim Hyŏn-sun, while his legal wife was suffering on her deathbed: "Even if love is important, is it more important than life?"[118] In another article,

Pak Ch'an-hŭi argued that the new women had not an iota of moral sense or consciousness; they not only had fallen into the chasm of vanity but were completely ignorant about the state of affairs of the nation.[119]

Despite many obstacles, women like Kim I-ryŏp challenged the ideal of the good wife and wise mother and the old marriage system, which made "women yield to power and not love" while "legislating against the development of affection in marriage."[120] She argued that the ideology of chastity was obsolete, and that for a woman to find her humanity and individuality, she needed to overcome the conventional norms of sexual morality.[121] "The trumpeted promiscuity of the modern girl who moved from man to man," Miriam Silverberg observes in the context of the Japanese *moga* (modern girl), "was thus but one of her self-sufficiency. She appeared to be a free agent without ties of filiation, affect, or obligation to lover, father, mother, husband, or children—a striking counterpoint to the state ideology of family documented in the Civil Code and in the ethics texts taught in the schools." [122]

Kim Wŏn-ju's short story "Chagak" (Awakening) sums up the contest over love, marriage, and divorce. The story, serialized in the *Tonga ilbo* in 1926, is written in epistolary form. [123] The protagonist, a young divorced woman, writes to her friend about her disillusionment with married life. Her complaints—cruel treatment at the hands of her in-laws and a shocking discovery of her husband's infidelity—would have been familiar to her readers:

> My first impulse was to pack up and leave my husband's house imme-
> diately. My in-laws, who valued keeping up appearances more than
> moral principles or compassion, pleaded with me to stay. Against
> their will, I left the house empty-handed, without even my travel
> gear, and returned to my parents. The love I had for him at first was
> nothing more than the fondness that arose naturally in my utterly
> inexperienced heart toward a new husband who had been forced on
> me by my parents and who treated me kindly as I stoically embarked
> on a marriage and began life with my in-laws. . . . You have no reason
> to see me as a contemptible wife, abjectly submissive to her heartless
> husband, who abuses and beats her, saying that she should die and

become the ghost of his household. You are silly to expect my return, knowing well that I would rather die ten times over rather than lead a humiliating life.[124]

A woman who had endured such humiliation deserved to leave her "doll's house" despite social norms that demanded silence and submission, because a marriage without love and faithfulness was but a sham.

Whereas a bad marriage could be handled by divorce, the new women faced a more difficult issue when it came to defining how a woman should live within a marriage and a home. Indeed, a survey conducted by the *Tonga ilbo* found that students at girls' schools unanimously found home economics among the most useless and uninteresting courses in the curriculum.[125] One editorial highlighted the contradictions and impracticalities of the traditional family order. How could a woman with an absentee husband (working abroad or in jail) be expected to conduct age-old traditional rituals like preparing foodstuffs for ancestor veneration and other sacrificial ceremonies, especially if she was working thirteen hours in fields or factory?[126]

Nationalist reformers argued that the concept of filiality, which was at the center of the old family, should be replaced with *hyoyul* (efficiency) in the new Korean family. They wanted to shift the emphasis from the drudgery of housework to the new woman's ability to execute her domestic duties efficiently. She would be a *hyŏnmyŏng chŏnŏp chubu* (wise and prudent professional wife), motivated less by filiality than by common sense in meeting the practical needs of her nuclear family, especially the education and upbringing of her sons.[127]

In their quest to modernize the home and promote the efficient mother and wife, nationalist reformers of the 1920s sought the aid of domestic science experts. First, they would improve domestic labor and the cult of domesticity (*kajŏng sungbae*) by advocating professionalization of housework and introducing bourgeois norms of efficiency and hygiene. Second, reformers sought to raise the ideology of housework to a higher plane, distinguishing it from the drudgery of the past and linking it to improvement in the nation's standard of living. In other words, the recreation of the nation was to start in the home.

Efforts to transform and elevate domesticity into a "modern profession" suitable for the "modern woman" figured prominently in this discourse. According to the *Tonga ilbo*, the Korean household would become a model of economics and efficiency—a spiritual retreat from the chaos and disorder of industrialization and social dislocation.[128] The key phrase was "domestic household scientific management," which included family, science, and time management.[129] A new respect had to be shown to female domesticity. As Mary Poovey has noted in a different context, "In producing a distinction between kinds of labor (paid and unpaid, mandatory versus voluntary, productive versus reproductive, alienated versus self-fulfilling), the segregation of the domestic ideal created the illusion of an alternative to competition; this alternative, moreover, was the prize that inspired hard work, for a prosperous family was the goal represented as desirable and available to every man."[130] This kind of professional cum scientific housewifery received some positive reactions from educated women. Ch'ae Maria, for example, concurred that impoverished women did not have the wherewithal to live "rational or ideal" lives and that traditional methods of housekeeping and livelihood that had been transmitted from mother to daughter for the past five thousand years were now antiquated. She argued that Korean women lacked sufficient knowledge of modern practices like hygiene, nutrition, and the purchase of clothing; to improve daily life based on a woman's use of "modern knowledge" was "a sign of power."[131]

The new order rested on a bourgeois model of the workplace and home, the separation of private and public. The home was to represent domestic rationality based on principles derived from economics and business. In this idealized perspective, home economics would teach a woman to apply her expertise, intelligence, and independence to her new home and family. It assumed a stable working class, a nuclear family supported by a male breadwinner, a dependent wife and children, and women's unpaid domestic labor. In other words, women would no longer have to seek dignity in the cold, impersonal, and degrading world of paid labor. The role of wife and mother now held new national meaning: she was responsible for scientific management of an orderly household for the modern nation, as well as rearing and training the children, who were the future citizens of the modern nation.

The application of bourgeois virtues like thrift, simplicity, hygiene, and knowledge of economics were critical to the professionalization of housewifery. This new family would be clean, healthy, and comfortable. At its center was the newly constructed housewife, who was well educated, scientifically oriented, managerial, and pedagogical, and free to select her own spouse. This model demanded thrift and creativity. Reformers criticized the traditional family for squandering precious resources on the idle entertainment of guests and called on women to take responsibility for managing the household savings.[132] Likewise, experts argued that the traditional family had too many attendants, whose presence disrupted the wife's role in the household. Hence, the first order of business was to eliminate servants and maids, who represented yet another household expense—the inverse of ideas in Western Europe, where domestic servants symbolized the efficient bourgeois household. Reformers argued that entrusting the duty of meal preparation to the maid was irresponsible.[133] To alleviate the wife's anxieties, reformers called for improvement in the traditional kitchen.[134] If the wife was not confident that she could satisfy her husband's tastes, she now had the new condiment MSG to enhance her meals.[135]

A woman's mastery of scientific ideas like hygiene and sanitation would make the kitchen more modern and efficient. A dish cloth, a clean knife, and a spotless chopping board were the wise wife's new tools, and would help her feel like she lived in the modern age while she performed her domestic duties.[136] Cleanliness was not a value in itself; it symbolized the increasing division of labor from and within the home. In other words, class boundaries could be seen in the standards of domestic cleanliness and purity.

The appearance of the modern housewife coincided with the inauguration of new domestic science courses taught at Ewha and other girls' schools.[137] "In the 1920s," Jihang Pak notes, "an increasing number of young men returned from the U.S. with college degrees and wanted to marry college-educated women. In response to this demand, the home economics department was set up to prepare Ewha women as desirable brides by teaching them how to cook western food. Understandably, the department soon acquired the nickname of the department of the daughter-in-law."[138] Eschewing rote memorization and useless courses, reformers insisted that scientific knowledge learned at school could be applied to the home. This new pedagogical curriculum would include modern nutritional science, especially useful for the housewife in her role as mother and wife.

Finally, reformers sought to provide housewives with advice columns and a home life section in the newspapers to assist them in rearing their children.[139] Newspapers and journals printed articles on child-rearing practices and encouraged housewives to follow them. In 1938, for example, a manual for housewives written by Professor Ujiie Hisako became available. It provided detailed chapters on time management and other important advice on managing the modern family.[140]

Thus nationalist reformers, with the active support of the new women, formulated a new vision of women's role in the family. Though it did not challenge traditional relationships, since it kept women in the kitchen and the home, the new ideology of the professional wife endowed women's domestic roles with a loftier purpose and significance in the struggle for the Korean nation.

The second part of the new ideology of Korean womanhood was the ideal of the "prudent and wise mother." The discussion of motherhood was complicated by the colonial government's policy of *umeyo fuyaseyo* (to give birth and multiply) and the reformulation of family law through civil ordinances that aimed to increase human resources.[141] For the state, the birthrate was a matter of national importance, particularly after 1930, when the government devoted more attention to the expansion of the empire.

While the Government-General stressed the necessity of demographic increase, Koreans debated the desirability of large families (especially in rural areas, where poverty was rampant) and the use of birth control.[142] Some Koreans agreed that a country's strength was gauged by its population. A decrease in population was evidence that the state had become weaker.[143] However, as the reformer Kim Kwang-sŏk put it, "Although a lot of families think that having a lot of children is a blessing, it is very difficult to support them if the family is in dire straits." He urged parents to limit themselves to two children so that they could "contribute to society and the improvement of the nation."[144] In another article, Cho Hyŏn-gyŏng, a schoolteacher at Hyŏpsŏng Girls' School, argued that if there was one area where women could agree with men, it was birth control. She also emphasized the dangers of frequent childbirth to a woman's body: "A weak body cannot bear a healthy child."[145] Nonetheless, as we will see, the new women differed greatly with male national reformers about who should use birth control.

The practice of limiting fertility was common among the European bourgeoisie (e.g., in Germany), where the "two-child system" was a sign of middle-class respectability.[146] In Korea, ideas about birth control began to circulate more broadly following Margaret Sanger's invitation to Japan by the Kaizō publishing group in 1922 and the publication of a Japanese translation of her book *Family Limitation*. Other influences were Ogino Kyūsaku's reports on periodic abstinence, and Ōta Tenrei's intrauterine device.[147] In the early 1920s, words like *sana chojŏl* (childbirth regulation), *sana chehan* (childbirth restriction), *usaenghak* (eugenics), and *wisaeng* (public hygiene) began to appear frequently in newspapers.[148]

Debates about fertility went hand-in-hand with a new discourse on eugenics. By the early 1930s, associations like the Chosŏn usaeng hyŏphoe (Korean Eugenics Association) and the Pokŏn undongsa (Sanitation Movement Society) were created.[149] One central question was whether Koreans should pursue "positive eugenics" (maximizing the meritorious stock) or "negative eugenics" (minimizing the propagation of undesirable strains).[150] In other words, science, in the opinion of these reformers, could now govern sexual behavior and choice in marriage.

The ideals of Lamarckian eugenics, which emphasized the ameliora-
tion of the environment through hygienic living and improvement in education, hit a responsive chord with many doctors and reformers.[151]
Chŏng Sŏk-t'ae, a doctor who had studied bacteriology in Germany,
agreed that the mass production of "inferior goods" (choje namjo) was
problematic and measures had to be taken to increase "superior" characteristics through birth control.[152] These advocates strongly believed
that women would play a critical role in breeding, rearing, and "improving
the racial stock of tomorrow." [153] Yi Kap-su, the founder of the Chosŏn
Eugenics Association, posited that a country's prosperity or decline
should be gauged not by measuring population fluctuations, but rather
by the "increase and decrease of eugenically superior citizens."[154]

If the goal was to create a nation of healthy citizens, reformers argued
that mothers would bear the primary responsibility for creating and nur-
turing offspring. Using the metaphor of a business, a Japanese reformer
living in Korea argued that children's health had to be systematically man-
aged. Mothers needed to become more vigilant in the protection of their
children's yukch'e (physical body) and provide aeho (love and protection).[155] Furthermore, he argued that one could not simultaneously love
and protect both the "superior stock" and an exceptionally "inferior
breed." Measures had to be taken to protect the former from the latter.[156]

The village became a target of reform, because the rural population
suffered most from high morality rates. Kim Myŏng-hŭi argued that
bearing too many children was "unproductive labor" and urged reformers and the state alike to find a way to control birth rates in the countryside.[157] At a roundtable discussion, Yi Ŭng-suk noted that rural families barely had enough to feed themselves, and if they continued to have
children, women's health would deteriorate.[158] One reformer blamed the
fall in fertility rates on the "evil practice" of early marriage, which forced
young girls with "feeble and immature bodies" to give birth in "reck-
less numbers." He warned that unless a solution could be found, young
women would create an excess of children who would be deformed with
low IQs.[159] An editorial in the Chosŏn ilbo urged young women to hold

off procreating until the age of twenty-five, when their bodies were fully developed.[160]

Male reformers also argued that the physical stress of work in the villages could permanently damage female reproductive activities. From the perspective of medical science, Chǒng Sǒk-t'ae argued that most mothers experienced direct or indirect trauma from childbirth; even if a woman's health was excellent, frequent births coupled with poor nutrition and hard labor would inevitably shorten her lifespan. He stated that the death rate of wives between eighteen and forty-five years of age was much higher than that of their husbands. Furthermore, according to Chǒng, it was critical for a woman's body to recuperate for a minimum of three years after giving birth, and he claimed he had medical evidence to corroborate his claims.[161]

The pressure to "protect motherhood" became increasingly urgent in the press debates as more impoverished families suffered from declining living conditions and the rural exodus. Records show that by 1930 infant mortality and the number of miscarriages had indeed increased, confirming the fears of reformers.[162] If motherhood was to regain its esteemed status as an "appointed task" (*samyǒng*) and a "divine calling" (*ch'ǒnjik*), birth control could, in the mind of some reformers, solve a wide range of social problems, such as poverty and feeblemindedness, and eliminate diseases like syphilis, Hansen's disease, imbecility, tuberculosis, and various heart ailments, as well as alleviating women's oppression.[163]

It must be noted that the issue of birth control raised numerous objections and cautionary tales. While male reformers lauded birth control as a way of liberating women from the yearly tyranny of pregnancy and birth, they were at pains to emphasize that only some women should have access to it. They believed that contraceptives (e.g., the pessary) should only be accessible to a small number of people. Widespread use without strict control, they argued, would have an adverse affect on the general population, triggering a "decay of public morality."[164] Moreover, the mixture of "pleasure-seeking moods" would create disorder in sexual relations.[165] Intellectuals like Yi Kwang-su, who admitted having used some kind of contraceptive, argued that a regulated birth-control method was acceptable for married couples, but it should be forbidden to young boys and girls.[166] Conservatives from religious circles contended that the increase in bearing children was part of the natural process, so any artificial control was an immoral act. Some socialist reformers posited that birth control was a tool of the bourgeoisie. For them, the solution to the birth crisis as well as other social ills, such as poverty and women's lack of education, lay in the destruction of capital and the creation of a society based on mutual assistance.[167]

Women became deeply engaged in the debate over their reproductive rights, in particular birth control. How could they be "good mothers" if their bodies were being abused? It was quite apparent that Japanese women gave birth with the assistance of professional midwives, which improved the chances for both mothers and infants; thus better health conditions for Korean women were not much to ask.[168] The average twenty-year-old Korean woman had at least two children, but Pak Ho-jin noted that "she continues to have more . . . and as her body starts to recuperate, she has yet another child." Pak noted that this phenomenon was not limited to the lower classes but was true of women from wealthy families as well. No matter how educated a woman was, "in this environment, she can not display an iota of her talents, and lets it rot."[169]

In an article entitled "The Expectations and Inconveniences of Being a Wife," a woman complained that she wanted to stop having children. She explained: "I am already thirty years old. . . . I have a total of five children. I had no choice. I am very unhappy about this. How can I continue to live if I keep having children?"[170] The popular journal *Samch'ŏlli* published the results of a 1930 poll on birth control. The subjects were renowned wives of intellectuals, such as Hŏ Yŏng-suk, the wife of Yi Kwang-su, the modern artist Na Hye-sŏk, and Kim I-ryŏp, the first editor of *Sin yŏja*. Aside from Yŏ Sun-ok, all the women supported birth control, saying the ideal number of children was two boys and one girl.[171] Unlike the male nationalist reformers who discussed the issue of reproduction and birth control in a nationalist and eugenics framework, the new women sought to humanize the debate by focusing on a woman's right to limit her fertility.

During the colonial period, public debate on the woman question centered around three discursive forces—the new women, national reformers, and the colonial state—each of which sought to engage, provoke, and change the others. The main priorities of the new women were to gain recognition of their humanity and to create a space for themselves, although they were conscious of the complexity, contradictions, and internal differences this entailed. They were not merely objects in prominent discourses but central agents in the crafting of a new Korean female identity. Though one can easily dismiss them as elitists, it is important to understand that these women had the choice of accepting the status quo. Although they were acutely aware of the risks—their vulnerability to moral suspicion, social ostracism, and ridicule—they sought to blur traditional gender roles and asserted a new form of subjectivity. The issues they raised, such as women's fashions, love and marriage, and reproduction, testified to the instability of tradition and prompted even the staunchest of male reformers to discuss, and even negotiate, gender identities and roles.

National reformers had to contend with the highly disciplined and penetrating apparatus of Japanese colonialism in their discussion of Korean women, especially in the area of birth control. In their discourse, they insisted that colonial oppression was shared by both men and women, and sought to enforce a single norm, often situating women as the metonymic extension of the nation. By constructing a national subjectivity, reformers attempted to deny and subordinate the independence and self-definition of the new women. They defined any attempt at liberation as selfish and vilified her cultural transformation as corrupt and materialistic. At the same time, nationalist reformers needed the support of the new women to promote a new patriarchy refashioned to meet the exigencies of the day. They had to accommodate women's modern sensibilities and include ideas such as the companionate marriage, sexual desire, and love in the "new home." By professionalizing housework and elevating married women to national importance, domestic science proclaimed that women could conduct traditional domestic work yet still maintain their modern sense of self. Although one could view the new ideology of "prudent mother, professional housewife" as a relinquishing of women's initiative, its very development reflects the influential role played by the new women in shaping the terms of Korean womanhood.

CHAPTER THREE

The Female Worker

From Home to the Factory

Two years before her untimely death from pulmonary tuberculosis, Song Kye-wŏl (1910–33), a reporter for *Sin yŏsŏng* (The new woman), penned a short story that foreshadowed her demise.[1] "News from a Factory" is one of the few works to address the plight of female workers in colonial Korea through the eyes of a displaced peasant worker.[2] The main character, Kim Ok-pun, in a final letter to her sister, describes the miseries of tuberculosis, which she contracted while working at a silk-reeling factory: "The clotting of blood in my mouth and the spitting up of rotten phlegm [signal that] my time is fleeting."[3] The empty cot in her ward is a reminder that her fifteen-year-old coworker, Kŭm-dol, has died of the same disease. Forced to enter the labor force by her father's desertion of the family for a *kisaeng* (female entertainer), Kim pronounces a scathing indictment of the harsh working conditions and merciless exploitation of countless Korean women: "[The factory] fattens [its profits] by squeezing our blood and sweat."[4]

Song's vivid factory narrative captured the wrenching turmoil spawned by rapid industrialization and rural impoverishment during the colonial period. The birth of the *yŏgong* (factory girl) introduced a new dynamic into the complex interaction between the Korean family structure, based

95

on Confucian patriarchy and values, and the new ideologies of woman-hood, which vied for dominance in colonial Korea. While many female workers sought to maintain the deep ties to their families out of filial loy-alty, they blazed an untrodden path as "workers" and "unskilled labor"—new social categories that embodied important political and social mean-ings. More broadly, the migration of peasant women from rural areas to industrial centers posed a threat to existing norms of social control and gender definitions, prompting multiple voices (from state authorities to women writers) to articulate competing visions of power relations.

This chapter examines the transition of Korean women from the home to the newly constructed factories—a process fraught with tension, as colonial authorities reorganized the labor force through an intense sex-ual division of labor based on marital and reproductive status. The fac-tory girl as a new *category* embodied a segment of the "political anatomy," constructed by multiple players (including the colonial state, Korean na-tionalists, educated women, and others). As a part of the greater social body, she was a cog in machinery that, to borrow Michel Foucault's phras-ing, was to function "with the techniques, the speed, and efficiency that [the industrialists] determined."[5] At the same time, the *yŏgong* was an in-dividual who often entered the wage market as part of a family strategy (like the fictional Kim Ok-pun), carefully negotiating the boundaries be-tween traditional ideologies and new discourses that sought to reshape her identity and role. More important, unlike elite women, commoner women had worked in the fields, cottage industries, and marketplace prior to the colonial period; as they adapted their skills to the demands of the new workplace, women workers forged new identities and subcultures through common hardships in the factories and dormitories, illness, and experiences of displacement and marginalization.

KOREAN WOMEN IN THE CHOSŎN ECONOMY

Korean women played a significant role behind the scenes in the fields and specialized in cottage industries during the Chosŏn period. The gendered division of labor among commoners placed the dual burden of household and agricultural work (or small trades) on women. Prior to the introduction of innovative techniques like *iangpŏp* (rice transplantation method) and new plowing methods in the second half of the Chosŏn period, women assumed the tedious task of preparing and sowing the rice seed by hand, as well as weeding the crop throughout the busy agricultural season. Following the autumn harvest, women sorted out the good seeds for the next harvest.[6] Women laboring in the rice paddies would have been a common sight to travelers passing through the Korean countryside during spring and summer. In Kwangbok (north Hamgyŏng Province), women also tended livestock, especially sheep, to help their husbands. With the mothers occupied in the fields, it fell to the young daughters to perform basic domestic tasks, such as fetching water from the well.[7]

After a long day in the fields, women prepared meals for their families— a labor-intensive chore because most staples, such as rice and grains, were unprocessed. While the more privileged families relied on a watermill to pound rice, commoners pulverized grain using a millstone pulled by a horse or donkey throughout the day. In the countryside, women often used a simple mortar to pound rice, barley, millet, and kaoliang, which often consumed an entire day's labor. Yi Nŭng-hwa captured the drudgery of women's lives in her own day: "No time to rest. Morning: rice to make; afternoon, following lunch: work in the field; and night: dry the barley and pound it in a mortar. . . . [T]he entire day [she] has no time to rest."[8] Not only were women responsible for feeding family members at home, but they also made frequent trips to the fields to bring meals to their husbands.[9] Paintings by Cho Yŏng-sŏk (1686–1761) and Kim Hong-do (1745–1810) captured the daily ritual of women who brought sustenance to their farmer husbands. In addition to feeding their households, women washed clothes by the barrelful for seven or eight hours at a time. One painting by Kim Hong-do depicts a group of women pounding clothing with wooden paddles on a fulling block. So important was laundry day in Korean life that a nineteenth-century French traveler described Seoul as "a huge laund012er house."[10]

Women of all classes engaged in cottage industries to supplement the income of the family and pay the taxes.[11] Although women were not paid laborers per se, the income from sales of their handicrafts was critical to the family budget. Cloth and garment production were particularly important handicrafts. Women cultivated silkworms and produced silk for market. They also spun their own yarn or thread from hemp, ramie, and cotton, and used whatever could not be sold at market to weave and embroider cloth or clothing. In Korean culture, good needlework was the measure of a woman's worth. As the old Chosŏn saying said, "A woman who is ignorant in the art of needlework or weaving is like a *yangban* man who neither knows how to write calligraphy and poetry nor is familiar with the six etiquettes."[12] Even wives in elite families engaged in needlework; custom dictated that her "seven friends" be "needles, thread, a ruler, a spool, iron, thimble, and scissors."[13] They had to resort to needlework and weaving, especially during the years when their husbands were preparing for the civil service examinations.[14]

The marketplace was a central site for the purchase and sale of products and food. Yi Nŭng-hwa observed that it was common in his day to see Korean women carrying wicker baskets on their heads to sell products at the market, and the "old records" revealed that it "had always been a popular practice."[15] The dominance of women in the marketplace was captured by the painter Sin Yun-bok (1758–1813), who portrayed women peddling dried fish, and Kim Tŭk-sin (1754–1822), who painted women carrying wares on their heads on the way to the market. Women were both consumers and producers: they needed to purchase enough food to feed their families, and they sold their handicrafts to pay for these items. Apart from anecdotal stories and paintings, little is known about the female culture of the marketplace and its language of bargaining, system of credit, or advertising of wares.[16]

In this proto-industrial context, the term *yŏgong* simply described women who worked, and *yŏgongp'um* referred to products made by women, including ramie and cotton cloth, silk fabric, woven goods, and needlecrafts.[17] In the colonial period, the term *yŏgong* would take on a new meaning—from "women's work" (a combination of the Chinese characters for "women" and "work"), it came to designate a new social category. The word *kong* no longer referred to work but specifically alluded to the *kong jang* (factory). These women were transformed from "women who worked" into "women factory workers."

JAPANESE ECONOMIC COLONIZATION: THE QUEST FOR WORKERS AND MARKETS

The transition of Korean female workers from their rural homes to the factory was a consequence of the belated but rapid industrialization that transformed the Korean economy. Just a month before the 1910 annexation, the American missionary Frank Brockman (1878–1929) lamented Korea's ignorance of the "Occidental trade," based on his two-month appraisal of the situation: "It is true that a few textiles are woven in homes, and rice is milled by hand, likewise little tanning of hides and curing of tobacco is carried on in the home. In brief it may be said, that there is no manufacturing in Seoul, only a few handicrafts. There is nothing in the industrial life of the city really worthy of the name: no factories, no mills; only a few workshops." Despite his critical tone, he had also observed a change in Korean society that was a result of the opening of the ports and the sudden infusion of Japanese products. "The most lamentable fact is that the result of their labors no longer satisfies the fancy of their own people," Brockman noted with dismay. "Whenever their goods stand in competition with the goods made abroad the Korean sees his own thrown aside." In his judgment, the cause was "lack of energy, insufficient stimulus for ambition, and centuries of official oppression."[18]

In spite of his misgivings, Brockman could not deny that something new was taking place before his eyes: "Korea is today facing an industrial revolution even in our lifetime such as she has never dreamed of, and it would be criminal for us Christian educators not to recognize the duty arising from this situation."[19] The Korean press also observed the changes. As an editorial in the *Maeil sinmun* proudly announced in 1913, Korea was "entering into a realm of advanced nations."[20] In 1935, a Japanese economist, Takahashi Kamekichi, noted in retrospect that the entry of Japanese capitalism into Korea was like "water breaking from a reservoir."[21]

The process of industrialization that followed Japan's annexation of the Korean peninsula in 1910 did not, of course, result in the overnight creation of factories and women workers. Exogenous factors coupled with shifts in the political economy played a critical role in shaping Japan's colonial policies. The World War I economic boom proved fortuitous for Japan as it took over European colonies in East Asia at minimal cost. Moreover, its international trade increased significantly during the years 1910–20, as it became a "full-fledged industrial nation."[22] Japanese yarn and cloth manufacturers quickly moved to fill the vacuum as European and U.S. cotton exports to Asia dwindled.[23] According to Kozo Yamamura, Japan became a major player in the world economy overnight as a supplier of industrial goods: "The number of industrial factories doubled, employment quadrupled in heavy and chemical industries, and tripled in light industry."[24] The demand for war materials increased trade between Japan and European states, and by 1914, Japan had not only eradicated its debt of 1.1 billion yen but had became a creditor nation, with more than 2.77 billion yen by the start of 1920.[25] However, as the war ended in Europe and the Western powers resumed their interest in Asian markets, exports fell drastically and Japan plunged into a depression as a result its declining role in international markets. Faced with balance of payment deficits, soaring inflation, and a shortage of grains, the Japanese government sought to permanently stem this crisis as quickly as possible.

Japan, which needed an outlet for the goods produced by its collapsing industries, turned to its neighbor Korea during this prolonged recession. At this nascent stage, the government offered Japanese firms state-sponsored loans with low interest rates to promote development.[26]

In 1919, in the aftermath of the March First Movement and nationwide protests in Korea, newly appointed Governor-General Saitō Makoto introduced reforms in the name of *bunka seiji* (cultural rule), including liberalization of the press and a new economic policy.[27] In pursuit of free trade, the government rescinded the Corporation Law of 1910, which had inhibited investment in nonagricultural sectors.[28] In addition, the Export Association Law of 1925 allowed large *zaibatsu* (conglomerates) like Mitsui, Mitsubishi, and Yasuda (all financed by state banks) to set up cement, paper, sugar, rice, and flour mills in Korea. At the same time, the Japanese companies Tōyō, Kanegafuchi, Dai-Nihon, Fuji-gasu, Nisshin, and Osaka-gōdō, otherwise known as the "Big Six," began to take control of the Korean textile market.[29]

With the entry of Japan's biggest *zaibatsu* coupled with the abundance of cheap labor power and raw materials, a viable market quickly arose on the peninsula.[30] Furthermore, the promotion of the *nai-sen kyōdo jigyō* (joint Korean-Japanese ventures) policy of September 1921 "opened the door to a limited but [real] efflorescence of Korean industrial capitalism."[31] According to Government-General statistics, the number of factories increased from 251 in 1911 to 1,900 in 1919 (table 1). Similarly, in his study of Japanese factories in Korea, Professor Ta Chen noted that Japan was no longer Korea's financier but its "leading customer." By the end of 1927, the number of factories in Korea had "increased 19.5 times, capital 51.1 times, employees 6.1 times, horsepower 19.4 times, and the value of industrial products 18.8 times."[32]

This rapid industrialization and modernization of the Korean economy had significant ramifications for the countryside, uprooting traditional communities and challenging social and cultural norms.

THE RURAL CRISIS IN KOREA:
JAPANESE POLICIES IN THE COUNTRYSIDE

Japanese policies in rural Korea were dictated by two primary concerns: the demands of its population at home and the need to maintain order

Table 1. Development of Industry

	Number of factories	Capital	Total workers	Korean workers
1911	251	10,613,830	14,575	12,180
1916	1,075	24,613,500	28,646	23,787
1919	1,900	129,378,761	48,705	41,873

SOURCE: Chōsen Sōtokufu, *Chōsen Sōtokufu tōkei nempō* (1924).

in the rural areas by creating obstacles to economic independence and prosperity. As a result, the fortunes of rural Koreans rose and fell, depending on the needs of the colonial power. For Japan, the Korean countryside represented an ideal source of tax revenues and food production. In fact, the new land tax levied in 1914 provided more than 45 percent of local government revenues. To ensure that Japan maximally utilized Korean resources, the cadastral survey of 1910–18 set up a modern administrative apparatus that collected tax revenues and confiscated crop surpluses on "an unprecedented scale."[33] By legalizing the private ownership of land (Civil Law of 1912) and giving landlords a better bargaining position through an annual contract system with tenants, the Government-General could secure high profits from the land.[34] More importantly, after mapping all plots of land, the new regulations stipulated that owners must provide evidence (e.g., title to their land) to the authorities.[35] While large landowners reported their claims, many "partial owners, tenants, [and] squatters with traditional cultivation rights" unfamiliar with the new reporting system failed to register their land and were displaced.[36]

As a result of the 1918 Rice Riots in Japan, caused by rice shortages and high prices, the central government set its sights on transforming Korea into a major food supplier, especially since agricultural output in Japan could no longer keep up with the rapid population growth. The Government-General initiated a thirty-year plan known as the Sanmai zōshoku keikaku (Rice Production Development Program) in the early 1920s. Importation of rice from Korea, which amounted to 300,000 tons at the outbreak of the First World War, increased to 771,086 tons. The Japanese sold this imported rice at 10 percent lower than the domestic price.[37]

Japan's demand for rice resulted in greater investment in the Korean rice industry. The replacement of traditional low-yield but drought-resistant seeds with higher-yielding seed varieties, combined with the introduction of new fertilizers and better irrigation techniques, led to a substantial increase in Korean paddy yields between 1910 and 1920. However, financial constraints caused by the agricultural recession of the 1920s coupled with discontent in Japan over "cheap imports" bought the ambitious expansion programs to an abrupt halt in 1934.[38]

At the behest of the Japanese government, newly appointed Governor-General Ugaki Kazushige (1868–1956) devised a new agricultural policy, better known as the "cotton in the south, sheep in the north" policy.[39] Ugaki believed that a twenty-year plan for cotton production and a ten-year plan for sheep raising would "intensify" and "diversify" the agricultural sector.[40]

However, Japan's aggressive march into China in 1937 created further rice shortages in Japan, setting in motion another policy revision, whereby Korea's agricultural sector reverted to its original task: rice production.

Impoverishment and Out-migration

The colonial government's economic and political policies had a profound impact on the countryside. Though intensification of labor, use of fertilizer, and better irrigation techniques brought about increased agricultural production during the initial phase of the rice production program, Korean agriculture "involuted or at best intensified, whereas both Taiwanese and Japanese agriculture developed."[41] One consequence of the cadastral survey and the rise of market relations was a rapid increase of "landownership in the hands of a few" and a "corresponding degradation of smallholders into tenants," which created a tenancy situation "with few parallels in the world."[42] The primary objective of Japanese agricultural policies, according to historian Kang Man-gil, was to transform the rural village into a supplier of food for the metropole, as well as to impede the growth of petty-middle landowners and independent farmers and to drive them into tenancy.[43]

In 1926, a survey conducted by the *Tonga ilbo* estimated the population of Korea at approximately 23 million, and 80 percent of those in rural areas identified themselves as tenant farmers. The reporter noted that "the average yearly income of a Korean household is only 102 *wŏn*. Most farmers are impoverished, miserable, and have no fixed tenancy rights, and members of each household are hiring themselves out."[44] A 1930 Government-General survey on tenant households showed that 75 percent of farmers were in serious debt. Thus, of 2,247,194 tenant households, nearly half (1,733,797 households) had an average debt of 60 *wŏn* 50 *chŏn*.[45] Likewise, in his contemporary study of the rural crisis, Kim Il-yong noted that an average tenant household's yield, which was 391 *wŏn* 76 *chŏn* in 1929, had spiraled down to 279 *wŏn* 57 *chŏn* by 1930. Given daily expenses (principally food), landlord rents, production expenditures, tilling expenses, tenant fees, social and ceremonial expenses, and other miscellaneous expenditures, tenants' debt kept mounting.[46] By 1931, according to a study of ten hamlets conducted by the *Chosŏn ilbo*, out of 26,161 households examined, 14,293—more than half the households—averaged a debt of 106 *wŏn* 91 *chŏn*.[47]

The economic depression of the 1920s created a crisis for the local rural population that, in the words of one Korean reporter, was "a hell on earth."[48] Even one Government-General study conceded that colonial economic policies had forced "Koreans [who had once] eaten rice to consume millet, who had rented a part of their house to someone else to rent rooms themselves." Their situation deteriorated further, as they went from "eating millet to the roots of grass, from renting rooms to living in tents . . . from tattered rags to nakedness." The Japanese study admitted, "[Our] economic policy has neglected the life of the Koreans.[49]

The cadastral survey and the Government-General's coercive rice aggrandizement policy inevitably led to a destabilizing process of out-migration. The mass export of rice, better known to Korean farmers as "starvation exports," led to an increase in the output of rice while rural earnings nose-dived. As a result, the rural population became "loosened from the land," and the first Korean peasant migrants began to head to urban areas and foreign destinations like Russia, northeast China, and Japan. The *Maeil sinmun* reported as early as 1914 that Korean female workers had joined their male counterparts in the Settsu Spinning Factory in faraway Osaka.[50] A Government-General report in the 1920s attributed this dislocation to problems of *chŏllyang nongga* (food shortage), *puch'ae* (debt), and *ch'ung'unggi* (spring starvation), forcing members of households to become *ch'ulga* (one who leaves home temporarily) or *t'alnong* (one who leaves the rural area for good).[51] Indeed, social investigators could cite concrete figures that showed a decline in the standard of living in the rural areas. A 1927 report showed that more than 150,000 farmers had left their farms because of "spring starvation."[52]

Out-migration involved not only adults of both sexes but also young children, many from the "rice bowl" provinces in the south.[53] For example, in the small hamlet of Talli in northern Kyŏngsang Province, which had fifty-nine households (a population of 250), forty men and sixteen women left their farms in search of work in 1936. Eighteen of the male migrants were eldest sons, while the female migrants were single and relatively young (between fourteen and sixteen). Strikingly, despite the out-migration of 22.4 percent of the village members, who sent remittances back home, this study concluded that families still found it difficult to subsist.[54]

The contemporary literature provided a human face for the official figures and warned readers of the dangers of out-migration. For example, in Han In-t'aek's story "Young Factory Girls," rumors circulate all around the country that Naeho (a region in Hamhŭng) is to become the next El Dorado. Elderly parents, young wives, and children accompany the men in search of this golden realm. Hundreds of people, even those from the remote southern provinces, sell whatever possessions they own to migrate to Naeho. Their efforts are in vain; the rumors turn out to be a hoax. Many migrants end up roaming the streets, and factory owners use middlemen to select workers from the lot. "This was just another quick profit scheme," the workers complain. "That is all these bastards seek." In the end, there is no gold cascading from the skies, only the unemployed who desperately try to sell their labor to the factories. The moral of the story is that going to the cities does not always guarantee employment, let alone a well-paid job.[55] Contemporaries like Kim Ungak, who idealized the peasant farmer, believed that the rural crisis had reached an extreme and reforms needed to be implemented to avert disaster: "In all honesty, besides the creator God who created life from nothing, it is the farmer [who creates life]."[56]

The Impact of the Rural Crisis on Women and the Family

The rural crisis generated upheavals in the family, especially among women. The Korean press was especially drawn to the plight of ordinary rural folk who resorted to desperate means to survive the difficult economic times. The appearance of the haggard peasant woman touched even the most casual observer: "Go and observe the rural woman and you will want to howl [in anguish]."[57] Countless articles described farmers who sought to make ends meet by engaging in *hwajŏn* (slash-and-burn) agriculture in the mountains, or the numerous *yumin* (drifters) who congregated in the cities looking for work.[58] Reporters claimed that some families even sold their children into slavery or prostitution to pay off a debt or simply to reduce the number of household members.[59] Likewise, a study conducted by the *Tonga ilbo* found that the number of women engaged in the sex trade, in particular as unlicensed prostitutes in the cities, increased precipitously by the day (see table 2).[60] Though such sensational stories captured headlines, the drudgery of survival through mundane work was more characteristic of rural Korean lives.

The out-migration of peasants from the southern rice bowl regions to the cities began to change the dynamics of gender roles and the family.[61]

Table 2. *Number of Japanese and Korean geisha/kisaeng,*
prostitutes, and barmaids

Newspaper reports	Japanese			Korean		
	Geisha	Prostitutes	Barmaids	Kisaeng	Prostitutes	Barmaids
Tonga ilbo, 9 May 1924	1,651	2,406	834	1,313	1,042	931
Tonga ilbo, 28 Sept 1927	1,702	2,178	624	1,521	1,034	941

As in most rural societies, the contribution of two partners was vital to family survival. The rhythm of the seasons, in particular during the harvest period, brought women out to the fields. The missionary Angus Hamilton observed during a trip to the countryside that "it is during the harvest that all available hands muster in the fields. The women cut the crops, the men fasten the sheaves, while the children load the rope panniers, suspended upon wooden frames from the backs of bulls."[62]

Korean contemporaries who studied the rural crisis observed that gender roles inevitably changed with the exodus of male household members to remote places like Manchuria and Japan. Korean women not only assumed greater responsibility in the fields but were forced to carry out other tasks that had traditionally been assigned to men.[63] Another reporter for the *Tonga ilbo,* who had been dispatched to write about the conditions in Ansŏng County, was shocked to see women performing intensive outdoor labor: "Women never engaged in rice-planting or weeding the dry fields. That [kind] of work is for the robust men! Although they are not fond of it, they are now doing this work."[64] In fact, women had performed some of these tasks prior to Japanese colonialization.

The absence of a male householder through migration (permanent or temporary) not only forced women to assume additional work in the fields, but ensured that they would be exhausted when they had to attend to their domestic duties. They conducted their household chores and engaged in side jobs, such as peddling sundry goods in the market or raising silkworms to ensure that every *ip* (mouth) was fed.[65] Significantly, the sudden collapse of cottage industries as a result of competition from factories deprived women of the one asset they had relied upon to supplement their resources. Many peasant women still engaged in *kilssam* (weaving by hand) of the cotton cloth that they had used since the sixteenth century to pay land taxes. A spool of yarn could be produced ten times faster by machines than by the traditional *chikcho*. As a result, the market for handicraft industries, which had provided a staple supplementary income for the family, began to dwindle, making subsistence even harder. Japanese policy to restrict rural cottage industries also contributed to the loss of this important source of income. According to Andrew Grajdanzev, "In some places [the state] forbade the use of handlooms in villages, while [in other places] handlooms were rendered useless by the obligation to use not more than ten *kin* (thirteen pounds) of yarn per person." The Japanese pursued this policy "ruthlessly . . . especially in respect to cotton and silk which were to be sold to Japanese agents at prescribed prices."[66]

Though there was no shortage of slogans in the Korean countryside— like "Let's not wear rayon," a nationalist call to rural women to resist the capitalist invasion—the reality was different.[67] Little wonder that more women began to hire themselves out as laborers to supplement the family economy. For instance, in one village, women worked at the Kaesŏng Ginseng Factory for twenty to thirty *chŏn* a day. One rural wife complained that she had not had time to take a bath for an entire month, or to cut her toe- or fingernails. With some irony, she declared, "Rural women are more useful than cows. [They] are stronger and have more perseverance than cows!" In short, women had a poor choice: they could work in the fields "where men once labored" and barely eke out a living, or they could join the rural exodus to the cities.[68]

New images of the laboring rural woman began to appear in the literature of the time. Though they may have simply reflected the writer's own perceptions, they did contain important recurring themes. For example, in "Drought," Pak Hwa-sŏng depicts Sŏng-sŏp's wife as a hard-working rural woman who labors ceaselessly throughout the story. Whether grinding the barley all night with a mortar and pestle, doing laundry, or weeding in the fields, her life is pure drudgery. In one episode, friends implore Sŏng-sŏp's wife to stop pounding the barley and take a rest: "The cock has crowed for two days. What are you going to do if you get ill?" However, for Sŏng-sŏp's wife, this kind of agonizing labor means survival.[69]

Notably, neither technology nor modern medicine (e.g., birth control methods) had made inroads into the countryside, and the physical burden of work began to take its toll on women's reproductive health. In his study of postpartum mothers in the rural villages, Ōno Tamotsu found that 90 percent of new mothers returned to work less than a week after giving birth. Approximately 42.7 percent of women had given birth on their own without the assistance of midwives. Moreover, 32.7 percent of all births were stillbirths, and 35 percent of babies died before age one.[70] The high infant mortality rate was detrimental to the family economy, which depended heavily on the labor of children. Given the multiple demands placed on women, children and the elderly assumed greater responsibility for domestic tasks.[71] "Ten-year-olds . . . fetch the water, make the rice, and do the laundry," the *Tonga ilbo* reported. The article went on to describe "six- or seven-year-olds who take care of the babies by putting them on their backs."[72]

Although the plight of rural women captured the sympathy of Korean intellectuals, the mass out-migration of women from the rural areas to the cities in search of better conditions was also alarming to them. As we will see in the next chapter, fears about the corruption of these "pure rural maidens" in the urban jungle fueled much debate in the press. In a typical appeal, Yi Hye-suk, a female writer, urged women to remain in the countryside: "Women of the rural villages, you are the women of this land. Those artificial women who wear powder and cream are not the [real] women of this land!"[73] Despite such calls, the number of young single girls (usually between twelve and sixteen) who left the rural areas as *ch'ulga* had increased significantly by 1930.[74] Indeed, their departure had been triggered by the rural crisis in Korea, which was generated to a large extent by Japan's need to feed its population at home at the expense of the local people and to subjugate the potentially unruly peasants. These policies not only led to increased impoverishment in the countryside but also transformed traditional gender and family structures, especially with the large out-migration to the cities.

GENDER AND INDUSTRIALIZATION

Unlike the "predisposed" farm girls in Massachusetts, who entered the Lowell mills as wage earners, the large number of single girls and women who sought employment in the mills in colonial Korea had a dual sense of obligation.[75] The dual necessities of supporting their families back home and earning enough to pay the *honsu* (marriage expenses) made female workers less committed to becoming permanent wage laborers. Society gradually accepted the necessity of this intermediary stage between adolescence and marriage; for young girls, it provided the sole opportunity to secure a *honsu*. Women sought employment at factories regardless of the low wages, strenuous work, and unsanitary conditions. For married women, commuting to a factory to supplement their family income was often a necessity. In many respects, work at a factory replaced the handicraft production that had been so vital to the household economy. Adapting to the new rules and codes of the workplace was a harsh, shocking process for Korean women workers; however, their hardships in the countryside had prepared them to some degree for the rigors of factory life.

Feminized Industries and the Sexual Division of Labor

In 1910, the Government-General reported that 151 factories, mostly small to medium, were fully operational, with a mixed workforce of 8,203.

By 1919, the number of factories had increased to 1,900 with a total workforce of 48,705.[76] In 1922, women comprised 20.4 percent of the total workforce (9,849); by 1936, 50,550 women, 33.3 percent of the workforce, worked in 5,937 factories.[77] Though these numbers might appear relatively modest, only eleven cities had a population of 14,000 in 1910. In the case of Kyŏngsŏng (Seoul), where 24 percent of the factories were located, there was a major demographic shift, as the population increased from 246,251 in 1914 to 929,872 in 1940.[78]

Like their counterparts in Europe, Korean female workers dominated light industries, such as textile and food-processing factories. However, the industrialization of Korea did not produce the "feminization" of certain factories—that is, the incursion of women into traditionally male-dominated arenas and the displacement of men from their positions. Unlike Europe, where feminization had led to fierce confrontations as men sought to protect their work from becoming defined as "women's work," select industries in Korea were feminized almost from the moment they were created (see table 3).[79]

Korean women dominated certain industries by the 1920s and 1930s. The statistics were quite striking: in 1921, female workers constituted 63.4 percent of the textile industry and 89.9 percent of the silk-reeling sector.[80] These numbers increased annually. There were other interesting features about female labor in the Government-General reports. A survey of 196 factories that employed fifty or more workers showed that female laborers worked the longest hours.[81] Moreover, a large number of women were married, unlike their counterparts in Europe, who were usually single. According to a survey conducted in 1930, roughly 80.8 percent of female workers in the chemical industries listed themselves as married.[82] Moreover, by 1936, more than 60.6 percent of female workers in textile factories with more than one hundred workers were illiterate.[83]

The sexual division of labor required conscious social engineering to obtain maximal results. Cultural ideas about the family and gender could be manipulated to justify employment practices. Employers described

Table 3. *Breakdown of jobs by age and gender*

Type of job	Factories	Workers below 16		Workers 16 to 50		Workers over 50		Total
		Male	*Female*	*Male*	*Female*	*Male*	*Female*	
Textile								
Silk-reeling	80	74	3,805	667	5,234	1	20	
Cotton fabric	24	80	661	898	1,277	1	1	
Silk fabric	15	6	36	113	341	0	0	
Knit fabric	53	250	80	707	257	6	3	
Cotton ginning	39	31	36	706	1,694	13	22	
	240	444	4,703	3,274	9,039	32	6	17,527
Metal	225	223	0	2,452	18	46	0	2,739
Machinery	218	163	0	3,813	1	53	2	3,402
Ceramics	314	224	7	5,120	373	108	4	5,856
Chemical	392	176	146	4,614	3,995	141	6	9,378
Lumber	152	128	23	2,942	36	29	1	3,159
Printing	208	271	4	3,778	64	31	0	4,148
Food processing	1,950	275	664	18,383	1,947	306	204	24,756
Gas/electric	75	0	0	815	0	0	13	838
Other	235	425	394	3,366	1,000	112	19	5,316
TOTAL	4,009	2,326	6,241	47,927	19,473	847	295	77,109

SOURCE: Chōsen Sōtokufu, *Chōsen Sōtokufu tōkei nempō* (1929), 192–97.

labor-intensive tasks in the factories as having inherently gendered qualities. In essence, they sought to justify the new gendered division of labor by arguing that nature had organized these roles according to gender traits. The industrialists argued that specific tasks required physical attributes like "delicate and nimble fingers," and traits like patience, agility, sharpness, and endurance, which were typical of females.[84] For instance, piecers needed supple fingers to repiece the broken threads back onto the spinning machines, a task rural women could easily adapt to because of their familiarity with weaving.[85] "Go and see for yourself," wrote one reporter. "The female worker's hand speed is unbelievable! You cannot follow their hand [movement] with your eyes! This requires dexterity!"[86] "Weaving is all about delicate hands," and it requires practice like that of soldiers, observed another journalist assigned to report on the Kyŏngsŏng Textile Company's apprentice school in Yŏngdŭngp'o.[87] Before the steam-powered looms could crank out hundreds of feet of silk, they required the tolerance and patience of female workers to fish the silk threads from scalding water, and delicate hands to coil the "silk threads as thin as a spider's web."[88] Yi Sŏng-hwan recalled his visit to a silk-reeling factory: "Anyone who goes there will get to know everything. . . . [F]emale workers as young as twelve or thirteen years old put their bare 'slender' hands into the scalding water to pull out the threads." The indispensable female trait of docility allegedly made it possible for women workers to work in very humid conditions, even during the dog days of summer, "for the sake of maintaining the gloss on the threads."[89]

Another essential trademark of the female textile worker was her ability to stand all day yet be alert enough to make sure that "a thousand strands of thread do not get tangled."[90] She then had to coil the fragile threads carefully "around a flat wooden-like spoon."[91] "Only the 'docile female' [*sunsilhan yŏja*] could do this kind of work," a reporter noted during his tour of the Kyŏngsŏng Textile Factory. "It is because they are from rural areas, they are 'naturally' accustomed to knitting and do not think of it as tedious"; despite the humid conditions and the putrid stench of rotting cocoons, they "hardly argue with Mayumi-san, the Japanese foreman."[92] Not surprisingly, female workers were also assigned tasks that were monotonous and repetitive—in other words, they occupied the least skilled jobs. Women who worked in the rice mills had the unenviable task of picking out rocks and unhulled rice one at a time, "like sparrows looking for insects"—a task that required the female trait of patience.[93] In many factories, employers assigned female workers the role of preparing raw materials for the machines.

Industrialization also exploited the domestic ideal to naturalize certain relations. Whereas a factory manager assigned male workers to operate the lathe or service the steam boilers (both relatively new skills that required some training and were not analogous to any premodern trade), female workers were always assigned tasks deemed "naturally suitable" to them. By deploying cultural stereotypes, industrialists called upon female workers to perform tasks analogous to "things done at home." Thus industrialists suggested that certain factory tasks were simply an extension of domestic duties. The only difference, according to a survey of workers conducted by the *Chosŏn ilbo*, was that workers now had to adapt to the speed of the machines.[94]

Assumptions about female work were formalized and institutionalized in various ways. Korean female workers from the rural areas did not become accustomed to factory work overnight and had to be "disciplined" into it. Disciplinary measures of this new capitalist economy were not confined to the shop floor, but also intruded into Korean daily life. The movement of females from the household economy to the factory invariably upset the rhythms of traditional life, as the factory assumed control over the women's daily calendar. Most striking was the rapid disappearance of rural handicraft skills, as women no longer had the time or incentive to pursue such activities. At the same time, factory work pushed women into monotonous tasks. The disassociation of the labor process from particular skills meant that female workers no longer needed to have a real understanding of work. By developing and naturalizing an automatic and mechanical instinct among workers, factories could easily allocate tasks to different groups of workers.

Government-General factory surveys often heralded the vast technological advancements of Japanese capitalism. For example, if the average horsepower utilized at a factory in Keijō (Seoul) registered at 10.8 in 1931, by 1939 it had increased to 152.5 or fourteenfold.[95] Indeed, by 1940, industrial output in Korea had surpassed agricultural output.[96]

Though factories, by their nature, produce standardized behavior, factory owners soon learned that all women workers complied equally with the needs of the industry. Age, marital status, the number of children, and the presence or absence of male support were also important in determining if a woman would be "obedient to the laws of the factory and the manager's instructions."[97] According to the Government-General annual report in 1929, of the 26,009 documented female workers, 6,241 were under sixteen years old. The average age of a female worker in the silk-reeling industry was sixteen.[98] However, Kwŏn T'ae-hwan notes that the number of girls from ten to fourteen leaving rural villages for the cities increased significantly between 1925 and 1935, and many juveniles began to work in textile mills.[99] Because of the cramped working space, managers used children to climb into engines to clean the machines. Many contemporaries highlighted the widespread use and abuse of children in the textile industry as the worst of the many exploitative features of Japanese colonialism. One writer lamented: "What is worse is that [our] children [are] 'purchased machines' used for profit!"[100] Factories favored children, much like female workers, because of their docility and dexterity.

Industrialization in Korea also transformed the language of labor. Workers became exposed to a new corporate jargon, which judged their work in terms of "efficiency," "costs," "rates," "speed," "competition," and so forth. Switching from task-based time to clock time proved extremely difficult, especially for rural migrant workers. It was a coercive measure by which work flowed to the laborers and not vice versa.[101] By breaking down production into minutes and assigning each worker a task, managers could increase productivity and optimize the labor of workers.

If a worker, in a moment of carelessness or fatigue, was hurt on the shop floor, managers treated her like a defective cog and quickly replaced her. Because of the abundance of workers, periodic replacements ensured "fresh parts." Likewise, a struggling factory could lay off its workers at any time. According to Chŏng Un-bing, ten or more workers were suddenly discharged from the Chongno "S" Socks Factory. They had been working there for more than fifteen years, but the style of shoes that went with their socks was no longer in demand. "It is understandable from the financial standpoint of the factory," Chŏng wrote, "but on the other hand, it is not that simple."[102]

Feminized Industries and Working Conditions

Precarious employment was only one of the risks borne by female workers. In primary feminized industries in Korea—the food processing, textile, and chemical industries—the working conditions for female workers were abysmal. Korean women's inferior position in these industries was based on both gender and nationality.

FOOD PROCESSING

In 1919, rice mills constituted more than 23 percent of the total number of factories.[103] The large number of rice mills reflected the state's intent to develop Korea into a principal supplier of rice. Of the 5,172 women hired in the food processing industry in 1921, 91.5 percent worked at the rice mills. Some tasks assigned to female workers mirrored their traditional roles in the fields, albeit in a mechanized setting. For example, the factory used female workers to sift through the harvested rice to remove stalks and foreign materials (i.e., dirt, stones, twigs) from the rough rice— a task women performed in the countryside. Mechanized factories with steam power performed the hulling and whitening (polishing) of the rice. As one female worker explained, "Rice spilled like an avalanche from the second floor. . . . The entire room would be filled with dust." In this factory, female workers, lined up cheek-by-jowl, assumed the monotonous task of sorting the polished rice on a glass plate.[104]

Not only were working conditions arduous, but wages were extremely

low—below subsistence level. One worker complained: "We work from
6 A.M. to 6 P.M., and earn [only] 60 *chŏn.*"[105] To exacerbate the situation,
working in the rice mills was a seasonal occupation. Many factories simply laid off their workers in October after the autumn harvest, closed
down the plant, and began rehiring in early February. According to a
Government-General report, rice mills operated for roughly 130 days
during the year.[106] A worker could hardly subsist in this sector of the economy without more steady work to carry her through lulls. It is not surprising, therefore, that rice mills were staffed primarily by married
women looking to supplement their family's income.

THE TEXTILE INDUSTRY

The textile industry was a profitable enterprise for Japanese investors,
who exploited the cheap labor and goods to increase their profits. During the first half of the colonial period, Japanese entrepreneurs concentrated their investments in the silk-reeling industry. By the late 1930s,
they had channeled their investments into the cotton industry, and by
1940, rayon had become the most favored industry for investment.[107]

The textile industries, in particular the silk-reeling factories, provided
the most stable employment for female workers. Silk-reeling factories
not only hired the greatest number of female workers but also had the
highest retention rate. According to a Government-General survey in
1938, 22.3 percent of the women remained in the factory for one to two
years.[108] One journalist posited that these factories preferred to hire
young, single females because "they were weak, docile, and cheap."[109] The
number of female workers in the textile industries remained relatively
consistent until Japan's war with China in 1937, when the state quickly
shifted from light to heavy industry to support the war effort.[110]

The division of labor in the textile industry and the scale of operation
were much more complex than in other sectors of the economy. Hosoi
Wakizō points out that aside from the "eight major processes, eighteen
subprocesses, eighteen different types of additional jobs/tasks and aux-
iliary processes, and chief supporting divisions (i.e., repair and mainte-

nance), an average factory had a total of fifty to seventy different tasks.[111] There was little hesitation in assigning female workers the most labor-intensive and dangerous tasks, which managers claimed could only be accomplished by those with feminine attributes. Silkworm cocoons, usually twenty-eight days old, were simmered in hot water to kill the chrysalis and loosen the sericin (glue), freeing the silk filaments. With their "supple" bare hands, female workers would fish for filaments, while at the same time trying to keep the thread continuous with an even thickness. Cocoons could have a thick surface with nothing inside or a thin surface with a thick body. Experienced workers knew which cocoon to fish for, while neophytes burned their hands extracting fruitless cocoons. Naturally, managers determined the wages by the quantity of silk strings fished from each cocoon, the gloss of the filament, and the thickness. The filaments were then attached to a spindle ready for spinning.

By the end of the 1930s, 88.4 percent of all silk-reeling factories had power looms. The Toyoda model 38 power loom with a more narrow iron or wood loom was much more durable than the traditional looms, and a weaver could operate six to seven looms at one time.[112] Filaments often snapped because of the tension and the speed of the looms. Workers had to quickly reconnect the strings, and this required alertness, dexterity, and patience—qualities that only women possessed, according to factory employers.[113] As we will see, such labor-intensive and dangerous working conditions were conducive to catastrophic accidents. No amount of feminine attributes could save inexperienced or even seasoned workers from burns and other injuries.

Textile factory recruiters sought to secure signatures from individuals who deceptively posed as parents with legal guardianship over the young girls. When a worker tried to bring in real authority figures (such as real parents, friends, and teachers) to resolve issues at the factory, the managers rejected their intervention, claiming that their names did not match the initial signature on the work contract. Han In-t'aek captured the consequences of this deception and abuse in his novel *Young Factory Girls*. A friend of Mr. W who arrives to visit the protagonist, Kŭmsŏm, at the Hamhŭng XX Silk-Reeling Factory has to argue for more than thirty minutes with the factory manager before being allowed to see her. The manager initially refuses because he is "not the parent or relative" who had signed the contract.[114] By signing contracts, female workers were often conned into working long periods of time.

THE CHEMICAL INDUSTRY

Among the various chemical-based industries (rayon, fertilizer, and rubber), the rubber shoe industry hired the most female workers. The majority of rubber factories were located in Pusan, Kyŏngsŏng (Seoul), and P'yŏngyang. Altering the shape of the *komusin* (rubber shoes) to resemble the traditional *chipsin* (straw shoes) for men and the *kosin* (pointed traditional *pŏsŏn*) for women, with its narrow toe and wide heel, proved to be a huge success for entrepreneur Yi Byŏng-tu. [115]

As rubber shoes became more popular and affordable than leather shoes, especially among young people, more businessmen began to invest in the industry and the number of factories increased. The number of factories increased from two in 1921 to seventy-two in 1933, with a net value of 9,845,000 *wŏn*.[116] The rubber industry started hiring female workers, ranging in age from sixteen to forty. According to one employee, the majority of workers were "mothers who left their crying babies at home," women "with swollen breasts," and emaciated women in their forties.[117] A survey conducted by the *Chosŏn chi kwang* in 1928 and a report conducted by the Government-General in 1935 (showing that 65.8 percent of the workforce were married) confirmed the large number of married women in the rubber factories.[118]

As in many mixed factories, there was a strict sexual division of labor. In most cases, male workers worked with the masticators or rollers and solvents to break down the polymer chains for vulcanization. Female workers participated in stirring and kneading the rubber in the vats after the solvents were added, but most were assigned to make the molds or assemble the soles. An experienced worker could make forty to fifty pairs a day, while a novice would complete roughly half that amount. Female workers often complained about the strain on their arms. Every time a sole was attached by the riveter, the finisher had to press down on the sole. Managers often penalized workers for any unevenness.[119]

The stress of producing perfect shoes paled in comparison to the psychological and physical stress of being a working mother. Although the number of communal or private *t'akaso*, or nurseries, was increasing, the majority of working women still had to bear the burden of rearing their children as well as providing income for the family.[120] Workers often carried infants on their backs, and one journalist reported her incredulity at seeing mothers breastfeed their babies in factories reeking of rubber fumes that were no doubt detrimental to their health.[121] For mothers who could not take their children to the factories, the mother-in-law or someone else in the household would bring the infant during break time for nursing.[122] Militant strikes for more breastfeeding time became quite prevalent among rubber workers, as will be discussed in the next chapter.

WAGES

To determine the wages of workers during the colonial period, historians have generally relied on the Government-General's records. However, the pay listed on paper was often higher than the real wages paid to workers, making the records highly unreliable. In the case of the rubber shoe industry, factories suspended operations for months during financial recessions or in the event of overproduction, causing a decline in the payment of wages.[123] The months from July to December marked the peak season for rubber shoe sales, because people purchased them as gifts for the harvest festival and other events. One year, the P'yŏngyang Rubber factory produced six million pairs of rubber shoes based on the previous year's sales; however, it only sold two million pairs, forcing the plant to suspend operations until May of the following year.[124] Workers put in more hours from July to December (twenty-six days per month) than from January to March (fifteen days per month), so their salaries

5. A textile factory.

6. A rice mill.

varied from month to month; as a result, the so-called average-wage index produced by the colonial government, which did not take into account special circumstances like cyclical downturns or periodic unemployment, was neither precise nor consistent. In the case of the rubber and silk-reeling factories, for instance, the data on wages did not reflect these irregularities.[125]

Factory owners resorted to other tactics to reduce wages and cut into the earnings of workers, who already suffered from the fluctuations of supply and demand and the instability of seasonal work. First, through a draconian system of *kangje chŏgŭm*, or forced savings, owners could withhold wages for a long period, often the duration of the worker's contract, keeping the wages in a savings account. Forced savings not only kept capital in the hands of the factory but assured managers that workers would remain for the duration of their promised contracts. If a worker decided to leave before his or her contract ended, the manager could keep whatever was left in the forced savings account. In the case of the Taech'ang Woven Goods Factory, managers hired workers for five years, knowing that many would quit before their contract ended; naturally they did not return any of the forced savings money to their workers.[126] Managers also kept a strict log of the number of days a worker showed up for work and could use it as a basis for deducting money from a worker's forced savings, on the pretext that the worker did not serve the full number of promised days.

Employers also resorted to the unscrupulous practice of meting out fines as punishment. The *pŏlgŭm chedo*, or penalty-fine system, not only deducted wages from workers and increased production, but also created competition among workers. Since workers did not have the right to file grievances, managers could withhold wages indefinitely. One common excuse for withholding wages was the poor quality of the product a worker produced. For example, in the textile industry, a worker's wages were determined by the gloss of the silk thread. A woman worker who worked at the Katakura Silk-Reeling Factory in Taegu complained that about seven hundred female workers in the three factories were not only subjected to unreasonable working conditions and terrible pay, but also judged according to the perfection of the product. Managers would levy a fine for any defect or mistake, making it practically impossible to make money. She complained bitterly that "after all that stress and excessive work, you end up with nothing, just debt."[127] Yuk Ji-su (1907–67), a professor at Yŏnhŭi College, notes that while most managers at the textile factories levied fines and blamed their workers for carelessness or lack of attention, in most cases (80 percent of the time), the failure to produce a first-grade product was due not to human error but to breakdown of the loom or inferiority of the silk threads.[128] Even if one did produce first-grade products on a daily basis, if one did not have a good rapport with the manager, "he would find a way to deduct wages."[129] The penalty system that forced female workers into debt proved to be a very effective control mechanism.

Even if female workers were able to save some money from their meager incomes, it was highly unlikely that all their remittances were sent home. Dorm inspectors often confiscated letters that contained money. A more common problem involved incoming girls who out of naïveté asked these inspectors to send their remittances home for them.[130] Needless to say, many of their families failed to receive the money. Female workers considered it their filial duty to work and save money to send back home. In fact, they justified their absence from home based on their duty to support their families. At the same time, they often voiced frustration, usually directed at their younger siblings, whom they believed had no appreciation of their sacrifices at the mills. As Kang Yang-sun, a textile worker, wrote to her siblings: "Do you know how hard I am working to pay for your education and to take care of our mother? Six years have already passed, and I still get up at six in the morning every day." Although Kang claimed that she felt no resentment toward her siblings and did not expect any monetary compensation in the future, she still wanted them to know the price of their comfort and the cost to her physical health: "All of my compatriots are toiling away, drenched in sweat, gasping for air, and our backs and legs are aching."[131] Despite the fatigue and sense of unfairness, the importance of supporting the family outweighed the suffering and physical toil at the factory. However, there was little left to send home in remittances after they paid their room and board, settled their penalty fines, and gave up a portion of their meager wages to the manager's forced savings accounts.

Another problem involved apprenticeship. Managers expected novices to serve three months to a year as apprentices. Although room and board was covered, the managers did not pay their workers during this time. In silk-reeling factories, for example, an average apprenticeship lasted six months.[132] During this time, an apprentice who put in thirteen hours at a spinning factory would be left with only one or two *wŏn* a month.[133] Han San-yŏ, a woman who began working at a tobacco factory when she was seventeen years old, attested to the difficulty of saving money: "I get up at four in the morning every day and spend my entire day wrapping cigarettes. I get paid 3 *chŏn* for wrapping ninety packs."[134] Those working at rubber shoe factories also complained about the long hours of work, the terrible pay, "and those penalty fines." A juvenile female worker who worked from 8 A.M. to 6 P.M. at the same factory concurred: "A single flawed shoe results in a big fine, usually worth half a day's work."[135]

While both married and single women felt enormous pressure to send remittances home to support their families, single women experienced the added burden of saving money for their *honsu* (marriage expenses). As a result of competition, women workers were not always amicable as each sought ways to earn an extra *wŏn*. A young female worker, frustrated with her low pay, felt that if she did not "curry favor with the manager" like some of the other girls, she would not be able to get her day's pay.[136]

The Government-General's price indices from 1926 to 1930 reveal that factories did not make any effort to increase the wages of their workers as the level of consumer prices consistently rose. If an item cost 29.3 *wŏn* in 1926, it would cost 36.23 *wŏn* in 1930.[137] A study conducted by the South Manchurian Railroad Company in 1933 noted that a monthly diet of barley, chestnut, and millet for a family of five cost between 15 and 21 *wŏn*.[138] Five years earlier, an *Tonga ilbo* survey noted that a monthly diet of only millet and salt for a family of three or four actually cost 20–25 *wŏn*. A single worker with the same diet would have to pay 9–12 *wŏn* a month, more than 70 percent of his or her wages.[139] Indeed, a simple computation of the average monthly pay of adult female workers at rubber and silk-reeling factories (roughly 12 *wŏn*) in 1932 minus penalty fines and remittances equaled an unsustainable living wage. In short, a worker could barely eke out a living for herself, let alone have enough to send money home without great sacrifice

Thirty-five years of colonial rule brought about significant economic and social transformations in Korea, including the establishment of several industries, the development of a modern financial sector, and the reorganization of agriculture. However, as this chapter has demonstrated, the changes that were set in motion both by exogenous shifts in the political economy and Government-General policies had profound consequences. These discursive processes challenged traditional gender relations and hierarchies in the family, workplace, and political sphere.

The exodus of thousands of young women and men from the rural areas to factories and mines in the cities not only had tremendous demographic and social implications but it destabilized notions of the natural division of labor, both in the city and in the countryside. As Raymond Williams has aptly noted, the "men and women who came from the country to the cities did not need to be told what they had lost, any more than they needed to be told what they might struggle to gain in their new world."[140] Migrants left the gaze of the rural community, only to be placed under the strict, often unforgiving surveillance of the modern factory. Control through a gendered division of labor, meager wages, long working hours, and even physical containment in dormitories proved profitable for the colonial state but detrimental to the well-being of the new Korean female workers. While the Korean press conscientiously portrayed these workers as victims of the greedy state, it also expressed ambivalence about the new female worker, who expressed discontent and independence, and challenged the social order. She justified her presence in the factories with references to her filial piety and her duty to support her family. At the same time, as we will see in the next chapter, the woman worker dared to express discontent with harsh working conditions. As women became more unruly in the eyes of both factory owners and educated society, the public began to debate the fate of the uncontrolled female worker. That discourse about class and race redefined and reconstituted the sexual domain of labor.

CHAPTER FOUR

Discoursing in Numbers
The Female Worker and the Politics of Gender

The prominence of the woman worker . . . came not so much
from an increase in their numbers or a change in the location,
quality or quantity of her work, as from contemporaries' preoccupation with gender as a sexual division of labor. This
preoccupation was not caused by objective conditions of industrial development; rather, it helped shape those conditions,
giving relations of production their gendered form, women
workers their secondary status, and home and work, reproduction and production, their oppositional meanings.

Joan Scott, "The Woman Worker in the
Nineteenth Century"

On 29 May 1931, as the sun slowly began to rise east of the Taedong
River, morning commuters noticed the silhouette of a woman standing
on top of the octagonal roof of the Ŭlmildae. The famous pavilion in
P'yŏngyang was visible for miles because of its strategic location on the
cliffs of the Ŭlmil-i Hill on Moran Peak. As people gathered around the
pavilion, the woman began to voice her grievances against the P'yŏngwŏn Rubber Factory. For nine hours before her arrest, she denounced
the abysmal working conditions and the plans for steep wage decreases

that threatened her and her coworkers. "I do not consider the loss of my life regrettable," she declared. "Of all the things I have learned, the most important one is that dying for the masses is honorable. . . . Until the owner comes out and retracts his statement about decreasing [our] wages, I will not come down. I am a representative of the working masses!"[1]

Kang Chu-ryong was one of the forty-nine female strikers who had staged a walkout and hunger strike on 16 May to protest the unexpected announcement of a wage cut, bringing production to a halt. The factory owner summoned Japanese gendarmes to disperse the striking workers and fired them for insubordination. Kang was moved to take her dramatic action in defense of some 2,300 rubber factory workers whose survival depended on their current wages. At first she contemplated suicide but opted for a public demonstration to reveal the injustices of the factory.[2]

This chapter explores the factors that generated discontent among Korean women workers and how they articulated and addressed their grievances. The image of the female worker in the Korean press was paradoxical: she was at once an innocent, exploited victim trapped in an oppressive factory system and an assertive activist who stirred up trouble. As a helpless victim, she could be assisted by philanthropy or reformed through work and discipline. But the public also needed to contend with the specter of a self-conscious woman fully capable of expressing discontent and organizing disobedience.

Kang Chu-ryong and others like her ignited broader public debates about the position of female workers in Korean society and in the empire more generally. At the most basic level, the workplace dynamics that pitted Korean male managers and police against female workers in a colonial context raised new questions: Should unequal gender relations be maintained even if it meant that Koreans would be forced to oppress their own compatriots? Who had the authority to police labor disputes? Was it acceptable for Korean authorities to take the side of industry and the colonial state over ordinary workers?

Serious questions about the female worker's status and role emerged with the rising demand for cheap unskilled labor: Should she be allowed to work outside the home or should she remain within traditional boundaries? Could she simultaneously work and fulfill her maternal duties? Would the "backward" Korean woman be able to adapt to the "modern, systematic, and orderly" life of the factory or was she, in the words of the social investigator Suzuki Masafumi, confined to a "medieval mindset"?[3] The question of how best to represent the female worker became a contentious matter as the state, social critics, and reformers of all persuasions sought to describe and document her.

CAUSES OF LABOR DISCONTENT

Despite their experiences in the fields and in cottage industries, Korean women's transition into the factories was a difficult one. Their plight caught the attention of the Japanese social investigator Ōyama Chōyō, who sharply criticized the appearance of the "shanty" buildings that housed modern industrial complexes: "Can you call this a factory?" He decried the lack of proper facilities, including restrooms, in factories in the western part of Seoul. Here the majority of workers were illiterate and were forced to accept substandard wages of 30 *chŏn* a day to "support a family of seven or eight people!"[4] No doubt the dire working conditions of the factory, compounded by an unfair wage system, had a detrimental impact on women's psychological and physical health. Yet, in the eyes of the factory owners, a vast reserve labor pool of female workers facilitated easy exploitation and abuse.

Through the 1920s, Korean workers who had expressed discontent could be pacified with limited concessions, which the Japanese colonial government was willing to make, in line with its more "lenient" cultural and economic policies. However, with the onset of the world depression in 1929 and the 1931 annexation of Manchuria, Japan "largely withdrew from the world system" and opted for a more self-contained, self-reliant economic strategy that not only generated "high industrial growth rates but changed the face of Northeast Asia."[5] As it entered a phase of heavy industrialization, setting up steel mills, petrochemical complexes, and hydroelectric facilities in North Korea and Manchuria, the colonial government had to enact draconian measures to secure its own interests. As a result, wages plummeted and working conditions deteriorated rapidly, forcing desperate Korean workers to become more articulate and militant about their grievances. In a paradoxical turn of events, the Japanese government's experiment in turning rural peasants into modern workers succeeded, as factory laborers who shared common experiences overcame gender biases and boundaries to unite in protest. Although gender inequality among workers was still prevalent, there were key moments when male workers accepted the leadership of female instigators or men sided with women to support a common cause.

The Dangers of Manual Labor and Mechanized Work

During the process of rapid industrialization, factories often neglected safety mechanisms, especially in low-paying, unskilled feminized industries. Work-related accidents were common in all industries and increased annually, according to a 1940 report in the *Tonga ilbo*. Absence as a result of work-related accidents rose from 31.66 percent in 1937 to 81.64 percent in 1939.[6]

A worker in a moment of carelessness or fatigue resulting from pressure to fulfill the daily quota was vulnerable to severe accidents and chronic illnesses. Women reported numerous gruesome accidents—from being hit by rocks flying from conveyor belts in the rice mills to getting hands stuck under rollers in a rubber factory.[7]

For example, in the silk-reeling factories, fishing barehanded in scalding water for the threads of silk led to skin disorders such as eczema.[8] Factory managers instructed novices to overcome the pain from their swollen hands because the next stage of production required even more concentration and agility. When the silk thread snapped, workers needed to grab the broken end quickly and reattach it to the spindle. With the looms rotating at high speed, workers often jammed their knuckles or sustained injuries from the flying shuttle.[9] In a factory with steam-powered machines, the possibility of the tanks exploding from overheating also posed a daily risk to the workers.[10] Despite the introduction of modern machinery, most factories could not dispense with manual labor, largely because the process of mechanization was still in its elementary stages.

Factory accidents in the silk industry were a staple theme in Korean literature. Writers employed the image of mangled, maimed body parts as a metaphor for the physical destruction of the female workers, who were as dispensable as useless fingers or limbs injured or severed during an accident. In her novel *News from a Factory* (1931), for example, Song Kye-wŏl explored the imagery of tortured flesh. Through the eyes of the protagonist, the reader sees a mother's sallow face and disheveled hair as she fishes in the scalding water for loose threads from the silk cocoons. Her moans of pain as her swollen and burned hands make contact with the water at regular intervals reflect the relentless rhythms of the factory, which drown out the sounds of human suffering.[11]

Lifeless fingers serve as a metaphor in Kang Kyŏng-ae's novel, *The Human Problem* (1933).[12] Sŏnbi, who has just begun her job at a silk-reeling factory, soon notices that her hands have turned bright red, scalded in the searing heat of the water as she fishes for silk threads. After she douses her hands in cold water, Sŏnbi observes in horror that all five fingers have turned white; one lifeless, dead finger hangs limp on "her living hand." Sŏnbi shudders as she thinks about how many other dead fingers have been discarded in this factory.[13] The Japanese economist Takahashi Kamekichi went so far as to characterize the Korean worker as an expendable piece of machinery that the factory discards when it becomes disabled: "The working conditions are inferior and the average serviceable years [of a worker] are [only] a year and six months!"[14]

Work-related injuries were especially prevalent in the textile industries, because female workers stood for thirteen hours a day in front of a loom. Monotonous work in a stooped posture led to chronic complaints about stiffness in the neck or severe cramping and bowing of the legs, which left some workers permanently disabled after several years.[15] According to one inspection report, stationary work, which causes "the retroversion of the uterus, irregular menstruation, and strain on the pelvis," caused serious complications during pregnancy. The report added that the drooping of the uterus caused mucous to form in the womb area, causing hyperemia (congestion of blood), which often led to heart complications.[16] Another study found that female laborers who worked during the midnight shift in textile factories suffered from more ailments than those who worked during the day shift.[17] Kojima Tsunehisa, who studied the impact of work on female health, added that the loss of body weight, especially among maturing girls who worked the midnight shift, was 638 grams a day.[18]

Social investigators who visited the factories remarked on the noxious odors and the deafening, jarring clanking of the machines. One worker at the Kyŏngsŏng Rubber Factory reported that one could go deaf for ten days or more and even become bedridden as a result of the noise.[19] Workers in chemical factories, especially fertilizer facilities, suffered from eye injuries caused by ammonium sulfate crystals and stomach problems caused by the odor. According to a survey conducted in the Hŭngnam Fertilizer Factory, of the 8,100 workers who fell ill annually, 1,300 died.[20]

The poor ventilation and oppressive heat in textile factories also contributed to the poor health of the laborers. One woman described the conditions inside factories that closed doors and windows during operating hours: "It is like the hottest day during the summer every day" because "the fragile silk threads will snap if there is too much air."[21] The airlessness also gave the threads a better luster.[22] According to another reporter for the *Chosŏn chung'ang ilbo*, "Young female workers labor in dark factories under the frightening gaze of the manager . . . in hundred-degree heat." The workers not only "suck in the hot air . . . [but] are working themselves to death." She was especially struck by the sallow ap-

pearance of the workers' faces, which reminded her of the visages of ter-
minally ill patients, and concluded that "this type of work makes you want
to pass out."[23]

The poor ventilation contributed to large amounts of dust, lint, flax,
and hemp and cotton fibers, which made workers vulnerable to chronic
respiratory problems, such as excessive coughing, wheezing, shortness
of breath, and diseases like byssinosis and tuberculosis.[24] The Government-General annual report also listed dysentery, typhoid, and diphtheria
as common factory-related diseases in Korea.[25] It concluded that more
than 81 percent of women working in factories in the south suffered from
some kind of health problem. In this report, Ishihara Yoshiharu suggested
that poor ventilation and circulation in the factories could be the reason
for the high number of illnesses. He noted, "The workers do not look
like they are alive. . . . In particular, the bodies of the apprentices are
shocking." Even though these juveniles were from peasant backgrounds,
they showed "dwarfed growth" from working in the factories for so long.
He added, "These girls are only twelve or thirteen years old, but they
look like twenty-year-olds." [26]

Despite the large number of work-related injuries and diseases, there
were almost no medical clinics or dispensaries in the factories.[27] If a factory had an infirmary, it was always full, and only those workers who
were extremely ill received time off to recuperate in the unsanitary wards.
A woman worker who went to visit her sick friend was astonished to see
so many women packed like sardines: "The ward was really crowded.
Women were lying down everywhere."[28] As we will examine more
closely in chapter 5, the crisis of women's health was a priority of Korean reformers, whose anxieties focused on the broader demographic
crisis.

Work Hours

Mechanization required workers to adjust to "clock time." The factory
clock not only regulated work hours but also cut into the daily lives of

workers. Those who lived in the dormitories often complained about the blaring siren that woke them up; this same obnoxious noise told them when it was mealtime and when it was time to return to work. One girl recalled, "When I first came, I thought the siren was a fire alarm, but then I realized it was a way to tell us it was time to work."[29]

Labor reforms were well under way in Japan, where government legislation had abolished the midnight shift (11 P.M. to 5 A.M.) for female and juvenile workers (fourteen and younger) and limited working hours to nine-hour shifts with thirty-minute breaks.[30] No such laws were enacted in Korea to assist working women. In fact, the absence of factory laws not only allowed managers to exercise power like a household patriarch but allowed them to maintain unbearable working conditions. As one factory worker complained, "We are forced to work like cattle . . . and do not even have time to wash our clothes!"[31] Owners often operated their factories for twenty-four hours in two twelve-hour shifts.[32] According to one government survey, 46.9 percent of female laborers worked for twelve or more hours. Female workers in the textile factories worked the longest hours, and 82.18 percent of all textile workers worked between 12 and 15.5 hours.[33]

The P'yŏngch'ang [Katakura] Silk-Reeling Factory, for example, required its female workers to wake up at 5 A.M. and start work by 5:30 A.M. Aside from one meal break, from 7 to 7:30 A.M., workers worked straight through until 7 P.M.[34] By 1935–36, female workers worked longer hours than their male counterparts in the low-skilled factories.[35]

According to the Government-General's Commerce and Labor Department in 1939, 65 percent of factories in Korea gave workers only 2.1 days off every month, while 81.25 percent of factories allotted no more than one and a half hours for rest time, which included two meal breaks. In the textile factories in Korea, the average break time for female workers was thirty minutes to one hour.[36] Inadequate leisure and rest time not only affected the morale of the workers but made them vulnerable to accidents as a result of chronic fatigue.

Violence and Sexual Harassment

Each plant hired male managers and foremen, primarily Japanese but also some Koreans, to oversee the work of female workers. In a survey conducted by the *Tonga ilbo*, certain factory managers explained why they preferred to hire female workers: they were docile, easy to manage, less likely to aggravate a situation, and commanded lower wages.[37] By maintaining a strict gender segregation policy, factories could subject female workers to special disciplinary rules, physical violence, and surveillance. Equally important, employers could engage in unscrupulous practices by manipulating long-standing patriarchal values. For example, managers could exploit a worker by virtue of her age, sex, and background (particularly if she was uneducated and from the countryside) through violent language, penalty fines, threats of layoff, or sheer physical violence.[38] Most factories deliberately set up their assembly lines so that workers could not see the managers. This way, the workers knew that they were under surveillance but could never be certain who was under the gaze of the manager at any given moment.[39] This system ensured that workers worked hard for fear of being watched and spared factories the cost of hiring many managers.

A manager's treatment of his workers differed from factory to factory; in general, however, overseers were extremely critical in descriptions of their workers. In her vivid diary entries, one female worker in a silk-weaving factory described the dictatorial and cruel personalities of the managers. On 7 August 1930, she wrote: "Pong-nyŏ got penalized!" The tired girl had been severely ill for several days but had continued to toil for thirteen hours a day like the rest of the girls. Exhausted, Pong-nyŏ made a mistake and immediately received a harsh penalty: the manager forced her to hold a bucket of water all day. Feeble and unable to hold onto the weight of the bucket of water, she dropped it and was brutally assaulted by her boss. The diary entry ended with a denunciation of the labor system: "The compensation [for our labor] is abuse and punishment!"[40]

The oppressive and inhumane treatment that Pong-nyŏ experienced was apparently a chronic problem at the factories. Exasperated by the offensive verbiage hurled at the workers, one woman asked a reporter in 1930, "How much longer do you expect us to remain patient? Our parents did not even use such insulting words."[41] Another female worker at a silk-reeling factory expressed outrage at the crude language employed by male managers: "These young girls are naïve and innocent and cannot really see the [shame] in all this. They steadfastly do their work day after day."[42] In another incident reported in the newspaper, three young girls at the Tongyang (Tōyō) Factory had their ankles severely lacerated by an abusive manager. Although they had difficulty walking, he ordered them to remain quiet and continue working at their stations.[43]

The frequency of sexual harassment and intimidation by managers and foremen was another unpalatable aspect of factory life. Male managers often seduced or raped the young girls, and for many this resulted in miscarriages, abortions, or stillbirths. Several factors contributed to the cycle of victimization. One major problem was corruption among law enforcement officers, who ignored the criminal behavior of Korean factory managers in return for bribes. In 1929, for instance, a victim reported being raped by a manager of a silk-reeling factory; with his resources, however, he easily curried favor with the police and subjected the victim to further humiliation by demanding that she expose her breasts and private parts for examination.[44] Clearly, such cases discouraged reporting by women who had been assaulted; they often faced inaction or, even worse, retribution by the very authorities whose responsibility it was to protect them. In very rare instances the publicity surrounding an assault case brought justice for a victim. In 1936, the *Tonga ilbo* reported Kim Mo's attempted rape of Chŏng Ae-ra. Chŏng was a married woman who worked at the Nambuk Cotton and Stocks Company in Suwŏn. Kim was a foreman infamous for preying on his workers. Mass resignations took place after this story leaked out to the other workers in the factory.[45] In this case, the press played an important role in exposing the crime and raising public awareness, but such instances were exceedingly rare.

Another factor that exacerbated sexual tensions in the factory was the desperate poverty of the women workers, who were under tremendous pressure to send their wages to their families. The seduction of female workers by overseers looking to buy sexual favors became a prominent theme in popular literature. While it is difficult to confirm that these tales had any basis in reality, it is certainly plausible that some workers may have resigned themselves to this fate for the sake of their families. The novels portrayed the "sacrifices" of these women in a sympathetic light, highlighting the economic plight of migrants from rural areas.

In Yu Chin-ho's *Female Factory Workers* (1931), Ok-sun reluctantly accepts money from the factory owner after refusing several times. The owner claims that the money comes with no strings attached and should be used to assist her father, who has been an invalid since falling at a construction site four years earlier. However, the owner reveals his true intentions upon handing her the money. She is to spy on Kun-ju, a fellow worker, and her secret reading group. The story revolves around Ok-sun's struggle with her conscience about spying on her fellow workers and her fear of getting caught as an informant. The price of taking the money is indeed high: the owner later rapes her and then fires her from the factory. At the end of the novel, as Ok-sun leaves the factory for the final time, she ponders: "Who is to blame? Is it the manager? The factory? No, it is because I was born a poor daughter. It was supposed to be like this. This was fate. I cannot live happily for this reason. . . . [T]ens of thousands, hundreds of thousands will be treading this same path."[46]

Despite the conspiratorial reading group in the background of the novel, which hints at resistance against the system, the author's resigned attitude reflects the pessimism that pervaded the early 1930s, despite labor's attempts to organize and the occurrence of militant strikes. More importantly, Yu Chin-ho, a male writer of proletarian literature, became frustrated with the lack of class consciousness among female workers, who placed family over the class struggle, the private over wider political goals. His statement that "hundreds of thousands will be treading this same path" expressed this sense of futility and hopelessness.

Song Kye-wŏl's novel, *News from a Factory*, explored the fate of factory workers who became pregnant after affairs with their managers or rapes. In a letter to her sister, Kim Ok-pun recalls the story of a young woman who had attempted suicide after she discovered that the manager who had promised to take full responsibility for their newborn child had taken a new mistress. Factory girls were a dime a dozen. As the popular folk song "Komu kongjang k'ŭnagi" (The rubber factory gal) teased, good looks could earn a factory girl free shoes:

> At the chill of early dawn, as the steam siren whistles . . .
> The rubber factory gal prepares her *bento*
> From morn 'til night, hunched over, fastens shoes together,
> Her heart pounding,
> For if she be a maiden with a pretty face, many pairs of shoes
>   shall be hers,
> [Just] a sweet smile and coquetry for the manager.
> The rubber factory gal's serge dress
> Says it's a gift from Sir Manager.
> Tucking the *bento* in her skirt, she leaves the factory,
> The shining stars from the eastern sky greet her.[47]

Girls who became pregnant were particularly dispensable, for they were the least desirable commodities in the workplace. Unfortunately there is little information about the frequency of pregnancy or on the fate of pregnant women, other than what we can infer from novels by Song Kye-wŏl and others who sought to expose the consequences of these abusive relationships: abandonment, shame, and dishonor.[48]

Factory women had to contend not only with abusive bosses in the workplace but also with predatory landlords who demanded sex in compensation for delinquent rent payments. In the absence of concrete data, it is impossible to assess how widespread this problem was, but it served as a common trope in the popular imagination. In Pak Hwa-sŏng's story, *The Evening before the Harvest Moon Festival*, Yŏng-sin, a factory worker who had just been verbally abused by her manager, comes home, only to be confronted by her Korean landlord, who had already raped her several times in lieu of rent. Angrily she responds, "I told you I would give it [the rent] to you tonight." Slamming her fists on the ground she screams: "He is a fellow countryman. . . . This is what this world is like. This is what people are really like. . . . What a dirty world!"[49]

The image of Koreans abusing their own compatriots, especially women, posed a serious dilemma for a nation under colonial rule. The worker's cry "He is a fellow countryman" spoke volumes about oppression by people who were themselves subjugated by the Japanese. Although the criticism is muted, the gendered imagery is an indictment: Koreans raped their own women, subjecting them to the humiliation that only foreign conquerors might inflict on their vanquished enemies. The image in Kang Kyŏng-ae's novel *The Human Problem*, of a Korean manager who thrashed new female workers on their buttocks, illustrates the hierarchical pyramid of race and class, the lowest figure being the Korean woman worker.[50] As we will see, social reformers, especially Korean nationalists, were keenly aware of this paradoxical display of power and its impact on the morale of the nation.

Living Conditions: Food and Living Arrangements

Female health was impacted not only by oppressive working conditions but by poor nutrition. Unappetizing meals with little nutritional value were the only reward for a difficult day of work at the factories. Workers generally ate only two meals a day; a common diet consisted of a bowl of low-grade rice, often mixed with millet or barley, and maggot-infested soybean paste soup. Though the meals were a little better than the herb roots, hulled millet, tree bark, and white clay from the mountains that their rural brothers and sisters were eating, two meals a day did not suffice for the long hours of arduous labor.[51] A juvenile worker complained bitterly: "Whenever I go to the cafeteria to eat, I cannot get up. I feel like a drunk and I always feel dizzy and my eyes automatically close.[52]

Not only was the quality of the food miserable, but the servings were extremely meager and the balance was poor. A Government-General report in 1933 reported that an average worker's diet was 59.5 percent rice, 12.7 percent barley and minor grains, 5.2 percent meat, and 12.5 percent vegetables.[53] This diet lacked the proper protein and vitamins required for good health. In addition, the mess halls and kitchens were filthy, and many women workers suffered from food poisoning. The *Tonga ilbo* reported one case in which eighty women workers at the Tongyang Silk-Reeling Factory in Sariwŏn suffered severe poisoning from the drinking water.

The spare, uncomfortable living quarters added to the miserable existence of women workers who had migrated from rural areas. Many of the large factories in Seoul with more than a hundred workers, in particular the textile mills, maintained their own dormitories. Factory owners, who emulated the dormitory system in Japan, offered their women workers housing in factory-owned dormitories. Commuting to work (the practice of half the workforce) was not possible for some women workers; according to the terms and conditions of their contracts, they agreed to reside in the dormitories for a duration of two to three years. This allowed the managers not only to maintain close control over these workers but also to prevent high rates of turnover in the factories. Managers developed a strict surveillance system to prevent girls from running away. For commuters, who for the most part lived in *t'omak* (mud huts or dens) near embankments, forests, or under bridges, the factory had a system of blaring the sirens at six in the morning to wake the workers. These "mud dwellers" differed from the *yumin* (drifters) who congregated in the cities looking for work.[54]

For rural families with far too many daughters, the dormitory accommodation appeared enticing, even though room and board was deducted from a worker's wages.[55] Factories often dispatched agents to remote rural areas, offering three-year contracts and small advances.[56] Unfamiliar with the realities of factory life, farmers felt reassured when the agents promised to supervise their daughters.[57] In Kyŏngsŏng Textile Factory, 90 percent of the female workers who lived in the company's dormitories identified themselves as *ch'ulga* (migrants who had left home temporarily).[58]

According to a 1938 Government-General survey, the living conditions were unsanitary and overcrowded.[59] Because of the two-shift system, two women would share roughly one *tatami* of space. In most cases, roughly ten women shared a room, and dormitory guards took shifts making sure nobody left the premises. Each dormitory had a *sagam* (dorm inspector), *sangdamwŏn* (counselor), and *silchang* (room chief).[60] A day off meant staying within the compound, despite strikes by workers who demanded time outside the factory gates. The majority of factories prevented their workers from leaving the premises until their contracts expired.[61]

To be sure, there were some leisure activities for workers. The dormitories, which most often were adjacent to the factories, had a yard where women could play ping-pong or swing on the swings once or twice a month. In some cases, managers would show films and even allow women to visit the bathhouse occasionally.[62] Some factories offered educational opportunities by hiring a factory clerk or staff member from a school to offer courses for the workers. Large factories even hired full-time instructors to teach short courses, offer technical training, or give lectures. Given the daily twelve-hour shifts, sleep or rest was much more desirable than an extra one or two hours of education; however, according to Yuk Ji-su (1907–67), a professor at Yŏnhŭi University, 40 percent of the female workers regularly attended these classes.[63] At the Kyŏngsŏng Textile Factory, lecturers offered courses on arithmetic, reading and writing, sewing, cooking, and cultural activities like the tea ceremony.[64]

Though such educational activities may have provided some escape from their monotonous jobs, female workers whose contracts enslaved them to the factory sometimes tried to flee the dormitories when the opportunity arose. Few succeeded, and those who were caught were punished and forced to resume their work.[65] Because of the strict surveillance, female workers attempted escapes during the middle of the night by jumping over the barbed wire fence or digging a hole under it.[66] Those who succeeded in escaping usually left their belongings behind.[67] In reality, due to their debts to the manager or the urgency of sending remittances home, the majority of female workers chose to stay; only when they suffered from a debilitating illness, such as tuberculosis, would the owner release them from the factory.[68]

FACTORY UNREST:
ACCOMMODATION AND RESISTANCE

Given the onerous conditions under which women workers labored, factory unrest was inevitable. Korean factory workers sought to redress their grievances through accommodation and resistance. As we have seen, some workers accommodated to the rigorous demands of the factory owners for the sake of their families, by remaining in the dormitories, eating the unpalatable food, and even surrendering to sexual advances. However, as discontent and anger erupted over unjust and criminal treatment, women workers began to resist by employing weapons of the weak or resorting to militant strikes.[69]

Although Korean women workers often acted on individual initiative without the help of organized unions, they also participated in the larger labor movement, which met the colonial government's growing repression with corresponding tactics. Kim Yun-hwan divides the labor movement into four major phases: 1920–24: the consolidation of labor groups, which gained momentum after the Fourth Congress; 1925–29: the development of labor groups and an increased number of strikes; 1930–36: strong and well-organized labor groups that staged numerous strikes; 1937–45: the hidden labor movement, which went underground as a result of repression.[70] Though the patterns of Korean women's resistance do not fit neatly into these categories, there was clearly a growing militancy in the 1920s that continued into the 1930s. Moreover, gendered grievances (such as the demand for breastfeeding breaks and regulation of sexual harassment) shaped the nature of the women's protests, for they had different needs than their male counterparts.

Absenteeism and Desertion

Dissatisfaction might be expressed by absenteeism or resigning from work altogether. For instance, the *Chosŏn sinmun* reported that the Kanebo Textile Factory in Keijō (Seoul) experienced a high rate of desertion: "Just today, seven female workers ran away. . . . Their ages ranged from thirteen to seventeen years, and this is disrupting factory [operations]."[71]

The Korean press and the Japanese state sought to explain the root causes of this phenomenon. Some social investigators argued that the high turnover rate resulted from the departure of workers who left in search of better conditions in a different factory. An investigator cited the 1926 testimony of one woman worker:

> I was hired at a tobacco company when I was seventeen years old. I was promised ten *chŏn* a day, but during my training session I only received six *chŏn* a day. Two years later, after I turned nineteen, I was told by someone that if I went to Pusan to a spinning company, I would get 15 *wŏn* a month (after deducting my room and board) during my training session and thereafter 50 *wŏn* a month. I cannot tell you how happy I was. Please, everybody, do not be shocked. I cannot hide my tears anymore.[72]

Not only had she been deceived, but she had worked longer hours for half the pay she had been promised. This worker left for another factory in Pusan with hopes for improved wages.[73]

It must be noted, however, that a government survey in 1940 found that more women left for family considerations than to find better work. Workers may have realized that conditions were no different in other factories. Based on this survey, 33.15 percent of those leaving their jobs cited family considerations (marriage or household duties), while 12.81 percent claimed illness.[74]

One writer blamed the food for the exodus from the factories: "The meals offered [to a female worker] are made of coarse grains—in a word, not edible. Daily wages are no more than 20 to 25 *chŏn*. Since it costs 15 *chŏn* to cover her expenses for food, it is inevitable that she ends up in debt, given the other daily expenses. It is natural for [her] to escape from that kind of environment!"[75] Indeed, in the case of the Chungnam Spinning Factory, women workers went on strike to protest the inferior quality of side dishes.[76]

Perhaps the most common cause of resignation was the endless cycle of poverty that resulted from the unfair wage system. According to reports in the late 1930s, poverty among workers had risen to crisis levels. Even if the workers "toiled in their sweat and blood day and night, to the point of death," the wages remained negligible, certainly not enough to support them or their families. "Our average income a month is between three and six *wŏn*," explained one worker. "For those who are single, they only have to worry about their meals. But for [people like myself] with a family of two or three, [we] can barely eke out a living."[77] Likewise, in a special report, Kim Ok-yŏ, a worker at the rubber factory, described her trials and tribulations as a female worker:

> I have been making rubber shoes day after day. The odor of the rubber gives you severe migraines and numbs your nose. My hands get swollen; [even though] I make several pairs of rubber shoes, I can barely eke out a living. What does the new year mean to [people like] us? What can we do? We are always without money [and] we are lucky if we do not starve. A New Year's meal would be fine. What will the young ones and my elderly mother wear? I am in big trouble. It is getting colder, and I have nothing to wear and nothing to eat. What can I do? Goodness, I am in debt again. My mother is in her sixties and stays at home. My daughter is ten years old this year and is working at a rice mill. My husband got involved in a strike last year and was accused of being an instigator and has remained behind bars for ten months.[78]

The *Kyŏngsŏng ilbo* reported on a big gathering of textile owners to discuss the sudden drop in the number of female workers in the late

1930s.[79] They pondered a global explanation: "Because of Japan's all-out war with China, many female workers are now working in munitions factories," one article explained. That was "why we have now entered a period [when] we are scrambling for female workers."[80] To be sure, the number of females working in men's jobs had increased significantly after 1937. According to a Government-General report, females working in the mines had increased from 3 percent in 1933 to 7.3 percent in 1941.[81] However, an editorial in the *Chosŏn sinmun* in 1937 begged to differ. "Was there not a surplus rural population?" the writer asked. "Then why is there this contradiction?" Unless factories eased up on their female workers, this writer believed that women were not going to continue working.[82]

Industrialists had also underestimated how rural families would respond to sexual problems in the workplace. Word about sexual assaults and harassment generated suspicion and anger among the public: "Women are simply wary about leaving the villages to work in the factories!"[83] The general public sentiment was that young girls lost their virginity and honor in the factories. Factories were becoming synonymous with sexual slavery.[84] In 1938, the Government-General noted that unless factories addressed this basic question, they risked being shut down regularly. Furthermore, incentives such as higher wages or better treatment of the workers had to be offered to counter negative images spawned by cases of impropriety and violence. At the same time, the report argued that if mores could not be changed at the factories, the Government-General should participate directly in the recruitment of female workers, even if it meant forced mobilization.[85]

Protests and Strikes

Just as the rates of absenteeism and desertion were high, the number of labor disputes also increased annually. Despite Government-General prohibitions against protests and public assembly, between 1920 and 1924, police reports documented 280 protests with 22,570 participants. From

1925 to 1928 there were 349 disputes and 29,952 participants.[86] In 1930 alone, there were 160 labor disputes and 18,972 participants. The following year, the number of disputes had increased to 201.[87]

Although it is tempting to argue that women's daily experiences with patriarchy and capitalism automatically produced a distinct shared or unified critical consciousness that led to collective resistance, the case was more complex. Perhaps we should understand Korean women's expression of discontent as "points of resistance," which are ubiquitous in power structures.[88]

Strikes represented various points of resistance to factory owners. They erupted all over the country, for a multitude of reasons that were not necessarily connected and had different ramifications for each participant. One common form was a spontaneous walkout as an immediate response to an outrage experienced by the workers. As in nineteenth-century France, such reactions were "more like public warnings to the owners—'we can be pushed only so far!'—than some concerted attempt to win specific concessions."[89] In the Korean context, the outrage usually involved an oppressive manager. In 1928, for instance, seventy female workers from the weaver's section at the Keijō Textile Factory walked out on their jobs to protest the behavior of their tyrannical Japanese manager.[90]

In the rice mills, there were walkouts when managers indiscriminately struck workers; the humiliation of physical punishment was not tolerated without some show of resistance. Other walkouts had a specific purpose. In 1924, over four hundred workers at a rice mill in Inch'ŏn picketed for the dismissal of an oppressive manager, and threatened the owner that they would resign en masse if he did not fire the miscreant.[91] If a strike failed and the leaders were dismissed, workers would strike again to reinstate the accused agitators. In August 1932, some three hundred female workers from the Chōsen Silk-Reeling Factory left their posts, demanding the reinstatement of two female workers who had been dismissed for their role in a previous strike. The reporter covering this strike noted that "the female workers displayed a tenacious attitude."[92]

Spontaneous strikes could also turn into more organized forms of protest, as in the famous P'yŏngwŏn Rubber Factory strike (29 May 1931), in which Kang Chu-ryong addressed the crowd from the roof of the Ŭlmildae. If factory owners perceived that it was an organized strike, they quickly sought assistance from the local police to arrest ringleaders like Kang. They also replaced the discharged workers immediately with fresh recruits.

Interestingly, in the P'yŏngwŏn Rubber strike, on 1 June the factory temporarily hired ten new male workers to replace the forty-nine female strikers, a revealing attempt to denigrate the value of female workers. Angered by this move, strikers moved their protest in front of the factory gates. Upon witnessing the Korean gendarmes throw crushed rocks at the female strikers, the new male recruits resigned from their new posts and joined the protestors.[93] In an ironic twist, the state's attempt to transform their identities from rural Koreans into modern workers had succeeded; at least for the moment, their common identification as workers overcame gender differences and united them against the factory owners. Although newspaper accounts do not reveal the internal gender dynamics that shaped the strikes, it is clear that women like Kang played a prominent, if not central, role—a fact that was accepted by male workers. In fact, the media valorized the leadership of the women and personalized the report by focusing on Kang as a worker and a widow. As one Japanese report admitted, "Although you hardly see a lot of strikes with good leadership, [the female protestors] are extremely brave."[94]

On 3 June, the P'yŏngwŏn Rubber Factory abandoned its tactic of employing men and hired eighteen new female recruits to resume operations. This time, the strikers assembled in front of the tram bringing the new recruits to the factory and blockaded the tracks with their bodies. Unable to move the prostrate female workers, factory operatives sought to transport their new recruits by car but failed when strikers lay down on the newly paved road. The owners called gendarmes to clear the road. Again, the specter of Koreans punishing compatriots raised the ire of bystanders witnessing the resolve of the young women, who wept openly but refused to acquiesce. Much to the chagrin of the factory, the bystanders sided with the strikers, hurling insults and rocks at the gendarmes who had dared to inflict suffering on Korean mothers and daughters for the sake of industrialists who served Japan's economic interests. Public opinion won in this case; the police released Kang Chu-ryong, who had fasted for seventy-six hours in jail as a sign of solidarity with strikers, despite her fear of reprisals by the police for this act of defiance.[95]

By the evening of 5 June, roughly a thousand workers had assembled to join Kang and forty-eight other strikers to prevent the recruitment of new women. So extensive was the scope and impact of the strike that the factory owners agreed to grant concessions. Wages would not be decreased if all the workers returned to work, but the factory demanded in exchange that Kang Chu-ryong and nineteen instigators of the strike be sacrificed. When the police arrested Kang and Ch'oe Yong-dŏk, most workers returned to work. Although Kang accepted the sacrifice for her fellow workers, she did not go quietly; for fifty-seven days, she staged a hunger strike in jail, which led to a digestive disorder and a severe nervous breakdown, at which point the police released her. Though Kang and her nineteen dismissed costrikers lived the rest of their lives together in P'yŏngyang's Sŏsŏngni district in abject poverty, they had achieved their goal: they had successfully blocked the rubber factories from cutting wages.[96]

Of course, not all strikes produced the desired result, especially when economic crises generated harsh repression by the colonial government. For instance, at the Hwandae Rubber Factory (Pusan) on 29 March 1932 (only a year after the P'yŏngwŏn Rubber Factory strike), six hundred female and three hundred male workers protested a reduction in their wages—a one *chŏn* reduction for each pair of shoes that they made. Kang Kum-do and Kim Suk-cha rejected this decision and posted the workers' demand for equitable wages on the factory bulletin board. In this case, the company decided to close the shop and lay off all the workers.[97]

The well-organized *asa tongmaeng*, or "death by starvation strike," was another method that female workers employed to generate a work stoppage. In July 1923, workers from four rubber factories in Kyŏngsŏng (Seoul) protested the tyrannical behavior of their manager and demanded his dismissal by organizing hunger strikes in front of the factory gates. The factory quickly called in the local police to disperse the strikers. Owners of fifteen rubber factories in Kyŏngsŏng met for an emergency meeting and decided to dismiss the strikers and their supporters. In this case, other workers helped sustain the strikers through organized charity funds from the Kyŏngsŏng socks workers, the Kyŏngsŏng leather shoe workers, and the P'yŏngsŏng Printing Workers Friends Association (P'yŏngsŏng inswae chikkong ch'inmokhoe). Funds came from as far away as Masan.[98] Although the strike took place in 1923, when militant strikes were not common, a high level of organization through emergency strike funds was clearly in place, or at least available through the mobilization of worker generosity.

Given the more lenient economic policies of the colonial state in the 1920s, concessions came quickly. After the tenth day of the strike in Kyŏngsŏng, the factory owners agreed to meet the demands of the strikers and reinstated everyone. In another case, more than four hundred workers (mostly female) walked off their jobs at Kyŏngsŏng Textile Factory in 1931 to protest their low wages. A group of women launched a hunger strike and submitted seventeen demands; although the stalemate lasted for a month, both sides compromised on several issues after promising not to "budge a tenth of an inch."[99]

Popular proletarian literature of the time not surprisingly valorized female strikers for their ability to articulate grievances and demands on paper. In Song Yŏng's novel *Osu-hyang* (1931), Osu-hyang, a *kisaeng*, falls in love with a customer, Cho Yong-t'ae. Cho is a labor activist who studied at Waseda University, and he teaches Osu-hyang about the labor movement before he is arrested. Osu-hyang disguises herself as a worker and becomes an important agitator in a strike of eight hundred workers. In a key moment, Osu-hyang writes out the demands for the workers and submits them to the factory. Thus the female activist not only voices the demands but physically delivers it to the factory.[100] In a short story by Yi Puk-myŏng, "The Factory Girl" (1933), the main character, Chong-hŭi, also plays an important role in writing up the demands for the factory owners.[101] A year earlier, a newspaper article had argued that there was a growing number of "disguised female workers, like Yi Kye-sun" who entered the factories and rural areas to "raise the consciousness of the workers."[102]

Breastfeeding

Finally, one experience unique to women workers led to militant rage: being denied the right to breastfeed infants at work. In general, the long hours robbed mothers of time with their children, a source of great distress and bitterness.[103] It was not uncommon for nursing mothers to bring their infants to work. One reporter described the double burden faced by these mothers: "Their faces looked weary and their arms swollen from pressing the soles of the rubber shoes with rollers. . . . Next to these women were young babies making a fuss, demanding breast milk from their mothers."[104] To evade the Government-General's censors, Yi Chŏk-hyo wrote a novel, *General Mobilization*, describing an August 1930 rubber factory strike in P'yŏngyang, in which he addressed the issue of breastfeeding. In detailed ethnographic terms, Yi portrayed mothers who nursed their babies before going to work; if the infant kept suckling, she would walk to work with the baby attached to her breast. Usually her mother-in-law or one of her children would accompany her to the factory, so that she could hand the baby to her at the factory gate. During her few breaks, the mother would go outside the factory gate to nurse her child.[105]

Strikers who sought more breastfeeding time employed the rhetoric of motherhood and patriarchy. If the factory was going to treat them as subordinates who needed to submit to male factory authorities, it had to give them the right to fulfill their role as mothers in this patriarchal paradigm. In a strike at the Kyŏngsŏng Textile factory in Yŏngdŭngp'o (1931), more than two hundred female and fifty male workers walked off their jobs, demanding longer breastfeeding time for female workers. Strikers asserted that breastfeeding was "an issue of humanity" and that the factory must acknowledge this right of a mother. That male workers protested alongside the women again demonstrated a solidarity among workers that cut across gender lines.[106]

Popular novels also sought to capture and personalize the hardships of employed mothers. In Pak Hwa-sŏng's novel *Two Passengers and a Bag* (1933), the heroine Chŏng, who is both a worker and mother, is forced to commute to a factory in Taegu after her husband goes to prison. Because she had to leave her infant at home, she must carry containers in her bag to pump breast milk. Constantly checking her breasts to see if she has enough milk, Chŏng feels pangs of guilt about her hungry baby. "Am I a competent mother?" she asks herself, as she questions the impossible choice between supporting her family and fulfilling her maternal role.[107]

While spontaneous walkouts, strikes, and hunger strikes produced hardships for all workers, they were especially difficult for married women and men, whose actions might destroy an already precarious household economy. As the economic crisis intensified in the Japanese empire, there was growing pressure to limit concessions to Korean workers. As a result, factory owners punished strikers using tactics similar to those used in Meiji Japan to quell the voices of opposition.[108] They deprived workers of their wages, fined them, blacklisted the main instigators as troublemakers so that other employers would refuse to hire them, and even had them arrested and charged with a crime. The deepening rift between Korean industrialists and workers, as well as the growing militancy of female workers, led to public debates about how to tame the *yŏgong.*

PUBLIC DEBATES OVER
"TAMING THE *YŎGONG*"

For educated society and the colonial government alike, the working woman and its most urgent manifestation, the *yŏgong* (factory girl), were an unstable element in Korean society that required discipline and direction. The most conservative elements of society contended that women's work outside the home was incompatible with their role in the traditional family. The *yŏgong* stood in direct opposition to the ideal *chubu* (housewife). Advocates of traditional marriage like Song Hwa-ja proposed concrete measures to prevent women from seeking employment in the factories. First, Koreans must create a strict gender division of labor for spouses: "Legally, it is the husband's duty to support his wife. If a husband does not fulfill this duty, a wife can now go as far as to divorce him." Second, Song sought to eliminate the "push factor"—the drudgery of housework, which she believed drove women to the factories. In a thoroughly bourgeois manner, Song aimed to professionalize household duties and assign some market value to domestic work. Song looked to places like England and the United States for models of compensation for female domestic labor.[109]

Naturally, proponents of a woman's right to work criticized Song's solution for ignoring the economic necessity that drove so many workers into the factories to support their families. In fact, they argued that more women should leave their hearth to enter the workforce in order to become economically independent. One writer for the *Tonga ilbo* declared: "Women of Korea are so unenlightened! [They] only know how to cook for the family, make clothes, and work in the fields. What else can they attend to 'outside'?"[110] To become like women in the West, Korean wives had to assume more responsibility for their own economic livelihood and break free from their traditional moorings. As long as a woman remained economically dependant on her husband, there was no hope of gender equality in marriage and the family.

Another reporter, summarizing the proceedings from a women's roundtable discussion, cited the miserable fate of a wife who endured a divorce from her primary breadwinner: "After a woman gets married, she [gives up her job and] takes care of the family. Men think this is proper. [However,] if a woman gets a divorce, then how is she to make a living? Economic independence is a necessity."[111] Similarly, Yi Hyŏn-gyŏng points out that whereas men previously had depended exclusively on women to manage all the household chores, in this new economy, a wife could ill afford to stay home. Yi cited the situation in the United States: "In America, [the entire] family works. The wife and daughter work in the factory. There are even cases [where] the husband is unemployed and takes care of the children and cooks."[112] Through work, traditional gender relations and family structures could be transformed.

The socialists, who represented an increasingly influential force in colonial Korea, were perhaps the most vocal in their criticism of the present condition of female workers. In broad Marxist terms, they blamed the feudal past for restricting women to unpaid, informal labor within the family and the current capitalist system for replicating that oppression by enslaving workers to a patriarchal factory.[113] In 1924, Kim Yun-gyŏng, a reporter for the *Sin yŏsŏng* (New woman), sought to elucidate the origins of the working woman in the European context for her Korean readers. Her article employed a Marxist trope: the power of the male householder in the traditional economy deprived women's labor in the family of any value.

Just like in Europe, the "production revolution" in Korea was really a euphemism for "submission," especially for women who now acquired two patriarchal masters—a husband and a boss.[114] As one writer put it, "Female workers are now no different from the slaves of yore. Their life and body are sold to the owner."[115] By welding the question of women working to the larger social question of the proletariat, Korean socialists could cast the female workers' oppression as the embodiment of the experience of the working class. As Chŏng Ch'un articulated the issue, "Women's existence should be understood by class difference. The upper class receives all the benefits, [but] liberation should not be limited to them. There are a large number of proletariat women and [we should] seek liberation for all."[116] In other words, gender identity was secondary to one's identification with the bourgeoisie or the proletariat. Indeed, some socialists were careful to distinguish between women's liberation and what they considered to be the more important struggle for class liberation.[117] They denigrated the feminist agenda to ensure women's economic independence as a needless bourgeois pursuit; the goal should rather be a struggle for livelihood that would unite all propertyless classes.[118]

Feminist socialists disagreed; uniting the two liberation movements—for women and for class—was bound to generate change.[119] Hwang Sin-dŏk (1898–1983), a vocal supporter of women's rights, contended that "women's liberation is after all about her economic independence. . . . To achieve that under the present capitalist economic structure is absolutely impossible." She added that women's liberation could not be divorced from the proletarian class movement and a socialist system.[120] Yamakawa Kikue, a respected Japanese feminist and Marxist, supported Hwang's position and decried the treatment of women as "a toy for men."[121] The liberation of women in the East would require a total overhaul of the capitalist system and its replacement with a socialist system.[122]

Starting in April 1921, socialist women's groups like the Chosŏn yŏja ch'ŏngnyŏnhoe (Korean Female Youth Association) began to emerge. Under the leadership of Pak Wŏn-hui (1899–1927), activists sought to raise consciousness among workers and assist them by visiting factories and organizing night schools, mutual assistance funds, and exhibitions, as well as holding rallies to commemorate National Woman's Day or Youth Day.[123]

Finally, socialists like Kim In-yu cast the problem in nationalist terms. He castigated the Japanese imperialists, "who have tormented us with their merciless exploitation and have strengthened their means of extraction. In this world [there is no] case parallel to ours." To blame Korean female workers for the ills caused by Japanese indulgence in violence and brutal politics was to blame the victims of racial, economic, and cultural subjugation.[124]

THE COLONIAL GOVERNMENT AND FACTORY
OWNER DISCOURSES

In contrast to the debate in Korean circles, colonial government and company discourse addressed the problem of the *yŏgong* through the lens of race. The state discourse for the most part depicted Korean workers (both men and women) as backward and unwilling or naturally incapable of overcoming their feudal mindsets.[125] Because they viewed the Korean worker in what Frantz Fanon has termed Manichean delirium, they believed him or her to be in need of moral and physical disciplining.[126] To exercise its power even in the most intimate matters of sexuality, marriage, and birth so as to maintain a system of difference, the Japanese state, at least up to the mid 1930s, consistently employed the Manichean allegory as a conceptual tool, not necessarily to pathologize Korean workers as bestial but to denigrate them enough to regulate their lives.

Government-General surveys commonly observed about Koreans of both sexes that they lacked a passion for work, responsibility, and a sense of duty; in short, they were plain lazy.[127] Because of the high ratio of job transfers recorded by social investigators, the state depicted Korean workers as incapable of settling down. According to a 1927 Government-General report, out of 48,043 workers in 664 factories, 16,694 stayed at one job for six months or less.[128] Japanese social investigators ascribed this restlessness and lack of loyalty to "racially common traits" in Korean workers. Koreans had a tendency to "follow people blindly"; if one worker left for greener pastures, others would quickly follow suit without considering the future. Moreover, Koreans resisted hard work, lacked the "spirit of saving," and took too many days off for holidays.[129] Another report described Korean workers as lacking a sense of shame, completely irresponsible, and incapable of overcoming their "thievish habits."[130] In addition, the Government-General reports noted that the appearance of physical maturity was deceptive, for "their mental capacity was only equivalent to that of a child."[131] Because of these mental impediments, Korean workers needed to be disciplined and transformed into "well-balanced and mentally capable" people before they could "serve the empire."[132]

Likewise, in his study of Korean *runpen* (vagrants), Sakurai Yoshiyuki, a social investigator, further elucidated the peculiar characteristics of Korean workers. They were unhygienic, *bushō* (indolent), and had little responsibility when it came to work. Moreover, they lacked education. In his mind, their insubordination was "fixed in their consciousness."[133] Furthermore, he observed that Korean workers did not stay in one job and "lived vagrant lives," which could explain the high rate of stealing among the workers.[134]

Oda Fumio conceded that Korean workers were indeed *bushō* but expressed a paternalistic admiration for the "remarkable progress" of Korean culture under the Government-General and the Oriental Development Company after annexation.[135] But in the final analysis, he expressed contempt for any attempt to compare Korean workers to the *naichi rōdōsha* (Japanese worker): "You can tell by a Korean's habit and disposition why their labor skills and efficiency are so low"; their racial characteristics simply could not be overcome.[136] Sakurai Yoshiyuki's study of miners concluded that Korean workers in general lacked the concept of time. Not only were they inefficient but they also lacked dedication to long hours of labor; breaks were disruptive because the workers found it difficult to resume work after a respite.[137] In their defense, the economist Takahashi Kamekichi (1894–1977) argued that the problem did not stem from the lack of a concept of time but from the low wages: "they were trying to get paid a little more" by stalling so that factory owners would not curtail their work hours.[138]

The colonial government criticized not only the racial characteristics of the Korean workers but their backward customs, especially early marriage, which they deemed harmful to productivity.[139] Indeed, Government-General reports in 1934 showed that 78 percent of Korean women were married before they turned nineteen. In 1922, Government-General Ordinance No. 13 fixed the minimum marriage age for a girl at fifteen and at seventeen for a boy. As a result, Korean girls started working earlier than

Japanese girls, which Takahashi argued influenced their working careers: "If a Japanese girl becomes employed at seventeen or eighteen years old, her service would be continuous; for Korean girls, if they get hired when they are fourteen or fifteen years old, one could never expect continuous service from them." After working for a year or so, Korean girls left the factories to get married and bear children. He continued: "If you look at the Keijō Spinning Factory in Yŏngdŭngp'o, the majority of the workers are between fifteen and twenty years old." That would mean the majority of these workers were potential brides. Thus the practice of early marriage was "unfavorable to industries in Korea."[140]

Internal company reports also utilized race and gender in their discourse on Korean workers. Being Korean (racial) and a woman (gender) signified inferiority and relegation to the bottom rung of the wage totem pole. A Japanese adult male worker made two times more than an adult Korean male, four times more than an adult Korean female, and six times more than a female juvenile worker.[141] At the same time, adult Japanese female workers made twice as much as Korean females and roughly 10 percent more than Korean adult males. Almost all of the Japanese male workers worked either in skilled factories or as managers. A Korean male typically made 1.46 times more than a Korean adult female. A skilled Korean male worker who worked at a lathe or welding factory made four times more than a female textile worker (see table 4).[142]

The colonial authorities and factory owners soon learned that it was more cost effective to hire Korean female workers whenever possible— a process that required some justification. As Takahashi pointed out, the abundance of female labor power at low wages had greatly benefited Japan: "Despite a great number of deficiencies, they have stout bodies in terms of their physical strength" and "can adapt to work" or "can be trained to be factory workers."[143] In Takahashi's view, Korean women were actually more useful to the empire than Korean men, because they could be molded more easily, their labor was cheap, and their gender was easily manipulated: "Korean women are like a cat's paw . . . [and] this [results from] the ingenuity of the Japanese."[144] The empire no longer re-

Table 4. *Wages based on race, sex, and age differences (1929)*
(in yen)

Race	Sex	Age	Avg. wage	Highest (type of industry)	Lowest (type of industry)
Japanese	Male	Adult	2.32	3.82 (munitions)	1.50 (confectionary)
		Child	0.71	1.00 (silk-reeling)	0.39 (needlework)
	Female	Adult	1.01	1.60 (rubber factory)	0.79 (match factory)
		Child	0.71	n/a	n/a
Korean	Male	Adult	1.01	1.80 (ship building)	0.70 (sardine factory)
		Child	0.44	0.65 (automobile)	0.25 (wig factory)
	Female	Adult	0.59	0.98 (socks)	0.35 (wig factory)
		Child	0.32	0.54 (rubber factory)	0.19 (needlework)

SOURCE: Yi Yŏ-sŏng and Kim Se-yong, *Sutja chosŏn yŏn'gu* (Kyŏngsŏng: Segwangsa, 1931), 80.

stricted women to the textile factories but utilized them in chemical, food processing, and other industries, making goods cheaper and more accessible. Indeed, factory reports justified the preference for female labor, stressing their work ethic. The Keijō Commerce and Industry Association praised Korean female workers at the Pusan Textile Factory for improving their skills on a yearly basis: "With such diligence and hard work, these female workers have shown excellent results this year." The same could be said about the female workers at a Japanese-owned tobacco company: "Their efficiency has been remarkably satisfactory."[145]

Employers also used racial terms to dehumanize, stereotype, or belittle Koreans when they recruited workers for skilled positions. Making work respectable for Japanese workers living in Korea without threatening existing gender and race hierarchies meant designing a labor system that would naturally subordinate Koreans. Concomitantly, it would disguise differences between Japanese men and women by emphasizing "a common racial bond" (*minzoku*). Although the language of racial difference (an ideology of inferiority) was critical in the colonial vocabulary and social fabric of everyday life, the state and employers had to continually construct and reinforce these racist views to eliminate ambivalence. Employers could make work respectable for their Japanese *naichi-jin* workers by valorizing their social status.

The race card could also be used to lower wages when hiring migrant Chinese workers. Likewise, companies deployed gender and race to deflect attention from potential class solidarity. For example, female workers in the rice mills and rubber factories often organized strikes to protest the hiring of Chinese workers. A reporter for the *Chosŏn ilbo* noted that the large number of migrant Chinese workers was posing a threat to the female workers working in the rice mills.[146] Chinese workers, fearful of deportation, often accepted meager wages. This mechanism of control created misunderstanding and hostility between two "inferior" races. The strategy of divide and conquer that we saw earlier in the conflicts that pitted Korean factory managers and police against Korean female workers was effectively used by the colonial government to control its subjects and reap the benefits of the empire's resources.

Korean women's lives underwent a dramatic transformation as Japan attempted to industrialize and modernize the peninsula at breakneck speed. The intense demands of production for high profits with minimal costs led many factories to employ predominantly female labor. The emergence of the *yŏgong* posed a difficult challenge to the existing social and economic order. Ava Baron's observation could not have summarized the situation in Korea better: "Gender is created not simply outside production but also within it."[147] Indeed, ideas of gender and nationality in the Korean case were deliberately structured into the factories and social relations at work. This new sexual division of labor in the factories needed to be legitimized within existing frameworks, such as Confucian patriarchy. These frameworks provided the factory owners and managers with the language of power and dominance, but it also gave Korean women workers a discourse for demanding their rights as mothers and wives, such as time to breastfeed or holidays to spend with their families.

At one level, the Japanese colonial government treated all Korean workers as a single inferior group whose racial characteristics and social customs, such as early marriage, made them inefficient cogs in the empire's machinery. At the same time, the colonial government gave lip service to the usefulness of Korean female workers, who could be utilized at a fraction of the cost of either Japanese or Korean male workers. By feminizing large segments of the industry, it exploited a large labor market but also challenged the social and cultural fabric of Korean society. Racial and gender stereotyping influenced the harsher treatment of workers in the 1930s and 1940s; only by brute force and mobilization could the colonial state get what it needed out of these "brutish" and ignorant workers. As concessions became rare, the cycle of militancy and repression became the story of the day, pushing more Koreans toward national and class liberation movements. Others, however, turned to modern education as the road to a better life and future.

CHAPTER FIVE

The Colonized Body

Korean Women's Sexuality and Health

This set of assumptions—that woman's reproductive function
defined her character, position, and value, that this function
was only one sign of an innate periodicity, and that this biological periodicity influenced and was influenced by an array
of nervous disorders—constructed the woman as essentially
different from man and, because of the quasi-pathological
nature of this difference, as a creature who needed constant
and expert superintendence by medical men. This set of
assumptions was also the physiological basis offered for what
was generally held to be woman's greater emotional volatility
and for her artfulness or cunning. Paradoxically, then, one
facet of authorizing medical practice consisted of representing
both menstruation and childbirth—the most "natural" of all
female functions—as disorders.

Mary Poovey, *Uneven Developments*

On 8 April 1931, approximately two kilometers from the Yŏngdŭngp'o
station, two young women committed suicide by hurling themselves in
front of an outbound Kyŏngin line train from Keijō (Seoul). Hong Og-im
was a twenty-one-year-old student from Ewha yŏja chŏnmun hakkyo, the
daughter of a prominent doctor and professor at Severance Medical Spe-

cial School. Her companion, nineteen-year-old Kim Yong-ju, also hailed from a privileged background; she was the daughter of the owner of Tŏkhŭng Bookstore and the wife of Sim Chong-il, the eldest son of a wealthy family in Tongmak.[1] In the suicide letter, Hong asked her father to forgive her for this selfish act, which she blamed on the hardships of life in a "futile world."[2] Though the suicide was newsworthy, it was the dark hints of a lesbian relationship between these privileged and educated women that inspired the riveting and sensational headlines.[3] Had Hong and Kim suffered from some hereditary disease or *hisŭt'eri* (hysteria)? Could a better moral upbringing have prevented their "same-sex love"? The public even entertained a conspiracy theory: perhaps the "deadly poisons" that had infected the two lovers could contaminate the entire nation, leading to moral depravity and decay.[4]

This chapter examines the discursive forces that competed to define Korean women's bodies within the framework of medical science. In particular, it focuses on reproductive biology, in which science sought to imbue the body with what Michel Foucault describes as the "mechanics of life."[5] Reproducing the nation was a top priority for modernizing countries but a particularly urgent goal for one under colonial occupation.

During the period under consideration, the Japanese state focused primarily on compiling detailed knowledge about the reproductive status of its colonial subjects. As earlier chapters have mentioned, in the 1920s the state and nongovernmental organizations conducted studies on indigenous practices, such as marriage practices and birth rates, to enhance the legibility of Korean society. However, it was not until after the Great Depression of 1929 and Japan's active involvement in Manchukuo in the 1930s that the state began to play a more proactive, albeit still limited, role in controlling the reproductive health of Korean women with a view to increasing the population.

If the state utilized official statistics later in the 1930s only to further its own agenda, these "tabulated facts" became a key source for Korean reformers, who drew on these numbers to articulate their concerns about the social in reproduction, and women's bodies in particular. If it wanted

to emerge victorious and independent, Koreans needed not only numbers but strong, healthy bodies and minds to rebuild the homeland. At
the heart of this critical task were the mothers of the nation. Korean and
Japanese social reformers concurred that what was needed was sexual education for the public, social reform of marriage, and new reproductive
knowledge and technologies to replace primitive practices. At the same
time, Koreans sought to assert control over the pace and nature of reforms, accommodating yet also resisting Japanese attempts to colonize
the Korean "national body."

TAMING THE DISCOURSE: CHANGING
ATTITUDES TOWARD SEXUALITY

On 31 March 1916, the editors of the *Maeil sinbo* chose not to print a
copy of *Haechilnyŏk* (Sunset) for fear of arousing the public's ire. This
award-winning painting was the work of Kim Kwan-ho, who had graduated at the top of his class from the renowned Tokyo School of Arts. As
a public gesture, the newspaper allowed a few remarks by the literary critic
Yi Kwang-su, who had just returned from Japan, where he had viewed
Kim's artwork; however, it refused to print the painting, saying its nu-
dity was culturally "inappropriate for our times."[6] The editors' attempt
to silence sex became an incitement to speak. Indeed, the 1920s witnessed
an unprecedented explosion of discourse on sex. Much like Japan, where
the "science of sex" was quickly gaining currency, social reformers and
medical doctors in Korea began to identify the category of sex as pivotal
to "debates about society and social reform, whether they feared for national security, demanded freedom or social control, or insisted on the
'truth of sex.'"[7]

Printing Sex

In 1927, a cartoon published in the popular magazine *Pyŏlgŏn'gon* sought
to capture the public's shifting views on sex. A young boy points to a paint-

ing of a nude woman at a museum and asks, "Mother, look at that painting. You do not take off your clothes and recline like that at home. Why
is she lying there naked so unabashedly? Are there really [women] like
that?" A man who overhears their conversation suppresses laughter, while
the mother hides her face in shame, admonishing the boy for his imper-
tinence. This cartoon revealed two significant changes that had taken
place since the turn of the century: first, in contrast to the *Haechilnyŏk*
incident, the nude painting was on public display, "giving it an analyti-
cal, visible, and permanent reality."[8] Second, it depicted an "ignorant"
mother confronted by a precocious child who was not ashamed to pose
questions about sexuality.[9] The cartoon frankly showed that a new generation of Koreans was moving beyond society's repression of sexuality
to a healthy curiosity about the subject.

Korean appetites for things sexual coincided with the printing boom
spawned by the liberalization of the press after the March First Movement. One visible change was the proliferation of sex-related advertising in newspapers and popular journals. According to Ch'ŏn Chŏng-
hwan, from 1920 to 1928, a total of eighty-five advertisements on
sex-related matters appeared in the *Tonga ilbo*, one of the most circulated
newspapers of the day.[10] Though Ch'ŏn does not provide the total number of advertisements in other newspapers, he notes that Japanese publishing houses like *Tōrinsha*, aware of the new commercial success of mail
order books, started to advertise similar products.[11]

Advertisements for erotic novels and scientific studies on sex dominated
the press. Tantalizing and sensual promotions of *Kekkon no tōya* (Wedding
night), an erotic book first published in 1926, appeared thirty-nine times
in the *Tonga ilbo*, and promotions of *Danjo no missho* (Secret letters of a
man and a woman) appeared twenty-three times during this eight-year
period. Sawada Junjirō, one of Japan's most prolific sexologists, was de-
lighted that advertisements for his treatise "Actual Contraception and
Possibilities of Limiting Births" appeared seven times in the *Tonga ilbo* and
that it was one of many Japanese books to be translated into Korean.[12]
"For less than two *wŏn*," one advertisement boasted, "you can now pur-

7. A cartoon from
Pyŏlgŏn'gon (1927),
depicting a conversation
between a boy and his
mother; the cartoon
captures the public's
shifting views about sex.

chase Sawada's other book, entitled *Illustrated Guide: The Sexual Lives of Maidens and Wives*, with 'new research' on sexual intercourse."[13] Titillating announcements like "Coitus Is the Foundation of Life" or "Sex Is the Greatest Pleasure of Human Beings," complete with enticing snippets, as well as the table of contents of Sawada's *A New Study of Male and Female Sexual Desire and Intercourse*, were very successful. Advertisers made the offers more appealing by reducing shipping and handling costs to less than 22 *chŏn* per customer. Explicit advertisements of "complete collections" of pictures of nude female bodies and "new illustrations of women's reproductive organs," which promised to "get any male or female excited," also appeared with greater frequency in the newspapers.[14] Shrewd advertisers combined eroticism with scientific writings about new sexual concepts and different methods of birth control.[15]

Appearing in all sizes—from as small as a business card to a quarter-page spread—these quasi-pornographic advertisements stirred up controversy from the start. Morally outraged Koreans went on a campaign to eliminate the so-called *ppalgan ch'aek* (red books), which symbolized

Japanese attempts to enslave Koreans to frivolous entertainment.[16] One writer criticized Japanese entrepreneurs for their secret plan to induce Koreans to squander their money on these alleged "rare books" and "illustrations of reproductive organs." By marketing this forbidden literature in erotic ways, they could exploit a hungry Korean consumer base. Another journalist argued that the "enthusiasm" or "reading fever" generated by these books was drawing attention away from more serious intellectual endeavors. The gender and political critique was overt: while he praised men for reading books by important socialist thinkers like Marx and Engels, as well as "important" literary works, he castigated women for indulging in books and articles on sex by Kuriyagawa Hakuson (*Modern Views on Love*), Sawada Junjirō, and August Bebel.[17] In the absence of surveys about readership, it is difficult to confirm whether women dominated the audience, as the writer claimed; more likely, Korean critics attempted to define the reading of such books as female so as to render it unworthy of respectable men. Concern for the moral character of its male citizens clearly informed the discourse that ascribed frivolous books on sex to women and more serious works on social theory to men.

Marketing Sexual Products and Advice

In the 1920s, Korea, like Western Europe, witnessed the development of sexology, which sought to cure abnormalities in sexuality through clinical treatment. Not surprisingly, medical products began to be marketed in tandem with books on sex. Whether hormonal products like diathermy and androgen for acute cases of uterine myoma, the magic bullet Salvarasan 606, which could "cure syphilis in a week," or a potion that "could enlarge a small male organ," pharmaceutical products outsold commodities like makeup and clothing.[18] Writers for the *Maeil sinbo*, for example, contributed more than 530 articles during the colonial period on infectious diseases ranging from leucorrhea to gonorrheal infections, leading anxiety-ridden readers fearing *segyun* (bacilli) to seek cures at their local pharmacies.[19] Indeed, a writer for the *Sinhan minbo* observed that medical products dominated two-thirds of all newspaper advertisements, making medicine the most profitable enterprise in the colony. He blamed the rush to the pharmacies on an unfortunate hypochondriac trait in Koreans, as well as on the poor health of young children, which the writer believed resulted from the harmful traditional practice of early marriage[20]

In addition to peddling sexual products and cures, newspapers and journals devoted significant space to advice columns. Ironically, though editors sought to provide greater information on sex to the Korean public, this venue of sex-confession played a significant role in the subjugation and control of sexuality. The inherent power relations in these exchanges were all the more significant because some of the so-called experts were Japanese; Koreans confessed their sexual practices to the very colonial authorities who sought to reform and control the Korean body. For example, the popular journal *Samch'ŏlli* published a question from a twenty-eight-year-old mother of four who was seeking birth control advice from a Japanese expert, Doctor Masayama. She questioned the effectiveness of the douche method and birth control medicine, which had failed to work, causing yet another unwanted pregnancy. Her confession informed the doctor that Korean women like her might be attempting to use birth control, a desirable practice from his point of view; however, the question also suggested the mother's lack of knowledge about the proper use of birth control or the physiological process that prevented pregnancy. Although he gave no guarantees, Dr. Masayama urged the woman to use both techniques to prevent her partner's sperm from entering her womb.[21] The power relations come in play when Korean women (the colonized) turn to colonial authorities as experts. The question is not about the advice he gave but the very interaction that took place: the colonized turning to colonial authorities for "knowledge" (to use Foucault's term).

Korean medical authorities who promoted the use of contraceptives but frowned upon the curtailment of male sexual pleasure made their views clear in their advice columns. Unlike Japanese doctors, who promoted the most effective contraceptives (i.e., condoms), Korean doctors often preferred the methods that were least inconvenient for men. For instance, a male reader who was fearful for his wife's health asked Dr. Pak Sun-ha of P'yŏngyang about the effectiveness of condoms and pessaries. Afraid that his unhealthy wife might bear a sick child, he asked if he should continue to use prophylactics. The doctor informed him that while the condom might prevent pregnancy, this device would also deprive him of sexual pleasure. Describing a pessary as a "device for closing the womb," Dr. Pak explained that it would definitely provide more pleasure for the husband but cautioned him to be careful that his sperm not enter her womb.[22]

In addition to advice columns, the press utilized questionnaires to assess public opinions, attitudes, and knowledge about a wide range of issues and to distinguish normative ideas about sex and sexuality from pathological aspects. In an attempt to gauge women's views of sex, a reporter from *Samch'ŏlli* visited a school in 1932 to survey female students. She divided her subjects into two major groups: the bourgeoisie (daughters of company directors, landlords, wealthy merchants, and nobility) and the proletariat (girls who would support their parents and siblings after graduating from school and daughters of middle-class families). She was surprised to learn that girls from both classes shared some attitudes: neither cared whether their male partners were virgins or felt the need to engage in premarital sex. However, when it came to issues of love and marriage, of the two hundred girls polled, 98 percent of the bourgeoisie camp expressed a need for love, as opposed to 67 percent of the proletarians.[23]

In attitudes toward work and motherhood, the reporter discovered distinct differences between the two groups. A large majority of proletarian women (73 percent) expressed an intent to seek employment, compared with a minority of their bourgeois counterparts (7 percent). In contrast, the privileged women declared that motherhood was their primary goal shortly after marriage (89 percent), while the working-class women did not consider children an immediate priority. In fact, only 9 percent asserted that starting a family right away was desirable; when asked if they wanted to have children within five years after marriage, 62 percent responded in the affirmative. The reporter also found a wide discrepancy in knowledge about birth control. Only 37 percent of proletarian girls but 79 percent of bourgeois girls claimed to know about contraceptives.[24] In some respects, this survey was not surprising; until the 1930s, knowledge about sexuality and reproduction was the sole domain of the privileged classes, who could read and had access to print literature. The concern was indeed primarily for what Foucault describes as the bourgeois "sexed and healthy body."[25]

However, starting in the 1930s, social reformers and activists embarked on a new mission to instill a desire for motherhood in the working classes and restore "the reproduction of bodies" to "natural levels." To ensure the well-being of the nation, fundamental reforms of the Korean family were needed to combat deep disillusionment with child bearing and rearing among the toiling masses.

REFORMING TRADITIONAL FAMILY PRACTICES FOR THE HEALTH OF THE NATION

Disparate groups with competing agendas scrutinized traditional Korean family practices and contributed ideas for reform to the Korean and Japanese press, as well as to the colonial state. One group included specialists employed by the Government-General's office to study the Korean population. It established key *kenkyūkai* (research institutes) and hired social investigators from various disciplines (statistics, economics, ethnography, and medicine) to compile data on the nation's vital statistics and collect ethnographic information about folk culture and the daily lives of peasants.

Additional information was provided by private nongovernmental agencies, conglomerates, and financial institutions, including the South Manchurian Railway Company, the Oriental Development Company, the Bank of Chōsen, the Industrial Bank of Chōsen, and Tōyō Keizai. These institutions all sponsored their own research bureaus and serial publications with the aim of learning more about the Korean people—their habits, customs, and demographic patterns—in order to maximize productivity. For example, Tōyō Keizai hired the famous economist Takahashi Kamekichi (1894–1977) to work for their research institute, while Keijō Imperial University sponsored faculty such as anthropologist Akiba Takashi (1888–1954) to conduct studies on folk culture. With previously untouched domains (marriage, childbirth, sex) reduced by the sleight of mathematics into new categories, the colonial state and Japanese companies could count, discuss, and ultimately manage the Korean masses more readily.

Another group of aspiring reformers included Korean medical and science professionals who sought to buttress and legitimize new social ideas and programs with scientific language and evidence. Though many shared similar ideas, it is unknown if any of these writers belonged to organized associations. Contributors to prominent newspapers and journals revealed little if anything about their individual identities—their upbringing, family and social background, or even education. In fact, these writers rarely used their real names, resorting instead to pen names or identifying themselves as anonymous researchers of *sŏngyokhak* (sexology)[26] or "doctors." According to Kim Mi-yŏng, 60 percent of the writers for the *kajŏng puin* (family wife) advice column in the *Chosŏn ilbo* were guest contributors who used pen names.[27] And in the rare instance where an individual employed a real name, the near absence of biographical information on medical professionals in the sources (in contrast to government officials or cultural figures) makes it difficult to create a composite portrait of these would-be Korean reformers.

The anonymity of Korean medical personnel clearly reflected their tenuous status in Korean society during the colonial period. Because of harsh Japanese policies, Koreans faced Herculean obstacles in their pursuit of a medical career. Upon annexation of the peninsula, the Government-General made a concerted drive to enroll Japanese students in the newly established medical schools in Korea. This was in part to alleviate the oversupply of qualified doctors in Japan. Rather than confront the stiff competition for positions at government hospitals in Japan, less-affluent Japanese medical students opted to begin their careers in Korea. In 1916, for instance, a third of the medical students at the Kyŏngsŏng chŏnmun hakkyo were of Japanese nationality.

Not only did Koreans compete with the Japanese (who enjoyed preferential status) for admission, but they faced stricter qualification requirements. The promulgation of the Doctors' Ordinance in November 1913 recognized only Korean doctors who had graduated from recognized Government-General medical schools and passed the state board examination, which was offered twice a year in Seoul.[28] By 1915, Korean students no longer enjoyed tuition waivers, making it impossible for many to enroll in the prestigious Government-General's medical *kangsŭpso* (training schools).[29] As late as 1943, the faculty and student breakdown at Keijō Imperial University Medical School showed 67 professors and 203 students of Japanese nationality and only 3 professors and 170 students of Korean nationality.[30]

The available data suggest that a few of the aspiring social reformers had received their medical and scientific education abroad. According to the Government-General's Revised Doctors' Ordinance in 1914, the state recognized doctors who had received medical degrees abroad. Students who had the financial means chose to study in Japan, Germany, or the United States rather than undergo the onerous state board exam in their homeland.[31] During the colonial period, 536 Korean students traveled abroad to complete medical degrees: 268 men and 101 women enrolled in Japanese medical degree programs, while 166 men enrolled in the Japanese doctoral programs in medicine; 14 (11 in the doctoral program) enrolled in the United States, 6 (all doctoral students) enrolled in Germany, and 1 university student went to Great Britain.[32]

In contrast, 150 students received their doctor of medicine degree from Keijō Imperial University in Korea. Yi Kap-su, a prominent social reformer, was born in Seoul in 1893. Upon graduation from Kyŏngsŏng Higher Common School in 1912, Yi attended Okayama Medical School and earned his degree in 1919. He spent four years conducting research in the department of physiology at Keijō Imperial University, where he received his doctorate in medicine in 1923. He was one of the first Koreans to be appointed as a full-time lecturer at this prestigious institution and was influential in the eugenics movement, as we will see.

Despite the paucity of biographical information, it is clear that these so-called reformers were knowledgeable about the contemporary debates over health and eugenics abroad. By identifying their ideas with the West and not Japan, Korean reformers could criticize traditional practices more vigorously and demand radical changes. They could avoid being labeled agents of the colonial state even though their views were in agreement with Japanese social investigators. These Korean medical specialists could claim that they had adapted Western models of health in the service of the Korean nation. Such attempts were especially notable in gynecology and obstetrics, which became a central focus of reformist zeal. By merging the social and the scientific, Korean reformers sought to promote new attitudes toward gender and health, often in a nationalistic context. Despite disagreements, the majority believed that the fundamental problems of Korean health stemmed from sexual practices like early marriage and primitive childbirth practices in the working classes.

Critiques of Early Marriage

Japanese social investigators and Korean reformers concurred that the traditional practice of early marriage had a detrimental impact on the reproductive and psychological development of young girls.[33] Despite attempts to reform family law and practices, traditional customs maintained a tenacious hold on the rural population. The Kabo Reforms of 1894, which had aimed to eliminate child marriage and permit widow remarriage, had had no visible impact in the countryside.[34] A study conducted by the *Sin yŏsŏng* in 1932 found that almost 70 percent of brides were between the ages of sixteen and nineteen, and almost 10 percent were under sixteen.[35] Moreover, even as late as 1937, of 11,008 married women in Kangwŏn Province alone, 31.9 percent were between fifteen and twenty.[36]

In large measure, early marriage persisted in the countryside because of the system of *minmyŏnŭri*. The *minmyŏnŭri* was a young girl who came to live with her future husband until she was ready to be married. After the marriage, the bride returned to her parents until the groom paid a bride-price for her return. During the Chosŏn period (1392–1910), the *minmyŏnŭri* system was economically profitable, because the young daughter-in-law worked for almost three years before she was legally married.[37] During the colonial period, poor farmers continued the practice by selling their daughters to wealthy families as *minmyŏnŭri*. As Kim Tu-hon notes, this in effect decreased the dowry.[38] In fact, the *minmyŏnŭri* system was better known in common parlance as *maemae kyŏlhon*, or "buying and selling of marriage." Little wonder that American missionaries like Charles Clark expressed outrage:

> Note the minimum ages fifteen and seventeen full years, not "*sals*." Fortunately, for us, the Japanese law on this point is the same as the church law. Non-Christians and others do continue to marry off tiny children just as they used to, but until each of the parties reaches their legal age of marriage cannot be registered, and if children are born before both of the parents are of legal age they must be registered as illegitimate children. The Christians are almost as stupid as the non-Christians about wanting early marriages, and a pastor has to wave the "big stick" pretty often if he wants to stop them.[39]

The tragic dramas of child brides played out on the front pages of the Korean press, which portrayed them as victims of the cruelest form of marriage.[40] The archetypal villain was the future mother-in-law, who wielded enormous power over the young *minmyŏnŭri*. In 1926 the *Tonga ilbo* reported the case of a seven-year-old *minmyŏnŭri* who died from an act of gratuitous violence. After visiting the bathroom one early morning, the girl had stopped by the kitchen to eat *kimch'i*, which was stored in the pantry. Caught red-handed by her future mother-in-law, the girl received a tongue lashing about her lack of prudence and manners. In her anger, the mother-in-law threw the girl down a flight of stairs, and the girl's head landed on a sharp stone. She died immediately from a cerebral hemorrhage.[41]

Husbands were no less cruel in their treatment of their *minmyŏnŭri*.[42] In 1929, the *Chosŏn ilbo* exposed the story of an eighteen-year-old *minmyŏnŭri* who fled to her uncle's house to escape relentless persecution at the hands of her future husband and mother-in-law during her four years of service. Upon her forcible return, the family accused her of having a lover and punished her by branding her fifty times with a soldering iron. The girl ended up in the hospital in critical condition.[43] Violent narratives of abuse that led to death were ubiquitous in the *Tonga ilbo*. Tales ranged from a twenty-three-year-old husband who murdered his twelve-year-old *minmyŏnŭri* for not satisfying his sexual desires (1928) to a thirty-year-old husband who beat his fourteen-year-old wife and buried her alive on the suspicion that she was having an affair (1929).[44] Another husband who suspected his wife of adultery cut her legs, and a husband of a ten-year-old *minmyŏnŭri* pummeled her to death with a pine tree club for disobeying him.[45] As these cases indicate, suspicion of adultery was a common reason cited for murder; whether or not the claim held validity, it was clearly a socially acceptable pretext for punishing wives. Given the social disdain for wayward wives, husbands could construct an acceptable excuse for their behavior.

Power struggles between an older woman and her "boy husband" (that is, a spouse who was considerably younger) could also lead to brutal scenes of violence. The *Tonga ilbo* reported the case of a sixteen-year-old husband who beat his twenty-two-year-old wife to death and then secretly buried her. He had resented her for treating him like a young boy.[46] Instead of tolerating abuse, a few girls decided to take matters into their own hands. The *Tonga ilbo* frequently reported incidents of young girls who attempted to escape from older spouses the night before the wedding.[47] Some contemplated a legal dissolution of their miserable union.

"By middle school, the thought of divorce was already in my head," re-marked a victim of abuse.[48] Suicide was another desperate alternative that women chose over their painful circumstances.[49] In 1923, a fifteen-year-old girl from Uiju County who had become a *minmyŏnŭri* to a twenty-four-year-old man at the tender age of eleven, fled from her husband to escape his sexual demands. When he found her working as a maid in a village, he forced her to return home; unwilling to live a life of bondage, the girl took her own life by jumping off a railroad bridge.[50] Others re-taliated against their husbands. One young *minmyŏnŭri* strangled her husband, and an older woman committed adultery although she knew she would be punished for it.[51]

The violent response of a fourteen-year-old *minmyŏnŭri* (and others like her) who conspired with her mother to commit arson inspired short stories like "Pul" (Fire) by Hyŏn Chin-gŏn.[52] In this tale, a fifteen-year-old *minmyŏnŭri* whose husband and mother-in-law forced her into sexual bondage and slave labor retaliates:

[Suni's] hips throbbed and twinged. When an iron club pushed her innards aside and thrust into her chest, her mouth fell agape, her body convulsed. Normally, this much pain would have roused her, but her daily rounds of labor—carrying a water crock on her head, pounding grain, treading the watermill's wheel, carrying meals to farmhands in the rice paddies—had worn her out, and she could not wake up much as she tried. That night, fire broke out in the eaves at the back of the room. Fanned by winds, the fire spread in an instant all over the thatched roof. Just outside the hedge of the next house, Suni stood, her face never more radiant than now. Her heart bursting with delight, she stamped and jumped with joy.[53]

In 1930, Government-General reports noted that women committed 60 percent of violent crimes, such as arson and murder, and attributed their motivation to the evils of early marriage.[54] Similarly, the *Chosŏn ilbo* showed that 98 percent of all women convicted in these crimes were illiterate and came from the lower class.[55] While these figures should be treated with caution, they suggest that many women had few avenues for their grievances and resorted to extreme measures to escape unbearable circumstances. Although the reports indicate that women of all ages committed these crimes, they do not reveal whether it was more youthful or older women who dominated the statistics. They do not tell us how long women waited before they decided to end their abuse and unhappy marriages. Moreover, the bare statistics do not include information about the number of children and other private details that might explain why they endured abuse and what factors led to their decision to adopt an extreme solution.

OBJECTIFYING THE FEMALE BODY THROUGH MEDICINE

Debates about early marriage coincided with the introduction to Korea of obstetrics and gynecology and their objectification of female bodies and reproductive capacities. "The dependence of the body of society on the reproductive practices and health of its constituent parts," David Horn has observed, "required both a heightened medical surveillance and new subordinations of bodies and rights to collective imperatives."[56] Each stage of a woman's biological life—puberty, menstruation, pregnancy, parturition, and menopause—had to be scrutinized by a medical expert.[57]

Little wonder that medical experts were so keen to participate in the discourse about early marriage; their agenda was to protect the physical health of girls so as to minimize risks to the future offspring of Korea.[58] In "Protecting the Pregnant Woman and Methods for Improving Mankind," Pak Ho-jin complained that Korean women's lives were overshadowed by frequent childbirth. Early marriage ensured that girls who were not even twenty years old gave birth to children in rapid succession. There was no period of postpartum recovery; only two or three months after giving birth, a woman would be pregnant with another child.[59] Kim Dong-ŭi, a doctor of internal medicine at Keijō Imperial University, argued that in addition to the danger of psychological disorders, this practice could damage girls' reproductive organs.[60] There was scientific proof to indicate that early marriages would have an adverse effect on a maturing girl's body.[61]

In the 1920s, newspapers started to publish new scientific knowledge about reproduction, particularly in matters of childbirth. *Pyŏlgŏn'gon*, a popular journal, sought to inform its readers about the biological aspects of pregnancy. Using a Darwinian model, one writer argued that all sexually reproducing species combine the genes of two individuals.[62] He used medical language to establish his authority: "One needs to understand the breakup of a cell and the two types of formations (e.g., the somatic cell and the reproductive) to understand conception." He explained the process of meiosis as well as the difference between spermatogenesis and the ovum. "If all human somatic cells have a full set of forty-six chromosomes . . . [then] they all have twenty-three matching pairs."[63]

The superiority and desirability of a male child, so central in Korean culture, also found its way into such scientific writings. The writer for the *Pyŏlgŏn'gon* explained that while everyone inherited one chromosome from each parent, it was the sex-determining chromosome in the male's sperm that would determine the sex of the baby. Equally important, the combination of twenty-two autosomes in the sperm and an X chromosome would result in a male child. If the sperm carried an "XX chromosome" (known as a Y chromosome today), the child would be female.[64] Thus the writer sought to entice his readers with knowledge by demystifying the conception of a male child—the most desirable sex.

Similar articles written by medical experts appeared frequently in newspapers. Korean reformers agreed on one point: if "all living things need a 'seed to propagate their species,'" it was imperative to understand and protect the "special characteristics" and "physiological functions" of both receptacles of the sexes.[65]

Pronatalist tracts by Korean nationalists, now infused with scientific rhetoric, emphasized the importance of the physical and psychological health of the mother. The *Chosŏn ilbo* predicated the happiness of a marriage on the woman's well-being, and encouraged her to obtain a physical examination prior to her wedding: "Many women get ill unexpectedly. If [they] are not healthy after [their] marriage, [their] entire life will be full of misery."[66] Likewise, the *Tonga ilbo* warned that "marriage can become life's tragedy" if the woman's body was not healthy.[67] Thus modern criteria for choosing a spouse should include a clean bill of health, including a complete disclosure of genetic illnesses in the family.

Others contended, however, that such careful actions did not guarantee success for a mother, who could easily "contract tuberculosis, [or] some brain or other contagious disease" and then pass it to her offspring. "Even if you come from a good family with a good genetic stock," wrote one observer for the *Tonga ilbo* in 1932, "that does not guarantee that you will be immune from diseases." In fact, he cited an example in which the husband's wanton lifestyle destroyed a woman's dreams of motherhood when he infected her with a venereal disease shortly after their marriage. She became infertile and could not contribute to the reproduction of the nation. The writer argued that preventive medicine was the only solution: women should find a "trustworthy doctor" and schedule frequent checkups to prevent future tragedies.[68] Here again, such writers manipulated the Korean desire for male offspring to drive home their point. As the *Chosŏn ilbo* warned darkly, the miscarriage rates of male fetuses were statistically higher than for female fetuses; therefore, women needed to protect their health.[69]

The new marriage criteria emphasized not only intelligence but also physical fitness, which defined female beauty in modern times. In the past, Korean women "did not get enough sun because they were afraid of looking like cooked bean sprouts."[70] "If being thin and haggard exemplified physical beauty in the past," wrote one reporter, a radiant, replenished, and healthy body represented the modern standard of beauty. "If you are not healthy," he warned, "you cannot be as beautiful as the woman in the picture of this article."[71] At the other end of the spectrum, obese women also were not tolerated, for their corpulent bodies were susceptible to disease. Besides, the obese body never attracted marital partners: "Even if a [woman] has academic credentials, money, or is the daughter of a wealthy man, she will not be able to get married."[72]

At the heart of the reproductive debate was the *chigŏp puin* (working woman) who attempted to balance work and family. The reality that young women were forced to seek employment in big cities had to be confronted.[73] The specific focus of social investigators was the *yŏgong* (factory girl), who worked under terrible conditions: "They stand in one position all day in pitch dark factories . . . breathing hot air."[74] These young girls, who ranged in age from fifteen to sixteen, had a "facial complexion" that resembled "seriously ill people."[75] Not only did they lack exercise and have a poor diet, but they refused to go outside "because they feared their faces would get dark and affect their beauty!"[76] Reformers argued that while factory reforms could ameliorate many health issues—another study claimed that female factory workers suffered from a host of pulmonary, stomach, and bowel ailments—it was equally important to reform the mentality of Korean women, who needed to be reeducated about their own health, especially their fear of fresh air and the sun.

Childbearing Techniques

Childbearing techniques were another contested site that preoccupied medical experts. In the 1920s, newspapers began to print doctors' columns for expectant mothers. Many experts stressed the importance of a woman's awareness of the physiological changes taking place in her body.[77] It was the woman's responsibility to prevent miscarriage or premature birth by taking precautions. As one doctor put it, "The fetus is in the mother's body . . . [therefore,] everything is in the hands of the pregnant mother." He advised the pregnant woman to be careful not to "traumatize or frighten" the fetus with spicy peppers, caffeine, tea, or any "cold food" that might disturb her stomach and intestines. Along with this new regimented diet, this medical practitioner encouraged women to exercise moderately and to take short, frequent baths.[78] These "scientifically proven" guidelines stressed the fourth month of pregnancy as the critical point when expectant mothers should change their eating and living patterns.[79] A physician, Dr. Yu Yŏng-jun, added his voice to the debate by urging women to adhere to these new hygienic and dietary practices.[80] Other medical tips ranged from checking one's urine for impurities to monitoring the frequency of urination each day to prevent bladder infection. [81]

One article even provided a guide to preparing a home delivery room that not only listed all the items necessary for childbirth but also discussed new conceptualizations of gender roles.[82] It was the woman's responsibility to obtain, prior to parturition, items such as a mattress, medicine, cotton, alcohol, a cushion, a basin, soap, a hot pad, towels, and powder.[83] Expectant fathers, who in the past had little or no role in childbirth, were now required to be actively involved in the birth of their children. Pronatalist reformers hoped that this paternal role would strengthen the chances of a healthy birth. At a practical level, doctors urged husbands to provide comfort and a "happy environment" to their wives. Emphasizing the importance of the mother's psychological well-being, one medical practitioner explained to his readers that in the long run it would be beneficial to the fetus. He also assigned to the husband the important task of selecting a good *sanp'a* (midwife), to demonstrate to his wife the sincerity of his intention to be a "responsible father." A good midwife, according this writer, should have several qualifications: "She must be skilled, experienced, and it would be best if she lived close by." If the midwife lived in another town, it was the responsibility of the husband to arrange transportation for her.[84] One writer suggested to his readers that after birth the husband should provide an honorarium to the midwife.[85]

The practice of midwifery, which had been instrumental in the standardization of modern and hygienic childbirth in Japan, became more popular in Korea with the arrival of Japanese immigrants. Although American missionaries had played an important role in bringing about qualitative changes in women's health by introducing obstetrics and nursing and establishing the first women's hospital, missionaries had found it very difficult to recruit and train Korean women to become nurses or midwives.[86] As Margaret Edmunds, a missionary nurse, observed in 1905:

Taken from the crude native environment of a home void of useful furniture such as beds, chairs, desks, tables and breakable dishes, they are suddenly transferred to a collection of buildings where, in addition to the very modest supply of the above mentioned articles, instruments, rubber appliances, thermometers, strange clothing, drugs and even the preparation of foreign diet is placed in the hands of these "anxious to learn" but sometimes confused nurses.[87]

According to Edmunds, a lack of knowledge of Western medicine and the idea of studying for six years came in conflict with "the custom of early marriages," making it very difficult to recruit "competent single young women for that long period of time."[88]

The colonial state held a contradictory position on Korean reproductive policies. On the one hand, it sought to increase the population for the utility of the empire. On the other hand, it set up obstacles for Korean medical practitioners that prevented them from intervening more effectively in childbirth or, for that matter, in other reproductive choices, such as abortions and infanticide. Though the Japanese state endorsed the practice of midwifery and even opened new centers to train midwives, it imposed strict regulations. Most important, the Government-General's license system, outlined in ordinances 108/109, required nurses and midwives to be at least twenty years old before they could qualify for the board examinations at designated government schools.[89] In an interview, Ch'oe Ae-do, one of the first midwives in Korea, told a reporter that she had to wait for one year, until she turned twenty, before she could take the board examination. Even after she got her license and started working in Kaesŏng, she had a very difficult time explaining to people her occupation as a *sanp'a*.[90]

A Government-General report in 1930 reveals that the number of midwives per 10,000 Korean women was only 1.3, as compared to 18.7 in Japan. Thus, at a macro level, according to a 1930 Government-General census, for 10,039,113 women, there were only 1,251 midwives.[91] And the *Maeil sinbo* reported in 1933 that the total number of doctors had only increased by twenty-seven since 1930.[92] Cognizant of the lack of medical facilities and staff, some questioned reformers who exhorted Korean women to consult midwives or obtain a checkup at a hospital.[93] The problem lay not with the ignorance of Korean women, the *Tonga ilbo* explained, but with the dearth of women doctors, who would ease the anxieties of their female patients and increase the likelihood of regular visits: "Even the educated 'new woman' dislikes an examination by male doctors."[94] However, because women were forced into marriage and motherhood at a young age, there was a small pool from which to draw midwives.

Doubts about the benefits of modern medicine for women were evident in a 1926 study for the *Chosŏn ilbo* by a former medical school student. The writer sought to inform the public about the three most common experiences ordinary people had with modern medicine. In the first case, he described the obstacles faced by a poor mother with an ill child when she went to consult a doctor. A trip to the hospital alone cost as much as she earned in a day.[95] The mother's inability to find such a huge sum to obtain medical services meant that her child would go untreated. In the second case, the writer pointed out that a mother would have to take her sick child to a hospital that was run either by a religious organization or by the government. If she went to a Christian hospital, she would need an introduction from a pastor. If she went to a government facility, she would need an introduction from an official at the police station or some other influential person. As the mother ran around town to obtain this paperwork, her child's condition would deteriorate. Critical of the government and so-called charitable organizations, the writer declared that Koreans like this mother were outsiders in their own country. Finally, if by happenstance the mother was able to obtain a proper introduction and hospital admission, she would have to sign away her right to determine what happened to her child in the event of his or her death. Authorities at the hospital would force her to sign a consent form that gave them authority to conduct an autopsy in the event of death or to use the cadaver as research material if death occurred during surgery.[96]

Not surprisingly, the idea of going to the hospital never crossed the minds of most Koreans. This relinquishment of power over the body, even after death, was unacceptable in a culture that valued elaborate death rituals and revered the departure of souls. As the writer for the *Chosŏn ilbo* study concluded, modern medical intervention did nothing to improve the health of the people; rather, it contributed to growing social problems like abandonment of infants and children and the deteriorating health of Korean mothers.[97]

Bodily Practices: Menstruation

Menstruation was another private female experience that was scrutinized in public as a decisive factor that shaped Korean women's sexuality and social behavior. First, a girl's entry into *sach'un'gi* (puberty) and first sexual stirrings marked a critical turning point. For Yi Kap-su, the first menarche should not be treated as a cultural initiation into womanhood but had to be understood as a specific biological stage of development requiring social and medical intervention. Yi explained that the stage of young adulthood began at sixteen and ended at thirty, when women transitioned into full adult maturity.[98] The *Choson ilbo* disagreed and warned parents that the onset of *sach'un'gi* could begin as early as thirteen for girls.[99]

According to medical experts, parental and public supervision of female menstruation was critical, because the sudden biological imbalance in a woman's womb often generated undesirable psychological responses.[100] Their opinions reflected notions about female periodicity that were prevalent in Victorian England. As Mary Poovey has shown, "The model of the human body implicit in this physiology [was] that of a closed system containing a fixed quantity of energy; if stimulation or expenditure occurred in one part of the system, corresponding depletion or excitation had to occur in another."[101] Indeed, Yi Kap-su stressed menstruation as a stimulation that led to both excitation (an "outburst of sexual desire" and a "lack of restraint") and depletion ("a weakening of the mind").

As in Western Europe, medical experts often associated menstruation with *hisŭt'eri* (a derivative of the Greek word *hustera*, or "womb") to explain a variety of disorders.[102] One writer linked "anemia, neuralgia, and hysteria" as symptoms related to the "absence of menarche" or other irregularities related to the uterus.[103] The term *unfit wombs* became a common diagnosis for unusual cases. For instance, in 1929 one doctor reported the case of a girl diagnosed with hysteria who had not experienced menarche by the age of seventeen. He explained that something "was blocking her uterus." In her case, the problems also included hematoma (blood clots) and related symptoms, in particular uterine bleeding, irregular ovulation, bladder dysfunction, and infertility.[104]

Yun Pong-gwŏn, a gynecologist at Keijō Imperial University Hospital, also highlighted symptoms of dysmenorrhea and its connection to the "retroflexion" of a woman's womb.[105] He explained to his readers that because of damage to the inner membranes of a woman's uterus through retroflexion, the nerves in her womb become oversensitive and trigger a nerve reaction.[106] Symptoms of this new ailment—neurasthenia—ranged from stress and anxiety to cold and clammy hands and feet. Dr. Yun also noted that dizziness directly affected women's emotions and psyche. Neurasthenics often experienced feelings of inadequacy and indifference, as well as physical fatigue.[107] "Essentially [a neurasthenic] becomes a sick person," another doctor explained, becoming prone to depression, temper tantrums, and other "abnormal" behavior.[108] More importantly, any woman diagnosed with a weak body and mind would most likely give birth to neurasthenic and hysteric infants.

Not surprisingly, doctors also related menstruation and hysteria to crime, including arson, murder, suicide, and vagrancy (i.e., prostitution).[109] In 1931, for instance, the *Chosŏn ilbo* featured the expert opinion of a Korean doctor who described the emotional turmoil that resulted from the monthly cycle: "Her feelings become more sensitive . . . and she loses her temper very quickly." This abnormal state of mind, in his opinion, inevitably led some women to "commit all sorts of crimes."[110] Another physician explained that due to changes in her body and emotions during *sach'un'gi* (puberty), "girls start to acquire a sexual consciousness and interest in men," which in turn develops into "an instinct for lying."[111]

Medical practitioners argued that the most efficient way to counter imbalances was to document a woman's menstrual activities to ensure normality. The main indicators of a healthy woman were regularity of the menstrual cycle (once a month), the quantity of blood lost (up to two hundred grams of blood), and the duration of menstruation (three days to a week of continual flow).[112] Moreover, medical experts played on men's anxieties to convince them of the necessity of intervention. One writer who praised the advances of science dangled an attractive incentive for becoming educated about these matters: "When you do not know whose child it is . . . you can now calculate the last day that she had her period [and figure out the paternity]." He explained that human conception took roughly ten months, or an average of 280 days (28 days per month) to be more numerically accurate. "If she is careless," the writer advised, "do the math and you can tell if she is deliberately hiding something from you!"[113]

In short, while menarche signified the "normality of women" at one level, it required that their "inherently unstable bodies" be subject to endless medical supervision. At another level, as Mary Poovey summarizes, the pathological hysteric "other" was "simultaneously the norm of the female taken to its logical extreme and a medical category that effectively defined this norm as inherently abnormal."[114]

SEX EDUCATION

The proliferation of discourse on sexuality and the medicalization of reproduction prompted Korean social reformers to channel their energies into the socialization of sex through pedagogy. Key thinkers such as Yu Hyŏng-suk urged a combination of moralism and science. In the journal *Sinsaeng* (1930), Yu asked her readers about their opinion of sex. "When we speak of 'sex,'" she observed, "men start to laugh instantly and girls put their heads down [in shame]." Challenging young men and women to think beyond "carnal matters," Yu defined sex as a "sacred institution" between men and women.[115] In reality, sex was not such a simple matter; social and medical reformers could not agree on the fundamental issues. At the most elementary level, what constituted sexual knowledge and how was *sŏngyok* (sexual desire) to be defined?[116] And which expert had the right to share the information with the public; should the entire complex of sex and medical experts be consulted? Moreover, what content would be considered appropriate for the public? Should sex education include topics such as the biology of reproduction, sexually transmitted diseases, and birth control? How could it be integrated into the school curriculum? Would this kind of pedagogy create an adverse effect, generating sexual deviance or interfering with a woman's procreative capacities?

The first order of the day was to address the growing "sexual licentiousness" among young people, despite their sexual ignorance. In a roundtable discussion of medical practitioners and gynecologists sponsored by the *Sin yŏsŏng* journal in 1933, Dr. Sin Paek-ho recollected an interesting experience he had with a young bride who had come to his clinic with her father-in-law. She claimed that while she was picking her teeth, she had swallowed the toothpick and it had become lodged in her stomach. After a full examination, Dr. Shin realized that the young bride was not being truthful and in fact had thrust an object up her vagina. To prevent further shame, he took her to the surgery room and removed the object. By sharing this anecdote, Dr. Shin wanted the public to know that masturbation was no longer a practice just among female palace attendants. [117]

The perception of serious problems with masturbation among female students prompted reformers to find a way to counter these acquired perversions. "The time has arrived for sex education," asserted the journal *Tonggwang*, to combat "unwanted pregnancies, the act of masturbation, the dangers of venereal disease, moral decay, and blind love."[118] Kim Yungyŏng also cited the rise in the number of illegitimate births and of prostitutes. "Despite the efforts to eradicate unlicensed prostitution," he observed, "their numbers [continue] to increase." Moreover, "the rising number of delinquencies among youths . . . [resulted in] adultery, rape, bigamy, and illegal matchmaking crimes." The death rate had also soared due to "abortions, infanticide, abandoned children, illicit love, jealousy, and grudges [among individuals]."[119]

There was plenty of blame to go around. Kim Yun-gyŏng blamed negligent parents for not taking responsibility for their children's actions.[120] Another reformer blamed the rebellious youth themselves: "Such audaciousness. They do not listen to their elders."[121] Kim Ch'ung, an advocate of sex education, blamed the sexual crisis on the traditional practice of separating the sexes at the age of seven, which began in the Chosŏn period. He argued that this sexual segregation "forced people secretly to suppress their sexual urges."[122] Some commentators blamed defective genes. Kim Ki-jin chose the example of Kim Myŏng-sun, a well-known poet and writer, to illustrate this "scientific" point. As the daughter of a *kisaeng*, she carried a "eugenic defect"; thus, it came as no surprise to Kim Ki-jin that she would be involved in sexual improprieties.[123]

Instead of repressing sex for the sake of morality or juridical purposes, Kim Ch'ung urged Koreans to reject the notion of sexuality as "illicit, shameful, or secretive."[124] A fellow proponent, Yi Kap-su, noted that the situation in Korea was similar to that in the West during the nineteenth century, "when sex education was neglected." Since then, the West had made tremendous strides in this area because of the large number of scholars engaged in "sexology" research.[125] Indeed, reformers aimed to take the mystery out of sex by teaching adolescents to accept their sexual desires as natural animal instincts to be tamed.[126] After all, Kim Yun-gyŏng explained, "sexual desire and instinct are facts one cannot deny."[127] Another educator described adolescent sexuality as that uncontrollable urge to plunge "into water or fire without even noticing it."[128]

Advocates of sex education argued that it would be beneficial on several levels. Pal Pong-sanin (a pseudonym) stressed the emotional aspect of the problem: "If you only have instinct and know nothing else," it leads to hollow romances. In nine out of ten cases, a girl will experience a broken heart, which could be detrimental to her psyche.[129] On a moral level, others argued that sex education could teach the importance of *sŏng todŏk* (sexual virtue) rather than *sŏngyok* (sexual desire).[130]

Most important, Kim Yun-gyŏng contended, ignorance about sexually transmitted diseases could harm not only the individual but also "the family and the nation."[131] Indeed, the fear that venereal disease would spread among young people and infect the general population was the most pressing concern. Yi Yŏng-jun informed his readers that venereal diseases were a global epidemic. He cited a report released by a sexual disease prevention association in France showing that a tenth of France's total population was infected with syphilis, leading to some forty thousand miscarriages each year. He also cited a study conducted by Tohoku Imperial University in Japan showing that 43.8 percent of mentally ill patients had syphilis. In addition, Yi provided statistics from Japan on the high abortion rates caused by syphilis (52 percent) and the loss of eyesight among syphilitic babies (60 percent).[132]

The *Chosŏn ilbo* also warned about the impact on offspring: "Because it is a congenital disease like tuberculosis, syphilis can be transmitted to the fetus." A woman's choices were unenviable: to undergo an abortion or risk "giving birth to a syphilitic child" with "bullous lesions on [his or her] palms and soles."[133] Another doctor warned readers that a syphilitic child might suffer from iritis; if not quickly treated, the child would become blind."[134] A Japanese physician stated that he would not raise objections to the marriage of two syphilitic individuals, but they had to be warned about the health risks, from severe congenital boils to premature births. In addition, reformers sought a connection between marriage and infidelity. They asserted that the source of *imjil* (gonorrhea)—the most prevalent form of venereal disease among women—was the husband, who passed it on to his wife.[135] The most "efficient course of action" to curb this epidemic, which "is endangering the entire human race," Chu Yo-han explained, "is through sex education."[136]

The pedagogization of sex also involved physical education and fitness training. Kim Po-yŏng wrote that women, who constituted nearly half of the Korean population (11,500,000), required better physical conditioning. The benefits of physical education included the physiological development and symmetry of a woman's body, and would provide her with more energy by "freeing up her mind."[137] The *Tonga ilbo* advised that schools should not simply focus on exercises that could alleviate one or two physical deficiencies, but also include those that could help a woman's mental state.[138] The newspaper enjoined Koreans not to ridicule women who played tennis, for the sport could serve the specific physical needs of women.[139] Kim Wŏn-ae, a female proponent of physical education, provided a nationalistic incentive. "If it is the calling of nature for a woman to bear a child," she noted, it was imperative for a healthy mother to bear "robust children for the nation." "Women constitute half the population," she stressed, and since "numbers equal power" for any country or ethnic people, "everything starts with health."[140]

The other pedagogical issue focused on the "biopolitics" of the population. Questions surrounding the issue of birth control generated great angst among reformers. Should birth control methods be introduced to students at school? A reporter for *Samch'ŏlli* interviewed the graduating class of one high school in Seoul. Of the 120 students polled, roughly half the girls had nothing to say when they were asked if they would like to restrict childbirth. Thirty-eight girls simply "blushed and put their heads down," proving to the reporter that Korean girls were ashamed to talk about this kind of topic. However, among those who responded, the reporter observed that the majority believed that fewer children per family would be economically beneficial and that the poor should not have so many children. One student said that parents who had too many children were irresponsible; unless they had the economic wherewithal to educate their children, they should expend their energies on the children they already had in order to educate them well. All the respondents concurred that having children right after marriage not only weakened the mother's body and imposed financial strains on the family but also infringed on the woman's mental well-being.[141] Similarly, in another women's magazine, a female teacher at Hyŏpsŏng yŏsin school urged contemporaries to come up with a concrete measure to inform the public, especially the youth, about birth control methods. "A large number of births," the writer explained, "will only weaken the [woman's] body . . . and a weak body will certainly not give birth to a healthy child."[142]

Government-General statistics showed 776,700 births and 4,430 deaths in 1930. Although these numbers were not alarmingly high, reformers argued that Koreans needed to "space the births apart." The *Tonga ilbo* even called for a national two-year moratorium on births. Drawing on the remarkable success of Margaret Sanger's birth control clinic in New York, the writer discussed the advantages of bringing fewer children into the world rather than accepting current birth and infant mortality rates.[143] The newspaper also highlighted Sanger's slogan, "Two Year Moratorium on Births," to demonstrate that contraceptive laws were scientifically proven. Moreover, it showed that excessive births not only destroyed a mother's body but also directly affected the health of subsequent fetuses.[144] In his article "Birth Control and the Health of the Mother," Li T'ae-gwi, a strong advocate of birth control, suggested that a woman should wait at least three years for her body to recuperate fully before having the next child. More importantly, Li urged fellow reformers to distribute contraceptives to all regardless of their class or health conditions.[145]

For socialists, the discussion of birth control had no meaning unless class oppression was first resolved. In 1927, the *Chung'oe ilbo* described the miserable fate of poor children whose parents sent them off to the factories to work instead of to school.[146] If the sole purpose behind Malthusian politics lay in "the exploitation of the proletariat class," one socialist reformer explained, how could one talk about birth control without connecting it to capitalism and its use of young boys and girls as "tools."[147] In other words, the socialists believed that the unequal economic system itself needed to be reformed before any attempts were made to educate the working class about sexual mores and birth control techniques.

Though female reformers recognized the need to introduce birth con-

trol methods to the population, they realized that "the population problem provided a setting for the redefinition of women's roles, status, and
rights in society."[148] Another female writer called for the "restriction of
childbirth" and the liberation of women from "unproductive labor."[149]
Noting that women constituted half the population, Yu Sang-kyu, an advocate for birth control, explained that the first order of business was to
"free the mother" so that she could choose her own husband and decide
how many children to bear. Yu argued that a woman needed to be given
adequate time to work on other abilities beyond her "reproductive capabilities."[150] "It is not as though [Korean women] had this sudden urge
for birth control," as one writer put it. "We have needed it for a long
time." [151] He insisted that a woman needed to have complete control of
her body and that it should be her decision to terminate a pregnancy.
Likewise, if Korea wanted to join the ranks of the Western world and
Japan as an advocate of birth control, it would have to make contraceptives like condoms and new medical knowledge, such as the douche tech-
nique and the rhythm method, available to the public.[152]

Nowhere was it more evident than in the field of medical science and
health that the female body was a site for regulation and control. Employing modern discourses and technologies, Korean intellectuals and
Japanese colonial authorities competed to define the boundaries of female sexuality and reproductive health. Medical science, with its privileged epistemological position, could be deployed to perpetuate certain
types of social relations. Despite attempts to modernize the Korean body
by reforming traditional family practices, such as early marriage and primitive childbirth, in many respects the colonial agenda did more to enforce
traditional patriarchal hierarchies and gender roles through medical
knowledge. In the view of the colonial power, a woman's status and health
were determined by her reproductive capabilities. A woman with irregular or unusual menstruation patterns, for instance, was now declared
unfit not only physically but mentally, since sexual health was linked to
mental health. Moreover, despite the utilization of modern medical dis-

course, the aim of the colonial state was not necessarily to improve the overall health and well-being of Korean women, but to reinforce colonial hegemony. In the case of birth control, the goal was not to provide access to easy, affordable means to limit pregnancies but to increase the subject population.

Careful scrutiny of the female body, which assisted the all-powerful medical establishment in regulating the population, also wedged open a space for a group of medical practitioners in the discipline of *sŏngyokhak* (sexology). Through the marketing of sexual products and advice columns, the public not only became acquainted with these sexologists (who were mostly male by default) but also learned about various aspects of sexuality (pleasures and psychosocial deviations). The public also gained a heightened awareness of new sexual disorders such as neurasthenia, although this diagnosis was often directed at women who posed a threat to established norms. In short, the colonized body became the site for a politically conservative and economically driven agenda that did not always bode well for Korean women despite the claims of progress by medical science.

Conclusion

> Beneath what one might call the "monotheistic" privilege that
> panoptic apparatuses have won for themselves, a "polytheism"
> of scattered practices survives, dominated but not erased.
>
> Michel de Certeau, *The Practice of Everyday Life*

A storm of criticism broke out prior to the release of the film *Blue Swallow* (2005), a fictionalized biography of Pak Kyŏng-wŏn (1901–33), one of the first Korean female aviators during the colonial period. The public was outraged that a "pro-Japanese traitor" who had flown promotional flights on behalf of the empire had been given a sympathetic movie about her life. Not only had she offered her services to the colonial powers but she had allegedly carried on a scandalous affair with Koizumi Matajiro, the minister of posts and telecommunications and grandfather of Koizumi Jun'ichiro, a former prime minister of Japan. In his defense of the film, director Yun Chong-ch'an contended that he wanted to explore the tragic life of a woman "who had chosen her dream over her country."[1]

The youngest daughter of a progressive wealthy farmer from Taegu, Pak was a precocious child who had enrolled at Sinmyŏng Higher Common School at the age of fourteen. Pak, who was gifted in mathematics, aspired to become an aviator from a young age—a career that was unattainable for most Koreans. After a lengthy apprenticeship in silk- and

hemp-reeling techniques at Kasahara Industrial Arts School in Yoko-
hama, Pak returned to Korea in 1920 and entered Chahye ŭiwŏn as a delivery nurse in the hopes of saving enough money to enroll at an aviation school in Japan. Pak was affable yet declined multiple marriage
requests.

As Pak's determination to become an aviator grew stronger, she
sought a way to achieve her dream.[2] In 1924, Pak applied to the Kabata
Driving School in Tokyo as a step toward preparing for flying lessons,
and subsequently moonlighted as a driver to earn money for her tuition.
She entered Tachikawa Flight School in April 1925 as one of six female
students in a class of thirty-three. Pak held her ground despite her inferior status as a colonial subject and a woman.[3] Unlike some of her compatriots living in Japan, she refused to change her name and showed pride
in her Korean nationality.

By 1928, Pak had earned her level-two aviator license, a significant
accomplishment for her time. She also participated in numerous aviation
competitions, winning all the female events. After graduating from flight
school at the top of her class, Pak flew several promotional flights with
the ultimate aim of flying to Europe or America. However, before em-
barking on a transpacific flight, she wanted to fulfill her lifelong dream
of flying from Japan to her homeland. On 7 August 1933, clad in her khaki
aviator cap and blue goggles, Pak confidently climbed into the cockpit
of the "Blue Swallow," her prized Salmonson 2A2 plane, and embarked
on her journey home. Fifty minutes after takeoff, as her plane reached
Hakone, Pak encountered fog. With a limited field of vision, she veered
off course, crashing into Mount Kurotake. The time on her wristwatch
said 11:25:30 A.M.[4]

As a woman and a colonial subject of Japan, Pak had to overcome
many more hurdles than An Ch'ang-nam (1900–30), the first male Korean aviator. As she reached the crossroads of her career, Japanese colonial policy switched from cultural accommodation to policies driven by
an all-out war with China. The totalizing effects of militarization re-

quired Koreans to change their names, speak Japanese, and worship at Shinto shrines under the dictates of Naisen ittai (Unity of Japan and Korea). Although Pak has been labeled a collaborator, her decision to place personal ambition over national interests was not unlike the decision made by many women discussed in this book. Embracing modernity meant gaining access to the "desirable domains of power and knowledge," even at the risk of being identified as a sympathizer or, worse, a traitor.

Indeed, in the context of colonial modernity, Korean women discovered new opportunities to articulate their sense of spatial location, craft new identities, and challenge the Confucian patriarchal system. One might argue that the self-conscious attempts of Korean women to redefine themselves and challenge gender roles and conventional norms of femininity were similar to trends in interwar Japan.[5] As in Japan, the emergence of the "new woman," professional housewife, working woman, and factory girl was intricately connected to rapid industrialization, an explosion of urban culture and values, and technological innovation. What distinguished Korean women's experiences, however, was their *dual* confrontation with modernity and colonial power, which was often concealed, disguised, and manipulated within newly demarcated spaces. The images of Korean women, as well as their self-definitions, could not be divorced from the colonial context and a growing nationalist movement that searched for a counternarrative and a voice.

COLONIALISM, SURVEILLANCE, AND THE KOREAN SOCIAL BODY

At the heart of these competing forces lay the power of modern surveillance, which made the new "terrain of the social" a more perilous path to navigate. As this study has shown, women responded in a variety of ways to colonial attempts to control the family, education, culture, work, and bodies.

Surveillance through the Family and Education

Under the gaze of the sort of disciplinary apparatus where "all noncon-formity became the focus," Koreans were under great pressure to police their own families and to redefine the boundaries between home and school.[6] Instructions on how to conform were ubiquitous, and the burden of surveillance lay on the shoulders of the mothers, who were at the heart of the family. Korean advice manuals about how to raise proper school-aged children, with the right friends, good hygiene, and values (diligence, respect for superiors) taught women how to create desirable imperial subjects who displayed deference, industry, and order.

Instructions on how to be good imperial subjects could also be found in Government-General manuals, such as a 1936 educational reader for Korean middle school girls. The motivations were transparent: the empire needed docile, moral, and obedient subjects. Domesticity and moral citizenship were stressed. Korean girls were encouraged to emulate Japanese female students and learn from their "sacrificial" spirit. Not only would this lifetime commitment to the "three obediences"—serving their parents-in-law, husband, and children—lead to prosperity, but it also would bring peace and harmony to the family.[7] This advice conveyed the spirit of Japanese traditional values, despite its modern language of citizenship.

Other forms of surveillance were more overt and public. Students now had to pledge their loyalty and obedience to the emperor by memorizing the Imperial Rescript on Education, which was redrafted for Koreans on 30 October 1931.[8] An oath of loyalty to the emperor, bowing in the direction of Tokyo, and compulsory visits to Shinto shrines (*sanpai*) became standard practice in schools, posing numerous problems for the remaining Christian schools. One goal of the *dōka* (assimilation policy) was to eradicate Korea's racial cultural heritage by abolishing all subjects related to Korean language, history, and geography.[9] The *Tonga ilbo* reported in 1938 that the Korean language course had been designated optional and would be replaced by other courses, such as horticulture and home economics.[10] Moreover, as Andrew Grajdanzev lamented, the problem with Korean education was the nationality of the teachers: "Teaching is conducted entirely in Japanese, a language strange to the ear of the Korean child. This might be mitigated to some extent by Korean teachers who would probably give some explanations in the Korean language, but Korean teachers are not numerous."[11]

At least in the eyes of Korean nationalists, it was incumbent on Korean women to receive an education and assume the role of the Korean teacher at home so as to undermine the controls established by the colonial power. Moreover, they could maintain some semblance of control over the mechanisms that aimed to remake their children at school by understanding the educational content, controlling children's peer groups, and teaching them how to mask hidden transcripts through orderly conduct and appearance. In other words, knowledge was one way to resist the surveillance of the state.[12]

Female education, however, was fraught with the potential for greater intervention into women's lives by the colonial power. Developing national character meant adhering to morals and disciplining oneself (*rensei* or *tanren*) to become a loyal imperial subject.[13] Grajdanzev criticized the new definition of morals as loyalty to the state: "As for 'morals,' they should not be mistaken for what we understand by the term. For us morals mean above all the guiding principles of human relations; official Japanese 'morals,' on the other hand, mean loyalty to the Emperor and state, and filial piety. Thus selling one's daughter to a brothel, according to this code of morals, is not immoral; but criticism of an official is."[14]

Despite the challenges, some women were able to take advantage of the educational system. Literacy, an area in which gender inequality was especially pronounced prior to the colonial period, became a central topic of public debate. Apart from a handful of literati women who were indoctrinated in the classical texts, women did not have access to education prior to the colonial period. From 1890 to 1910, Korea witnessed an unprecedented growth in private missionary schools, with the most noteworthy expansion occurring in primary girls' schools.[15] At minimum,

Protestant missionary schools provided an opportunity for ordinary women to learn how to read and write. More importantly, these schools broke new ground in female education and instilled a love of learning in a population that had heretofore been excluded from the world of letters. Although their numbers were few, many of the first generation of students who graduated from these missionary schools would emerge in the early 1920s to challenge the Confucian patriarchal system and to articulate new goals for women's education.[16]

A new class of educated women who had sojourned in Japan and the West had acquired new knowledge and sought to negotiate their own vision of modernity. These "new women" demanded authority over their own personhood—the freedom to choose modern hairstyles, clothing, and definitions of beauty. Although the public outrage over bobbed haircuts and short skirts was cast in the press as a "culture war" (glorification of the West over native culture), perhaps it was more a reflection of discomfort with the blurring of gender identities.

New knowledge also fostered the quest for female emancipation, even at the expense of liberation for all the Korean people. In the context of colonial modernity, women's pursuit of personal ambitions—whether higher education or an aviator's license—was often judged by the public according to its contribution to the private family (by daughter, wife, or mother) or the national cause. When modern aspirations clashed with traditional norms of Korean womanhood, the critique was sexual—both in language and content. Terms like "the other woman" and "seductive temptress" were employed to describe the threat that the new woman's assertiveness posed to accepted gender roles in Korean society. The public obsession with aviator Pak Kyŏng-wŏn's supposed sexual relationships with Japanese authorities is a case in point. Cartoons and caricatures of the new woman were equally denigrating in sexual terms.

That many prominent women, including painter Na Hye-sŏk, poet Kim Myŏng-sun, singer Yun Sim-dŏk, and pilot Pak Kyŏng-wŏn, died tragically or obscurely has been interpreted by many scholars as evidence of their failure to overcome the shackles of an ironclad patriarchy. For

Korean nationalist scholars, these women's ambitions for a career, self-expression, or free love were inappropriate during a time of colonial exploitation. These scholars bemoan narcissistic tendencies that precluded any national consciousness; these new women were at best a disgrace, because they put the personal over the national. Others have argued that the new women were failures because they entertained naïve notions that Western liberalism would somehow free them. Some scholars have even argued that the chasm between traditional Korea and modernity during the colonial period and the modern era was so deep that any attempt to embrace colonial modernity was destined to fail.[17] As this study has shown, though the impact of Korea's modern women on patriarchal structures and ideas may have been negligible during the colonial period, their articulation of a new vision of Korean womanhood and the controversies they ignited by their personal example laid the foundations for an eventual reevaluation of gender and identity in Korea.

Surveillance in the Workplace

The accelerated pace of industrialization and urbanization that accompanied Japan's colonization of the peninsula altered women's lives on many levels. It generated a crisis in rural areas, which witnessed a sharp decline in cottage industries and the mass migration of peasants to cities in search of work. As I have shown, female workers in Korea did not usurp traditional male occupations (thus feminizing labor); rather, new positions, such as telephone operator, postal worker, and bank clerk, became available to female workers in the urban centers right from the beginning.[18]

Workers in these occupations were almost always female, according to newspaper accounts. Factory employers deployed gender categories that relegated their female operatives to menial, monotonous, labor-intensive, low-skilled, and low-paying jobs. If women received unequal wages for their work, employers explained, it was because of the biological differences of their sex.

Surveillance of young workers in the factories came in the guise of

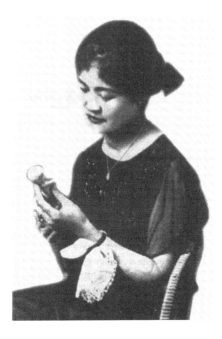

8. The singer Yun Sim-dŏk
(1920).

factory managers who sought to assert patriarchal authority over their employees. The image of the Korean manager beating his female workers in Kang Kyŏng-ae's novel *In'gan munje* (The human problem) followed the hierarchical pyramid of race and class that often kept workers from organizing resistance and demanding basic reforms.[19]

Women's visibility in the public sphere fueled debates about women and work among contemporaries who lamented the demise of the traditional family. As nuclear families became more prevalent in the cities and the middle class expanded, contemporaries worked to rejuvenate the domestic sphere by promoting a new ideology of the *hyŏnmyŏng chŏnŏp chubu* (wise and prudent professional wife).

Policing the Body

Another arena of surveillance involved the health and bodies of Korean women. Public debates about the modernization of childbirth, the introduction of birth control, and the improvement of hygiene wedged open a new arena of discourse on sex. These new discursive sites (medico-juridical, economic, and pedagogical) sought to impose normative ideas about women's bodies, sexuality, and reproductive capacity. As we have seen, there were competing agendas for control of women's bodies: for Korean nationalists, the central goal was to reproduce a fit and healthy nation that could declare its independence from colonial authorities. To that end, the reformers sought to transform traditional marital practices (such as the *minmyŏnŭri* system) in order to extend the life expectancy of young women, increase fertility, and prevent severe social tensions in the family. Through these reforms, they sought to medicalize and "nationalize" menstruation, conception, pregnancy, and childbirth. By elevating motherhood as a national ideal that required scientific instruction and precision, the reformers inadvertently provided the basis for intrusive policing of women's bodies. Cervixes were to be prodded with care, breasts examined for milk production, and body weight accurately measured. Ideally, births were to take place in a hospital under the supervision of doctors and midwives. To be sure, such recommendations were more an ideal than a reality in colonial Korea; however, changes were taking place as medical science entered the private terrain of the female body.

The colonial authorities maintained a contradictory stance on Korean reproductive policies. Although they welcomed population increase for the utility of the empire, they frequently obstructed Korean medical practitioners who sought to intervene more effectively in childbirth or prevent abortions and infanticide. One way to maintain control over their colonial subjects was to construct their bodies as unhealthy and in need of supervision and treatment. This construction of illness was gendered female, with the attendant deficiencies of Koreans—corporeal weakness and inferiority—thus justifying their subjugation and subordination. In particular, the colonial state's interest in genetic diseases (including mental illness) and sexually transmitted diseases reinforced the "biological truth" of their inferiority. Although it is difficult to know how these cultural constructions of illness impacted the actual health of Korean women, they may have left them more vulnerable to violence (i.e., sexual slavery) and intervention.

KIM HWAL-LAN: NAVIGATING
THE NEW TERRAIN

The legacy of colonialism is still one of the most important and sensitive issues in Korean society today. Despite ideological differences, many Korean scholars (on both ends of the peninsula) view the Japanese occupation as a result of the failure of a corrupt ancient regime to reform and defend a nation with a five-hundred-year history of sovereignty and cultural superiority against aggressive colonialism. They argue that the occupation "intervened, derailed, and hijacked" Korea's drive toward modernity.[20] Yet, as this study has shown, for Korean women, colonialism both opened up new possibilities and subjugated them as colonial subjects.

The life story of Kim Hwal-lan perhaps best encapsulates the contradictions that characterized the encounters of Korean women with colonial modernity. On 25 March 2005, students at Ewha Womans University congregated around the bronze statue of Kim Hwal-lan, the first president of the school, denouncing her pro-Japanese activities and calling on the administrators to eradicate all vestiges of Japanese imperialism by replacing Kim with Yu Kwan-sun, an independence movement "righteous martyr" and a revered alumnus.[21] Several years earlier, the General Students Association had organized a similar rally on campus to condemn the administration for commemorating the achievements of "a Japanese sympathizer" by inaugurating the Helen Kim Award, which recognized the efforts of women activists around the world. Given the negative public perception of Kim's role as a collaborator, university officials quickly scrapped the award. How could such a luminary figure, respected for her pioneering efforts in advancing women's rights and access to education, be equally infamous for her collaboration with the colonial government? This was the paradox of the Korean women who embraced colonial modernity to gain access to power and knowledge.

Born in Chemulp'o (Inch'ŏn) on 27 February 1899 to Christian parents, Helen's life changed when her family moved to Seoul in 1907. She entered Ewha haktang with a full scholarship when she was eight years old and graduated from high school at fourteen. In 1918, under the supervision of Ms. Lulu E. Frey, Helen graduated from Ewha College and became active in Christian groups like the YWCA while working as an instructor. In 1924, after securing a three-year scholarship, she went abroad to earn a bachelor's degree at Ohio Wesleyan University and a master of arts in philosophy at Boston University. After several years of teaching English at Ewha haktang, Kim became the first Korean woman to earn a doctorate from Columbia University Teachers College (1930), at the urging of Alice Appenzeller, then president of Ewha College. Upon her return to Korea, she was appointed dean of Ewha College in 1931 and served as president of the university from 1939 until her retirement in 1961.[22]

Despite her activism in feminist and Christian circles, as well as her efforts to revitalize the countryside in the 1930s, Kim Hwal-lan, like so many other Korean intellectuals, found herself faced with a choice between survival through cooperation with the Japanese authorities and imprisonment during the latter half of colonial rule, a particularly repressive period. A year after the outbreak of the second Sino-Japanese War, Governor-General Minami Jirō issued the Third Educational Ordinance (1938–43), which expedited the transformation of Koreans through *kōminka* (imperialization) and a rigorous curriculum of *dōka* (assimilation). The new objective of the state was "to secure peace and happiness in East Asia" for its *teikoku shinmin* (imperial subjects).[23] As Japan's involvement deepened in the Pacific War, Governor-General Koiso Kuniaki issued the fourth and final Educational Ordinance (1943–45), which ultimately closed the doors on liberal education.

Kim Hwal-lan, who changed her name to Yamagi Katsuran in 1941, found herself working with pro-Japanese groups like the *Imjŏn taech'aek hyŏmnyŏkhoe* (Countermeasures for going into battle mutual association) and the Chosŏn imjŏn poguktan puindae (Korean Patriotic Going into Battle Women's Association).[24] In editorials and speeches, she appealed to her Korean "compatriots" to "fulfill their duties as citizens" by enlisting in the Japanese imperial army or voluntary corps to assist in the war effort.[25]

By 1943, the state promulgated the Gakuen senji hijō sochi hōsaku (Wartime Emergency Measures for Schools), which reduced the period of secondary schooling to four years. Whatever lip service the government had given to education disappeared; the need to conscript able-bodied Koreans revealed the colonial power's disdain for the intellectual and cultural needs of its subjects. The government mobilized boys and girls under the Kokumin seishin sōdōin undō (National Spiritual Mobilization Movement) ordinance to serve in volunteer groups like the Josei teishintai (Female Volunteer Corps). Such volunteer groups were fronts for wartime conscription. Many students ended up as laborers or soldiers, and some were conscripted to serve as *ianfu* (comfort women) in Japanese military brothels. In 1944, the state closed down Ewha Woman's College and all remaining mission schools. The Seito kinrō rei (Student Labor Act) of 1944 dispatched female students to factories or assigned them to administrative duties. A slogan during this period of extreme uncertainty and repression captured the despair: "Today's work rather than tomorrow's graduation."[26]

In 1941, "some 1.4 million Koreans were in Japan, of whom 700,000 were in the labor force: 220,000 were in construction work, 208,000 in manufacturing, 94,000 in mining, and the remainder in agriculture. Yet at least half a million more were sent to Japan thereafter so that by the end of the war Koreans comprised one-third of the industrial labor force in Japan; 136,000 worked in the mines, often in the harshest forms of labor."[27] Approximately 80,000 to 200,000 Korean women were conscripted to serve in Japanese military brothels—a tragic chapter in the story that had seen the emergence of the "new women," professional housewives, factory workers, and modern working women.[28]

In the final analysis, the life of Kim Hwal-lan reveals the limitations that Korean women confronted in their struggle to become modern. Even though not all Korean women cooperated with the colonial authorities, they all lived their lives within the context of colonialism and its mechanisms of power. This is not to argue that women lost their agency altogether, for they played a critical role in negotiating and defining their role and status in Korean society. At the same time, the underlying pressures of colonialism drew the boundaries within which Korean women could assert themselves or define their womanhood in public. These limitations led women to perform their public gender roles meticulously while expressing dissent in more subtle ways. In moments of conflict, however, they sometimes discarded these performances and crossed boundaries (for instance, in strikes), actions fraught with severe consequences.

Women also had to contend with their male compatriots. While Korean reformers hailed women's participation in the modernization of Korea, they expressed ambivalence at the new assertiveness and independence that accompanied women's acquisition of education or their ability to earn a salary, albeit a modest one. In the end, many male reformers wanted to contain the new woman within the boundaries of domesticity, where she could be controlled and directed. Although Korean society still remained largely traditional in its gender relations and structures, some cracks had begun to appear that were irreversible and momentous.

NOTES

INTRODUCTION

1. *Tonga ilbo*, 9 Aug. 1926, 14 Aug. 1926.

2. Miriam Silverberg, "Remembering Pearl Harbor, Forgetting Charlie Chaplin, and the Case of the Disappearing Western Woman: A Picture Story," in *Formations of Colonial Modernity in East Asia*, ed. Tani Barlow (Durham, NC: Duke University Press, 1997), 255.

3. Ko Yŏng-han, "Sinmun kija ro pon 10-yŏn chosŏn" [Ten years of Korea seen through the eyes of a newspaper reporter], *Pyŏlgŏn'gon* (Jan. 1930), cited in Kim Chin-song, *Sŏul e ttaensŭhol ŭl hŏhara* [Permit a dance hall in Seoul] (Seoul: Hyŏnsil munhwa yŏn'gu, 1999), 40–41.

4. Bruce Cumings, *Korea's Place in the Sun: A Modern History* (New York: Norton, 1997), 152.

5. Michel Foucault, *The History of Sexuality: An Introduction*, trans. Robert Hurley (New York: Vintage, 1990), 145–46.

6. James Scott, *Seeing Like a State* (New Haven, CT: Yale University Press, 1998), 4–5, 77.

7. Michel Foucault, *History of Sexuality*, 36–37.

8. Ibid., 141.

9. William H. Sewell Jr., *Logics of History: Social Theory and Social Transformation* (Chicago: University of Chicago Press, 2005), 135–36.

10. Michel Foucault, *Discipline and Punish: The Birth of the Prison*, trans. Alan Sheridan (New York: Vintage Books, 1995), 138–39.

11. Tom Conley, introduction to Michel de Certeau, *The Writing of History*, trans. Tom Conley (New York: Columbia University Press, 1988), ix–x.

12. Ibid., xiv–xv.

13. Ibid., x.

14. Pak Yong-ok, "Nondan: Han'guk yŏsŏng yŏn'gu ŭi tonghyang" [Research note: Trends in women's studies in Korea], *Ewha sahak yŏn'gu* 9, no. 3 (1976): 30–34.

15. By December 1974, the institute had published thirteen volumes, with thirty-five articles devoted to Korean women history and culture. Ibid., 30–31.

16. Earlier in June 1958, a group of scholars organized a festschrift commemorating Kim Hwal-lan's forty years of service to Ewha Womans University. Participants contributed eleven important essays on women's history and culture.

17. Han'guk yŏsŏngsa p'yŏnch'an wiwŏnhoe, *Han'guk yŏsŏngsa* [The history of Korean women], 3 vols. (Seoul: Ewha yŏja taehakkyo ch'ulp'anbu, 1972).

18. In 1977, a group of prominent women professors founded the Korean Women's Institute (KWI) and launched the first undergraduate Women's Studies program in Korea at Ewha Womans University. Although the institute often faced the daunting task of serving as an "umbrella" for various outside organizations and despite conflicting demands on its time and resources, it succeeded in fulfilling its stated goals: it hired a faculty of twenty professors from various disciplines and worked on developing a curriculum for college students. In 1982, the university launched Korea's first master's program in Women's Studies. Many of the original authors and their students started to publish their works in journals, such as *Yŏsŏnghak nonjip* [Women's studies review] (1984–present), *Yŏsŏng* [Women] (1985–89), and *Yŏsŏng kwa sahoe* [Women and society] (1990–present).

19. Denise Riley, *"Am I That Name?" Feminism and the Category of 'Women' in History* (Minneapolis: University of Minnesota Press, 1988), 2.

20. The 19 April 1960 "Student Revolution" marked the beginning of the *minjung* antiauthoritarian democracy movement.

21. Bruce Cumings, "Bringing Korea Back In: Structured Absence, Glaring Presence, and Invisibility," In *Pacific Passage: The Study of American-East Asian Relations on the Eve of the Twenty-First Century*, ed. Warren I. Cohen (New York: Columbia University Press, 1996), 355.

22. The term *yŏsŏng haebang* (women's liberation) emerged from the *minjung* movement in the 1970s.

23. Yi Hyo-jae, "Ilcheha han'guk yŏsŏng nodong yŏn'gu" [Research on Korean female labor under Japanese rule], *Han'guk hakpo* 4 (1976): 141–88.

24. *Subaltern* refers to subordination "in terms of class, caste, gender, race, language and culture and signifies the dichotomy of dominant/dominated relationship in history." See Gyan Prakash, "Subaltern Studies as Postcolonial Criticism," *American Historical Review* 99 (Dec. 1994): 1477.

25. Gail Hershatter, "The Subaltern Talks Back: Reflections on Subaltern Theory and Chinese History," *positions* 1, no. 1 (Spring 1993): 103–30.

26. Gayatri C. Spivak, "Subaltern Studies: Deconstructing Historiography," in *Selected Subaltern Studies*, ed. Ranajit Guha and Gayatri C. Spivak (New York: Oxford University Press, 1988), 11.

27. Dipesh Chakrabarty, "Conditions for Knowledge of Working-Class Conditions: Employers, Government and the Jute Workers of Calcutta, 1890–1940," in *Selected Subaltern Studies*, ed. Guha and Spivak, 179.

28. Kim Yun-hwan, *Han'guk nodong undongsa* [A history of the Korean labor movement], vol. 1 (Seoul: Ch'ŏngsa, 1982); Kim Kyŏng-il, *Ilcheha nodongsa* [A history of labor under Japanese colonial rule] (Seoul: Ch'angjak kwa pip'yŏng, 1992); Cho Sŭng-hyŏk, *Han'guk kong'ŏphwa wa nodong undong* [The industrialization of Korea and labor movements] (Seoul: P'ulbit, 1984).

29. Gerda Lerner, "Reconceptualizing Difference among Women," *Journal of Women's History* 3 (Winter 1990): 107.

30. Chŏng Hyŏn-baek, "Yŏsŏngsa yŏn'gu ŭi iron kwa pangpŏp" [Research on women's history: Theory and practice], *Yŏksa pip'yŏng* (Autumn 1994): 376–77.

31. Sewell, *Logics of History*, 48.

32. Judith Butler, *Gender Trouble: Feminism and the Subversion of Identity* (New York: Routledge, 1990), x.

33. Han'guk yŏsŏng yŏn'guhoe yŏsŏngsa pun'gwa, "Han'guk yŏsŏngsa ŭi yŏn'gu tonghyang kwa kwaje: Kŭndae p'yŏn" [Research trends and issues in Korean women's history (modern section)], *Yŏsŏng kwa sahoe* 5 (1994): 297–327.

34. Mun So-jŏng, "Ilcheha han'guk nongmin kajok e taehan yŏn'gu—1920–30-yŏndae pinnongch'ŭng ŭl chungsim ŭro" [Research on Korean rural families under Japanese occupation: Focusing on the 1920s–1930s poor peasant class], (Ph.D. diss., Seoul National University, 1991); Cho Ŭn, "Ilcheha hyangch'on pan'ga ŭi kajok saenghwal kwa pyŏnhwa" [The livelihood of rural elite families and changes under Japanese colonial rule], in *Yŏsŏng kajok sahoe* [Women, family, society], ed. *Yŏsŏng han'guk sahoe yŏn'guhoe p'yŏn* (Seoul: Yŏlŭmsa, 1991), 61–83.

35. An Yŏng-sŏn, "Han'guk singminji chabonjuŭihwa kwajŏng esŏ yŏsŏng nodong ŭi sŏnggyŏk e kwanhan yŏn'gu: 1930-yŏndae pangjik kong'ŏp ŭl chungsim

ŭro" [Research on the characteristics of women's labor during the formation of colonial capitalism in Korea: Focusing on the textile industries during the 1930s] (Master's thesis, Ewha Womans University, 1988); Chŏng Chin-sŏng, "Singminji chabonjuŭihwa kwajŏng esŏ ŭi yŏsŏng nodong ŭi pyŏnmo" [The transformation of women's labor under colonial capitalistic processes], *Han'guk yŏsŏnghak* 4 (1988): 49–100; Sin Yŏng-suk, "Ilcheha han'guk yŏsŏng sahoesa yŏn'gu" [A social history of Korean women under Japanese colonial rule] (Ph.D. diss., Ewha Womans University, 1989); Yi Chŏng-ok, "Ilcheha kong'ŏp nodong esŏ ŭi minjok kwa sŏng, 1910–1945" [Race and Sex in industrial labor under Japanese colonial rule, 1910–1945] (Ph.D. diss., Seoul National University, 1990).

36. Kang I-su, "1930-yŏndae myŏnbang tae kiŏp yŏsŏng nodongja ŭi sangt'ae e kwanhan yŏn'gu: Nodong kwajŏng nodong t'ongje rŭl chungsim ŭro" [Research on the conditions of female workers in the large-scale cotton industry during the 1930s: Focusing on the labor process and labor control] (Ph.D. diss., Ewha Womans University, 1992).

37. Han'guk yŏsŏng yŏn'guhoe yŏsŏngsa pun'gwa, "Han'guk yŏsŏngsa ŭi yŏn'gu tonghyang kwa kwaje: kŭndae p'yŏn," 305–7.

38. Kim Ŭn-ju, "Han'guk kyohoe yŏsŏng kyoyuk ŭi yŏksa wa munje e taehan yŏn'gu: Kamni kyohoe yŏsŏng kyoyuk ŭl chungsim ŭro" [A study on the history and problems of Korean church women: Focusing on women's education and the Methodist Church] (master's thesis, Ewha Womans University, 1985).

39. Yun Hye-wŏn, "Kaehwagi yŏsŏng kyoyuk" [Women's education during the enlightenment period], in *Han'guk kŭndae yŏsŏng yŏn'gu* [Research on modern Korean women], ed. Asea yŏsŏng munje yŏn'guso (Seoul, 1987), 113–83; Kim Sŏng-ŭn, "1930-yŏndae chosŏn yŏsŏng kyoyuk ŭi sahoejŏk sŏnggyŏk" [Women's education and its societal characteristics in Korea during the 1930s] (master's thesis, Ewha Womans University, 1992).

40. Han'guk yŏsŏng yŏn'guhoe yŏsŏngsa pun'gwa, "Han'guk yŏsŏngsa ŭi yŏn'gu tonghyang kwa kwaje: Kŭndae p'yŏn," 297.

41. Kwŏn Podŭrae, *Yŏnae ŭi sidae: 1920-yŏn ch'oban ŭi munhwa wa yuhaeng* [An era of love: Culture and trends/fashion in the early 1920s] (Seoul: Hyŏnsil munhwa yŏn'gu, 2003); Ch'oe Hye-sil, *Sin yŏsŏngdŭl ŭn muŏt ŭl kkum kkuŏnnŭn'ga?* [What were the new women dreaming about?] (Seoul: Saenggak ŭi namu, 2000); Chŏn Kyŏng-ok, Pyŏn Sin-wŏn, Pak Chin-sŏk, and Kim Ŭn-chŏng, eds., *Han'guk yŏsŏng munhwasa* [A cultural history of Korean women], 4 vols. (Seoul: Sukmyŏng yŏja taehakkyo ch'ulp'an'guk, 2004); Kim Kyŏng-il, *Yŏsŏng ŭi kŭndae, kŭndae ŭi yŏsŏng* [The modernity of women, women of modernity] (Seoul: P'urŭn yŏksa, 2004).

42. V. N. Voloshinov, *Marxism and the Philosophy of Language*, trans. Ladislav

Matejka and I. R. Titunik (Cambridge, MA: Harvard University Press, 1986), 105.

1. WOMEN IN CHOSŎN KOREA

1. Henry Savage-Landor, *Corea or Cho-sen: The Land of the Morning Calm* (New York: MacMillan, 1895), 60.

2. Though the history of Korean [women] does not have a long-standing historiographic tradition within which interpretations can be debated, there are several important books on which to base a discussion of gender. I have relied in particular on Martina Deuchler, *The Confucian Transformation of Korea: A Study of Society and Ideology* (Cambridge, MA: Harvard University Press, 1992); Kim Tu-hon, *Han'guk kajok chedo yŏn'gu* [A study of the Korean family system] (Seoul: Sŏul ch'ulp'ansa, 1968); Yi Hyo-jae, *Kajok kwa sahoe* [Family and society] (Seoul: Minjosa, 1968); and Yŏksa Hakhoe, ed., *Han'guk ch'injok chedo yŏn'gu* [A study of the Korean kinship system] (Seoul: Ilchogak, 1992). In 1949, Kim Tu-hon completed his study of kinship relations, which examined the evolution of the family system and documented the transformations. Kim's monograph is still widely read by sociologists and historians. Although functionalist and statistically based on empirical research, it has contributed greatly to our understanding of the diversity in family structures and the relationship of women to other aspects of social life.

3. Ernest Oppert, *A Forbidden Land: Voyages to the Corea* (New York: G. P. Putman's Sons, 1880), 105.

4. Louis Dumont, *Homo Hierarchicus: The Caste System and Its Implications*, trans. Mark Sainsbury, Louis Dumont, and Basia Gulati (Chicago: University of Chicago Press, 1980), 65–66; also see Bruce Cumings, *Korea's Place in the Sun* (New York: W. W. Norton, 1997), 13.

5. Martina Deuchler, "The Tradition: Women during the Yi Dynasty," in *Virtues in Conflict: Tradition and the Korean Woman Today,* ed. Sandra Mattielli (Seoul: Royal Asiatic Society, Korea Branch, 1977), 2.

6. Bruce Cumings, *Korea's Place in the Sun: A Modern History* (New York: Norton, 1997), 13.

7. The *ajŏn* or *yamen* (clerks) also were part of the *chungin* class. Many of the *sŏja*, illegitimate children born to women other than legal wives, were part of this class. Hesung-Chun Koh, "Religion, Social Structure and Economic Development in Yi Dynasty" (Ph.D. diss., Boston University, 1953), 85–86.

8. One became a slave through destitution, conviction of a heinous crime, being sold in the market by one's parents, or as a "seed slave" (the child of a slave parent).

9. Yung-Chung Kim, ed., *Women of Korea: A History of Ancient Times to 1945* (Seoul: Ewha Womans University Press, 1976), 21, 47–48.

10. Deuchler, *The Confucian Transformation of Korea*, 9.

11. Ibid., 57–81.

12. Jahyun Kim Haboush, "Filial Emotions and Filial Values: Changing Patterns in the Discourse of Filiality in Late Chosŏn Korea," *Harvard Journal of Asiatic Studies* 55, no. 1 (June 1995): 130.

13. Chŏng To-jŏn, *Sambong-jip*, 231, cited in Martina Deuchler, *The Confucian Transformation of Korea*, 244–45.

14. In Korea, age is counted by the years during which one has lived. For example, a newborn child is said to be one year old, and another year is added after each lunar new year.

15. Yung-Chung Kim, ed., *Women of Korea*, 94–95.

16. Only those from the upper class were subject to these restrictions, since the majority of commoners did not have surnames. As a result, commoners possessed more freedom of choice in their marriages.

17. Deuchler, *The Confucian Transformation of Korea*, 236–37.

18. Ibid.

19. Ibid., 237.

20. Chung Yo-sup, "Women's Social Status in the Yi Dynasty," in *Women of the Yi Dynasty*, ed. Asian Women Research Center (Seoul: Sookmyung Women's University Press, 1986), 162–63.

21. There were two types of secondary wife: (1) *yang ch'ŏp* (commoner background); (2) *ch'ŏn ch'ŏp* (*ch'ŏnmin* background). A *yangban teril sawi* (married-in son-in-law) would change his surname to his wife's surname and live with her. See Hesung Chun Koh, "Religion, Social Structure and Economic Development in Yi Dynasty," 54.

22. All adoptions had to be approved, and the Yejo (Board of Rites) kept a record, called the *kyuju-tŭngnok* (register of adoptions). See Mark Peterson, "Women without Sons: A Measure of Social Change in Yi Dynasty Korea," in *Korean Women: View from the Inner Room*, ed. Laurel Kendall and Mark Peterson (New Haven, CT: East Rock Press, 1983), 34–38; Mark Peterson, *Korean Adoption and Inheritance: Case Studies in the Creation of a Classic Confucian Society* (Ithaca, NY: East Asia Program, Cornell University, 1996).

23. I base my account on information in the excellent study Yi Hyo-jae offers

in *Chosŏnjo sahoe wa kajok* [Society and family in the Chosŏn dynasty] (Seoul: Hanŭl, 2003), 143–49, 183–95.

24. Ibid., 147.

25. Ibid., 183.

26. Ibid., 183–95; see also Kyung Moon Hwang, *Beyond Birth: Social Status in the Emergence of Modern Korea* (Cambridge, MA: Harvard University Asia Center, 2005).

27. Ibid., 259.

28. Michelle Zimbalist Rosaldo, "A Theoretical Overview," in *Woman, Culture, and Society,* ed. Michelle Zimbalist Rosaldo and Louise Lamphere (Stanford, CA: Stanford University Press, 1974), 21.

29. Homer B. Hulbert, *The Passing of Korea* (New York: Paragon Book Gallery, 1906), 349–56.

30. Ibid., 366.

31. Savage-Landor, *Corea or Cho-sen,* 67.

32. William Elliott Griffis, *Corea: The Hermit Nation* (New York: Charles Scribner's Sons, 1885), 244.

33. Charles Gutzlaff, *Journal of Three Voyages along the Coast of China in 1831, 1832, and 1833 with Notices of Siam, Corea, and the Loo-Choo Islands* (London: Frederick Westley and Att. Davis, 1834), 322.

34. Hulbert, *The Passing of Korea,* 359.

35. J. Robert Moose, *Village Life in Korea* (Nashville, TN: Publishing House of the M. E. Church, 1911), 74–75.

36. Louise Jordan Miln, *Quaint Korea* (New York: Charles Scribner's Son's, 1895), 94.

37. Savage-Landor, *Corea or Cho-sen,* 65–66.

38. Koh, "Religion, Social Structure and Economic Development in Yi Dynasty," 60.

39. Ibid., 369.

40. Miln, *Quaint Korea,* 77–79.

41. Cho Haejong, "Male Dominance and Mother Power: The Two Sides of Confucian Patriarchy in Korea," in *Confucianism and the Family,* ed. Walter H. Slote and George A. DeVos (Albany: SUNY Press, 1998), 190.

42. Horace Underwood, *Fifteen Years among the Top-Knots or Life in Korea* (Boston: American Tract Society, 1904), 50.

43. Angus Hamilton, *Korea* (New York: Charles Scribner's Son, 1904), 48.

44. Rev. George W. Gilmore, *Korea from Its Capital with a Chapter on Missions* (Philadelphia: Presbyterian Board of Publication, 1892), 107.

45. Cho Haejong, "Male Dominance and Mother Power: The Two Sides of Confucian Patriarchy in Korea," 190.

46. Yung-Chung Kim, ed., *Women of Korea*, 145–45.

47. First tested in the Kyŏnggi province in 1608, it took one hundred years to fully implement it across the peninsula. Ki-baik Lee, *A New History of Korea*, trans. Edward Wagner with Edward J. Shultz (Cambridge, MA: Harvard University Press, 1984), 224.

48. Peter Lee, ed., *Sourcebook of Korean Civilization*, vol. 2 (New York: Columbia University Press, 1996), 86.

49. Chu Yŏng-ha, Kim So-hyŏn, Kim Ho, and Chŏng Ch'ang-jŏn, eds., *19-segi chosŏn saenghwal kwa sayu ŭi pyŏnhwa rŭl yŏtpora* [A look into the changes in life and thought in nineteenth-century Chosŏn] (Seoul: Tolbege, 2005), 47.

50. Chŏng Kyŏng-suk, "Kaehwagi yŏsŏnggwan ŭi pyŏnmo wa kyoyuk kuguk undong" [The changing view of women during the enlightenment period and the 'save the nation' educational movement], in *Uri yŏsŏng ŭi yŏksa* [Our women's history], ed. Han'guk yŏsŏng yŏn'guso yŏsŏngsa yŏn'gusil (Seoul: Ch'ŏngnyŏnsa, 1999), 251.

51. Chŏng Hae-ŭn, "Chosŏn hugi yŏsŏng sirhak cha pinghŏgak yi-ssi" [Late Chosŏn period's female *sirhak* scholar *pinghŏgak* Ms. Yi], *Yŏsŏng kwa sahoe* 8 (1997): 299–300.

52. Pak Ok-ju, "Pinghŏgak yi-ssi ŭi kyuhapch'ongsŏ e taehan munhŏnhak chŏk yŏn'gu" [A philological study of Pinghŏgak yi-ssi's *Kyuhapch'ongsŏ*], *Han'guk kojŏn yŏsŏng munhak yŏn'gu* 1 (2000): 271–304.

53. Ibid.

54. Chŏng Hae-ŭn, "Chosŏn hugi yŏsŏng sirhakcha pinghŏgak yi-ssi," 298. Another interesting woman cited in the *Chosŏn wang jo sillok* (The veritable records of the Chosŏn Dynasty) is Kim Man-dŏk (1739–1812), a female merchant from Cheju Island. At a very young age, Kim became adept in reading commodity price fluctuations and started a wholesale business exporting Cheju's abalone, seaweed, and mandarins to the mainland. However, during 1792 and 1795, a series of storms triggered a string of bad harvests. Instead of hoarding her wealth, Kim purchased grain from merchants in Chŏlla Province and had them ship it to Cheju and distribute it to the islanders at her expense. Upon hearing of Kim's benevolent act through a memorial sent by a local official, King Chongjo offered a monetary reward (which she politely declined), bestowed upon her an official rank to be remembered in posterity, and on 25 November 1796, granted Kim a special travel permit to visit the mainland to fulfill her lifelong dream of touring the Kumgang (Diamond) Mountains. See Chŏng Hae-ŭn, "Ponggŏn ch'eje ŭi tong'yo wa

yŏsŏng ŭi sŏngjang" [Unrest in the feudal system and the rise of women], in *Uri yŏsŏng ŭi yŏksa* [Our women's history], ed. Han'guk yŏsŏng yŏn'guso yŏsŏngsa yŏn'gusil (Seoul: Ch'ŏngnyŏnsa, 1999), 241–42.

55. Chŏng Hae-ŭn, "Ponggŏn ch'eje ŭi tongyo wa yŏsŏng ŭi sŏngjang," 247.

56. Ibid., 248.

57. In *Yongdam yusa* (Hymns from Dragon Pool), Ch'oe stressed the importance of *namnyŏ p'yŏngdŭng* (equality between the sexes) and *kahwaron* (harmony in the family). See Chŏng Kyŏng-suk, "Kaehwagi yŏsŏnggwan ŭi pyŏnmo wa kyoyuk kuguk undong," 252.

58. Pak Yong-ok, *Han'guk yŏsŏng kŭndaehwa ŭi yŏksajŏk maengnak* [The modernization of Korean women and its historical interconnections] (Seoul: Chisik sanŏpsa, 2001), 184.

59. Ibid., 157–59, 254.

60. Chŏng Kyŏng-suk, "Kaehwagi yŏsŏnggwan ŭi pyŏnmo wa kyoyuk kuguk undong," 253.

61. Pak Yong-ok, *Han'guk yŏsŏng kŭndaehwa ŭi yŏksajŏk maengnak*, 138, 154–57.

62. Gilmore. *Korea from Its Capital*, 149.

63. Lulu Frey, "Higher Education for Korean Girls," *The Korea Mission Field* 10, no. 10 (Oct. 1914), 307. Isabella Bird Bishop, a frequent visitor to Korea, observed that there were no native schools for girls. She estimated that there were only two Korean women in a thousand who could read. See Isabella Bird Bishop, *Korea and Her Neighbors: A Narrative of Travel with an Account of the Recent Vicissitudes and Present Position of the Country* (1895; reprint, Seoul: Yonsei University Press, 1970), 342.

64. Yung-chung Kim, ed., *Women of Korea*, 154.

65. *Naehun* [Instruction for Women] (1475), as found in Haejong Cho, "Korean Women and Their Experience in the Traditional World," in *Korean Women and Culture*, ed. Research Institute of Asian Women (Seoul: Sookmyung Women's University Press, 1998), 28.

66. Deuchler, *The Confucian Transformation of Korea*, 258; Yung-chung Kim, ed., *Women of Korea*, 156.

67. On 21 September 1876, Korean garrisons fired upon the *Unyo Kan*, one of the three Japanese battleships, while they were ostensibly conducting a survey along the Korean coastline. This hostile interaction between the two countries led to the signing of the Kangwha Treaty of 1876.

68. *Heathen Woman's Friend* 16, no. 7 (1885): 158–59, cited in Hyae-weol Choi, "Women's Literacy and New Womanhood in Late Chosŏn Korea," *Asian*

Journal of Women's Studies 6, no. 1 (March 2003): 92–93. Yi Su-jŏng was baptized in April 1883. He taught Korean at Tokyo University and prepared a textbook entitled *Chōsen nihon senrin kōwa* [For the sake of peaceful neighborly relations between Korea and Japan] in August 1884. See Yi Kwang-nin, *Han'guk kaehwasa yŏn'gu* [A study of the history of Korean enlightenment] (Seoul: Iljogak, 1969), 234–43.

69. National History Compilation Committee, ed., *Yun Ch'i-ho's Diary*, vol. 2 (Seoul, 1974), 139.

70. Ibid., 215.

71. Sŏ Chae-pil (1866–1951) was one of the progressive intellectuals involved in the *Kapsin* coup d'etat. Banished to Japan in 1884, Sŏ went to America to study medicine and became a naturalized U.S. citizen. Philip Jaisohn (after his naturalization) returned to Korea in 1896. See Vipan Chandra, *Imperialism, Resistance, and Reform in Late Nineteenth-Century Korea: Enlightenment and the Independence Club* (Berkeley: Institute of East Asian Studies, University of California, 1988).

72. *Tongnip sinmun*, 21 April 1896.

73. Ibid., 5 September 1896.

74. If man is identical to god, then one must treat others as though one was serving god. See Benjamin B. Weems, *Reform, Rebellion, and the Heavenly Way* (Tucson: University of Arizona Press, 1964).

75. *Tongnip sinmun*, 13 Sept. 1896.

76. Ibid., 12 May 1896.

77. Ibid., 7 Sept. 1896.

78. The Kabo Reforms of 1894 sought to reform the government, abolish slavery, and eliminate many old customs, such as the cutting off of the topknot, child marriage, and strictures on widow remarriage.

79. Residency-General in Korea, *Administrative Reforms in Korea* (Keijō, 1907), 4.

80. *Tongnip sinmun*, 10 Sept. 1896.

81. Ibid., 13 Nov. 1898; 5 July 1898.

82. *Sŏu*, 1 Dec. 1906, 10.

83. *Tae Chosŏn tongnip hyŏphoe hoebo*, 2 July 1896.

84. Horace N. Allen, *Things Korean: A Collection of Sketches and Anecdotes Missionary and Diplomatic* (New York: Fleming H. Revell Company, 1908), 188.

85. Ibid.

86. Lee Hyo-chae, "Protestant Missionary Work and Enlightenment of Korean Women," *Korea Journal* 17, no. 11 (Nov. 1977): 40.

87. "Severence Hospital," *Korea Review* 6, no. 2 (Feb. 1906): 62–63.

88. "Po Ku Nyo Koan," *Report Read at the Seventh Annual Session of the Korea Woman's Conference of the Methodist Episcopal Church* (June 23–27, 1905), 59. The literal translation of the name is "Salvation for All Women Institution."

89. Maren Bording, "Konju Infant Welfare and Public Health," *Thirtieth Annual Report of the Korea Woman's Conference of the Methodist Episcopal Church* (Oct. 1928): 19.

90. Various Protestant groups opened missions during the late 1880s: the Presbyterian (North) in 1884, the Methodist Episcopal (North) in 1885, the Canadian Baptists in 1889, the Church of England in 1890, the Presbyterian (South) in 1892, the Canadian Presbyterian in 1893, and the Methodist Episcopal (South) in 1896. The number of evangelical Protestant missionaries surged from 934 in 1890 to 5,000 at the turn of the century and 20,000 by end of the 1920s. In 1893, the Methodist Episcopal mission (South) and the Northern Presbyterian Mission signed the "Territorial Partition Agreement," which stated that open ports and towns with a population over 5,000 should be opened for "common occupation." Seoul was partly placed under the auspices of the Methodists, while the Presbyterians concentrated on the citizens of P'yŏngyang. Harry A. Rhodes, *History of the Korean Mission Presbyterian Church U.S.A., 1884–1934*, vol. 1 (Seoul: Choson Mission Presbyterian Church, U.S.A., 1925), appendix A. In general, missionaries had a college education, and additional higher training—theological or professional—was required. Most women missionaries had at least a high school education or its equivalent. See Dae Young Ryu, "Understanding Early American Missionaries in Korea 1884–1910: Capitalist Middle-Class Values and the Weber Thesis," *Archives de Sciences Sociales des Religions* 113 (Jan.–Mar. 2001): 93.

91. Mary F. Scranton, "Women's Work in Korea," *Korean Repository* 3, no. 1 (Jan. 1896): 2–3.

92. Allen, *Things Korean*, 206.

93. Yung-Chung Kim, ed. *Women of Korea*, 204: "Whenever a male teacher gave a lesson, he would have to sit in a chair facing the blackboard and keep his back to the student at all times." Furthermore, whenever he entered the classroom, "the girls would all turn around and face the back of the room until he signaled them with a cough that he was seated in his chair facing the blackboard." Richard Rutt, *Modern Transformation of Korea* (Seoul: Sejong Publishing Company, 1970), 114.

94. L. George Paik, *The History of Protestant Missions in Korea 1832–1910* (P'yŏngyang: Union Christian College Press, 1929), 126.

95. Jean Comaroff and John Comaroff, *Of Revelation and Revolution: Chris-

tianity, Colonialism, and Consciousness in South Africa (Chicago: University of Chicago Press, 1991), 233.

96. "The Educational Needs in Korea," *Korea Review* 4, no. 10 (Oct. 1904): 444.

97. Yun Ch'i-ho, "Women's Education," *Korean Mission Field* 31, no. 7 (July 1935): 135.

98. *Report of the Woman's Foreign Missionary Society of the Methodist Episcopal Church for 1885,* cited in Paik, *The History of Protestant Missions in Korea 1832–1910,* 125.

99. Mary Scranton, "The Gospel in all Lands for 1888," cited in Paik, *The History of Protestant Missions in Korea 1832–1910,* 373.

100. "Ladies Commercial Association," *Korea Review* 6, no. 2 (Feb. 1906): 51.

101. Ibid.

102. Louise C. Rothweiler, "Our Work in Korea," *Korea Mission Field* 5, no. 10 (Oct. 1909): 166.

103. Annie Ellers Bunker, "Personal Recollections of Early Days," in *Within the Gate: Comprising the Addresses Delivered at the Fiftieth Anniversary of Korean Methodism First Church,* ed. Charles A. Sauer (Seoul: Korean Methodist News Service, 1934): 66.

104. D. L. Gilford, "Education in the Capital of Korea," *Korean Repository* (Aug. 1896), 409–10.

105. Paik, *The History of Protestant Missions in Korea,* 191.

106. *Hwangsŏng sinmun,* 17 Sept. 1908.

107. James S. Gale, *Korea in Transition* (New York: Young People's Missionary Movement of the United States and Canada, 1909), 144.

108. George Thompson Brown, *Mission to Korea* (Nashville, TN: Board of World Missions, Presbyterian Church U.S., 1962), 68.

109. William Scott, *Canadians in Korea: Brief Historical Sketches of Canadian Mission Work in Korea* (Toronto: Board of World Missions, United Church of Canada, 1975), 62.

110. Annabel Major Nisbet, *Day In and Day Out in Korea* (Richmond, VA: Presbyterian Committee of Publications, 1919), 126; *Korea Woman's Conference* (Seoul, 1911), 23; Missionaries often referred to non-Christians as "heathens" or "different from ourselves." See Everett Nichols Hunt, Jr., *Protestant Pioneers in Korea* (New York: Orbis Books, 1980), 90.

111. *Korea Woman's Conference,* 22.

112. Ibid.

113. *Korea Review* 1, no. 10 (Dec. 1919): 155.

114. This kind of activity was known as "missionary itinerating." The aim was to avoid overconcentration in the cities. Classes were often held in a household's *sarangbang*, the "reception for guests" room. At one time it was called *sarangbang* education. In 1905, it became known as *sagyŏnghoe*, or "Bible class," after a uniform curriculum was designed. See Dr. William Scott, *Canadians in Korea; Korean Mission Field* 2, no. 10 (Oct. 1906): 238.

115. Mrs. Myrtle Elliott Cable, "Evangelical Work on the West Korea District," *Report Read at the Seventh Annual Session of the Korean Woman's Conference of the Methodist Episcopal Church* (Seoul, June 23–27, 1905), 32.

116. Ibid., 33.

117. *Reports read at the Ninth Annual Session of the Korea Woman's Conference of the Methodist Episcopal Church* (Seoul, July 19–27, 1907), 12.

118. Millie M. Albertson, "The Bible Woman's Training School," *Korea Woman's Conference* (Seoul, 1911), 17.

119. The Society for Women's Education had a membership of roughly 280 wives. A group of some forty wives opened the Yangyu Ŭisuk Girls' School. See *Hwangsŏng sinmun*, 18 May 1906, 1 Nov. 1906.

120. They were also known as *Yangsŏngwŏn* (training schools).

121. *Hwangsŏng sinmun*, 13 Oct. 1898.

122. Yung-Chung Kim, ed., *Women of Korea*, 223–24.

123. *Tongnip sinmun*, 10 Dec. 1898.

124. Ibid., 9 Sept. 1898.

125. "Ladies Commercial Association," *Korea Review* 6, no. 2 (Feb. 1906): 51–57.

126. Ibid., 55.

127. Ibid., 57

128. By 1910, there was one government girls' high school and fifteen private schools. See *Taehan minbo*, 13 May 1910.

129. *Cheguk sinmun*, 14 Nov. 1906.

130. Ibid., 8 Jan. 1907.

131. Chŏng Yŏng-t'aek, "Yŏja kyoyungnon" [A discussion of women's education], *Yŏjagye* 2 (1918), 8–10.

2. THE "NEW WOMAN" . . .

1. *Tonga ilbo*, 24 June 1922.

2. *Tonga ilbo*, 8 Oct. 1926.

3. Na Kyŏng-hŭi, "Ilcheha han'guk sinmun e nat'anan yŏsŏng undonggwan" [An outlook on the women's movement in Korean newspapers under Japanese colonial rule] (master's thesis, Korea University, 1987), 17.

4. Henri Lefebvre, *The Production of Space*, trans. Donald Nicholson-Smith (Oxford: Blackwell, 1993), 51.

5. Kim Kyŏng-il, *Yŏsŏng ŭi kŭndae, kŭndae ŭi yŏsŏng* [The modernity of women, women of modernity] (Seoul: P'urŭn yŏksa, 2004), 287, 303; Yi Man-gyu, *Chosŏn kyoyuksa* [The history of education in Korea], vol. 2 (Seoul: Kŏrŭm, 1988), 215–17.

6. Residency-General in Korea, *Administrative Reforms in Korea* (Keijō, 1907): 4.

7. Shidehara Taira. *Chōsen kyōiku ron* [Discussion on the education of Korea] (Tokyo, 1919), 46.

8. One of the features of colonization is that the colonizing nation implements its own form of schooling within its colonies. This process is "an attempt to assist in the consolidation of foreign rule." See Gail P. Kelly and Phillip G. Altbach, "The Four Faces of Colonialism," in *Education and the Colonial Experience*, ed. Gail P. Kelly and Phillip G. Altbach (New Brunswick, NJ: Transaction, 1984), 1–5. While moral and intellectual suasion was important for governance, cultural assimilation was perhaps the most effective form of political action. See Gauri Viswanathan, "Currying Favor: The Politics of British Educational and Cultural Policy in India, 1813–1854," in *Dangerous Liaisons: Gender, Nation, and Postcolonial Perspectives*, ed. Anne McClintock, Aamir Mufti, and Ella Shohat (Minneapolis: University of Minnesota Press, 1997), 113–29.

9. Government-General of Chōsen, *Annual Report: Reforms and Progress in Chōsen (Korea) 1911–1912* (Keijō, 1912), 201. The Japanese residents in Seoul had their own schools since the opening of the ports. A school was opened in Pusan in 1877 and later in other port cities, including Wŏnsan (1882) and Chemulp'o (1885). See Horace Underwood, *Modern Education in Korea* (New York: International Press, 1926), 11.

10. W. Carl Rufus, "The Japanese Educational Policy in Korea," *Korea Review* 2, no. 11 (Jan. 1921): 12–13.

11. Shidehara Taira, *Chōsen kyōiku ron*, 201–3.

12. The case was also referred to as the "Christian Conspiracy Case." See Allen D. Clark, *A History of the Church in Korea* (Seoul: Christian Literature Society, 1971), 186–90.

13. The private school ordinance was revised in 1915. "Paichai Methodist Higher Common School was the first Christian institution to make an application to become a recognized school under the ordinance of 1915, preferring to

omit the Bible from the curriculum rather than to incur the displeasure of officials by holding out against the government during the ten years of grace." *Korea Review* 3, no. 1 (March 1921): 15.

14. *Maeil sinbo*, 10 Sept. 1910.

15. James Earnest Fisher, "Democracy and Mission Education in Korea" (Ph.D. diss., Columbia University, Teachers College, 1928), 7.

16. Government-General of Chōsen, *Annual Report*, 211.

17. Although many schools were given a ten-year grace period to make changes, many still could not meet the standards. According to another Government-General report conducted in 1917, the number of private schools ranged from 4,000 to 5,000 schools prior to 1908. However, by July of 1910, the number had dropped significantly, to around 2,000 schools. *Korea Review* 2, no. 12 (Feb. 1921), 13. Chōsen Sōtokufu hen, *Chōsen no hogo oyobi heigō* [The protection and annexation of Korea] (Keijō, 1917), 165.

18. J. C. Crane, "The Evolution and Execution of a School," *Missionary Survey* (March 1917): 203.

19. T. Stanley Soltau, *Korea: The Hermit Nation and Its Response to Christianity* (Toronto: World Dominion Press, 1932), 49–50.

20. William Scott, *Canadians in Korea. Brief Historical Sketches of Canadian Mission Work in Korea* (Toronto: Board of World Missions, United Church of Canada, 1975): 121.

21. Fisher, "Democracy and Mission Education in Korea," 6.

22. Chŏng Ch'ung-nyang, *Ewha 80-yŏnsa* [The eighty-year history of Ewha] (Seoul: Ewha yŏdae ch'ulp'ansa, 1967), 247–48.

23. *Tonga ilbo*, 17 Feb. 1934.

24. "Yŏja kyoyuk ŭi sŏkkŭmgwan" [Outlook on girls' education today and yesterday], *Sin yŏsŏng* (April 1926): 9–10.

25. Andrew Nahm, *Korea: A History of the Korean People* (Elizabeth City, NJ: Hollym, 1988), 250.

26. Ibid., 251.

27. Rufus, "The Japanese Educational Policy in Korea," 12.

28. Government-General of Chōsen, *Annual Report on the Administration of Chōsen 1926–1927* (Keijō, 1928), 96–97.

29. According to one of the clauses in the Revised Educational Regulations of 1922, twelve volumes would be included in the curriculum with the aim of "making [the students] masters of the national language." Yung-Chung Kim, ed., *Women of Korea: A History from Ancient Times to 1945* (Seoul: Ewha Womans University Press, 1976), 233.

30. Carter J. Eckert, Ki-baik Lee, et. al., *Korea Old and New: A History* (Cambridge: Korea Institute, Harvard University, 1990), 262.

31. Ibid., 97.

32. Pak Tal-sŏng, "Iphak yŏllyŏng ŭi chanyŏ rŭl tun kajŏng ege" [To the families with girls entering school age], *Sin yŏsŏng* (March 1924): 99.

33. *Tonga ilbo*, 6 March 1922.

34. Pak Tal-sŏng, "Iphak yŏllyŏng ŭi chanyŏ rŭl tun kajŏng ege," 99.

35. Jihang Pak, "Trailblazers in a Traditional World: Korea's First Women College Graduates, 1910–1945," *Social Science History* 14, no. 4 (Winter 1990): 537.

36. *Tonga ilbo*, 1 May 1920.

37. *Korea Review* 3, no. 1 (March 1921): 14.

38. You Kak Kyunghee, "Seoul Young Women's Christian Association," *Korea Mission Field* 21, no. 6 (June 1925): 132.

39. Melissa Kim, "The Korean Women's Educational Association," *Korea Mission Field* 16, no. 10 (Oct. 1920): 207.

40. Cho Wŏn-suk, "Kyogyu t'ako tomang olttae" [When running away in a palanquin], *Pyŏlgŏn'gon* (Aug. 1927): 57–58.

41. *Tonga ilbo*, 14 April 1920. In 1937, Kim Mirisa changed her name to Cha Mirisa.

42. The twelve cities were: Keijō (Seoul), Chemulp'o (Inch'ŏn), Kunsan, Mokp'o, Taegu, Pusan, Masan, P'yŏngyang, Chinamp'o, Sinŭiju, Wŏnsan, and Chungjin.

43. This meant that the total population in the twelve cities was 652,608. See Helen Kim, "Rural Education for the Regeneration of Korea" (Ph.D. diss., Columbia University, 1931), 25.

44. The majority of primary school teachers were still Korean.

45. Helen Kim, "Rural Education for the Regeneration of Korea," 31.

46. Kil An-ae, "Yŏng'a ŭi ilnyŏn kan" [During the first year of a newborn child], *Uri kajŏng* (Oct. 1936): 61–63.

47. Kim Sang-dŏk, "Ŏmŏni tokpon, dae 5-ke, chajangga" [Mother's reader, fifth lesson, lullabies], *Kajŏng ŭi u* (Aug. 1938): 45–49.

48. "Hakkyo e taninŭn adong ŭl tusin pumo ege" [To parents of the child attending school] *Uri kajŏng* (Oct. 1936): 25–26.

49. Ibid. "Public transcript" refers to the open, public interaction between the dominant power and the oppressed. "Hidden transcript" refers to what takes place offstage, beyond public visibility. For more on hidden transcripts, see James

Scott, *Weapons of the Weak: Everyday Forms of Peasant Resistance* (New Haven, CT: Yale University Press, 1985).

50. Ibid., 131–32.

51. Government-General of Chōsen, *Annual Report: Reforms and Progress*, 204.

52. Sukmyŏng yoja taehakkyo, *Sukmyŏng 70-yŏnsa* [The seventy-year history of Sookmyung] (Seoul: Sukmyŏng yŏja chung-kodŭng hakkyo, 1976), 62.

53. According to this study, there were a total of 16,063 Korean students (11,866 boys and 4,197 girls).

54. Ch'oe Yŏng-su, "Hakkyo nŭn nunmul in'ga? Hansum in'ga?" [Is school something to cry about or something to sigh about?], *Sin tonga* (June 1936), 18–19.

55. *Tonga ilbo*, 22 Feb. 1931. Unlike the countryside, where parents did not really have a choice, in bigger towns and cities, competition in placing one's child at a higher common school was rather stiff. See Yi Chŏng-ho, "Iphak sihŏm kwa ŏmŏni ŭi chuŭi" [The entrance examination and what a mother should pay attention to], *Sin yŏsŏng* (March 1932): 60–63.

56. *Fifty Years of Light: Prepared by Missionaries of the Woman's Foreign Missionary Society of the Methodist Episcopal Church in Commemoration of Fifty-Years of work in Korea* (Seoul, May 1938), 24.

57. Ada B. Hall, *Thirty third Annual Report of the Members of the Woman's Foreign Missionary Society in Korea* (Seoul, Sept. 1931), 38.

58. Ibid.

59. *Tonga ilbo*, 1 Jan. 1928.

60. Ibid, 6 April 1920.

61. Ibid.

62. Pak Sa-jik, "Puin kyoyuk munjero tongŭi haya" [Reaching a consensus on the woman's education problem], *Kaebyŏk* (March 1921), 35.

63. Kil Myŏk-sok [pseud.], "Chorŏp hu iljunyŏn" [A full year after graduation], *Sin yŏsŏng* (Aug. 1924), 51–52.

64. Han So-je, "Kŭriun kŭ yennal" [Yearning for the past], *Sin kajŏng* (June 1936), 164.

65. Na Hye-sŏk, "Isangjŏk puin" [The ideal lady], *Hak chi kwang* (March 1914), 13–14.

66. "Ch'ŏlhak paksa Kim Hwal-lan yang" [Doctor of philosophy Kim Hwal-lan], *Sin tonga* (Feb. 1932), 67.

67. Chu Yo-sŏp, "Chosŏn yŏja kyoyuk kaesinan" [A plan to reform Korean women's education], *Sin yŏsŏng* (Oct. 1933), 12–17

68. Yi Kwang-su, "Nae ka yŏhakkyo tanggukcha i'myŏn: Mosŏng chungsim

ŭi yŏja kyoyuk" [If I was the principal of a girls' school: Education centered around mothercraft], *Sin yŏsŏng* (Jan. 1925), 19.

69. Min T'ae-wŏn, "Nae ka yŏhakkyŏ tanggukcha i'myŏn" [If I was the principal of a girls' school], *Sin yŏsŏng* (Jan. 1925), 17–18.

70. Il kija [a journalist], "Yŏsŏng p'yŏngnon" [A critique of women], *Sin yŏsŏng* (March 1926), 17–18.

71. In 1920, a student from X Girls' School committed suicide, fearing that she would be accused of stealing a gold ring. That same year, a student at *Ewha yŏja chŏnmun hakkyo* committed suicide for stealing 20 *wŏn*. Another student at Kyŏngsŏng Girls' Trade School committed suicide after slandering her teacher. Sin Yŏng-suk, "Ilcheha han'guk yŏsŏng sahoesa yŏn'gu" [A social history of Korean women under Japanese colonial rule] (Ph.D. diss., Ewha Womans University, 1989), 39.

72. *Tonga ilbo*, 3 April 1920.

73. "C" kija [pseud.], "Hakkyo pang'mungi" [Reflecting on my visit to a school], *Haktŭng* (Nov. 1935), 14–15.

74. By the 1920s, the number of Korean female students going to Japan rose significantly. The majority enrolled in higher normal schools or special medical schools for women. See Pak Chŏng-ae, "1910–1920-yŏndae ch'oban yŏja ilbon yuhaksaeng yŏn'gu" [A study of students studying abroad in Japan during the first half of the 1920s] (master's thesis, Sookmyung Women's University, 1999), 24. Hwang Sin-dŏk, Kim Myŏng-sun, and Na Hye-sŏk all studied in Japan. Ko Myŏng-ja was the first Korean women to study at Moscow State University. Kim Hwal-lan was the first Korean woman to receive a doctoral degree from Columbia University. See Kim Cha-hye, "P'yŏngyang e naŭn sin yŏsŏng" [New women from P'yŏngyang], *Sin kajŏng* (March 1933), 120.

75. *Tonga ilbo*, 1 March 1924.

76. "Yŏhaksaeng ŭi segaji p'yep'ung" [Three bad habits of female students], *Sin yŏsŏng* (April 1926), 17–18.

77. *Tonga ilbo*, 24 June 1922. Sang Sŏp, "Yŏja tanbal munje wa kŭ e kwallyŏn hayŏ" [The female bobbed hair problem and related matters], *Sin saenghwal* (July 1922), 49–50.

78. "X yŏhakkyo KY saeng: tanbal han kamsang" [Student KY at X girls' school: Impressions on bobbed hair], *Tonggwang* (Sept. 1932), 61.

79. "Tanbal munje ŭi sibi" [The rights and wrongs of the bobbed hair problem], *Sin yŏsŏng* (Aug. 1925), 37–38.

80. Kim Hwal-lan, "Yŏja tanbal e: ka han'ga pu han'ga?" [Regarding a woman's bobbed hair: Should we approve or disapprove?], *Pyŏlgŏn'gon* (Jan. 1929): 128–33.

81. Kang 'X' Hwan, "Che-2 ho in'gan tŭl" [Second class human beings], *Pyŏl-gŏn'gon* (Aug. 1927): 69.

82. *Chosŏn ilbo*, 21 July 1929.

83. "Kyŏngsŏng myŏngmullyŏ tanballang mihaenggi" [A shadower's account of famous women with bobbed hair in Seoul], *Pyŏlgŏn'gon* (Dec. 1926), 70.

84. "Sŏul hakkyo kongbu" [Studying at a school in Seoul], *Sin yŏsŏng* (June 1925), 33.

85. Yi In-sŏn, "Yŏhaksaeng chalmot, namhaksaeng chalmot: Nae nun ŭro pon yŏhaksaeng ŭi haengdong" [Mistakes by female students, mistakes by male students: The conduct of female students seen through my eyes], *Sin yŏsŏng* (July 1924), 42–43. Yi W.S., "Yŏhaksaeng chŭk sach'i tŏngŏri" [Female students, namely a chunk of extravagance], *Sin yŏsŏng* (July–Aug. 1924), 46–47.

86. *Tonga ilbo*, 11 June 1924.

87. *Pyŏlgŏn'gon* (Dec. 1927), 12.

88. *Chosŏn ilbo*, 29 Sept. 1928.

89. The first advertisement of the "two-piece outfit" was published in the *Taehan maeil sinbo* on 7 April 1909. The *Tonga ilbo* published an advertisement of the "Oxford Shoes" on 22 June 1920.

90. *Tonga ilbo*, 14 Oct. 1921.

91. *Tonga ilbo*, 10 April 1924.

92. *Tonga ilbo*, 28 Sept.–2 Oct. 1921.

93. *Chosŏn ilbo*, 29 Sept. 1928.

94. Henrik Ibsen, *A Doll's House* (New York: Dover Publications, 1991).

95. Laura Raspilica Rodd, "Yosano Akiko and the Taisho Debate over the 'New Woman,'" in *Recreating Japanese Women 1600–1945*, ed. Gail Lee Bernstein (Berkeley: University of California Press, 1991), 175.

96. *Tonga ilbo*, 8 Oct. 1926.

97. *Tonga ilbo*, 11 July 1921.

98. *Tonga ilbo*, 26 March 1924.

99. This cartoon was a scathing critique of Na Hye-sŏk, Korea's first female artist, who professed to have had an affair while studying in Paris. "Nobumo ullyŏ yuhak hago toraon yuji sinsa wa sin sungnyŏ" [Makes aged parents cry, goes abroad and returns: A sympathetic gentleman and new lady], *Pyŏlgŏn'gon* (Dec. 1927), 23.

100. Ch'oe Chun, *Han'guk sinmunsa* [The history of the Korean newspaper] (Seoul: Ilchogak, 1960), 301.

101. Ellen Key was first introduced to Korea by No Cha-yŏng. See No Cha-yŏng, "Yŏsŏng undong ŭi cheil inja elen kk'ei" [The most renowned personal-

ity in the women's movement, Ellen Key], *Kaebyŏk* (Aug. 1921), 46–50. Articles on Ellen Key's ideas also appeared in newspapers and journals: *Chosŏn ilbo*, 12 Dec. 1933, 28–29 April 1936, 1 May 1936. "Pulgŭn yŏnae chuin'gongdŭl" [The protagonists of radiant love], *Samch'ŏlli* (July 1931), 13. Iwanami Press translated and published Key's *Love and Marriage* into Japanese (*Ren'ai to kekkon*) in 1930. Frederick Engels's *Origins of the Family, Private Property and the State* was published in segments in the *Chosŏn kyohwa wŏlbo* in 1934 (vols. 79–84). Ōtake Hirokichi's translation of works by Alexandra Kollontai also appeared in bookstores in 1936. Another very popular book among Koreans studying in Japan was Kuriyagawa Hakuson's *The Modern View on Love*. See Kim Ŭl-han, *Sillok tonggyŏng yuhaksaeng* [A record of a student studying abroad in Tokyo] (Seoul: T'onggudang, 1986), 61.

102. The Kabo Reforms of 1894 sought to eliminate child marriage and allow widow remarriage. See Lew Young-ick, "The Kabo Reform Movement: Korean and Japanese Reform Efforts in Korea, 1894" (Ph.D. diss., Harvard University, 1972). In 1922, the colonial state promulgated the Chōsen Civil Code Ordinance Number 13, which set the minimum age for marriage at seventeen for boys and fifteen for girls. This was in conformity with the old Japanese Civil Code, articles 765, 780, and 781. Divorce was legalized under the condition that couples agreed to it and reported it to the head of their county or the mayor of their city of residence. However, couples could not get a divorce without the consent of their parents. A divorce by trial could be filed on grounds of bigamy, adultery, imprisonment, ill treatment, or if a spouse was missing for three years. Yung-chung Kim, ed., *Women of Korea*, 267–70.

103. Tae Hŏ [pseud.], "Chosŏn ŭi honin chosa" [A study of marriage in Korea], *Sin yŏsŏng* (Sept. 1933), 54–57.

104. Hong Nan, "P'yŏngnon: ihon sosong kyŏkchŭng" [An editorial comment on the sudden increase in divorce litigations], *Sin yŏsŏng* (Feb. 1925), 13.

105. Pak "X" Hŭi, "Na ŭi kyŏlhon ch'amhoe" [My marriage confession], *Pyŏlgŏn'gon* (May 1930), 15.

106. Kim Song-ŭn, "Ihon munje e taehayŏ" [Regarding the problem of divorce], *Kaebyŏk* (May 1923), 39–40.

107. Kim Ki-jin, "Kyŏlhon kwa ihon e taehayŏ" [Regarding marriage and divorce], *Sin yŏsŏng*, May 1924, 30–37.

108. Chŏn Ŭn-jŏng, "Kŭndae kyŏnghŏm kwa yŏsŏng chuch'e hyŏngsŏng kwajŏng" [The modern experience and the process of women's subjectivity formation], *Yŏsŏng kwa sahoe* 11 (Nov. 2000): 37.

109. Frederick Engels, *The Origins of the Family, Private Property, and the State* (New York: Pathfinder, 1972), 117.

110. Min Pyŏng-hŭi, "Kyegŭp undong kwa aeyok munje" [Class struggle and the problem of passion], *Pip'an* (Feb. 1932), 77–79. Yamakawa Kikue (1890–1980), a member of *Seitō* (Blue stockings), had a big impact on many Korean female intellectuals. She argued in "Women as Bargain Goods with Giveaway Premiums" that in capitalist society "married women" were constructed by the capitalist marriage relationship. She noted that "within it, wives, as economic dependents of husbands" were merely "prostitutes just like women who sold sexual services for cash to a variety of male customers." E. Patricia Tsurumi, "Visions of Women and the New Society in Conflict: Yamakawa Kikue Versus Takamure Itsue," *Japan's Competing Modernities: Issues in Culture and Democracy 1900–1930*, ed. Sharon Minichiello (Honolulu: University of Hawai'i Press, 1998), 339.

111. "Nampy'ŏn choeŏk mangmyŏng chung ch'ŏ ŭi sujŏl munje" [The problem of a spouse remaining faithful while her husband is imprisoned or has fled the country], *Samch'ŏlli* (Nov. 1930), cited in Chŏn Ŭn-jŏng, "Kŭndae kyŏnghŏm kwa yŏsŏng chuch'e hyŏngsŏng kwajŏng," 35.

112. Hwang Sin-dŏk, "Pubuae, chŏngsa, sŏng kyoyuk" [Love among couples, double suicides, sex education], *Samch'ŏlli* (May 1930), 52.

113. Kim P'yŏn-ju, "Ch'ŏngsang ŭi saenghwal" [The life of a young widow], *Sin yŏja* (June 1920), 13.

114. Im In-sik, "Yŏngwŏn ŭi han p'umŭn 'S' nŭn wae chasal haenna?" [S's harboring eternal resentment. Why did she commit suicide?], *Pip'an* (Sept. 1931), 85–88.

115. Ellen Key, *Love and Marriage*, trans. Arthur G. Chater (New York: G. P. Putman's Sons, 1912), 13–16.

116. Pang In-kŭn, "Kyŏlhon ŭn yŏnae ŭi chŏngch'ajang" [Marriage is the stopping point for love], *Samch'ŏlli* (Nov. 1932), 94.

117. Yun Sŏng-sang, "Kyŏlhon ŭn yŏnae ŭi kyŏlsil igirŭl minnŭnda" [Believing that the realization of love is marriage], *Yŏsŏng* (May 1938), 31–35.

118. Yi Chŏng-hwan, "An Ki-yŏng, Kim Hyŏn-su sagŏn kwa hyŏndae yŏnae sajo ŭi pip'an" [Criticism of the Yi Ki-yŏng and Kim Hyŏn-su incident and the current public opinion of free love], *Sin yŏsŏng* (June 1933), 10–13.

119. Pak Ch'an-hŭi, "Sin yŏja ege han kaji put'ak" [Requesting one favor from the new woman], *Pyŏlgŏn'gon* (Dec. 1927), 86–87.

120. Tsurumi, "Visions of Women and the New Society in Conflict," 339.

121. Kim I-ryŏp, "Uri ŭi isang" [Our ideal], *Punyŏ chi kwang* (Aug. 1924), 10.

122. Miriam Silverberg, "The Modern Girl as Militant," in Bernstein, *Recreating Japanese Women*, 246.

123. *Tonga ilbo* 19–20 June 1926.

124. Kim Wŏn-ju, "Awakening," trans. Yunghee Kim, *Korean Studies* 21 (1997): 28–29.

125. *Tonga ilbo*, 7 Jan. 1928.

126. *Tonga ilbo*, 19 Nov. 1929.

127. *Tonga ilbo*, 5 Feb. 1928; 7 Feb; 1928.

128. *Tonga ilbo*, 25 May 1923.

129. Kim Hye-gyŏng, "Kasa nodong tamnon kwa han'guk kŭndae kajok: 1920, 1930-yŏndae rŭl chungsim ŭro" [Discourses on domestic labor and the modern Korean family: Focusing on the 1920s and 1930s], *Han'guk yŏsŏnghak* 15 (1999): 164.

130. Mary Poovey, *Uneven Developments: The Ideological Work of Gender in Mid-Victorian England* (Chicago: University of Chicago Press, 1988),10.

131. Ch'ae Maria, "Kasa chŏnmun iyagi" [A discussion on the professionalization of housekeeping], *Ewha* (April 1929), cited in Kim Hye-gyŏng, "Kasa nodong tamnon kwa han'guk kŭndae kajok," 155.

132. *Tonga ilbo*, 16 March 1925.

133. Ibid., 12 March 1938.

134. Ibid., 1 Nov. 1938, cited in Kim Hye-kyŏng, "Kasa nodong tamnon kwa han'guk kŭndae kajok," 165.

135. "Ajinomoto" [MSG], *Sin yŏsŏng* (Sept. 1933), 114.

136. Kim Hye-gyŏng, "Kasa nodong tamnon kwa han'guk kŭndae kajok," 165–66.

137. The first sewing textbook was published in 1925 and used at the Kyŏngsŏng Girls' Common School. *Chosŏn ilbo*, 27 March 1925.

138. Pak Jihang, "Trailblazers in a Traditional World," 537.

139. "Yŏja chigŏp anhae" [Woman, work, wife], *Pyŏlgŏn'gon* (March 1927), 101.

140. Ujiie Hisako, *Saishin katei kanri to kaji kezai* [Recent family management and household economies] (Tokyo: Genbunsha, 1938), 385–88.

141. Article 11 of Civil Ordinance 7 introduced aspects of Japanese civil law in areas such as legal age for marriage, judicial divorce, and inheritance. The principle of registration was introduced in the event of birth, death, marriage, and adoption with the promulgation of the Ordinance of the Family Registration on 18 December 1922. For an excellent discussion of family law during the colonial period, see Hyunnah Yang, "Envisioning Feminist Jurisprudence in Korean Fam-

ily Law at the Crossroads of Tradition and Modernity" (Ph.D. diss., New School for Social Research, 1998), 37–66.

142. Chōsen Sōtokufu, "Jinkō zōshoku oyobi seisan fusoku" [The increase of population and insufficiency in production], *Hantō jiron* 1–4 (July 1917), cited in Kang Pyŏng-sik, "Ilcheha han'guk esŏ ŭi kyŏlhon kwa ihon mit ch'ulsan silt'ae yŏn'gu" [Research on Marriage, divorce, and birth conditions in Korea under Japanese colonialism], *Sahak chi* 28 (1995), 42.

143. Hyŏn Sang-yun, "Ingu chŭngsik p'ilyonon" [Discussion on the need for increasing the population], *Hak Chi kwang* (July 1917), cited in So Hyŏn-suk, "Ilche singminji sigi chosŏn ŭi ch'ulsan t'ongje tamnon ŭi yŏn'gu" [A study on the discourse of birth control under Japanese colonial rule] (master's thesis, Hanyang University, 1999), 9.

144. Kim Kwang-sŏk, "Munje ŭi munje: Ahe rŭl manhi nach'i malja" [One problem after another: Let's not give birth to many children], *Pyŏlgŏn'gon* (Nov. 1930), cited in So Hyŏn-suk, "Ilche singminji sigi chosŏn ŭi ch'ulsan t'ongje tamnon ŭi yŏn'gu," 15.

145. Cho Hyŏn-gyŏng, "Sana chehan ŭl haeya hana? Modudŭl haeya handamnida" [Should we allow birth control? Everybody says we should], *Yŏsŏng* (April 1936), cited in Son Hyŏn-suk, "Ilche singminji sigi chosŏn ŭi ch'ulsan t'ongje tamnon ŭi yŏn'gu," 21.

146. John Knodel, *The Decline of Fertility in Germany, 1871–1939* (Princeton, NJ: Princeton University Press, 1974). Also see James Woyche, *Birth Control in Germany, 1871–1933* (London: Routledge, 1988).

147. *Nihon sanji chōsetsu hyakunenshi* [A hundred-year history of birth control in Japan], (Tokyo: Shuppan kagaku sōgōkenkyūkai, 1976), 348.

148. Both editorials urged the state to legalize birth control. *Tonga ilbo*, 13 Nov. 1921, 24 Oct. 1924. Phrases like *jinshū no kairyō* (improving the race) and *shakai kairyō* (improving of society) also began to appear in Japanese newspapers and journals. See Sabine Frühstück, "Transforming Sex into a Discourse: Managing the Truth of Sex in Imperial Japan," *Journal of Asian Studies* 59, no. 2 (May 2000): 336.

149. The *Chosŏn ŭisa hyŏphoe* (Chosŏn Doctor's Association) was established in 1930, the *Pogŏn undongsa* (Sanitation Movement Society) in 1932, and the *Chosŏn usaeng hyŏphoe* (Chosŏn Eugenics Association) in 1933. Kim Hwal-lan was a member of the Chosŏn Eugenics Association. *Tonga ilbo*, 8 June 1932.

150. In the case of Europe, Lynne Frame notes: "In the wake of the First World War, these discourses of urban decay, 'degeneration,' and its proposed antidote 'racial hygiene' (eugenics), shifted from the realm of philosophical specu-

lation and medical investigation to that of political practice. Biomedical schemes for boosting the 'quality and quantity' of the population came to inform state legalization and administration, creating policies that focused largely on women and their role in reproduction." Lynne Frame, "Gretchen, Girl, Garçonne? Weimar Science and Popular Culture in Search of Ideal Woman," in *Women in the Metropolis: Gender and Modernity in Weimar Culture*, ed. Katharine Von Ankum (Berkeley: University of California Press, 1997), 14.

151. Lamarkian eugenics emphasized changes in the environment, such that these changes would be passed down to future generations biologically. If men and women had the same education, for example, "their natures would converge more rapidly." See Ellen Key, *The Century of the Children* (New York: G. P. Putnam's Sons, 1909); Allen Buchanan, Dan W. Brock, Norman Daniels, and Daniel Wilker, *From Chance to Choice: Genetics and Justice* (Cambridge: Cambridge University Press, 2000), 30–31.

152. *Chosŏn ilbo*, 29 May 1930.

153. *Tonga ilbo*, 25–27 Jan. 1929; *Chosŏn ilbo*, 20–24 May 1930.

154. Yi Kap-su, "Usaenghakchŏk sana chehan non" [Discourse on eugenical birth control], *Sin yŏsŏng* (August 1933), 76–79.

155. *Aigo* and *nikutai* in Japanese.

156. Kudo Takeki, "Jidō aigo no konpon mondai" [The fundamental problem of *aigo* in children], *Chōsen shakai jigyō* 8–5 (1930), cited in Kim Hye-gyŏng, "Ilcheha ŏrinigi ŭi hyŏngsŏng kwa kajok pyŏnhwa e kwanhan yŏn'gu" [A study of the formation of childhood and the transformation of the Korean family under Japanese colonial rule] (Ph.D. diss., Ewha Womans University, 1997), 75.

157. Kim Myŏng-hŭi, "Sip'yŏng" [Comments on current events], *Sin yŏsŏng* (Jan. 1925), 10.

158. Idong chwadam, "Nae ka isang hanŭn namp'yŏn" [My ideal type of husband], *Sin yŏsŏng* (Dec. 1932), 46.

159. Yi Sŏng-hwan, "Kin'gŭp tongŭi hamnida: Nongch'on yŏsŏng munje e taehayŏ" [An urgent consensus is needed: Regarding the problems of women in the rural villages], *Sin yŏsŏng* (Jan. 1925), 4–9.

160. *Chosŏn ilbo*, 10 May 1929.

161. *Chosŏn ilbo*, 28 May–14 June 1930.

162. Pak Yong-hae, "Sana chojŏl ŭi sahoejŏk koch'al" [A social inquiry into regulating childbirth], *Hak Chi kwang* (Aug. 1930), cited in So Hyŏn-suk, "Ilche singminji sigi chosŏn ŭi ch'ulsan t'ongje tamnon ŭi yŏn'gu," 17.

163. *Chosŏn ilbo*, 28 May, 6 June 1930.

164. *Maeil sinbo*, 28 Dec. 1929.

165. *Tonga ilbo*, 18–19 Nov. 1929.

166. Yi Kwang-su, "Mosŏng" [Motherhood], *Yŏsŏng* (May 1936), 12–13.

167. Nam Sang-hŭi, "Sana chehan" [Birth control], *Kat'ollik chŏngnyŏn* (Feb.–March 1934), 10–11.

168. Chōsen Sōtokufu Gakumyukyoku Shakaika, "Ninsampu hogo ni kan suru chōsa" [A study concerning the protection of expecting and nursing mothers], *Chōsen shakai jigyō* 11 (1933): 53.

169. Pak Ho-jin, "Sana chehan ŭi chŏlgyu" [A call for birth control], *Samch'ŏlli* (April 1930), cited in So Hyŏn-suk, "Ilche singminji sigi chosŏn ŭi ch'ulsan t'ongje tamnon ŭi yŏn'gu," 17.

170. Kim Ki-jŏn, "Anhae e taehan hŭimang, anhae e taehan pulp'yŏn" [Regarding the expectations and inconveniences of a wife], *Sin yŏsŏng* (April 1931), 78–80.

171. "Myŏngnyu puin kwa sana chehan" [Renowned wives and birth control], *Samch'ŏlli* (Sept. 1930), 23–25.

3. THE FEMALE WORKER

1. The author was best known for "Chŏlmŭn ŏmŏni" [The young mother]—a collaborative effort with Pak Hwa-sŏng, Kang Kyŏng-ae, Ch'oe Chŏng-hŭi, and Kim Hye-ja—which was serialized in the journal *Sin kajŏng* [New family] from January to April 1931.

2. By the 1920s, Korean writers split into two ideological camps: national and class literature. Kwŏn Yŏngmin notes that the writers' obsession with class struggle inevitably "took on a fixed pattern with stereotyped main characters" and "focused mostly on the organized struggle and mass resistance of the working class." Kwŏn argues that it is difficult to find works that embody "the positive meaning of labor or the true value of a worker's life." Many proletarian writers joined Kim Ki-jin (1903–1985) and Pak Yŏng-hŭi's (1901–?) Chosŏn p'ŭrollet'aria yesul tongmaeng-Korea artista proleta federatio (KAPF). See Kwŏn Yŏngmin, "Early Twentieth-Century Fiction by Men" in *A History of Korean Literature*, ed. Peter Lee (Cambridge: Cambridge University Press, 2004), 390–411.

3. In Sŭng-hyŏn, *Han'guk nodong sosŏl chŏnjip (1930–1932)* [Collection of Korean working-class novels], vol. 2 (Seoul: Pogosa, 1995), 273.

4. Ibid., 274.

5. Michel Foucault, *Discipline and Punish: The Birth of the Prison*, trans. Alan Sheridan (New York: Vintage Books, 1995), 138.

6. Yi Hyo-jae, *Chosŏnjo sahoe wa kajok* [Society and family in the Chosŏn dynasty] (Seoul: Hanŭl, 2003), 151.

7. Kim Sŏng-hŭi, "Chŏnt'ong sahoe yŏsŏng ŭi sajŏk yŏngyŏk kwa kongjŏk yŏngyŏksŏ ŭi nodong" [Women's labor in the private and public spheres in traditional Korean society], *Han'guk kajŏng kwalli hak hoeji* 20, no. 6 (2002): 25–36.

8. Kim, Sang-ŏk. *Yi Nŭnghwa chŏnjip: Chosŏn yŏsokko* [Complete works of Yi Nŭng-hwa: Korean folk women]. (Seoul: Tosŏ ch'ulp'ansa, 1990), 383.

9. Yi Hyo-jae. *Chosŏnjo sahoe wa kajok*, 157.

10. Kim Sŏng-hŭi, "Chŏnt'ong sahoe yŏsŏng ŭi sajŏk yŏngyŏk kwa kongjŏk yŏngyŏksŏ ŭi nodong," 33.

11. Ibid., 34. The *Taedongpŏp* (universal land tax law) stipulated that for each adult male, the state could levy up to two rolls of cotton cloth, equivalent to twelve *tu* of rice.

12. Ibid., 32.

13. Ibid.

14. Yi Chun-gu, *Chosŏn sidae yŏsŏng ŭi il kwa saenghwal* [Women's work and livelihood during the Chosŏn period] (Seoul: Ch'ŏngnyŏnsa, 1999), 191.

15. Kim Sang-ŏk, *Chosŏn yŏsokko*, 382–83.

16. Kim Sŏng-hŭi, "Chŏnt'ong sahoe yŏsŏng ŭi sajŏk yŏngyŏk kwa kongjŏk yŏngyŏksŏ ŭi nodong," 33–34.

17. Kim Sang-ŏk, *Chosŏn yŏsokko*, 368, 370.

18. Frank M. Brockman, "Some of the Problems of Industrial Education in Korea," *Korean Mission Field* 7 (July 1910): 172.

19. Ibid.

20. *Maeil sinmun*, 8 Feb. 1913.

21. Takahashi Kamekichi. *Gendai chōsen keizai ron* [A discourse on the economy of contemporary Korea] (Tokyo: Chikura Shobō, 1935), 346.

22. H. Rosovsky and K. Ohkawa, "A Century of Japanese Economic Growth," in *The State and Economic Enterprise in Japan: Essays in the Political Economy of Growth*, ed. William W. Lockwood (Princeton, NJ: Princeton University Press, 1965), 77–83.

23. Mikiso Hane, *Modern Japan: A Historical Survey* (Boulder: Westview Press, 1986), 12.

24. Kozo Yamamura, "The Japanese Economy, 1911–1930: Concentration, Conflicts, and Crises," in *Japan in Crisis: Essays on Taishō Democracy*, ed. Bernard S. Silberman and H. D. Harootunian (Ann Arbor: Center for Japanese Studies, University of Michigan, 1999), 300.

25. Ibid., 302.

26. Ibid.

27. More than half a million Koreans participated in nationwide demonstrations. For more on the March First Movement, see Frank Baldwin Jr., "The March First Movement: Korean Challenge and Japanese Response" (Ph.D. diss., Columbia University, 1969).

28. The Chōsen Kaisha Rei (Company law of Korea), drafted in 1910, restricted both Japanese and Koreans from creating modern industrial factories. It was abolished in March 1920.

29. "The Exporters Association Law created export unions [*yushutsu kumiai*] in particular product lines among the medium and smaller enterprises. It authorized these associations to accept products for export on consignment from members, and to control quantities, qualities, and prices of export goods." See Chalmers Johnson, *MITI and the Japanese Miracle: The Growth of Industrial Policy, 1925–1975* (Stanford, CA: Stanford University Press, 1982), 98. Soon-won Park, *Colonial Industrialization and Labor in Korea* (Cambridge, MA: Harvard University Asia Center, 1999).

30. The Nihon Ginkō (Bank of Japan) and six *nōkō ginkō* (regional agricultural and industrial banks), most notably the Chosen shokusan ginkō (Industrial Bank of Chōsen), provided credits and low interest rates to these *zaibatsu* (conglomerates) to construct large modern factories for production. This "mighty trio" monitored all investments with great efficiency and latitude, ensuring that their projects moved "swiftly and sequentially." See Jung-en Woo, *Race to the Swift: State and Finance in Korean Industrialization* (New York: Columbia University Press, 1991), 19–42.

31. Carter Eckert, *Offspring of Empire: The Koch'ang Kims and the Colonial Origins of Korean Capitalism 1876–1945* (Seattle: University of Washington Press, 1991), 49.

32. Ta Chen, "The Labor Situation in Korea" *U.S. Department of Labor Bureau of Labor Statistics* 31, no. 5 (Nov. 1930): 26.

33. The Land Tax Law of 1914 levied a tax on all landowners. See Bruce Cumings, *The Origins of the Korean War*, vol. 1 (Princeton, NJ: Princeton University Press, 1981): 41. The cadastral survey served more as a means of enhancing the legibility of existing land ownership patterns. It was really the operation of economic forces that was most responsible for land-tenure change during the colonial period. These legible blueprints of indigenous practices made it easier for companies like the Oriental Development Company (chartered in 1907) to re-

organize agriculture efficiently in the countryside. See Edwin H. Gragert, *Landownership under Colonial Rule: Korea's Japanese Experience 1900–1935* (Honolulu: University of Hawai'i Press, 1994).

34. The competition for tenancy rights and higher rents transferred more of the production costs to tenants, guaranteeing high profits.

35. Kang Man-gil, *Singminji sigi sahoe kyŏngje han'guksa* [Social and economic history of Korea during the colonial period] (Seoul: Han'gilsa, 1994), 221.

36. Carter J. Eckert, Ki-baik Lee, Young Ick Lew, Michael Robinson, and Edward W. Wagner, *Korea Old and New: A History* (Cambridge, MA: Korea Institute, Harvard University, 1990), 265.

37. Kozo Yamamura, "The Japanese Economy, 1911–1930," 304. By the end of the 1920s, 40 percent of the total rice production being exported to Japan came from Korea. See Bruce F. Johnstone, *Japanese Food Management in World War II* (Stanford, CA: Stanford University Press, 1953), 51.

38. Sang-chul Suh, *Growth and Structural Changes in the Korean Economy, 1910–1940* (Cambridge, MA: Harvard University Press, 1978), 34.

39. The policy of *Nammyŏn pugyang* (Cotton in the south, sheep in the north) was also referred to as *Puksŏn kaech'ŏk* (Cultivating the northern frontiers) and *San'gŭm changryŏ* (Promoting gold mining). See Kang Man-gil, *Singminji sigi sahoe kyŏngje han'guksa*, 294.

40. Andrew J. Grajdanzev, *Modern Korea* (New York: John Day Company, 1944), 93.

41. Gi-Wook Shin, *Peasant Protest and Social Change in Colonial Korea* (Seattle: University of Washington Press, 1996), 45.

42. Bruce Cumings, *Origins of the Korean War*, 43.

43. Kang Man-gil, *Ilcheha pinmin saenghwal yŏn'gu* [A study on the livelihood of the poor under Japanese colonial rule] (Seoul: Ch'angjak kwa pip'yŏng ch'ulp'ansa, 1987), 23, 105.

44. *Tonga ilbo*, 8 Dec. 1926.

45. Chōsen Sōtokufu, *Chōsen no kosaku kankō* [Tenancy customs in Korea] (Keijō, 1930), 146. By the end of 1927, an average household comprised five people. See Ch'oe Kwang-mo, "Chosŏn ŭi nong'ŏp hyŏnsang" [The condition of agriculture in Korea], *Nongmin* (Sept. 1930), 4–5.

46. Kim Il-yong, "Chosŏn nongch'on kyŏngje ŭi chŏnmyŏnjŏk koch'al" [An extensive study of the Korean rural economy], *Nongmin* (June 1931), 11–13.

47. *Chosŏn ilbo*, 12 April 1931. According to a study conducted by Himeno Minoru, 68.1 percent of farmers classified themselves as tenants in 1930, and 48.3 percent of farmers suffered from "spring starvation." See Himeno Minoru, *Chō-*

sen keizai zuhyō [A chart of Korea's economy] (Keijō: Chōsen Tōkei Kyŏkai, 1940), 191. More than 60 percent of farmers could not pay taxes in 1935. See Fuji Chō-jiro, "Chōsen musan Kaikyō kenkyū" [A study of the propertyless class in Korea], *Chōsen oyobi manshū* (May 1935), 95.

48. *Chung'oe ilbo*, 7 June 1925.

49. Chōsen Sōtokufu Kambō Bunshoka Murayama Chijun Chōsa, *Chōsen no genron to sesō* [Views and social conditions in Korea] (Keijō, 1927), 82–83.

50. Bruce Cumings notes that it was in the aftermath of the cadastral survey (1910–1918) that the first great migrations began. With the establishment of legal contracts and land titles, traditional practices of "verbal tenancy rights" became less secure, allowing landowners to misinform peasants. He calls these peasants "hybrids" because they were displaced yet hoped to return to their hometowns after working. Cumings, *Origins of the Korean War*, 32. Through the *enko tokō* system (entry or recruitment through social connections), the first large wave of young Korean men headed to Japan in 1910. With the growing number of workers migrating to Japan, the colonial government sought to curb immigration by requiring applicants to be proficient in Japanese and have more than ten yen in addition to a travel fee and, by 1927, requiring migrants to produce an original copy of their census register and a signature from their district police precinct. Chin-sung Chung, "Colonial Migration from Korea to Japan" (Ph.D. diss., University of Chicago, 1984), 135. *Maeil sinmun*, 8 April 1914. See also Michael Weiner, *Race and Migration in Imperial Japan* (London: Routledge, 1994), 45, 112.

51. Most of the women *ch'ulga* headed to cities such as Keijō (Seoul) to work in textile factories, while their male counterparts sought work in mines and engaged in hard labor. Chōsen Shokusan Ginkō, *Shokugin chōsa geppō* 45 (Keijō, 1942), 20. Mun So-jŏng, "Ilcheha nongch'on kajok e kwanhan yŏn'gu" [A study of the rural village family under Japanese colonial rule], in *Han'guk sahoesa yŏn'guhoe nonmunjip* [A collection of articles by the Korean social history research association], vol. 12 (Seoul: Munhak kwa chisŏngsa, 1988), 96–98.

52. Of the 150,000 or so migrants, 69,644 farmers headed to Japan or Manchuria to find work. *Tonga ilbo*, 12 April 1927. Of those *inong* (farmers who were leaving permanently), 73.4 percent left for a place other than their hometowns to find work (i.e., at a factory, in commerce, or in other miscellaneous employment), 16.9 percent went to Japan, 2.1 percent to Manchuria, and 0.7 percent to Siberia. See Chōsen Sōtokufu, *Chōsen no shōsaku shūkan* [Tenanting practices of Koreans] (Keijō, 1929), 40–41.

53. A higher percentage of males migrated to faraway places like Manchuria

or Japan, whereas female migrants to cities outnumbered males by the 1920s. Kwŏn T'ae-hwan, "Ilche sidae ŭi tosihwa" [Urbanization during the Japanese colonial period], in *Han'guk ŭi sahoe wa munhak* [Korean society and literature], vol. 11 (Seoul: Han'guk chŏngsin munhwa yŏn'guwŏn, 1990), 270.

54. Chōsen Nōson Shakai Eisei Chōsakai, *Chōsen no nōson eisei* [Sanitation in Korean farming villages] (Tokyo: Iwanami Shoten, 1940), 143–45. Many of those leaving the village were young; ages ranged from twelve to sixteen years. Even in 1935, the *Fusan shinpo* [Pusan daily] noted the impact of the "spring starvation" crisis and natural disasters on the rural family. Apart from the forty-six reported broken marriages in town, the police precincts reported more than 23,332 household members "leaving the home unannounced," and 2,069 leaving home as *dekasegi* (working away from home). *Fusan shinpo*, 3 March 1935.

55. Han In-t'aek, "Chŏgŭn yŏgong" [Young factory girls], *Pip'an* (April 1932), cited in An Sŭng-hyŏn, ed., *Han'guk nodong sosŏl chŏnjip* [Collection of Korean labor novels], vol. 2 (Seoul: Pogosa, 1995): 293–96.

56. Kim Un-gak, "Uri nongch'on ŭi kaejo" [Reconstructing our rural villages], *Kaebyŏk* (April 1922), 98–101.

57. Yi Sŏng-hwan, "Chosŏn ŭi nongch'on yŏsŏng" [The rural women of Korea], *Chosŏn nongmin* (March 1927), 2.

58. In 1933, the *Tonga ilbo* noted that there were 266 waifs and 164 orphans wandering the streets of Seoul. *Tonga ilbo*, 6 April 1933.

59. Countless newspaper accounts reported that a growing number of farmers resorted to selling young girls to brothel masters and restaurant owners in the cities, as well as to customers in distant places like Manchuria. *Tonga ilbo*, 26 Nov. 1924. Ae Hyang-nyu, "Nongch'on ch'ŏnyŏ p'allinŭn imyŏn" [The inside story of selling a farm girl], *Sil saenghwal* (Oct. 1931), 29–31.

60. *Tonga ilbo*, 2 July 1925, 24 Nov. 1925. *Yu-gwak*, red-light districts, were established in Pusan (1902), Inch'ŏn (1902), Wŏnsan (1903), and Kyŏngsŏng (1904). Two red-light districts were set up in Kyŏngsŏng (Keijō), at Sinch'ŏng (Shinmachi) and Sillimdong. The *Tōkanfu* (resident-general) sought to regulate prostitution by maintaining official "licensed" districts where *kongch'ang* (licensed prostitutes) could engage in their trade after paying a union fee. Although the ordinance on public prostitution promulgated in 1908 and revised in 1916 set the legal age at seventeen, many peasant girls, driven by poverty and unable to afford a license, engaged in illicit prostitution (i.e., working as a *chakpu* or barmaid). Yamashida Yŏng-ae, "Singminji chibae wa kongch'ang chedo ŭi chŏn'-gae" [Colonial control and the development of the prostitution system], *Sahoe*

wa yŏksa 51 (1997): 159–60. According to one reporter, a Japanese prostitute charged four times more than a Korean prostitute. *Tonga ilbo*, 15 Nov. 1920.

61. *Tonga ilbo*, 6 April 1922.

62. Angus Hamilton, *Korea* (New York: Charles Scribner's Sons, 1904), 48, 121.

63. Pae Sŏng-yŏng, "Chibang ŭi nongch'on p'ungsŭp" [Customs of farming villages in the countryside], *Nongmin* (June 1932), 55–57.

64. *Tonga ilbo*, 17 Sept. 1933. Another journalist, shocked to see so many women in the field, notes, "I have never seen so many female bodies!" *Tonga ilbo*, 25 June 1932. Ōno Tamotsu also noted that because of the absence of their husbands, wives would harvest the rice during *nong pŏn-gi* (farmers' busy season). Ōno Tamotsu, "Chōsen nōgyō no jittaiteki kenkyū" [A study of the actual conditions of agriculture in Korea], *Manshū gyōsei gakkai, ronsō dai 4 shu* (Keijō, 1941): 194–95.

65. Han Hŭg-u, "Nongch'on puin ŭn kodalp'ŭda" [It is weary being a wife in a farming village], *Yŏsŏng* (Jan. 1940), 96.

66. Grajdanzev, *Modern Korea*, 152.

67. "Injogyŏn kwa nongch'ŏn" [The rural village and rayon], *Nongmin* (June 1930), 29.

68. *Tonga ilbo*, 10 Oct. 1932.

69. Pak Hwa-sŏng, "Hankwi" [Drought], *Cho kwang* (Nov. 1935), cited in *1920–1930-yŏndae minjung munhaksŏn* [Selection of minjung literature from 1920 to 1930], ed. Chu Chong and Yi Chŏng-ŭn, vol. 1 (Seoul: T'apch'ulp'ansa, 1990), 101–14.

70. Ōno Tamotsu, "Chōsen nōgyō no jittaiteki kenkyū" 347–48.

71. *Tonga ilbo*, 19 July 1933.

72. *Tonga ilbo*, 14 June 1935.

73. Yi Hye-suk, "Nongch'on ŭi yŏsŏngdŭl" [Women in the rural villages], *Nongmin* (May 1930), 35.

74. Many young girls who were not able to enter the factories worked as maids or *ch'imo* (seamstresses). Kwŏn T'ae-hwan, "Ilche sidae ŭi tosihwa," 27.

75. Thomas Dublin, *Transforming Women's Work: New England Lives in the Industrial Revolution* (Ithaca, NY: Cornell University Press, 1994).

76. Tōkanfu, *Tōkanfu tōkei nenpō* [Annual statistical report of the residency-general of Korea] (Keijō, 1910). Chōsen Sōtokufu, *Chōsen Sōtokufu tōkei nenpō* [Statistical yearbook of the Government-General of Korea] (Keijō, 1919–1940). It was only after 1922 that women workers were separately tabulated as a category in Government-General records.

77. Chōsen Sōtokufu, *Chōsen Sōtokufu tōkei nenpō*, 1922, 1936; Takahashi, *Gendai chōsen keizai ron*, 430.

78. Keijō Shōkō Kaigisho, *Keijō ni okeru kōjō chōsa* [A survey of factories in Seoul] (Keijō, 1937), 115–16.

79. For a good example of the feminizing of industries, see Kathleen Canning, *Languages of Labor and Gender: Female Factory Work in Germany, 1850–1914* (Ithaca, NY: Cornell University Press, 1996).

80. Yi Chŏng-ok, "Ilcheha kongŏp nodong esŏ ŭi minjok kwa sŏng, 1910–1945" [Race and sex in industrial labor under Japanese colonial rule 1910–1945] (Ph.D. diss., Seoul National University, 1990), 275.

81. *Chosŏn sinmun*, 2 July 1930.

82. Chōsen Sōtokufu, *Kokusei chōsa hōkoku* [A study of the state of affairs of Korea: A report] (Keijō, 1935), cited in Sŏ, Hyŏng-sil, "Singminji sidae yŏsŏng nodong undong e kwanhan yŏn'gu: 1930-yŏndae chŏnban'gi komu chep'um chejo'ŏp kwa chesa'ŏp ŭl chungsim ŭro" [A study of the women's labor movement under Japanese colonialism: Centering on the rubber and silk-reeling industry during the first half of the 1930s] (Ph.D. diss., Ewha Womans University, 1989), 36–38.

83. Chōsen Shōkō Kaigisho, *Chōsenjin shōkkō ni kan suru kōsatsu* [An inquiry into Korean commerce/industry] (Keijō, 1936), 27.

84. Ibid.

85. *Chosŏn ilbo*, 14 Feb. 1925.

86. "Yakchin hanŭn chŏ chejo kong'ŏp sahoe pangmun'gi," 114.

87. "Sŏmsŏm oksuro tchanŭn pangjik yŏhakkyo" [Weaving with delicate hands: A woman's textile school], *Samch'ŏlli* (Jan. 1936), 141.

88. *Sin tonga* (June 1932), 68.

89. Yi Sŏng-hwan, "Puin kwa chigŏp chŏnsŏn" [Women and the work front], *Sin yŏsŏng* (March 1932), 13.

90. Ibid.

91. The female workers at Sawada Silk Reeling Factory had to work for thirteen hours or more a day to earn twenty to thirty *chŏn*. *Tonga ilbo*, 12 Dec. 1924.

92. *Chosŏn ilbo*, 12 Feb. 1925.

93. "Chitpalp'in chŏngmi yŏjikkong ŭi sogim ŏmnŭn kobaek kwa hoso" [An honest confession and complaint by a trampled-down rice-polishing female factory worker], *Pyŏlgŏn'gon* (June 1931), 28; *Tonga ilbo*, 1 Jan. 1925.

94. *Chosŏn ilbo*, 2 Feb. 1925.

95. Keijō Shōkō Kaigisho. *Keijō ni okeru kōjō chōsa*, 41–42.

96. See Chōsen Ginkō, *Chōsen kezai nempō* [The annual economic report of Korea] (Seoul, 1948).

97. Pyŏng Ch'ŏl [pseud.], "Nodongja ka bon puin nodongja ŭi saenghwal munje" [The problems of livelihood among married woman workers seen through the eyes of a male worker], *Pip'an* (March 1933), 64–65.

98. Chōsen Sōtokufu, *Chōsen Sōtokufu tōkei nenpō*, 1929, 192–97.

99. Kwŏn T'ae-hwan, "Ilche sidae ŭi tosihwa," 27.

100. "Sonyŏn chikkong" [A juvenile factory worker], *Chosŏn chi kwang* (June 1922), 366–74.

101. The organization of time and control of time space was an important aspect of Fordist production. See David Harvey, *The Condition of Postmodernity* (Cambridge, MA: Blackwell Publishers, 1990), 125–29.

102. Chŏng Un-bing, "Yangmal chigŏp ŭi chaeg'ŭi" [Dispute at a socks company], *Samch'ŏlli* (May 1931), 352.

103. There were 440 rice mills among 1,352 factories. Chōsen Sōtokufu, *Chōsen Sōtokufu tōkei nempō*, 1919, n.p.

104. Chitpalp'in chŏngmi yŏjikkong ŭi sogim ŏmnŭn kobaek kwa hoso," 28

105. Ibid.

106. Keijōfu Sangyō Chōsakai, *Orimono kōgyō ni kansuru chōsa* [A survey of the weaving industry] (Keijō, 1937), 69.

107. Kawai Akitake. *Chōsen kōgyō no gen dankai* [The present stage of Korean industries] (Keijō: Tōyō keizai shinpōsha Keijō shikyoku, 1943), 273–75.

108. Textile industries included *meriyasu* (knit fabric), cotton spinning, weaving, twisted yarn, cloth, dyeing, and processed cotton. Of the 2,459 workers profiled, the shortest time a worker stayed was three months or less (17.3 percent) and the longest was four or more years (9.4 percent). Yuk Ji-su, "Seishi rōdō ni tsuite" [Regarding silk-reeling labor], *Chōsen Sōtokufu chōsa geppō* 9, no. 6 (Sept. 1938): 27–28; 34–35.

109. *Tonga ilbo*, 25 June 1927; In the case of England, based on an 1851 census, 27 percent of the female workers toiling in the seven Lancashire districts were married. Margaret Hewett, *Wives and Mothers in Victorian Industry* (London: Rockcliff, 1958), 14.

110. The workers declined from 32 percent in 1937 to 31.5 percent in 1940. Female workers shifted to munitions factories or chemical industries. See Chōsen Sōtokufu, *Chōsen Sōtokufu tōkei nenpō*, 1937–44.

111. Hosoi Wakizō, *Jokō aishi* [The pitiful history of female factory workers] (Tokyo: Kaizōsha, 1925), 25–29. In the cotton industry, female workers were assigned to carding, drawing, rovering, and spinning, while their male counterparts would work with the rollers or in the transportation sector.

112. One should note, however, that Toyoda's N-type (1920) looms or his

G-type (1927) automatic loom, though popular in Japan, were not necessary in Korean factories because of cheap labor. The looms in Korean factories were much inferior in speed and quality to those in Japan. Kojima Tsunehisa, *Hataraku josei hyakunen no ayumi* [The course of one hundred years of working women] (Tokyo: Kawade Shōbōshinsa, 1983), 3.

113. Yuk Ji-su, "Seishi rōdō ni tsuite," 27–28.

114. Han In-t'aek, "Chŏgŭn yŏgong" [Young factory girls], *Pip'an* (April 1932), cited in An Sŭng-hyŏn, ed., *Han'guk nodong sosŏl chŏnjip*, 293–96.

115. By the 1920s, Yi's Korean-style rubber shoes outsold *mit'uri* (hemp-cord sandals) and *namaksin* (wooden clogs worn during the rainy season). Yi, working as an errand boy at a Japanese sundry goods shop in P'yŏngyang, had tried peddling Japanese rubber shoes without much success. Puzzled at the lack of interest from Korean consumers, Yi decided to sojourn in Japan and learn firsthand how to set up a rubber factory. By the early 1920s, entrepreneurs started advertising rubber shoes designed by Yi in the newspapers. Kim T'ae-su, *Kkot kach'i p'iŏ maehokk'e hara: sinmun kwanggoro bon kŭndae ŭi p'unggyŏng* [Bloom like a flower, make it enchanting: Looking at the modern landscape through the lens of newspaper advertisements] (Seoul: Hwangsojari, 2005), 34–35.

116. Ibid., 36.

117. *Chosŏn nongmin* (Oct. 1929): 15–16.

118. "Kyŏngsŏng yŏsŏng yŏjikkong t'onggye" [Statistics of female factory workers in Seoul], *Chosŏn chi kwang* 8 (May 1928): 51.

119. Workers often had dark bruises on their arms. Keijōfu, *Gomu kōgyō ni kansuru chōsa* [A study of the rubber industry] (Keijō, 1935), 63, 68.

120. In 1929 there were 2,104 nurseries in Korea. Sin Yŏng-suk, "Ilcheha han'guk yŏsŏng sahoesa yŏn'gu" [A social history of Korean women under Japanese colonial rule], (Ph.D. diss., Ewha Womans University, 1989), 146.

121. "Komin ŭi kobaek: ŏnŭ puin kija ŭi ilgi" [An agonized confession: Diary of a certain married woman journalist], *Sin kajŏng* (Feb. 1935), 33–36.

122. Yi Chŏk-hyo, "Ch'ongdongwŏn" [General mobilization], *Pip'an* 3 (Aug. 1931), cited in An Sŭng-hyŏn, ed., *Han'guk nodong sosŏl chŏnjip*, 213–37. The reporter profiled a household where the husband took care of the infant while the wife worked at a rice mill. The husband had been laid off and could not find any work. The author notes: "The [father] feeds and holds the baby. . . . When would you have this kind of comfort [and] luxury?" Also see "Chitp'alp'in chŏngmi yŏjikkong ŭi sogim ŏmnŭn kobaek kwa hoso," 28

123. *Tonga ilbo*, 28 July 1933.

124. *Chosŏn chung'ang ilbo*, 10 Sept. 1933.

125. Keijōfu, *Gomu kōgyō ni kansuru chōsa*, 63.

126. *Tonga ilbo*, 22 Jan. 1930.

127. *Tonga ilbo*, 4 July 1935.

128. Yuk Ji-su, "Seishi rōdō ni tsuite," 34–35.

129. *Tonga ilbo*, 1 Sept. 1932.

130. U Sun-ok, "Ŏnŭ chesa yŏgong ilgi" [A diary of some silk-weaving factory girl], *Pyŏlgŏn'gon* (May 1930), 72–73.

131. Chigŏp sonyŏdŭl ŭi kaji kaji sŏlum" [Juvenile girl factory workers' various griefs], *Ŏrini* (June 1929), 14

132. *Chosŏn chung'ang ilbo*, 9 April 1930. At the Tongyang Reeling factory, even when the workers went on strike, apprentices remained on the job, knowing that they would have to start their apprenticeships over again or be fired. *Chosŏn sinmun*, 8 Dec. 1930.

133. *Tonga ilbo*, 1 Sept. 1932.

134. "Chigŏp sonyŏdŭl ŭi kaji kaji sŏlum," 14.

135. "Kongjang sonyŏn sunbanggi" [My account of my visit to a boys' factory], *Ŏrini* (June 1929), 24.

136. *Tonga ilbo*, 3 Nov. 1926.

137. Chōsen Sōtokufu, *Chōsen Sōtokufu chōsa geppō* [Korean Government-General monthly investigation report] (May 1931), 111.

138. Minami Manshū Tetsudō Kabushiki Gaisha Keizai Chōsa Dai ichibu (Hen), *Chōsenjin rōdōsha ippan jijō* [The general review of Korean workers] (Keijō: Tairen, 1933), 71.

139. *Tonga ilbo*, 30 Nov. 1926

140. Raymond Williams, *The Country and the City* (New York: Oxford University Press, 1973), 271.

4. DISCOURSING IN NUMBERS

1. *Chosŏn ilbo*, 16 May 1931, 28–31 May 1931, 12 June 1931. Muho Hyang-in [pseud.], "Ŭlmildae ŭi ch'e kongnyŏ yŏryu t'usa Kang Chu-ryong hoekyŏn'gi" [An account of my meeting with Kang Chu-ryong, Ŭlmildae's female factory worker and champion], *Tonggwang* (July 1931), cited in Yŏsŏngsa yŏn'gu moim kilbak sesang, *20-segi yŏsŏng sagŏnsa* [Historical women's events during the twentieth century] (Seoul: Yŏsŏng sinmunsa, 2001), 99.

2. She rejected the idea of suicide because the public would interpret the act as a private atonement for her husband's death. When Ch'oe Chŏn-bin (five years

her junior) joined an independence group, he became ill and died in her arms. Her in-laws had branded her the "bitch who killed her husband," and sent her to jail. *Chosŏn ilbo*, 16 May 1931.

3. Suzuki Masafumi, *Chōsen keizai no gen dankai* [The current stage of the Korean economy] (Keijō: Teikoku Chihō Gyōsei Gakkai Chōsen Honbu, 1938), 193.

4. Ōyama Chōyō, "Nishibu keijō ni okeru kōjō rōdōsha no chōsa: Itashiki jokō no aiwa" [A study of factory workers in western Keijō: The pitiful stories of female factory workers], *Chōsen jiron* (April 1927), 20.

5. Bruce Cumings, "Northeast Asian Political Economy," *International Organization* 38, no. 1 (Winter 1984): 12.

6. *Tonga ilbo*, 30 April 1940.

7. "Komin ŭi kobaek" [An agonized confession], *Sin kajŏng* (March 1935), 33–36. Murakami Nobuhiko, *Meiji joseishi* [The history of Meiji women], vol. 1 (Tokyo: Rironsha, 1971), 168–71.

8. Chŏng Yo-sŏp, "Ilcheha yŏsŏng undong ŭi saeroun chŏn'gae" [New developments in the women's movement under Japanese colonial rule], in *Han'guk yŏsŏng tongnip undongsa* [The history of the Korean women's independence movement], ed. 3.1 yŏsŏng tongjihoe munhwabu p'yŏn (Seoul, 1980), 312.

9. Hosoi Wakizō, *Jokō aishi* [The pitiful history of female factory workers] (Tokyo: Kaizōsha, 1925), 145.

10. Yi Puk-myŏng, "Ch'ulgŭn chŏngji" [Stoppage of work], *Munhak kŏsŏl* (Dec. 1932), cited in An Sŭng-hyŏn, ed., *Han'guk nodong sosŏl chŏnjip* [Collection of Korean labor novels], vol. 2 (Seoul: Pogosa, 1995), 428–36. In this novel, the author highlights the daily fears that the factory might close down because the tank blows up.

11. Song Kye-wŏl, "Kongjang sosik" [News from a factory], *Sin yŏsŏng* (Dec. 1932), cited in An Sŭng-hyŏn, *Han'guk nodong sosŏl chŏnjip*, vol. 2, 273.

12. *Tonga ilbo* serialized the work in 1933.

13. Kang Kyŏng-ae, "In'gan munje" [The human problem], in Kim Sŭng-ok, ed., *Han'guk hyŏndae munhak chŏnjip* [A collection of Korean modern literature], vol. 11 (Seoul: Samsŏng ch'ulp'ansa, 1978), 222.

14. Takahashi notes that 47 percent of female workers in the silk-reeling industry worked for less than one year. Takahashi Kamekichi, *Gendai chōsen keizai ron* [A discourse on the economy of contemporary Korea] (Tokyo: Chikura Shobō, 1935): 428.

15. *Sin tonga* (June 1932), 69.

16. *Tonga ilbo*, 8 Aug. 1939. Female workers suffered from physical deformities, delayed puberty, dysmenorrhea, and anemia as a result of the long and in-

tense hours. For a comparative view, see Gita Sen, "The Sexual Division of Labor and the Working Class: Towards a Conceptual Synthesis of Class Relations and the Subordination of Women," *Review of Radical Political Economics* 12, no. 2 (Summer 1980): 76–86.

17. *Chosŏn chung'ang ilbo,* 2 July 1935.

18. Kojima Tsunehisa, *Hataraku jōsei hyakunen no ayumi* [The course of one hundred years of working women] (Tokyo: Kawade Shōbōshinsa, 1983): 40.

19. *Tonga ilbo,* 1 Jan. 1925.

20. Ibid., 1 Aug. 1936; Yi Puk-myŏng, "Chilso piryo kongjang" [The nitrogen fertilizer factory], *Chosŏn ilbo,* 29–31 May 1932. In this short story, Munho, the protagonist, suffers from various ailments while working at a chemical factory.

21. *Tonga ilbo,* 3 Nov. 1926.

22. *Chosŏn ilbo,* 2 Jan. 1931.

23. *Chosŏn chung'ang ilbo,* 2 July 1936.

24. In'gansa p'yŏnjipsil pŏnyŏk, ed., *Ŏnŭ yŏgong ŭi norae* [A factory girl's song] (Seoul: In'gansa, 1983), 105.

25. Andrew Grajdanzev, *Modern Korea* (New York: International Secretariat, Institute of Pacific Relations, 1944), 259.

26. Ishihara Yoshiharu, "Nansen chihō ni okeru rōdō jihō no dōkō to rōdō kanri no iro mondai" [The trends in the condition of labor in southern Korea and the various problems of labor management], *Chōsen shakai jigyō* 6 (Keijō, 1941), 28, 42.

27. Chōsen Sōtokufu Gakumukyoku Shakaika, *Kōjō oyobi kōzan ni okeru rōdō jōkyō chōsa* [A study of the labor conditions in factories and mines] (Keijō, 1933): 89.

28. U Sun-ok, "Ŏnŭ chesa yŏgong ilgi" [A diary of a textile factory girl], *Pyŏlgŏn'gon* 5 (1930): 72–73.

29. "Sigol kyesin ŏmŏnim kke" [To my dear mother in the countryside], *Ŏrini* (Dec. 1930), 38.

30. Arno Pearse, *The Cotton Industry of Japan and China* (Manchester: International Cotton Federation, 1929), 102–3.

31. *Chosŏn ilbo,* 24 April 1930.

32. *Yŏsŏng* (July 1938), 86.

33. Yi Yŏ-sŏng and Kim Se-yong, *Sutcha chosŏn yŏn'gu* [Research on statistics in Korea] (Kyŏngsŏng: Segwangsa, 1931), 84–87, 98–100.

34. *Chosŏn ilbo,* 15 Oct. 1934.

35. *Tonga ilbo,* 18 Nov. 1937.

36. Keijō Shōkō Kaigisho, *Keijō ni okeru kōjō chōsa* [A survey of factories in Seoul] (Keijō, 1939), 111.

37. *Tonga ilbo*, 10 Nov. 1933.

38. *Tonga ilbo*, 25 June 1927. In one labor dispute case at the Kyŏngsŏng chesa factory, female workers demanded that managers stop using physical violence. Also see *Tonga ilbo*, 8 Jan. 1931, 9 Aug. 1932, 28 Sept. 1933.

39. *Chosŏn sibo*, 30 July 1931.

40. U Sun-ok, "Ŏnŭ chesa yŏgong ilgi," 72–73.

41. *Chung'oe ilbo*, 11 Aug. 1930.

42. *Tonga ilbo*, 2 Oct. 1929.

43. Ibid., 9 May 1926.

44. Ibid., 3 Nov. 1929.

45. Ibid., 18 Feb. 1936.

46. Yu Chin-ho, "Yŏjikkong" [Female factory workers], *Chosŏn ilbo*, 1–24 March 1931, cited in An Sŭng-hyŏn, *Han'guk nodong sosŏl chŏnjip*, vol. 2, 151–87.

47. Kim T'ae-su, *Kkot kach'i p'iŏ maehokk'e hara: Sinmun kwanggoro bon kŭndae ŭi p'unggyŏng* [Bloom like a flower, make it enchanting: Looking at the modern landscape through the lens of newspaper advertisements] (Seoul: Hwang-sojari, 2005):41.

48. An Sŭng-hyŏn, *Han'guk nodong sosŏl chŏnjip*, vol. 2, 273–74.

49. Pak Hwa-sŏng, "Ch'usŏk chŏnya" [The evening before the harvest moon festival], *Chosŏn mundan* (Jan. 1925), cited in *1920–1930-yŏndae minjung munhaksŏn* [Selection of minjung literature from 1920 to 1930], ed. Chu Chong and Yi Chŏng-ŭn, vol. 2 (Seoul: T'apch'ulp'ansa, 1990), 91–102. Other representative works by Pak include *Paekhwa* (White flower, 1932), *Hongsu chŏnhu* (Before and after the flood, 1934), and *Kohyang ŏmnŭn saramdŭl* (People without a native land, 1936).

50. Kang Kyŏng-ae, "In'gan munje," 202, 221.

51. *Tonga ilbo*, 8 June 1927.

52. "Sigol kyesin ŏmŏnim kke," 38.

53. Chōsen Sōtokufu Gakumukyoku Shakaika, *Kōjō oyobi kōzan ni okeru rōdō jōkyō chōsa*, 112.

54. Keijō Teikoku Daigaku Eisei Chōsabu Hen, *Dobakumin no seikatsu eisei* [Sanitation in the life of mud dwellers] (Keijō, 1942), 43–45.

55. *Chōsen Orimono Kyōkai*, "Chōsen orimono kyōkai shi" [A history of the Korean textile association], vol. 11 (Aug. 1939): 25.

56. *Tonga ilbo*, 22 March 1923.

57. Kim Hyo-dong, "Han'guk myŏn pangjik kong'ŏp ŭi sachŏk kochal" [An

investigation on the success of the cotton textile industry in Korea], in *Kyŏng jesa munhŏn charyo* [A history of the Korean economy: Documentary records], vol. 3 (Sept. 1972), 39.

58. Yuk Ji-su, "Seishi rōdō ni tsuite" [Regarding silk-reeling labor], *Chōsen Sōtokufu chōsa geppō* 9, no. 6 (Sept. 1938): 11.

59. Chōsen Sōtokufu, *Chōsen Sōtokufu chōsa geppō*, July 1938, cited in An Yŏn-sŏn, "Han'guk singminji chabonjuuihwa kwajŏng esŏ yŏsŏng nodong ŭi sŏng-gyŏk e kwanhan yŏn'gu: 1930-yŏndae pangjik kong'ŏp ŭl chungsim ŭro" [Research on the characteristics of women's labor during the formation of colonial capitalism in Korea: Focusing on the textile industries during the 1930s] (master's thesis, Ewha Womans University, 1988.

60. *Chosŏn chung'ang ilbo*, 2 July 1936. According to Pak Ho-jin, a reporter for the *Kunuhoe*, more than two hundred female workers lived in unsanitary conditions in the dormitories at the Chosŏn Textile Factory and "seven or eight workers would have to share a room that is the size of two tatami." Pak Ho-jin, "Yŏjikkong pangmun'gi" [Observations on my visit to a female factory], *Kunuhoe* (1929), 72.

61. In the Kyŏngsŏng Taech'ang Textile Company strike, strikers demanded that they be allowed to spend time outside the factory gate. *Tonga ilbo*, 2 June 1933.

62. *Tonga ilbo*, 20 Feb. 1936.

63. Yuk Ji-su, "Seishi rōdō ni tsuite," 11.

64. Kyŏngsŏng Pangjik Chusik Hoesa, *Kyŏngsŏng pangjik osimnyŏn* [Fifty years of Kyŏngsŏng textiles] (Seoul, 1969), 187–88.

65. *Tonga ilbo*, 25 June 1927.

66. Ibid., 24 Jan. 1930, 5 April 1935; *Chosŏn chung'ang ilbo*, 9 July 1936.

67. An Sŭng-hyŏn, *Han'guk nodong sosŏl chŏnjip*, vol. 2, 275. In the letter to her sister "S," Kim Ok-bum notes that female workers who escaped from the factory often wrote letters asking the factory owner to return their belongings. However, not only did the owner keep their belongings, but they did not get a penny of the wages the company owed them for that month.

68. Han In-t'aek, "Chŏgŭn yŏgong" [Young factory girls], *Pip'an* (April 1932), cited in An Sŭng-hyŏn, ed., *Han'guk nodong sosŏl chŏnjip*, vol. 2, 293–96.

69. James C. Scott, *Weapons of the Weak: Everyday Forms of Resistance* (New Haven, CT: Yale University Press, 1985).

70. Kim Yun-hwan, *Han'guk nodong undongsa* [A history of the Korean labor movement], vol. 1 (Seoul: Ch'ŏngsa, 1982), 17.

71. *Chosŏn sinmun*, 4 Feb. 1938.

72. *Tonga ilbo*, 3 Nov. 1926.

73. Ibid.

74. Keijō Shokugyō Shōkaijo, *Keijō shokugyō shōkaijo shohō* [Keijō employment agency's report] (Keijō, 1940), 64–65.

75. *Tonga ilbo*, 27 Oct. 1929.

76. Chōsen Sōtokufu Keimukyoku, *Saikin ni okeru chōsen chian jōkyō* [The recent conditions of the public security in Korea] (Keijō, 1933), 142.

77. *Chosŏn ilbo*, 5 Nov. 1931.

78. Kim Ok-yŏ, "Ton ŏpsido paehol manhan nodong yahak e issŏtsu myŏn" [If there was a good enough night school for workers to study for free], *Sin yŏsŏng* (Jan. 1926), 14–15.

79. *Kyŏngsŏng ilbo*, 26 Jan. 1936.

80. *Tonga ilbo*, 19 Nov. 1935.

81. Chōsen Sōtokufu Gakumukyoku Shakaika, *Kōjō oyobi kōzan ni okeru rōdō jōkyō chōsa* [A study of the labor conditions in factories and mines] (Keijō, 1930), 376.

82. *Chosŏn sinmun*, 16 June 1937

83. Ibid.

84. Chōsen Sōtokufu, *Chōsen Sōtokufu jikyoku taisaku chōsakai shimon tōshin-sho* [The final report of the Chōsen Government-General commission on policy for the current situation] (Keijō, 1938), cited in Kang I-su, "1930-yŏndae myŏnbang tae kiŏp yŏsŏng nodongja ŭi sangt'ae e kwanhan yŏn'gu: Nodong kwajŏng kwa nodong t'ongje rŭl chungsim ŭro" [Research on the conditions of female workers in the large-scale cotton industry during the 1930s: Focusing on the labor process and labor control] (Ph.D. dissertation, Ewha Womans University, 1992), 132.

85. Ibid.

86. Chōsen Sōtokufu, Keimukyoku, *Saikin ni okeru chōsen chian jōkyō*, 139–52. *Chosŏn ilbo* questioned the conservative numbers offered by the Government-General office. According to their surveys, from 1920 through 1926, there were 1,260 strikes and 325,881 participants. *Chosŏn ilbo*, 20 July 1927. These protests occurred even though the Peace Preservation Law of May 1925 "provided the police with broadened powers to control political life in the colony." Carter J. Eckert, et. al., *Korea Old and New* (Cambridge, MA: Korea Institute, Harvard University, 1990), 299.

87. Chōsen Sōtokufu Keimukyoku, *Saikin ni okeru chōsen chian jōkyō*, 139–52.

88. Michel Foucault, *The History of Sexuality*, trans. Robert Hurley (New York: Vintage Books, 1990), 95–96.

89. William H. Sewell Jr., "Artisans, Factory Workers, and the Formation of

the French Working Class, 1789–1848," in *Working-Class Formation: Nineteenth Century Patterns in Western Europe and the United States*, ed. Ira Katznelson and Aristide R. Zolberg (Princeton, NJ: Princeton University Press, 1986), 68.

90. *Keijō nippō*, 2 June 1928.

91. *Tonga ilbo*, 19 Nov. 1924; *Chosŏn ilbo*, 19 Nov. 1924.

92. *Tonga ilbo*, 31 Aug. 1932, 2 Sept. 1932.

93. *Chosŏn ilbo*, 16 May 1931–12, June 1931.

94. *Sangyō rōdō jihō* [Industry and labor report] (Oct. 1931, rpt. Tokyo: Hōsei Daigaku Shuppankyoku, 1986), 81.

95. Ibid.

96. Ibid.

97. *Tonga ilbo*, 29 Oct. 1933; *Chosŏn ilbo*, 29 Oct. 1933.

98. *Tonga ilbo*, 9 July 1923, 17 July 1923, 18 July 1923.

99. *Chosŏn ilbo*, 20 May 1931.

100. Song Yŏng, "Osuhyang," *Chosŏn ilbo*, 1–26 March 1931.

101. Yi Puk-myŏng, "Yŏgong" [The factory girl], *Sin kyedan* (March 1933), cited in An Sŭng-hyŏn, ed., *Han'guk nodong sosŏl chŏnjip*, vol. 3, 40–52.

102. *Chosŏn chung'ang ilbo*, 18 Feb. 1932.

103. *P'yŏngnam maeil sinmun*, 2 Aug. 1933.

104. *Sin tonga* (June 1932), 71.

105. Yi Chŏk-hyo "Ch'ongdongwŏn" [General mobilization], *Pip'an* (March 1931), cited in An Sŭng-hyŏn, ed., *Han'guk nodong sosŏl chŏnjip*, vol. 2, 213–37.

106. *Tonga ilbo*, 31 April 1931.

107. Pak Hwa-sŏng, "Tu sŭnggaek kwa kabang" [Two passengers and a bag], *Chosŏn munhak* (Oct. 1933), 198–99.

108. E. Patricia Tsurumi, *Factory Girls: Women in the Thread Mills of Meiji Japan* (Princeton, NJ: Princeton University Press, 1990), 89.

109. *Chosŏn ilbo*, 4 Jan. 1925.

110. *Tonga ilbo*, 11 July 1921.

111. "Yŏsŏng munje e taehan yŏsŏng chwadamhoe" [A woman's roundtable discussion regarding the woman's problem], *Sin tonga* (April 1932), 74.

112. Yi Hyŏn-gyŏng, "Kyŏngje sangt'ae ŭi pyŏnch'ŏn kwa yŏsŏng ŭi chiwi" [Changes in the economic conditions and the position of women], *Hyŏndae p'yŏngnon* (May 1927), 51–56.

113. Kim Chŏng-il, "Kŭnse chosŏn ŭi sahoe kyegŭp" [The social classes of contemporary Korea], *Sin tonga* (Oct. 1934), 52.

114. Kim Yun-gyŏng, "Puin chigŏp munje" [The problem of the working woman], *Sin yŏsŏng* (Nov. 1924), 33–38.

115. Kim Ŭn-hŭi, "Musan punyŏ ŭi undong ŭn ŏdaero kanya" [Where is the proletarian women's movement going], *Samch'ŏlli* (Feb. 1932), 104.

116. Chŏng Ch'un, "Puin haebang undong taehaya" [Regarding the liberation movement of women], *Kye* (Aug. 1923), 22–30. Socialists used two important texts—Engels's *Origins of the Family* (1884) and Bebel's *Woman under Socialism* (1879)—to analyze the woman question. These texts influenced the debates among members of the Second International. See June Hannam and Karen Hunt, *Socialist Women: Britain, 1880s to 1920s* (New York, Routledge, 2002), 17.

117. *Sidae ilbo*, 16 May 1924.

118. Ibid.

119. *Tonga ilbo*, 20–21 April 1927.

120. Hwang Sin-dŏk, "Chosŏn puin undong ŭi kwagŏ hyŏnje mit changnae" [The Korean women's movement's past, present, and future], *Chosŏn mit chosŏn minjok* [Korean class, Korean problem] 1 (1927): 175. Slogans like "Yagyuk kangsik" (Strong preying on the weak) or "Namjon yobi" (Treatment of women as inferior) could be used together as rallying points.

121. "Changnae chosŏn ŭi yŏsŏng" [The future of Korean women], *Ch'ŏngnyŏn* 7 (May 1927): 338.

122. *Tonga ilbo*, 3 Jan. 1925.

123. Ibid., 19 Dec. 1925, 6 March 1926.

124. Kim Min-yu, "Chosŏn e issŏsŏ XX chŏk koyang kwa XX tang ŭi inmu" [Because it is in Korea, XX to exhalt and duty to the XX party], *Musanja P'anp'ŭllet* 3 (March 1931), cited in Kim Kwang-un, "1930-yŏn chŏnhu chosŏn ŭi chabon imnodong kwan'gye wa ilche ŭi nodong t'ongje chŏngch'aek" [Korea's capital, wage labor relations, and labor management policies under Japanese colonial rule before and after 1930], edited by Kuksa p'yŏnch'an wiwŏnhoe. Kuksagwan nonch'ong [National History Institute, collection of materials] (Seoul, 1992), 38:177–201.

125. Chōsen Sōtokufu, *Chōsenjin no shisō to seikaku* [The thoughts and characteristics of Koreans] (Keijō, 1927), 189–90.

126. According to the Afro-Caribbean theorist Frantz Fanon, the Western Manichean delirium (i.e., good versus bad, black versus white, etc.) manifests itself in various ways, often creating an "imago" of the black as "The Other." See Frantz Fanon, *The Wretched of the Earth* (New York: Grove Press, 1968), 169–83.

127. The descriptions of the Korean worker had many similarities to descriptions of the Korean farmer. Laziness was often applied to both the farmer and the factory worker. "Chōsen nōson no jōkyō" [The conditions of the Korean rural village], *Chōsen minpō*, 18 Sept. 1928.

128. Chōsen Sōtokufu Kanbō Bunshoka Murayama Chijunchōsa, *Chōsen no gun-shū* [Korean crowds] (Keijō, 1926), 62.

129. Chōsen Sōtokufu, *Chōsen Sōtokufu chōsa geppō* [Korean Government-General monthly investigation report] (March 1936): 7.

130. *Chōsen doboku kenchiku kyōkai kaihō* [Civil engineering and construction association bulletin] 102 (Nov. 1926): 1–3.

131. Rōmu Kōsei Kenkyūshō, "Chōsenjin rōmu kanri no yōryō" [Points on Korean labor management], *Rōsei jihō* 782 (Keijō, 1943), cited in Kang I-su, "1930-yŏndae myŏnbang tae kiŏp yŏsŏng nodongja ŭi sangt'ae e kwanhan yŏn'gu: Nodong kwajŏng nodong t'ongje rŭl chungsim ŭro," 133.

132. Chōsen Sōtokufu Shokusankyoku, *Chōsen ni okeru kōfu rōdō jihō* [A review of Korean miners] (Keijō, 1930), cited in Kang I-su, "Kongjang ch'eje wa nodong kyuyul" [The factory system and labor discipline], in Kŭndae chuch'e wa singminji kyuyul kwŏllyŏk [Modern subjectivity and colonial disciplinary power], ed. Kim Chin-gyun and Chong Kun-sik (Seoul: Munhwakwahaksa, 1997), 134.

133. Sakurai Yoshiyuki, *Chōsen no runpen: Hantō ni tsuite runpen seikatsu no tokushō* [Korean vagrants: The typical characteristics of vagrants in the peninsula] (Keijō, 1934), 56. The etymological origin of the word *runpen* is "lumpen" or "lumpenproletariat."

134. Ibid.

135. Oda Fumio, "Chōsenjin rōdōsha mondai" [The problem of the Korean worker], in *Chōsen keizai no kenkyū* [A study of Korea's economy], by Funada Kyōji hen (Tokyo: Tōe Shoin, 1929), 2–27.

136. Ibid.

137. Sakurai Yoshiyuki, *Chōsen ni tsuite kōzan rōdō jōkyō* [The condition of Korean mine workers] (Keijō, 1934), 231

138. Takahashi Kameikichi, *Gendai chōsen keizai ron*, 393–403.

139. Ibid., 407.

140. Ibid.

141. See Chōsen Sōtokufu, *Chōsen Sōtokufu tōkei nenpō* (1929–45), cited in Yi Chŏng-ok, "Ilcheha kong'ŏp nodong esŏ ŭi minjok kwa sŏng, 1910–1945" [Race and sex in industrial labor under Japanese colonial rule, 1910–1945] (Ph.D. diss., Seoul National University, 1990), 131.

142. Yu Pong-ch'ŏl, "Ilcheha ŭi kungmin saenghwal sujun" [The living standard of citizens under Japanese colonial rule], in *Ilcheha ŭi minjok saenghwalsa* [History of the livelihood of Koreans under Japanese colonial rule], ed. Cho Ki-jun (Seoul: Minjung sŏgwan, 1971), 476.

143. Takahashi Kameikichi, *Gendai chōsen keizai ron*, 393–403.

144. Ibid., 407.

145. Ibid.

146. *Chosŏn ilbo*, 5 May 1925.

147. Ava Baron, "Gender and Labor History," in *Work Engendered: Toward a New History of American Labor*, ed. Ava Baron (Ithaca, NY: Cornell University Press, 1991), 37.

5. THE COLONIZED BODY

1. Kim had been attending Tongdŏk Higher Common Girls' School but was forced to drop out after her parents married her off to Sim. After their marriage, Sim packed his bags and left for Tokyo to pursue his studies. *Tonga ilbo*, 10 April 1931.

2. Kim Ki-jŏn, "Ch'ŏngch'un tu yŏsŏng ŭi ch'ŏldo chasal sagŏn kwa pip'an" [A critique of the railroad suicide incident of two young women], *Sin yŏsŏng* (May 1931), 30–38. *Tonga ilbo*, 14 April 1931.

3. In the *Tonga ilbo* report, the writer criticized both women for falling into sentimental nihilism and criticized Kim as mentally fragile and weak-minded for not being able to wait for her husband's return from Tokyo. *Tonga ilbo*, 10, 14 April 1931.

4. Yi Kap-su, "Sŏng kyoyuk e taehaya" [Regarding sex education], *Ch'ŏngnyŏn* (Feb. 1931), 8–11.

5. Michel Foucault. *The History of Sexuality*, trans. Robert Huxley (New York: Vintage Books, 1990), 139.

6. Pak Suk-cha, "1920-yŏndae yŏsŏng ŭi yukch'e e taehan namsŏng ŭi sisŏn kwa hwansang" [The male gaze and fantasy of women's bodies in the 1920s], *Han'guk kŭndae munhak yŏn'gu* 5, no. 1 (April 2004): 166–67.

7. Sabine Frühstück, *Colonizing Sex: Sexology and Sexual Control in Modern Japan* (Berkeley: University of California Press, 2003), 102.

8. Foucault, *History of Sexuality*, 44.

9. *Pyŏlgŏn'gon* (July 1927), cited in Kwŏn Podŭrae, *Yŏnae ŭi sidae: 1920-yŏn ch'oban ŭi munhwa wa yuhaeng* [An era of love: Culture and trends/fashion in the early 1920s] (Seoul: Hyŏnsil munhwa yŏn'gu, 2003), 159.

10. Ch'ŏn Chŏng-hwan, *Kŭndae ŭi ch'aek ilki* [Reading books in the modern period] (Seoul: Tosŏch'ulp'an p'ŭrŭn yŏksa, 2003), 186–87.

11. In the case of Japan, Frühstück notes that it was common practice for

newspapers to allow publishing houses to advertise their products, knowing that they would boost their circulation numbers. Frühstück, *Colonizing Sex*, 103.

12. Other popular books were *Yoru no tamatebako* [Pandora's box at night, 1926] and *Joshi no himitsu* [A woman's secret, 1928]. See Ch'ŏn Chŏng-hwan, *Kŭndae ŭi ch'aek ilki*, 186–87.

13. Sawada Junjirō, *Ch'ŏnyŏ mit ch'ŏ ŭi sŏngjŏk saenghwal* [The sexual lives of women and wives], cited in Kwŏn Podŭrae, *Yŏnae ŭi sidae*, 165.

14. *Tonga ilbo*, 24 Oct. 1923, 10 Dec. 1923, 7 Sept. 1924, 7 March 1924, 20 Nov. 1924. *Danjo zukai seishokuki shinsho* [Illustrations of men and women's reproductive organs: New pictures, 1926]; *Bijin ratei himitsu shashin* [Secret pictures of beautiful nude bodies, 1926]. Also see Ch'ŏn Chŏng-hwan, *Kŭndae ŭi ch'aek ilki*, 186–87.

15. *Chosŏn ilbo*, 18 March 1927.

16. "Pŏlgŏsung'i namnyŏ ŭi sajin" [Pictures of a nude male and female], *Pyŏlgŏn'gon* (Dec. 1927), cited in Kwŏn Podŭrae, *Yŏnae ŭi sidae*,168.

17. *Chosŏn ilbo*, 10 April 1929. Kuriyagawa Hakuson's essay, *Modern Views on Love*, "published in 1920 and widely read by young women [in Japan], links the ideal of marriage to the underlying ethos implicit in self-cultivation: 'Only love has the total power to join two individuals mentally and physically and influence the formation of their character.'" Barbara Sato, *The New Japanese Woman: Modernity, Media, and Women in Interwar Japan* (Durham, NC: Duke University Press, 2003), 144.

18. *Chosŏn ilbo*, 24 Oct. 1934; *Tonga ilbo*, 14 March 1923; *Chosŏn ilbo*, 15 July 1921; *Pyŏlgŏn'gon* (Nov. 1931), 62–65.

19. Ko Pyŏng-ch'ŏl, "Ilche sidae kŏn'gang tamnon kwa yak ŭi kuwŏnnon: maeil sinbo yak kwanggo punsŏk ŭl chungsim ŭro" [Discourses on health and the soteriology of medicine under Japanese imperial rule: An analysis of medicine advertisements in the *Maeil sinbo*], *Chonggyo yŏn'gu* 30 (2003): 288.

20. *Sinhan minbo*, 19 May 1927.

21. Dr. M. B [pseud.],"Sana chojŏlso" [Place for regulating birth], *Samch'ŏlli* (March 1929), cited in Son Hyŏn-suk, "Ilche singminji sigi chosŏn ŭi ch'ulsan t'ongje tamnon ŭi yŏn'gu" [A study of the discourse of birth control under Japanese colonial rule] (master's thesis, Hanyang University, 1999), 22.

22. Ibid.

23. "Puro wa ppurŭ yŏhaksaeng ŭi chŏngjo wa yŏnaegwan" [An overview of chastity and love among female students of the proletariat and bourgeoisie], *Samch'ŏlli* (Dec. 1932), cited in Kim Chin-song, *Sŏul e ttaensŭhol ŭl hŏhara* [Permit a dance hall in Seoul] (Seoul: Hyŏnsil munhwa yŏn'gu, 1999), 335–37.

24. Ibid.

25. Michel Foucault, *History of Sexuality*, 1–49, 115–31.

26. Yi Myŏng-sŏn, "Singminji kŭndae ŭi 'sŏng kwahak' tamnon kwa yŏsŏng ŭi sŏng" [Sexology discourse and female sexuality under colonial modernity], *Yŏsŏng kŏn'gang* 2 (2001): 98.

27. Kim Mi-yŏng, "Ilcheha 'chosŏn ilbo' ŭi kajŏng puin-nan yŏn'gu" [A study of the *Chosŏn ilbo*'s family wife column under Japanese colonial rule], *Hyŏndae munhak yŏn'gu* 16 (2004): 230.

28. *Maeil sinbo*, 22 Nov. 1913; Pak Yun-jae, *Han'guk kŭndae ŭihak ŭi kiwŏn* [The origin of Korea's modern medical system] (Seoul: Hyean, 2005), 304–5, 310–11.

29. Ibid., 279.

30. Pak Sŏng-nae, Sin Tong-wŏn, and O Tong-hun, *Uri kwahak 100-yŏn* [Our science, one hundred years] (Seoul: Hyŏnsamsa, 2001), 128.

31. Pak Yun-jae, *Han'guk kŭndae ŭihak ŭi kiwŏn*, 310–11.

32. Ibid. Chi Sŏk-yŏng was one of the first Koreans to study Western medicine abroad (1883); Sŏ Chae-p'il (also known as Philip Jaisohn) graduated from Columbia Medical College in 1889 (and later George Washington University Medical School). Kim Chŏm-dong (also known as Esther Park) was the first Korean woman to study medicine abroad. She accompanied her mentor, Dr. Rosetta Sherwood Hall, back to America and enrolled at the Baltimore Women's Medical College in 1896. Tokyo Women's Medical College was the most popular destination for Korean female students (fifty-nine students). Ki Chang-dŏk, "Ŭihakkye ŭi haeoe yuhaksaeng" [Korean medical students studying abroad], *Ŭisahak* 3, no. 2 (Dec. 1994): 170–92.

33. "Sōkon, chihōkon, kaikyūkon, rankon no hei" [The evil custom of early marriages, local marriages, class marriages, and lavish marriages], *Chōsen shisō tsūshin* (May 1926), 66.

34. Lew Young-ick, "The Kabo Reform Movement: Korean and Japanese Reform Efforts in Korea, 1894" (Ph.D. diss., Harvard University, 1972).

35. *Sin yŏsŏng* (Sept. 1933), cited in Sin Yŏng-suk, "Ilcheha han'guk yŏsŏng sahoesa yŏn'gu" [A social history of Korean women under Japanese colonial rule], Ph.D. diss., Ewha Womans University, 1989, 65.

36. *Tonga ilbo*, 19 Oct. 1938.

37. Yung-Chung Kim, ed., *Women of Korea: A History from Ancient Times to 1945* (Seoul: Ewha Womans University Press, 1976), 44, 94.

38. Kim Tu-hon, *Han'guk kajok chedo yŏn'gu* [A study of the Korean family system] (Seoul: Sŏul taehak ch'ulp'ansa, 1968), 454–55.

39. Charles Allen Clark, "Marriage Questions in Chōsen," *Korea Mission Field*

(Aug. 1919), 161. In Korea, "man" or "full year" refers to the Western way of counting age. *Sal* refers to the Korean way, in which a newborn baby is one year old and another year is added on each lunar New Year.

40. So Ch'un [pseud.], "Minmyŏnŭri hakdae munje e taehayŏ," [Regarding the problem of the cruel treatment of the *minmyŏnŭri*], *Sin yŏsŏng* (Oct. 1926), 8–10.

41. *Tonga ilbo*, 9 Oct. 1926.

42. Yi Yŏng-ae, "Yŏin sip'yŏng: Chohon ŭi pigŭk" [Comments on current events regarding women: The tragedy of early marriages], *Sin yŏsŏng* (Jan. 1934), 26–29.

43. *Chosŏn ilbo*, 24 Oct. 1929.

44. *Tonga ilbo*, 3 April 1928, 16 March 1929.

45. *Maeil sinbo*, 27 Aug. 1937; *Tonga ilbo*, 7 Feb. 1926.

46. *Tonga ilbo*, 21 July 1937.

47. Ibid, 16 May 1931.

48. *Chosŏn nongmin* (Sept. 1928), 33.

49. Yi Yŏng-ae, "Yŏin sip'yŏng: Chohon ŭi pigŭk," 26–29; *Chosŏn ilbo*, 24 Oct. 1929.

50. *Tonga ilbo*, 13 July 1934.

51. Yi Yŏng-ae, "Yŏin sip'yŏng. Chohon ŭi pigŭk," 26–29; *Tonga ilbo*, 21 July 1937.

52. Ibid, 6 April 1927.

53. Hyŏn Chin-gŏn, "Fire," in *Flowers of Fire: Twentieth-Century Korean Stories*, ed. Peter Lee (Honolulu: University of Hawai'i Press, 1974), 8–9.

54. From 1910 through 1923, ten girls under the age of eighteen were sent to jail for committing murder. In 1926, fourteen girls were convicted of murder and only one boy. Yu Sŭng-hyŏn, "Ilcheha chohon ŭro inhan yŏsŏng pŏmchwae" [Female crimes caused by early marriage under Japanese colonial rule], in *Yŏsŏng kwa hyŏnsil* [Women and reality], ed. Pak Yong-ok (Seoul: Kukhak charyowŏn, 2001), 374–79.

55. *Chosŏn ilbo*, 16 Feb. 1933.

56. David Horn, *Social Bodies: Science, Reproduction, and Italian Modernity* (Princeton, NJ: Princeton University Press, 1994), 64.

57. Mary Poovey, *Uneven Developments: The Ideological Work of Gender in Mid-Victorian England* (Chicago: University of Chicago Press, 1988), 28.

58. Kim Chŏng-jin, "Chohon p'aeji" [Eliminating early marriage], *Sahae kongnon* (May 1935), 50–51.

59. Pak Ho-jin, "Sanmo poho wa illyu kaeryang pangmyŏn" [Protecting the pregnant woman and methods for improving mankind], *Samch'ŏlli* (May 1930), 40.

60. *Tonga ilbo*, 1 March 1932.

61. Ibid., 3 Oct. 1933.

62. Kim T'ae-hun, "Saengni kangjwa namnyŏ sŏngjing ŭi kyŏljŏng che ich'a sŏngjing" [A course on physiology: Determining the sexual characteristics of M/F, the secondary sex], *Pyŏlgŏn'gon* (March 1930), cited in Chŏn Kyŏng-ok, Pyŏn Sin-wŏn, Pak Chin-sŏk, and Kim Ŭn-jŏng, eds., *Han'guk yŏsŏng munhwasa* [A cultural history of Korean women], vol. 2 (Seoul: Sukmyŏng yŏja taehakkyo ch'ulp'an'guk, 2004), 293–95.

63. Ibid.

64. Ibid.

65. *Chosŏn ilbo*, 21 March 1930.

66. Ibid., 24 Oct. 1934.

67. *Tonga ilbo*, 26 Aug. 1929.

68. Ibid., 16 March 1932.

69. *Chosŏn ilbo*, 14 Aug. 1937.

70. "Kŭndae yŏsŏng mi ŭi haebu" [An analysis of a modern woman's beauty], *Sin tonga* (March 1933), 92–94.

71. Ibid.

72. *Tonga ilbo*, 29 July 1926.

73. Chōsen Sōtokufu, *Chōsen kokusei chōsa hōkoku* [A study of the conditions of Korea] (Keijō, 1930), 46–49.

74. *Chosŏn chung'ang ilbo*, 2 July 1936.

75. Ibid.

76. *Chosŏn ilbo*, 7 June 1931.

77. Yun T'ae-gwŏn, "Imsin chung ŭi sŏpsaengpŏp, imsin tokpon" [The rules of hygiene during pregnancy: A pregnancy reader], *Pyŏlgŏn'gon* (June 1934), cited in Chŏn Kyŏng-ok, Pyŏn Sin-wŏn, Pak Chin-sŏk, and Kim Ŭn-jŏng, eds., *Han'guk yŏsŏng munhwasa*, 295.

78. *Chosŏn ilbo*, 12 May 1925.

79. Ibid., 20 May 1931.

80. Ibid., 10 May 1926.

81. Sŏk I-gyŏng, "Imsin ttae ŭi sŏpsaengpŏp" [The rules of hygiene during childbirth], *Samch'ŏlli* (Feb. 1935), 150.

82. *Chosŏn ilbo*, 27 April 1928.

83. Ibid., 28 April 1928.

84. Ibid., 25 April 1928.

85. Ibid., 26 April 1928.

86. Cutler M. Edmunds, "PokuNyokwan," in *Korea Woman's Conference An-*

nual Report (1899), 26. Also see Yi Kkott-mae, *Han'guk kŭndae kanhosa* [The history of the modern nurse] (Seoul: Tosŏnch'ulpan, 2002).

87. Margaret Edmunds, "Po Ku Nyo Koan: Hospital, Dispensary and Nurses' Training School, Seoul," in *Reports Read at the Seventh Annual Session of the Korean Woman's Conference of the Methodist Episcopal Church* (Seoul, 23–27 June 1905), 60.

88. Missionaries turned to widows hoping that they would have the time to get the proper training. Ibid., 61.

89. Chōsen Sōtokufu, *Chōsen eisei jihō yōran* [Review on Korea's hygiene: An outline] (Keijō, 1922), 14.

90. *Tonga ilbo*, 15 Jan. 1926.

91. Chōsen Sōtokufu, *Chōsen Sōtokufu tōkei nenpō* [Statistical yearbook of the Government-General of Korea] (Keijō, 1915, 1920, 1930, 1940).

92. In 1933, there were 1,998 doctors in Korea: 1,052 Koreans, 915 Japanese, and 31 foreigners. *Maeil sinbo*, 27 Dec. 1933.

93. Ibid. In 1933, there were 133 hospitals in Korea: government (4), public (45), and private (84).

94. *Tonga ilbo*, 3 Aug. 1932.

95. In 1929, the average daily wage of a Korean factory worker was 1 to 2.5 *wŏn*. If they were admitted to a Government-General hospital, workers had to pay 2,000 *wŏn* for hospitalization and 700 *wŏn* for outpatient service. Pak Sŏng-nae, Sin Tong-wŏn, and O Tong-hun, *Uri kwahak 100-yŏn*, 121–24.

96. *Chosŏn ilbo*, 17 Jan. 1926.

97. Pak Sŏng-nae, Sin Tong-wŏn, and O Tong-hun, *Uri kwahak 100-yŏn*, 121–24.

98. Yi Kap-su, "Sŏng kyoyuk e taehaya" [Regarding sex education], *Ch'ŏngnyŏn* (Feb. 1931), 8–11.

99. "Ch'ŏnyŏ sidae ŭi wisaeng" [Hygiene during the virginal stage], *Tonggwang* (June 1931), 56.

100. *Chosŏn ilbo*, 2–4 April 1931.

101. Mary Poovey, *Uneven Developments*, 36.

102. *Chosŏn ilbo*, 24 Oct. 1934

103. Pak Ch'an-hun, "T'ŭkhi chuŭihal yŏsŏng kwa kŭmyok saenghwal" [Something women need to pay special attention to: Women and the ascetic life], *Pyŏlgŏn'gon* (Feb. 1929), 73.

104. *Tonga ilbo*, 25 Aug. 1929.

105. *Chosŏn ilbo*, 30 April 1930, 1 May 1930.

106. Ibid., 24 Oct. 1934.

107. *Tonga ilbo*, 1 March 1932.

108. Kim Yun-gyŏng, "Sŏng kyoyuk ŭi chuch'ang" [Advocating sex education], *Tonggwang* (March 1927), 26–29.

109. Yi Kap-su, "Sŏng kyoyuk e taehaya," 8–11.

110. *Chosŏn ilbo*, 2–4 April 1931.

111. Kim Sŭng-sik, "Ch'ŏnyŏ sidae ŭi simli" [A mental state during a girl's virginal stage], *Sin yŏsŏng* (Oct. 1931), 21–24.

112. *Chosŏn ilbo*, 2–4 April 1931.

113. Ibid., 11 Oct. 1928.

114. Mary Poovey, *Uneven Developments*, 37.

115. Yu Hyŏng-suk, "Sŏng ŭi yŏnggam" [Sacred intuition of sex], *Sinsaeng* (Dec. 1930), 30.

116. Yu Hyŏng-suk, "Sŏng ŭi suyang" [Cultivating sex], *Sinsaeng* (April 1929), 18.

117. The roundtable discussion featured Kim Kyu-t'aek, Hŏ Sin, Sin Paek-ho, Yun T'ae-gwŏn, and Yang Yun-sik. "Sŏng munje rŭl chungsim ŭro han che ilhoe puin kwa ŭisa chwadamhoe" [A roundtable discussion among gynecologists centering around the question of sex], *Sin yŏsŏng* (May 1933), 16–26.

118. "Sŏng e kwanhan munje ŭi t'oron" [A debate on matters related to sex], *Tonggwang* (Dec. 1931), 34–38.

119. Kim Yun-gyŏng, "Yŏrŏ kaji mosun ŭro saengginŭn pigŭk kwa haedok" [The many contradictions that create tragedy and harm], *Tonggwang* (April 1927), 27.

120. Kim Yun-gyŏng, "Sŏng kyoyuk ŭi chuch'ang," 26–29.

121. Yun Chi-hun, "Modŏn yŏsŏng sipkyemyŏng" [The ten commandments of the modern girl], *Sin yŏsŏng* (April 1931), 70–72.

122. Kim Ch'ung, "Sŏng kyoyuk ŭi chuch'ang" [Promoting sex education], *Tonggwang* (April 1927), cited in Chŏn Kyŏng-ok, Pyŏn Sin-wŏn, Pak Chin-sŏk, and Kim Ŭn-jŏng, eds., *Han'guk yŏsŏng munhwasa*, 298.

123. Kim Ki-jin, "Kim myŏngsun ssi e taehan konggaejang" [An open letter regarding Kim Myŏng-sun], *Sin yŏsŏng* (Nov. 1924), 46–50.

124. Kim Ch'ung, "Sŏng kyoyuk ŭi chuch'ang," 298.

125. Yi Kap-su, "Sŏng kyoyuk e taehaya," 8–11. The *Chosŏn ilbo* also highlighted activities in Tokyo in which civic groups carefully planned the introduction of sex education in girls' schools. *Chosŏn ilbo*, 25 April 1927.

126. Yi Yong-ho, "Sŏng wisaeng" [Sex hygiene], *Tonggwang* (May 1931), 85.

127. Kim Yun-gyŏng, "Sŏng kyoyuk ŭi chuch'ang," 26–29.

128. "Sŏng kyoyuk silsi pangch'aek" [Sex education and enforcing measures], *Pyŏlgŏn'gon* (Feb. 1929), 54.

129. Pal Pong-sanin [pseud.], "Kŭnil ŭi yŏsŏng kwa hyŏndae ŭi kyoyuk" [Today's women and today's education], *Sin yŏsŏng* (June–July 1925), 62.

130. Yiji Kija [pseud.], "Yŏhaksaeng ŭi yuhok munje haebu" [Analysis of a female student's seduction problem], *Sin yŏsŏng* (Oct. 1926), 33–38.

131. "Sŏng kyoyuk silsi pangch'aek," 54.

132. Yi Yŏng-jun, "Chosŏnin kwa sŏngbyŏng" [Koreans and venereal disease], *Sin tonga* (Nov. 1932), 130–31.

133. *Chosŏn ilbo*, 4 Oct. 1930.

134. Ibid., 28 Feb. 1930.

135. Ibid., 26 March 1930.

136. Chu Yo-han, "Sŏng e kwanhan che munje" [The many problems regarding sex], *Tonggwang* (Dec. 1931), cited in Kim Chin-song, *Sŏul e ttaensŭhol ŭl hŏhara*, 298–99.

137. Kim Po-yŏng, "Yŏsŏng ch'eyuk e taehayŏ" [Regarding women's physical education], *Man'guk puin* (Jan. 1931), cited in Chŏn Kyŏng-ok, Pyŏn Sin-wŏn, Pak Chin-sŏk, and Kim Ŭn-jŏng, eds., *Han'guk yŏsŏng munhwasa*, 110–12.

138. *Tonga ilbo*, 18 Nov. 1927.

139. Ibid., 30 June 1923.

140. Kim Wŏn-ae, "Yŏja wa ch'eyuk" [Women and physical education], *Sin tonga* (March 1934), 46–48.

141. "Yŏhaksaengdŭl ŭn sana chehan ŭl sowŏn hanya?" [Do female students want to have birth control?], *Samch'ŏlli* (May 1933), 97.

142. Cho Hyŏn-gyŏng, "Sana chehan ŭl haeya hana?" [Do we have to restrict childbirth?], *Yŏsŏng* (April 1936), 66.

143. *Tonga ilbo*, 4 Oct. 1931.

144. Ibid., 11 March 1931.

145. Li T'ae-gwi, "Sana chehan kwa ŏmŏni ŭi kŏn'gang" [Birth control and the health of the mother], *Ch'ŏngnyŏn* (May 1927), cited in Son Hyŏn-suk, "Ilche singminji sigi chosŏn ŭi ch'ulsan t'ongje tamnon ŭi yŏn'gu," 12.

146. *Chung'oe ilbo*, 13 June 1927.

147. *Tonga ilbo*, 30 March 1925.

148. Frühstück, *Colonizing Sex*, 119.

149. Kim Myŏng-hŭi, "Sip'yŏng," [Comments on current events], *Sin yŏsŏng* (Jan. 1925), 10–13.

150. Ryu Sang-kyu, "Chosŏn yŏsŏng kwa sana chehan" [Korean women and birth control], *Sin yŏsŏng* (March 1932), 8–11.

151. Pae Sŏng-nyong [pseud.], "Kyŏngje chŏngse wa hyŏnsilsŏng" [The economic conditions and reality], *Samch'ŏlli* (April 1930), 30.

152. Ibid.; Chŏng Sŏk-t'aek, "Sana chehan ŭi chŏlgyu" [A great shout for birth control], *Samch'ŏlli* (April 1930), cited in Chŏn Kyŏng-ok, Pyŏn Sin-wŏn, Pak Chin-sŏk, and Kim Ŭn-jŏng, eds., *Han'guk yŏsŏng munhwasa*, 296.

CONCLUSION

1. Kim Tae-jong, "Blue Swallow Faces Turbulence," *Korea Times*, 1 June 2006.

2. *Tonga ilbo*, 8 July 1925.

3. Ibid., 12 Dec. 1925.

4. Han'guk yŏsŏng kaebalwŏn, ed., *Han'guk yŏksa sok ŭi yŏsŏng inmul* [Female personalities in Korean history] (Seoul: Mundŭk inswae, 1998), 37–38.

5. For a good discussion of femininity and gender roles during the interwar period in Japan, see Barbara Sato, *The New Japanese Woman: Modernity, Media, and Women in Interwar Japan* (Durham, NC: Duke University Press, 2003).

6. Michel Foucault, *Discipline and Punish: The Birth of the Prison*, trans. Alan Sheridan (New York: Vintage Books, 1995), 299.

7. Chōsen Sōtokufu, "Joshi chōsengo chūtō kyōiku tokuhon" [Girls' Korean language middle school educational reader], in *Han'guk kyoyuk saryo chipsŏng* [Compilation of historical documents on Korean education], ed. Han'guk chŏngsin munhwa yŏn'guwŏn (Seoul, 1994), 88–91.

8. The Imperial Rescript on Education, drafted 30 October 1890, emphasized a return to Confucian values and mores. Theodore Wm. de Bary, Ryusaku Tsunoda, and Donald Keene, eds., *Sources of Japanese Tradition* (New York: Columbia University Press, 1964), 646–47.

9. Kim Ki-hong, "Ilcheha chŏnsi ch'ongdongwŏn ch'ejegi (1938–1945) hwangminhwa kyoyuk yŏn'gu" [A study of the wartime general mobilization system phase under Japanese colonial rule, 1938–1945] (master's thesis, Yonsei University, 2000), 1–40.

10. *Tonga ilbo*, 2 April 1938.

11. Andrew Grajdanzev, *Modern Korea* (New York: International Secretariat, Institute of Pacific Relations, 1944), 266.

12. Ibid. See James Scott, *Weapons of the Weak: Everyday Forms of Peasant Resistance* (New Haven, CT: Yale University Press, 1985).

13. *Rensei* (*yŏnsong*) and *tanren* (*tanryŏn*) were used interchangeably. Both meant training or disciplining.

14. Grajdanzev, *Modern Korea*, 269.

15. For more on the history of Korean women's education, see Lulu Frey, "Higher Education for Korean Girls," *Korea Mission Field* 10 (1914): 307; James Earnest Fisher, "Democracy and Mission Education in Korea" (Ph.D. diss., Columbia University, Teachers College, 1928); Yung-Chung Kim, ed., *Women of Korea: A History from Ancient Times to 1945* (Seoul: Ewha Womans University Press, 1976).

16. Lee Hyo-chae, "Protestant Missionary Work and Enlightenment of Korean Women," *Korea Journal* 17, no. 11 (Nov. 1977): 33–50.

17. Insook Kwon, "The New Women's Movement' in 1920s Korea: Rethinking the Relationship between Imperialism and Women," *Gender and History* 10, no. 3 (Nov. 1998): 381–405.

18. *Chosŏn ilbo*, 21 March 1925.

19. Yi Sang-gyŏng, *Kang Kyŏng-ae chŏnjip* [A collection of Kang Kyong-ae's works] (Seoul: Somyŏng ch'ulp'an, 1999), 135–413.

20. Bruce Cumings, *Parallax Visions: Making Sense of American–East Asian Relations at the End of the Century* (Durham, NC: Duke University Press, 1999), 70–73.

21. *Ohmynews*, 25 March 2005.

22. *Chung'ang ilbo*, 10 Feb. 2003.

23. Chōsen Sōtokufu, *Chōsen Sōtokufu kanpo* 4 [The official gazette of the Government-General of Korea] (March 1938), 2.

24. Chŏng Un-hyŏn, *Na nŭn hwang'guk sinmin iro soida* [I am hereby an imperial subject] (Seoul: Kaema kowŏn, 1999), 144–49; *Maeil sinbo*, 18 Jan. 1939, 25 Dec. 1943.

25. Kim Hwal-lan, "Chingbyŏngje wa pando yŏsŏng ŭi kago" [The conscription system and the preparedness of women on the peninsula], *Sin sidae* (Dec. 1942), cited in Yi Hye-jŏng, "Ilche malgi Kim Hwal-lan ŭi ilche hyŏmnyŏk paegyŏng kwa nolli" [The background and reasoning behind Kim Hwal-lan's cooperation during the latter period under Japanese colonial rule], *Yŏsŏnghak nonjip* 21, no. 2 (2004): 65–66.

26. Yung-Chung Kim, ed., *Women of Korea*, 240.

27. Bruce Cumings, *Korea's Place in the Sun: A Modern History* (New York: W. W. Norton, 1999), 177.

28. See Yoshimi Yoshiaki, *Comfort Women: Sexual Slavery in the Japanese Military during World War II* (New York: Columbia University Press, 2000).

GUIDE TO ROMANIZATION

Korean and Japanese words and names in the text are romanized by the McCune-Reischauer and Hepburn systems, respectively, except those with their own divergent orthography. Korean and Japanese names cited in the text are given full names (surname first, no comma).

Abe Isoo	安部磯雄
aeho	愛護
ajinomoto (MSG)	아지노모도
ajŏn	衙前
An Myŏng-gŭn	安明根
anch'ae	안채
asa tongmaeng	餓死同盟
Asea yŏsŏng munje yŏn'guso	亞細亞女性問題研究所
budan seiji	武斷政治
bushō	無精
chagak	自覺
Chahye ŭiwŏn	慈惠醫院
Ch'ae Maria	채 마리아
Ch'angyang-hoe	贊襄會
chapkwa	雜科
Cheguk sinmun	帝國新聞
Cheju	濟州
Chemulp'o	濟物浦

chian yuji pŏp	治安維持法
chigŏp puin	職業婦人
chikcho	織造
ch'ilgŏ chiak	七去之惡
ch'ima chŏgori	치마 저고리
Chinmyŏng puin-hoe	進明婦人會
ch'in-yŏng	親迎
Ch'oe Che-u	崔濟愚
Ch'oe Si-hyŏng	崔時亨
chŏgori	저고리
choje namjo	粗製濫造
chŏn	錢
Ch'ŏndogyo	天道敎
Chŏng To-jŏn	鄭道傳
Chŏng Yag-yong	丁若鏞
ch'ŏnjik	天職/賤職
chokpo	族譜
Chŏlla	全羅
Chŏllyang nongga	絶糧農家
ch'ŏn ch'ŏp	천첩
chongpŏp	宗法
Ch'ŏnhak ch'oham	天學初函
ch'ŏnmin	賤民
ch'ŏp	妾
Chosŏn	朝鮮
Chosŏn ilbo	朝鮮日報
Chosŏn sinmun	朝鮮新聞
Chosŏn usaeng hyŏphoe	朝鮮優生協會
Chosŏn wangjo sillok	朝鮮王朝實錄
Chosŏn yŏja ch'ŏngnyŏnhoe	朝鮮女子靑年會
chubu	主婦
ch'ulga	出嫁
Ch'unhyang-jŏn	春香傳
chungin	中人
ch'un'gunggi	春窮期
Chu Yo-sŏp	朱燿燮
dōka	同化
Ewha haktang	梨花學堂

futsū	普通
Haejilnyŏk	해질녘
Hakpu	學部
han'gŭl	한글
Han'guk yŏsŏngsa p'yŏnch'an wiwŏnhoe	韓國女性史編纂委員會
Hansŏng	漢城
Hara Kei	原敬
hisŭt'eri	히스테리
Hŏ Chŏng-suk	許貞淑
Hŏ Yŏng-suk	許永淑
hojŏk tŭngbon	戶籍謄本
Hong Kyŏng-nae	洪景來
Hong Og-im	洪玉姙
honsu	婚需
Hosoi Wakizō	細井和喜藏
hwajŏn	火田
Hwang Sin-dŏk	黃信德
Hwangsŏng sinmun	皇城新聞
hyanggyo	鄕校
hyŏnmo yangch'ŏ	賢母良妻
hyŏnmyŏng chŏnŏp chubu	賢明傳業主婦
hyoyul	效率
imjil	淋疾
Imjin waeran	任辰倭亂
ilbu ilch'ŏ	一夫一妻
il myŏn il kyoje	一面一敎制
ingyŏk	人格
Inhyŏng ŭi chip	人形의家
innae ch'ŏn	人乃天
Jiali	家禮
jitsugyō	實業
jōsei teishintai	女性挺身隊
Kabo	甲午
Kaebyŏk	開闢
kaekchu	客主
Kaesŏng	開城
kajok	家族
Kajŏng puin	家庭婦人

kajŏng sungbae	家庭崇拜
Kanebō	鐘紡
Kanegafuchi	鐘淵
Kang Chu-ryong	강주룡
Kang Hyang-nan	강향난
Kang Kyŏng-ae	姜敬愛
Kanghwa	江華
kangje chŏgŭm	強制貯金
kangsŭpso	講習所
Keijō	京城
kilssam	길쌈
Kim Hong-jip	金弘集
Kim Hwal-lan	金活蘭
Kim I-ryŏp	金一葉
Kim Kwan-ho	金觀鎬
Kim Man-dŏk	김만덕
Kim Mirisa	김미리사
Kim Myŏng-sun	金明淳
Kim U-jin	金祐鎮
Kim Wŏn-ju	金元周
Kim Yun-gyŏng	金允經
kiuje	祈雨祭
kisaeng	妓生
Koiso Kuniaki	小磯國昭
Kojong	高宗
kogong	雇工
kōminka	公民化
komusin	고무신
kongnobi	公奴婢
Koryŏ	高麗
Kōtō keisatsu	高等警察
Kuriyagawa Hakuson	廚川白村
Kuunmong	九雲夢
Kwanghyewŏn	廣惠院
Kwanŭm posal	觀音菩薩
kyŏl	결
kyŏlnap	結納
Kyŏnggi	京畿

Kyŏngguk taejŏn	經國大典
Kyŏngsŏng	京成
Kyŏngsŏng ilbo	京成日報
kyoyuk	教育
Liji	禮記
Maeil sinbo	每日新報
maemae kyŏlhon	賣買結婚
manmin p'yŏngdŭng	萬民平等
Min Tae-wŏn	閔泰瑗
Minbi	閔妃
minjok	民族
minjung	民衆
minmyŏnŭri	민며느리
Mitsui	三井
mŏsŭm sŏbang	머슴 서방
mudang	무당
Musanja	無産者
Na Hye-sŏk	羅蕙錫
Nae chasin wihae	네 자신 위해
Naehun	內訓
naichi	內地
naichi rōdōsha	內地勞動者
Naimushō	內務省
naisen ittai	內鮮一體
Namin	南人
namnyŏ p'yŏngdŭng	男女平等
nissen yūwa	日鮮融和
nobi	奴婢
oegŏ nobi	外居奴婢
Ogino Kyūsaku	荻野久作
Ojuyŏnmun changjŏnsan'go	五洲衍文長箋散稿
ŏnmun	諺文
Ōno Tamotsu	大野保
Ota Tenrei	太田典禮
Paejae haktang	培材學堂
paego-in sakkŏn	100人事件
paekchŏng	白丁
Pak Che-ga	朴齊家

Pak Chi-wŏn	朴趾源
Pak Hwa-sŏng	朴花城
Pak Kyŏng-wŏn	朴敬元
Pak Wŏn-hŭi	朴元熙
pan ch'in-yŏng	半親迎
Pang In-kŭn	方仁根
Pinghŏgak Yi-ssi	빙허각 李氏
Pogu yŏgwan	保救女館
pŏlgŭm chedo	罰金制度
pongsahon	奉仕婚
pon'gwan	本貫
ppalgan ch'aek	빨간책
puch'ae	負債
Pusan	釜山
p'yŏng	坪
Pyŏlgŏn'gon	別乾坤
P'yŏngyang	平壤
rensei	鍊成
rump'en	룸펜
Sa ŭi ch'anmi	死의贊美
sach'un'gi	思春期
sahwa	士禍
Saitō Makoto	齊藤實
sagam	舍監
sagyŏnghoe	查經會
Samch'ŏlli	三千里
Samgang haengsilto	三綱行實圖
Samgang oryun	三綱五倫
samjong chido	三從之道
sam myŏn il kyoje	三面一校制
sambulgŏ	三不去
sana chehan	産兒制限
sana chojŏl	産兒調節
sangdamwŏn	相談院
sangmin	常民
sanobi	私奴婢
sanp'a	産婆
sarangbang	舍廊房

sarye	四禮
Sasojŏl	士小節
Sawada Junjirō	澤田順次郎
se	歲
sekyun	細菌
senmon	專門
shiritsu gakko rei	私立學校令
Sidae ilbo	時代日報
Sim Ch'ŏng	심청
sin	新
sinhaeng	新行
sinhŭng	新興
Sin tonga	新東亞
Sin yŏja	新女子
Sin yŏsŏng	新女性
Sin'ganhoe	新幹會
Sinminhoe	新民會
sinsa yuram-dan	紳士遊覽團
Sinsaenghwal	新生活
sirhak	實學
Sŏ Chae-p'il	徐載弼
sŏdang	書堂
sŏhak	西學
Sohye	昭惠
sŏja	庶子
solgŏ nobi	솔거노비
sŏng	性
Song Kye-wŏl	宋桂月
sŏng todŏk	性道德
sŏngbyŏlsa	性別史
sŏngyokhak	性慾學
Sōtoku	總督
sŏwŏn	書院
ssibaji	씨받이
sugong	手工
Sookmyung	淑明
sunsilhan yoja	純實한女子
taedongp'o	大同布

taedong-pŏp	大同法
taedongjŏn	大同錢
Taewŏn'gun	大院君
Takahasi Kamekichi	高橋龜吉
t'alnong	脫農
tanbal	短髮
tanren	鍛鍊
teikoku shinmin	帝國臣民
Terauchi Masatake	寺內正毅
teril sawi	대릴사위
tomak	土幕
Tonga ilbo	東亞日報
Tonggyŏng taejŏn	東經大全
Tonghak	東學
Tongnip sinmun	獨立新聞
Toyotomi Hideyoshi	豊臣秀吉
Tsuda Sen	律田仙
tu	斗
ugwi	于歸
Ŭigwan	醫官
Ŭlmildae	乙密臺
usaenghak	優生學
wisaeng	衛生
wŏn	원
Yamakawa Kikue	山川菊榮
yangban	兩班
yangch'ŏn kyŏlhon	良賤結婚
yangmin	良民
yejo	禮曹
yen	圓
Yi Kap-su	李甲洙
Yi Kwang-su	李光洙
Yi Kyu-gyŏng	李圭景
Yi Nŭng-hwa	李能和
Yi Puk-myŏng	李北鳴
Yi Sŏng-gye	李成桂
Yi Su-jŏng	李樹廷
Yi Tŏng-mu	李德懋

Yi Wŏn-ik	李元翼
Yŏgye	女界
Yŏja kyoyuk-hoe	女子教育會
yŏgak	旅閣
yŏgong	女工
Yŏllyŏ-jŏn	烈女傳
yŏnae	戀愛
Yongdam yusa	龍潭遺詞
Yŏngdŭngp'o	永登浦
Yŏnhŭi chŏnmun hakkyo	延禧傳門學校
Yŏsŏng	女性
yŏsŏngsa	女性史
Yu Kil-chun	俞吉濬
yukch'e	肉體
Yuk Ji-su	陸之修
Yun Ch'i-ho	尹致昊
Yun Hyo-chŏng	尹孝定
Yun Sim-dŏk	尹心悳
yusin	維新
Zhu Xi	朱熹

BIBLIOGRAPHY

NEWSPAPERS AND JOURNALS

Cheguk sinmun
Cho kwang
Ch'ŏngnyŏn
Chōsen shakai jigyō
Chōsen shiron
Chosŏn chi kwang
Chosŏn chung'ang ilbo
Chosŏn ilbo
Chosŏn nongmin
Chōsen oyobi manshū
Chosŏn sinmun
Chung'oe ilbo
Ewha
Fusan shinpo
Hak chi kwang
Haktŭng
Hwangsŏng sinmun
Hyŏndae p'yŏngnon
Kaebyŏk
Kajŏng ŭi u
Kat'orik ch'ŏngnyŏn

Keijō nippō

The Korea Times

Kunu

Kyegŭp t'ujaeng

The Korea Review

The Korean Mission Field

Korean Repository

Maeil sinbo

The Missionary Survey

Nongmin

Ohmynews

Ŏrini

Pip'an

Punyŏ chi kwang

Pyŏlgŏn'gon

Sahae kongnon

Samch'ŏlli

Sidae ilbo

Sin kajŏng

Sinsaeng

Sil saenghwal

Sin saenghwal

Sin sidae

Sin tonga

Sin yŏja

Sin yŏsŏng

Sinhan minbo

Sisa ilbo

Tae Chosŏn tongnip hyŏphoe hoebo

Taehan minbo

Tonga ilbo

Tonggwang

Tongnip sinmun

Uri kajŏng

Yŏja kye

Yŏsŏng

MISSIONARY DOCUMENTS

Korea Woman's Conference. Seoul, 1911.

Eighteenth Annual Report of the Korea Woman's Conference of the Methodist Episcopal Church. Seoul, March 9–14, 1916.

Fifty Years of Light: Prepared by Missionaries of the Woman's Foreign Missionary Society of the Methodist Episcopal Church in Commemoration of the Completion of Fifty-Years of Work in Korea. Seoul: The Society, May 1938.

Fourteenth Annual Report of the Korean Women's Conference of the Methodist Episcopal Church. Seoul, March 6–12, 1912.

Report Read at the Ninth Annual Session of the Korea Woman's Conference of the Methodist Episcopal Church. Seoul, July 19–27, 1907.

Report Read at the Seventh Annual Session of the Korea Woman's Conference of the Methodist Episcopal Church. Seoul, June 23–27, 1905.

Thirtieth Annual Report of the Korea Woman's Conference of the Methodist Episcopal Church. Seoul, Oct. 1928.

Thirty-first Annual Report of the Korean Woman's Conference of the Methodist Episcopal Church. P'yŏngyang, June 1929.

Ada B. Hall. *Thirty-third Annual Report of the Members of the Woman's Foreign Missionary Society in Korea.* Seoul, Sept. 1931.

STATE AND COMPANY DOCUMENTS

Chōsen doboku kenchiku kyōkai kaihō [Civil engineering and construction association bulletin] 102 (Nov. 1926).

Chōsen Ginkō. *Chōsen keizai nenpō* [The annual economic report of Korea]. Seoul. 1948.

Chōsen Menshifushō Rengōkai. *Chōsen mengyōshi* [A history of the cotton industry in Korea]. Keijō, 1929.

Chōsen Nōson Shakai Eisei Chōsakai. *Chōsen no nōson eisei* [Sanitation in Korean farming villages]. Tokyo: Iwanami Shoten, 1940.

Chōsen Orimono Kyōkai. "Chōsen orimono kyōkai shi" [A history of the Korean textile association]. Vols. 11–12. 1939.

Chōsen Shōkō Kaigisho. *Chōsenjin shōkō ni kansuru kōsatsu* [An inquiry into Korean commerce/industry]. Keijō: 1936.

Chōsen Sōtokufu. *Chōsen eisei jihō yōran* [Review on Korea's hygiene: An outline]. Keijō, 1922.

———. *Chōsenjin no shisō to seikaku* [The thoughts and characteristics of Koreans]. (Keijō, 1927).

———. *Chōsen kokusei chōsa hōkoku* [A study of the conditions of Korea: A report]. Keijō, 1930.

———. *Chōsen no kosaku kankō* [A consideration of Korean tenants]. Keijō, 1932.

———. *Chōsen no shōsaku shūkan* [Tenanting practices of Koreans]. Keijō, 1929.

———. *Chōsen Sōtokufu chōsa geppō* [Korean Government-General monthly investigation report]. May 1931, March 1936, July 1938.

———. *Chōsen Sōtokufu jikyoku taisaku chōsakai shimon tōshinsho* [A final report of the Chōsen Government-General commission on policy for the current situation]. Keijō, 1938.

———. *Chōsen Sōtokufu kanpō* [The official gazette of the Government-General of Korea]. Volume 4 (March 1938).

———. *Chōsen Sōtokufu tōkei nenpō* [Statistical yearbook of the Government-General of Korea]. Keijō, 1919–40.

Chōsen Sōtokufu Gakumukyoku Shakaika. *Kōjō oyobi kōzan ni okeru rōdō jōkyō chōsa* [A study of the labor conditions in factories and mines]. Keijō, 1933.

———. "Ninsampu hogo ni kan suru chōsa" [A study concerning the protection of expecting and nursing mothers]. *Chōsen shakai jigyō* 11 (1933).

———. *Shisei sanjūnen shi* [The thirty-year history of the administration]. Keijō, 1940.

Chōsen Sōtokufu hen. *Chōsen no hogo oyobi heigō* [The protection and annexation of Korea]. Keijō, 1917.

Chōsen Sōtokufu Kanbō Bunshoka Murayama Chijunchōsa. *Chōsen no genron to sesō* [Views and social conditions in Korea]. Keijō, 1927.

———. *Chōsen no gunshū* [Korean crowds]. Keijō, 1926.

Chōsen Sōtokufu, Keimukyoku. *Saikin ni okeru chōsen chian jōkyō* [The recent conditions of the public security in Korea]. Keijō, 1933.

Chōsen Sōtokufu Shokusankyoku. *Chōsen ni okeru kōfu rōdō jihō* [A review of Korean miners]. Keijō, 1930.

Chōsen Tetsudō Kyōkai. *Chōsen ni okeru rōdōsha sū oyobi sono bunpu jōkyō* [The number of workers in Korea and the conditions in their distributions]. Keijō, 1929.

Chōsen Tetsudō Yonjūnen Ryakushi [A brief forty-year history of Korean railroads]. Keijō, 1940.

Government-General of Chōsen. *Annual Report: Reforms and Progress in Chōsen (Korea), 1911–1912*. Keijō, 1912.

Government-General of Chōsen. *Annual Report on the Administration of Chōsen, 1926–1927.* Keijō, 1928.

Inch'ŏnbu, *Inch'ŏnsa* [The history of Inch'ŏn]. Keijō, 1933.

Keijōfu. *Gomu kōgyō ni kansuru chōsa* [A study of the rubber industry]. Keijō, 1935.

Keijōfu Sangyō Chōsakai. *Orimono kōgyō ni kansuru chōsa* [A survey of the weaving industry]. Keijō, 1937.

Keijō Shōkō Kaigisho, *Keijō ni okeru kōjō chōsa* [A survey of factories in Seoul]. Keijō, 1937.

Keijō Shokugyō Shōkaijo. *Keijō shokugyō shōkaijo shohō* [Keijō employment agency's report]. Keijō, 1940.

Keijō Teikoku Daigaku Eisei Chōsabu Hen, *Dobakumin no seikatsu eisei* [Sanitation in the life of mud dwellers]. Keijō, 1942.

Kyŏngsŏng Pangjik Chusik Hoesa. *Kyŏngsŏng pangjik osimnyŏn* [Fifty years of Kyŏngsŏng textiles]. Seoul, 1969.

Minami Manshū Tetsudō Kabushiki Gaisha Keizai Chōsa Dai ichibu (Hen). *Chōsenjin rōdōsha ippan jijō* [The general review of Korean workers]. Keijō: Tairen, 1933.

Residency-General in Korea. *Administrative Reforms in Korea.* Keijō, 1907.

Rōmu Kōsei Kenkyūshō. "Chōsenjin rōmu kanri no yōryō" [Points on Korean labor management]. *Rōsei jihō* Vol. 782. Keijō, 1943.

Sangyō rōdō jihō [Industry and labor report]. Oct. 1931. Reprint, Tokyo: Hōsei Daigaku Shuppankyoku, 1986.

Tōkanfu, *Tōkanfu tōkei nenpō* [Annual statistical report of the residency-general of Korea]. Keijō, 1910.

Tōyō bōseki kabushiki gaisha. *Tōyō bōseki 70 nenshi* [A seventy-year history of the Tōyō spinning company]. Tokyo, 1953

Zaidan Hōjin Kekkaku Yobōkai Chōsen Chihō Honbu. *Chōsen ni okeru kekkaku no genjō* [The current conditions of tuberculosis in Korea]. Keijo, 1943.

BOOKS AND ARTICLES IN JAPANESE

Fuji Chōjiro. "Chōsen musan kaikyū kenkyū" [A study of the propertyless class in Korea]. *Chōsen oyobi manshū* (May 1935).

Himeno Minoru (hen). *Chōsen keizai zuhyō* [A chart of Korea's economy]. Keijō: Chōsen Tōkei Kyōkai, 1940.

Hosoi Hajime. *Senman no keirei* [The management of Koreans and Manchurians]. Keijō, 1929.

Hosoi Wakizō. *Jokō aishi* [The pitiful history of female factory workers]. Tokyo: Kaizōsha, 1925.

Kawai Akitake. *Chōsen kōgyō no gen dankai* [The present stage of Korean industries]. Keijō: Tōyō keizai shinpōsha Keijō shikyoku, 1943.

Kojima Tsunehisa. *Hataraku josei hyakunen no ayumi* [The course of one hundred years of working women]. Tokyo: Kawade Shōbōshinsa, 1983.

Murakami Nobuhiko. *Meiji joseishi* [The history of Meiji women]. 4 vols. Tokyo: Rironsha, 1971.

Nihon sanji chōsetsu hyakunenshi [A hundred-year history of birth control in Japan]. Tokyo: Shuppan kagaku sōgōkenkyūkai, 1976.

Oda Fumio. "Chōsenjin rōdōsha mondai" [The problem of the Korean worker]. In *Chōsen keizai no kenkyū* [A study of Korea's economy], by Funada Kyōji. Tokyo: Tōe Shoin, 1929.

Ōno Ken'ichi. "Chōsen kyōiku mondai kanken" [A personal view of the Korean education problem]. *Chōsen Sōtokufu gakumuka.* Keijō: Chōsen kyōikukai, 1936.

Ōno Tamotsu. "Chōsen nōgyō no jittaiteki kenkyū" [A study of the actual conditions of agriculture in Korea]. *Manshū gyōsei gakkai, ronsō dai 4 shu.* Keijō, 1941.

Sakurai Yoshiyuki. *Chōsen ni tsuite kōzan rōdō jōkyō* [The condition of Korean mine workers]. Keijō, 1934.

———. *Chōsen no runpen: Hantō ni tsuite runpen seikatsu no tokuchō* [Korean vagrants: The typical characteristics of vagrants in the peninsula]. Keijō, 1934.

Sampei Kōko. *Nihon mengyō hattatsu shi* [History of the development of the Japanese cotton industry]. Tokyo: Keiō shobō, 1941.

Shidehara Taira. *Chōsen kyōiku ron* [Discussion on the education of Korea]. Tokyo, 1919.

"Sōkon, chihōkon, kaikyūkon, rankon no hei" [The evil custom of early marriage, local marriages, class marriages, and lavish marriages]. *Chōsen shisō tsūshin* (May 1926): 66.

Suzuki Masafumi. *Chōsen keizai no gen dankai* [The current stage of the Korean economy]. Keijō: Teikoku Chihō Gyōsei Gakkai Chōsen Honbu, 1938.

Takahashi Kamekichi. *Gendai chōsen keizai ron* [A discourse on the economy of contemporary Korea]. Tokyo: Chikura Shobō, 1935.

Ujiie Hisako. *Saishin katei kanri to kaji keizai* [Recent family management and household economies]. Tokyo: Genbunsha, 1938.

Yuk Ji-su. "Seishi rōdō ni tsuite" [Regarding silk-reeling labor]. *Chōsen Sōtokufu chōsa geppō* 9, no. 6 (Sept. 1938).

BOOKS AND ARTICLES IN KOREAN

An Sŭng-hyŏn, ed. *Han'guk nodong sosŏl chŏnjip* [Collection of Korean labor novels]. 3 vols. Seoul: Pogosa, 1995.

An Yŏn-sŏn. "Han'guk singminji chabonjuuihwa kwajŏng esŏ yŏsŏng nodong ŭi sŏnggyŏk e kwanhan yŏn'gu: 1930-yŏndae pangjik kong'ŏp ŭl chungsim ŭro" [Research on the characteristics of women's labor during the formation of colonial capitalism in Korea: Focusing on the textile industries during the 1930s]. Master's thesis, Ewha Womans University, 1988.

Cho Sŭng-hyŏk. *Han'guk kong'ŏphwa wa nodong undong* [The industrialization of Korea and labor movements]. Seoul: P'ulbit, 1984.

Cho Un. "Ilcheha hyangch'on pan'ga ŭi kajok saenghwal kwa pyŏnhwa" [The livelihood of rural elite families and changes under Japanese colonial rule]. In *Yŏsŏng kajok sahoe* [Women, family, society], edited by Yŏsŏng han'guk sahoe yŏn'guhoe p'yŏn, 61–83. Seoul: Yŏlumsa, 1991.

Ch'oe Hye-sil. *Sin yŏsŏngdŭl ŭn muŏt ŭl kkum kkuŏnnŭn'ga?* [What were the new women dreaming about?] Seoul: Saenggak ui namu, 2000.

Ch'oe Chun. *Han'guk sinmunsa* [The history of the Korean newspaper]. Seoul: Ilchogak, 1960.

Ch'ŏn Chŏng-hwan. *Kŭndae ŭi ch'aek ilki* [Reading books in the modern period]. Seoul: Tosŏch'ulp'an p'urŭn yŏksa, 2003.

Chŏn Kyŏng-ok, Pyŏn Sin-wŏn, Pak Chin-sŏk, and Kim Un-jŏng, eds. *Han'guk yŏsŏng munhwasa* [A cultural history of Korean women]. 4 vols. Seoul: Sukmyŏng yŏja taehakkyo ch'ulp'an'guk, 2004.

Chŏn Ŭn-jŏng. "Kŭndae kyŏnghŏm kwa yŏsŏng chuch'e hyŏngsŏng kwajŏng" [The modern experience and the formation process of women's subjectivity]. *Yŏsŏng kwa sahoe* 11 (Nov. 2000): 29–45.

Chŏng Chin-sŏng. "Singminji chabonjuŭihwa kwajŏng esŏ ŭi yŏsŏng nodong ŭi pyŏnmo" [The transformation of women's labor under colonial capitalistic processes]. *Han'guk yŏsŏnghak* 4 (1988): 49–100.

Chŏng Ch'ung-nyang. *Ewha 80-yŏnsa* [The eighty-year history of Ewha]. Seoul: Ewha yŏdae ch'ulp'ansa, 1967.

Chŏng Hae-ŭn. "Chosŏn hugi yŏsŏng sirhakcha pinghŏgak yi-ssi" [Late Chosŏn period's female sirhak scholar pinghŏgak Ms. Yi]. *Yŏsŏng kwa sahoe* 8 (1997): 297–317.

———. "Ponggŏn ch'eje ŭi tong'yo wa yŏsŏng ŭi sŏngjang" [Unrest in the feudal system and the rise of women]. In *Uri yŏsŏng ŭi yŏksa* [Our women's history], edited by Han'guk yŏsŏng yŏn'guso yŏsŏngsa yŏn'gusil, 225–74. Seoul: Ch'ŏngnyŏnsa, 1999.

Chŏng Hyŏn-baek. "Yŏsŏngsa yŏn'gu ŭi iron kwa pangpŏp" [Research on women's history: Theory and practice]. *Yŏksa pip'yŏng* (Autumn 1994): 375–91.

Chŏng Kyŏng-suk. "Kaehwagi yŏsŏnggwan ŭi pyŏnmo wa kyoyuk kuguk undong" [The changing view of women during the enlightenment period and the 'save the nation' educational movement]. In *Uri yŏsŏng ŭi yŏksa* [Our women's history], edited by Han'guk yŏsŏng yŏn'guso yŏsŏngsa yŏn'gusil, 251–74. Seoul: Ch'ŏngnyŏnsa, 1999.

Chŏng Un-hyŏn. *Na nŭn hwang'guk sinmin iro soida* [I am hereby an imperial subject]. Seoul: Kaema kowŏn, 1999.

Chu Chong, and Yi Chŏng-ŭn, eds. *1920–1930-yŏndae minjung munhaksŏn* [Selection of minjung literature from 1920 to 1930]. Seoul: T'apch'ulp'ansa, 1990.

Chu Yŏng-ha, Kim So-hyŏn, Kim Ho, and Chŏng Ch'ang-jŏn, eds. *19-segi chosŏn saenghwal kwa sayu ŭi pyŏnhwa rŭl yŏtpora* [A look into the changes in life and thought in nineteenth-century Chosŏn]. Seoul: Tolbege, 2005.

Han'guk chŏngsin munhwa yŏn'guwŏn ed. *Han'guk kyoyuk saryo chipsŏng* [Compilation of historical documents on Korean education]. Seoul, 1994.

Han'guk yŏsŏng kaebalwŏn, ed. *Han'guk yŏksa sok ŭi yŏsŏng inmul* [Female personalities in Korean history]. Seoul: Mundŭk inswae, 1998.

Han'guk yŏsŏngsa p'yŏnch'an wiwŏnhoe. *Han'guk yŏsŏngsa* [The history of Korean women]. 3 vols. Seoul: Ewha yŏja taehakkyo ch'ulp'anbu, 1972.

Han'guk yŏsŏng yŏn'guhoe yŏsŏngsa pun'gwa. "Han'guk yŏsŏngsa ŭi yŏn'gu tonghyang kwa kwaje: Kŭndae p'yŏn" [Research trends and issues in Korean women's history (modern section)]. *Yŏsŏng kwa sahoe* 5 (1994): 297–327.

In Sŭng-hyŏn. *Han'guk nodong sosŏl chŏnjip (1930–1932)* [Collection of Korean working-class novels]. 2 vols. Seoul: Pogosa, 1995.

In'gansa p'yŏnjipsil pŏnyŏk, ed. *Ŏnŭ yŏgong ŭi norae* [A factory girl's song]. Seoul: In'gansa, 1983.

Kang I-su. "1930-yŏndae myŏnbang tae kiŏp yŏsŏng nodongja ŭi sangt'ae e kwanhan yŏn'gu: Nodong kwajŏng kwa nodong t'ongje rŭl chungsim ŭro" [Research on the conditions of female workers in the large-scale cotton industry during the 1930s: Focusing on the labor process and labor control]. Ph.D. dissertation, Ewha Womans University, 1992.

———. "Kongjang ch'eje wa nodong kyuyul" [The factory system and labor discipline]. In *Kŭndae chuch'e wa singminji kyuyul kwŏllyŏk* [Modern subjectivity and colonial disciplinary power], edited by Kim Chin-gyun, Chŏng Kŭn-sik, 117–67. Seoul: Munhwakwahaksa, 1997.

Kang Man-gil. *Han'guk hyŏndaesa* [A modern history of Korea]. Seoul: Ch'angjak kwa pip'yŏng ch'ulp'ansa, 1984.

———. *Ilcheha pinmin saenghwal yŏn'gu* [A study on the livelihood of the poor under Japanese colonial rule]. Seoul: Ch'angjak kwa pip'yŏng ch'ulp'ansa, 1987.

———. *Singminji sigi sahoe kyŏngje han'guksa* [Social and economic history of Korea during the colonial period]. Seoul: Han'gilsa, 1994.

Kang Pyŏng-sik. "Ilcheha han'guk esŏ ŭi kyŏlhon kwa ihon mit ch'ulsan silt'ae yŏn'gu" [Research on marriage, divorce, and birth conditions in Korea under Japanese colonial rule]. *Sahakchi* 28 (1995): 39–67.

Ki Chang-dŏk. "Ŭihakkye ŭi haeoe yuhaksaeng" [Korean medical students studying abroad]. *Ŭisahak* 3, no. 2 (Dec. 1994): 170–92.

Kim Chin-gyun and Chŏng Kŭn-sik, eds. *Kŭndae chuch'e wa singminji kyuyul kwŏllyŏk* [Modern subjectivity and colonial disciplinary power]. Seoul: Munhwakwahaksa, 1997.

Kim Chin-song. *Sŏul e ttaensŭhol ŭl hŏhara* [Permit a dance hall in Seoul]. Seoul: Hyŏnsil munhwa yŏn'gu, 1999.

Kim Chŏng-hwa. *Tambae iyagi* [The story of tobacco]. Seoul: Chiho, 2000.

Kim Hye-gyŏng. "Kasa nodong tamnon kwa han'guk kŭndae kajok: 1920, 1930-yŏndae rŭl chungsim ŭro" [Discourses on domestic labor and the modern Korean family: Focusing on the 1920s and 1930s]. *Han'guk yŏsŏnghak* 15 (1999): 153–84.

Kim Ki-hong. "Ilcheha chŏnsi ch'ongdongwŏn ch'ejegi (1938–1945) hwangminhwa kyoyuk yŏn'gu" [A study of the wartime general mobilization phase under Japanese colonial rule]. Master's thesis, Yonsei University, 2000.

Kim Kwang-un. "1930-yŏn chŏnhu chosŏn ŭi chabon imnodong kwan'gye wa ilche ŭi nodong t'ongje chŏngch'aek" [Korea's capital, wage labor relations, and labor management policies under Japanese colonial rule before and after 1930], edited by Kuksa p'yŏnch'an wiwŏnhoe. *Kuksagwan nonch'ong* [National history institute, collection of materials], vol. 38. Seoul, 1992.

Kim Kyŏng-il. *Ilcheha nodongsa* [A history of labor under Japanese colonial rule]. Seoul: Ch'angjak kwa pip'yŏng, 1992.

———. *Yŏsŏng ŭi kŭndae, kŭndae ŭi yŏsŏng* [The modernity of women, women of modernity]. Seoul: P'urŭn yŏksa, 2004.

Kim Mi-yŏng. "Ilcheha 'chosŏn ilbo' ŭi kajŏng puin-nan yŏn'gu" [A study on the *Chosŏn ilbo*'s family wife column under Japanese colonial rule]. *Hyŏndae munhak yŏn'gu* 16 (2004): 221–76.

Kim Sang-ŏk. *Yi Nŭnghwa chŏnjip: Chosŏn yŏsokko* [Complete works of Yi Nŭnghwa: Korean folk women]. Seoul: Tosŏ ch'ulp'ansa, 1990.

Kim Sŏng-hŭi. "Chŏnt'ong sahoe yŏsŏng ŭi sajŏk yŏngyŏk kwa kongjŏk yŏngyŏksŏ ŭi nodong" [Women's labor in the private and public spheres in traditional Korean society]. *Han'guk kajŏng kwallihak hoeji* 20, no. 6 (2002): 25–36.

Kim Sŏng-ŭn, "1930-yŏndae chosŏn yŏsŏng kyoyuk ŭi sahoejŏk sŏnggyŏk" [Korean women's education and its societal characteristics in Korea during the 1930s]. Master's thesis, Ewha Womans University, 1992.

Kim Sŭng-ok, ed. *Han'guk hyŏndae munhak chŏnjip* [A collection of Korean modern literature]. Vol. 11. Seoul: Samsŏng ch'ulp'ansa, 1978.

Kim T'ae-su. *Kkot kach'ip'iŏ maehokk'e hara: Sinmun kwanggoro bon kŭndae ŭi p'unggyŏng* [Bloom like a flower, make it enchanting: Looking at the modern landscape through the lens of newspaper advertisements]. Seoul: Hwangsojari, 2005.

Kim Tu-hon. *Han'guk kajok chedo yŏn'gu* [A study of the Korean family system]. Seoul: Sŏul taehak ch'ulp'ansa, 1968.

Kim Ŭl-han. *Sillok tonggyŏng yuhaksaeng* [A record of a student studying abroad in Tokyo]. Seoul: T'onggudang, 1986.

Kim Ŭn-ju. "Han'guk kyohoe yŏsŏng kyoyuk ŭi yŏksa wa munje e taehan yŏn'gu: Kamni kyohoe yŏsŏng kyoyuk ŭl chungsim ŭro" [A study on the history and problems of Korean church women: Focusing on women's education and the Methodist Church]. Master's thesis, Ewha Womans University, 1985.

Kim Yun-hwan. *Han'guk nodong undongsa* [A history of the Korean labor movement]. Vol. 1. Seoul: Ch'ŏngsa, 1982.

Ko Pyŏng-ch'ŏl. "Ilche sidae kŏn'gang tamnon kwa yak ŭi kuwŏnnon: maeil sinbo yak kwanggo punsŏk ŭl chungsim ŭro" [Discourses on health and the soteriology of medicine under Japanese colonial rule: An analysis of medicine advertisements in the maeil sinbo]. *Chonggyo yŏn'gu* 30 (2003): 285–310.

Kwŏn Podŭrae. *Yŏnae ŭi sidae: 1920-yŏn ch'oban ŭi munhwa wa yuhaeng* [An era of love: Culture and trends/fashion in the early 1920s]. Seoul: Hyŏnsil munhwa yŏn'gu, 2003.

Kwŏn T'ae-hwan. "Ilche sidae ŭi tosihwa" [Urbanization during the Japanese colonial period], in *Han'guk ŭi sahoe wa munhak* [Korean society and literature]. Vol. 11. Seoul: Han'guk chŏngsin munhwa yŏn'guwŏn, 1990.

Mun So-jŏng. "Ilcheha han'guk nongmin kajok e taehan yŏn'gu—1920–30-yŏndae pinnongch'ŭng ŭl chungsim ŭro" [Research on Korean rural families under

Japanese colonial rule: Focusing on the 1920s–1930s poor peasant class]. Ph.D. dissertation, Seoul National University, 1991.

———. "Ilcheha nongch'on kajok e kwanhan yŏn'gu" [A study of the rural village family under Japanese colonial rule]. In *Han'guk sahoesa yŏn'guhoe non-munjip* [A collection of articles by the Korean social history research association]. Vol. 12. Seoul: Munhak kwa chisŏngsa, 1988.

Na Kyŏng-hŭi. "Ilcheha han'guk sinmun e nat'anan yŏsŏng undonggwan" [An outlook on the women's movement in Korean newspapers under Japanese colonial rule]. Master's thesis, Korea University, 1987.

Pak Chŏng-ae. "1910–1920-yŏndae ch'oban yŏja ilbon yuhaksaeng yŏn'gu" [A study of students studying abroad in Japan during the first half of the 1920s]. Master's thesis, Sookmyung Women's University, 1999.

Pak Ok-ju. "Pinghŏgak yi-ssi ŭi kyuhapch'ongsŏ e taehan munhŏnhak chŏk yŏn'gu" [A philological study of Pinghŏgak yi-ssi's Kyuhapch'ongsŏ]. *Han'guk kojŏn yŏsŏng munhak yŏn'gu* 1 (2000): 271–304.

Pak Sŏng-nae, Sin Tong-wŏn, and O Tong-hun. *Uri kwahak 100-yŏn* [Our science, one hundred years]. Seoul: Hyŏnsamsa, 2001.

Pak Suk-cha. "1920-yŏndae yŏsŏng ŭi yukch'e e taehan namsŏng ŭi sisŏn kwa hwansang" [The male gaze and fantasy of women's bodies in the 1920s]. *Han'guk kundae munhak yŏn'gu* 5, no. 1 (April 2004): 166–93.

Pak Yong-ok. "Nondan: Han'guk yŏsŏng yŏn'gu ŭi tonghyang" [Research note: Trends in women's studies in Korea]. *Ewha sahak yŏn'gu* 9, no. 3 (1976): 30–34.

———. "Yangsŏngwŏn ŭi chojik kwa hwaltong" [The organization and activities of Yangsŏngwŏn]. *Sahak yŏn'gu* 34 (1982): 81–107.

Pak Yun-jae. *Han'guk kŭndae ŭihak ŭi kiwŏn* [The origin of Korea's modern medical system]. Seoul: Hyean. 2005.

Sin Yong-ha. *Han'guk kundae sahoesa yŏn'gu* [A study of the history of modern Korea]. Seoul: Iljisa, 1987.

Sin Yŏng-suk. "Ilcheha han'guk yŏsŏng sahoesa yŏn'gu" [A social history of Korean women under Japanese colonial rule]. Ph.D. dissertation, Ewha Womans University, 1989.

Sŏ Hyŏng-sil. "Singminji sidae yŏsŏng nodong undong e kwanhan yŏn'gu:1930-yŏndae chŏnban'gi komu chep'um chejo'ŏp kwa chesa'ŏp ŭl chungsim ŭro" [A study of the women's labor movement under Japanese colonialism: Centering on the rubber and silk-reeling industry during the first half of the 1930s]. Ph.D. dissertation, Ewha Womans University, 1989.

Son Che-sŏn. "16-segi myŏnp'o ŭi hwap'ae kinŭng" [The function of cotton cloth as currency during the sixteenth century]. In *Pyŏn T'ae-sŏp paksa hoekap kinyŏm sahak nongch'ong* [Commemorating Dr. Pyŏn Tae-sŏp's sixtieth birthday: Collected historical essays], 389–430. Seoul: Sam Yŏngsa, 1985.

Son Hyŏn-suk. "Ilche singminji sigi chosŏn ŭi ch'ulsan t'ongje tamnon ŭi yŏn'gu" [A study of the discourse of birth control under Japanese colonial rule]. Master's thesis, Hanyang University, 1999.

Sukmyŏng yŏja taehakkyo. *Sukmyŏng 70-yŏnsa* [The seventy-year history of Sukmyŏng]. Seoul: Sukmyŏng yŏja chung-kodŭng hakkyo, 1976.

Yamashida Yŏng-ae. "Singminji chibae wa kongch'ang chedo ŭi chŏn'gae" [Colonial control and the development of the prostitution system]. *Sahoe wa yŏksa* 51 (1997): 143–81.

Yi Chŏng-ok. "Ilcheha kong'ŏp nodong esŏ ŭi minjok kwa sŏng, 1910–1945" [Race and sex in industrial labor under Japanese colonial rule, 1910–1945]. Ph.D. dissertation, Seoul National University, 1990.

Yi Chun-gu. *Chosŏn sidae yŏsŏng ŭi il kwa saenghwal* [Women's work and livelihood during the Chosŏn period]. Seoul: Ch'ŏngnyŏnsa, 1999.

Yi Hyo-jae. *Chosŏnjo sahoe wa kajok* [Society and family in the Chosŏn dynasty]. Seoul: Hanŭl, 2003.

———. "Ilcheha han'guk yŏsŏng nodong yŏn'gu" [Research on Korean female labor under Japanese colonial rule]. *Han'guk hakpo* 4 (1976): 141–88.

———. *Kajok kwa sahoe* [Family and society]. Seoul: Minjosa, 1968.

Yi Hye-jŏng. "Ilche malgi Kim Hwal-lan ŭi ilche hyŏmnyŏk paegyŏng kwa nolli" [The background and reasoning behind Kim Hwal-lan's cooperation during the latter period under Japanese colonial rule]. *Yŏsŏnghak nonjip* 21, no. 2 (2004): 45–76.

Yi Kkot-mae. *Han'guk kŭndae kanhosa* [A history of nursing in contemporary Korea]. Seoul: Tosŏnch'ulp'an, 2002.

Yi Kwang-nin. *Han'guk kaehwasa yŏn'gu* [A study of the history of Korean enlightenment]. Seoul: Iljogak, 1969.

Yi Myŏng-sŏn. "Singminji kŭndae ŭi 'sŏng kwahak' tamnon kwa yŏsŏng ŭi sŏng" [Sexology discourse and the construction of female sexuality under colonial modernity]. *Yŏsŏng kŏn'gang* 2 (2001): 97–124.

Yi Yŏ-sŏng and Kim Se-yong. *Sutcha chosŏn yŏn'gu* [Research on statistics in Korea]. Kyŏngsŏng: Segwangsa, 1931.

Yŏksa Hakhoe, ed. *Han'guk ch'injok chedo yŏn'gu* [A study of the Korean kinship system]. Seoul: Ilchogak, 1992.

Yŏsŏngsa yŏn'gu moim kilbak sesang. *20-segi yŏsŏng sagŏnsa* [Historical women's events during the twentieth century]. Seoul: Yŏsŏng sinmunsa, 2001.

Yu Sŭng-hyŏn. "Ilcheha chohon ŭro inhan yŏsŏng pŏmchwae" [Female crimes caused by early marriage under Japanese colonial rule]. In *Yŏsŏng kwa hyŏnsil* [Women and reality], edited by Pak Yong-ok, 357–93. Seoul: Kukhak charyo-wŏn, 2001.

Yun Hye-wŏn. "Kaehwagi yŏsŏng kyoyuk" [Women's education during the enlightenment period]. In *Han'guk kŭndae yŏsŏng yŏn'gu* [Research on modern Korean women], edited by Asea yŏsŏng munje yŏn'guso, 113–83. Seoul, 1987.

BOOKS AND ARTICLES IN ENGLISH

Abu-Lughod, Lila. "Introduction: Feminist Longings and Postcolonial Conditions." In *Remaking Women: Feminism and Modernity in the Middle East.* Princeton, NJ: Princeton University Press, 1998.

Ahearne, Jeremy. *Michel de Certeau: Interpretation and Its Other.* Stanford, CA: Stanford University Press, 1995.

Albisetti, James C. *Schooling German Girls and Women: Secondary and Higher Education in the Nineteenth Century.* Princeton, NJ: Princeton University Press, 1988.

Allen, Horace N. *Things Korean: A Collection of Sketches and Anecdotes Missionary and Diplomatic.* New York: Fleming H. Revell Company, 1908.

Althusser, Louis. *Lenin and Philosophy and Other Essays.* New York: Monthly Review Press, 1971.

Anderson, Benedict. *Imagined Communities.* London: Verso, 1993.

Appadurai, Arjun. *Modernity at Large: Cultural Dimensions of Globalization.* Minneapolis: University of Minnesota Press, 1996.

Baldwin, Frank, Jr. "The March First Movement: Korean Challenge and Japanese Response." Ph.D. dissertation, Columbia University, 1969.

Barnes, J. A. "Genealogies." In *The Craft of Social Anthropology,* edited by A. L. Epstein, 101–27. London: Taustock Publications, 1967.

Baron, Ava, ed. *Work Engendered: Toward a New History of American Labor.* Ithaca, NY: Cornell University Press, 1991

Baverman, Harry. *Labour and Monopoly Capital.* New York: Monthly Review Press, 1974.

Berman, Marshall. *All That Is Solid Melts into Air: The Experience of Modernity.* New York: Penguin Books, 1988.

Bernstein, Gail Lee, ed. *Recreating Japanese Women, 1600–1945.* Berkeley: University of California Press, 1991.

Bibby, Martin. "Feminism, Criticism and Foucault." *New German Critique* 27 (Fall 1982): 3–30.

Bishop, Isabella Bird. *Korea and Her Neighbors: A Narrative of Travel with an Account of the Recent Vicissitudes and Present Position of the Country*. 1895. Reprint, Seoul: Yonsei University Press, 1970.

Block, Fred, and Margaret Somers. "Beyond the Economic Fallacy: The Holistic Social Science of Karl Polanyi." In *Visions and Methods in Historical Sociology*, edited by Theda Skocpol, 47–84. Cambridge: Cambridge University Press, 1984.

Brandt, Vincent. *A Korean Village: Between Farm and Sea*. Cambridge, MA: Harvard University Press, 1971.

Brown, George Thompson. *Mission to Korea*. Nashville, TN: Board of World Missions, Presbyterian Church U.S., 1962.

Buchanan, Allen, Dan W. Brock, Norman Daniels, and Daniel Wilker. *From Chance to Choice: Genetics and Justice*. Cambridge: Cambridge University Press, 2000.

Burke, Martin J. *The Conundrum of Class: Public Discourse on the Social Order in America*. Chicago: University of Chicago Press, 1995.

Butler, Judith. *Bodies That Matter: On the Discursive Limits of "Sex."* New York: Routledge, 1993.

———. *Excitable Speech: A Politics of the Performative*. New York: Routledge, 1997.

———. *Gender Trouble: Feminism and the Subversion of Identity*. New York: Routledge, 1990.

Callaghan, Karen A. *Ideals of Feminine Beauty: Philosophical, Social, and Cultural Dimensions*. Westport: Greenwood Press, 1994.

Canning, Kathleen. *Languages of Labor and Gender: Female Factory Work in Germany, 1850–1914*. Ithaca, NY: Cornell University Press, 1996.

Chakrabarty, Dipesh. "Conditions for Knowledge of Working-Class Conditions: Employers, Government and the Jute Workers of Calcutta, 1890–1940." In *Selected Subaltern Studies*, edited by Ranajit Guha and Gayatri C. Spivak, 179–230. New York: Oxford University Press, 1988.

Chandra, Vipan. *Imperialism, Resistance, and Reform in Late Nineteenth-Century Korea: Enlightenment and the Independence Club*. Berkeley: Institute of East Asian Studies, University of California, 1988.

Chatterjee, Partha. "Colonialism, Nationalism, and Colonized Women: The Contest in India." *American Ethnologist* 16, no. 4 (November 1989): 622–33.

———. *Nationalist Thought and the Colonial World: A Derivative Discourse*. Minneapolis: University of Minnesota Press, 1993.

———. *The Nation and Its Fragments: Colonial and Postcolonial Histories.* Princeton, NJ: Princeton University Press, 1993.

Cheal, David. *Family and the State of Theory.* Toronto: University of Toronto Press, 1991.

Cho, Haejong. "Korean Women and Their Experience in the Traditional World." In *Korean Women and Culture*, edited by the Research Institute of Asian Women, 25–51. Seoul: Sookmyung Women's University Press, 1998.

Cho, Hyoung, and Pil-wha Chang, eds. *Gender Division of Labor in Korea.* Seoul: Ewha Woman's University Press, 1994.

Chodorow, Nancy. *The Reproduction of Mothering: Psychoanalysis and the Sociology of Gender.* Berkeley: University of California Press, 1978.

Choi, Hyae-weol. "Women's Literacy and New Womanhood in Late Chosŏn Korea." *Asian Journal of Women's Studies* 6, no. 1 (March 2003): 88–115.

Choi, Jang-jip. *Labor and the Authoritarian State: Labor Unions in South Korean Manufacturing Industries, 1961–1980.* Seoul: Korea University Press, 1989.

Chung, Chai-sik. *A Korean Confucian Encounter with the Modern World: Yi Hang-no and the West.* Berkeley: Institute of East Asian Studies, University of California, 1995.

———. "Chŏng Tojŏn: 'Architect' of the Yi Dynasty Government and Ideology." In *The Rise of Neo-Confucianism in Korea*, edited by Wm. Theodore de Bary and JaHyun Kim Haboush, 59–88. New York: Columbia University Press, 1985.

Chung, Sei-wha, ed. *Challenges for Women: Women's Studies in Korea.* Translated by Shin Chang-hyun, et al. Seoul: Ewha Womans University Press, 1986.

Chung, Yo-sup. "Women's Social Status in the Yi Dynasty." In *Women of the Yi Dynasty*, edited by Asian Women Research Center, 139–72. Seoul: Sookmyung Women's University Press, 1986.

Clark, Allen D. *A History of the Church in Korea.* Seoul: Christian Literature Society, 1971.

Clark, Anna. *The Struggle for the Breeches: Gender and the Making of the British Working Class.* Berkeley: University of California Press, 1997.

Comaroff, Jean, and John Comaroff. *Of Revelation and Revolution: Christianity, Colonialism, and Consciousness in South Africa.* Chicago: University of Chicago Press, 1991.

Conroy, Hilary. *The Japanese Seizure of Korea 1868–1910: A Study of Realism and Idealism in International Relations.* Philadelphia: University of Pennsylvania Press, 1974.

Cook, Harold. *Korea's 1884 Incident*. Seoul: Royal Asiatic Society, Korea Branch, 1972.

Cooper, Frederick, and Ann Laura Stoler, eds. *Tensions of Empire: Colonial Cultures in a Bourgeois World*. Berkeley: University of California Press, 1997.

Cumings, Bruce. "Bringing Korea Back In: Structured Absence, Glaring Presence, and Invisibility." In *Pacific Passage: The Study of American-East Asian Relations on the Eve of the Twenty-First Century*, edited by Warren I. Cohen, 337–74. New York: Columbia University Press, 1996.

———. "The Legacy of Colonialism." In *The Japanese Colonial Empire, 1895–1945*, edited by Ramon Myers and Mark Peattie, 478–96. Princeton, NJ: Princeton University Press, 1984).

———. *Korea's Place in the Sun: A Modern History*. New York: Norton, 1997.

———. *The Origins of the Korean War*. Vol. 1. Princeton, NJ: Princeton University Press, 1981.

———. "Northeast Asian Political Economy." *International Organization* 38, no. 1 (Winter 1984): 1–40.

———. *Parallax Visions: Making Sense of American–East Asian Relations at the End of the Century*. Durham, NC: Duke University Press, 1999.

Dallet, Charles. *Traditional Korea*. 1874. Reprint, New Haven: Human Relations Area Files, 1954.

Davidoff, Leonore, and Catherine Hall, eds. *Family Fortunes: Men and Women of the English Working Class, 1780–1850*. Chicago: University of Chicago Press, 1987.

de Bary, Theodore Wm., and JaHyun Kim Haboush, eds. *The Rise of Neo-Confucianism in Korea*. New York: Columbia University Press, 1985.

de Bary, Theodore Wm., Ryusaku Tsunoda, and Donald Keene, eds. *Sources of Japanese Tradition*. New York: Columbia University Press, 1964.

de Certeau, Michel. *Heterologies: Discourse on the Other*. Translated by Brian Massumi. Minneapolis: University of Minnesota Press, 1997.

———. *The Practice of Everyday Life*. Translated by Steven Rendall. Berkeley: University of California Press, 1984.

———. *The Writing of History*. Translated by Tom Conley. New York: Columbia University Press, 1988.

Deuchler, Martina. *The Confucian Transformation of Korea: A Study of Society and Ideology*. Cambridge, MA: Harvard University Press, 1992.

———. "Neo-Confucianism in Action: Agnation and Ancestor Worship in Early Yi Korea." In *Religion and Ritual in Korean Society*, edited by Laurel Kendall and Griffin Dix, 26–55. Berkeley: Institute of East Asian Studies, University of California, 1987.

———. "The Tradition: Women during the Yi Dynasty." In *Virtues in Conflict: Tradition and the Korean Woman Today*, edited by Sandra Mattielli, 1–47. Seoul: Royal Asiatic Society, Korea Branch, 1977.

di Leonardo, Micaela, ed. *Gender at the Crossroads of Knowledge: Feminist Anthropology in the Postmodern Era*. Berkeley: University of California Press, 1991.

Donzelot, Jacques. *The Policing of the Families*. Translated by Robert Hurley. Baltimore, MD: Johns Hopkins University Press, 1979.

Dublin, Thomas. *Transforming Women's Work: New England Lives in the Industrial Revolution*. Ithaca, NY: Cornell University Press, 1994.

Duby, Georges, and Michelle Perrot, eds. *A History of Women in the West: Toward a Cultural Identity in the Twentieth Century*. Vol. 5. Cambridge: Belknap Press, 1994.

Dumont, Louis. *Homo Hierarchicus: The Caste System and Its Implications*. Translated by Mark Sainsbury, Louis Dumont, and Basia Gulati. Chicago: University of Chicago Press, 1980.

Duus, Peter. *The Abacus and the Sword: The Japanese Penetration of Korea, 1895–1910*. Berkeley: University of California Press, 1995.

Ebrey, Patricia Buckley. *The Inner Quarters: Marriage and the Lives of Chinese Women in the Sung Period*. Berkeley: University of California Press, 1993.

Eckert, Carter. *Offspring of Empire: The Koch'ang Kims and the Colonial Origins of Korean Capitalism 1875–1945*. Seattle: University of Washington Press, 1991.

Eckert, Carter J., Ki-baik Lee, Young Ick Lew, Michael Robinson, and Edward W. Wagner. *Korea Old and New: A History*. Cambridge, MA: Korea Institute, Harvard University, 1990.

Engel, Barbara Alpern, *Between Fields and the City: Women, Work, and Family in Russia, 1861–1914*. Cambridge: Cambridge University Press, 1996.

———. *Mothers and Daughters: Women of the Intelligentsia in Nineteenth Century Russia*. Evanston, IL: Northwestern Press, 1983.

Engels, Frederick. *The Origin of the Family, Private Property, and State*. New York: Pathfinder Press, 1972.

———. *The Condition of the Working Class in England*. Chicago: Academy Chicago Publishers, 1969.

Enstad, Nan. *Ladies of Labor, Girls of Adventures: Working Women, Popular Culture, and Labor Politics at the Turn of the Twentieth Century*. New York: Columbia University Press, 1999.

Fanon, Frantz. *Black Skin, White Masks*. Translated by Charles Lam Markmann. New York: Grove Press, 1967.

Felski, Rita. *The Gender of Modernity.* Cambridge, MA: Harvard University Press, 1995.

Fisher, James Earnest. "Democracy and Mission Education in Korea." Ph.D. dissertation, Columbia University, Teachers College, 1928.

Forrest, Derek W. *Francis Galton: The Life and Work of a Victorian Genius.* London: Elek, 1974.

Foucault, Michel. *Beyond Structuralism and Hermeneutics.* Translated by Hubert L. Dreyfus and Paul Rabinow. Chicago: University of Chicago Press, 1983.

———. "The Confession of the Flesh." In *Michel Foucault: Power/Knowledge*, edited by Colin Gordon, 194–228. Hemel Hempstead: Harvester, 1980.

———. *Discipline and Punish: The Birth of the Prison.* Translated by Alan Sheridan. New York: Vintage Books, 1995.

———. *The History of Sexuality: An Introduction.* Translated by Robert Hurley. New York: Vintage, 1990.

Frader, Levine. "From Muscles to Nerves: Gender, 'Race' and the Body at Work in France 1919–1930." In *Complicating Categories: Gender, Class, Race, and Ethnicity*, edited by Eileen Boris and Angélique Janssen, 123–48. Cambridge: Cambridge University Press, 1999.

Frader, Laura L., and Sonya O. Rose, eds. *Gender and Class in Modern Europe.* Ithaca, NY: Cornell University Press, 1996.

Frame, Lynne. "Gretchen, Girl, Garçonne? Weimar Science and Popular Culture in Search of the Ideal Woman." In *Women in the Metropolis: Gender and Modernity in Weimar Culture*, edited by Katharine Von Ankum, 12–40. Berkeley: University of California Press, 1997.

Frevert, Ute. *Women in German History: From Bourgeois Emancipation to Sexual Liberation.* Oxford: Oxford University Press, 1989.

Frühstück, Sabine. *Colonizing Sex: Sexology and Sexual Control in Modern Japan.* Berkeley: University of California Press, 2003.

———. "Transforming Sex into a Discourse: Managing the Truth of Sex in Imperial Japan." *Journal of Asian Studies* 59, no. 2 (May 2000): 332–58.

Furth, Charlotte. *A Flourishing Yin: Gender in China's Medical History, 960–1665.* Berkeley: University of California Press, 1999.

Gale, James S. *Korea in Transition.* New York: Young People's Missionary Movement of the United States and Canada, 1909.

———. *Korean Sketches.* Chicago: Fleming H. Revell, 1898.

Gallagher, Catherine, and Thomas Laqueur, eds. *The Making of the Modern Body: Sexuality and Society in the Nineteenth Century.* Berkeley: University of California Press, 1987.

Garon, Sheldon. *The State and Labor in Modern Japan.* Berkeley: University of California Press, 1987.

Geertz, Clifford. *The Interpretation of Cultures.* New York: Basic Books, 1973.

Gifford, Daniel C. *Everyday Life in Korea: A Collection of Studies and Stories.* Chicago: Fleming H. Revell Company, 1898.

Gilman, Charlotte Perkins. *Women and Economics: A Study of the Economic Relations between Male and Women as a Factor in Social Evolution.* New York: Harper and Row, 1966.

Gilmore, W. *Korea from its Capital with a Chapter on Missions.* Philadelphia: Presbyterian Board of Publication, 1892.

Glenn, Evelyn Nakano. "The Social Construction and Institutionalization of Gender and Race: An Integrative Framework." In *Revisioning Gender,* edited by M. M. Ferree, J. Lober, and B. B. Hess, 3–43. Thousand Oaks, CA: Sage Publications, 1999.

Gordon, Andrew. *The Evolution of Labor's Relations in Japan: Heavy Industry, 1853–1955.* Cambridge, MA: Harvard University Press, 1988.

Gragert, Edwin H. *Landownership under Colonial Rule: Korea's Japanese Experience 1900–1935.* Honolulu: University of Hawai'i Press, 1994.

Grajdanzev, Andrew. *Modern Korea.* New York: International Secretariat, Institute of Pacific Relations, 1944.

Gramsci, Antonio. *Selections from Cultural Writings.* Edited by David Forgacs and Geoffrey Nowell-Smith and translated by William Boelhower. Cambridge, MA: Harvard University Press, 1985.

Griffis, William Elliott. *Corea: The Hermit Nation.* New York: Charles Scribner's Sons, 1885.

Guha, Ranajit, and Gayatri Chakravorty Spivak, eds. *Selected Subaltern Studies.* New York: Oxford University Press, 1988.

Gutzlaff, Charles. *Journal of Three Voyages along the Coast of China in 1831, 1832, and 1833 with Notices of Siam, Corea, and the Loo-Choo Islands.* London: Frederick Westley and Att. Davis, 1834.

Haaland, Bonnie. *Emma Goldman: Sexuality and the Impurity of the State.* Montreal: Black Rose Books, 1993.

Haboush, Jahyun Kim. "Filial Emotions and Filial Values: Changing Patterns in the Discourse of Filiality in Late Chosŏn Korea." *Harvard Journal of Asiatic Studies* 55, no. 1 (June 1995): 129–77.

———. "The Confucianization of Korean Society." In *The Confucian Heritage and Its Modern Adaptations,* edited by Gilbert Rozman, 84–110. Princeton, NJ: Princeton University Press, 1991.

———. *The Memoirs of Lady Hyegyŏng: The Autobiographical Writings of a Crown Princess of Eighteenth-Century Korea.* Berkeley: University of California Press, 1996.

Hacking, Ian. *The Taming of Chance.* Cambridge: Cambridge University Press, 2001.

Hall, John R., ed. *Reworking Class.* Ithaca, NY: Cornell University Press, 1997.

Hamilton, Angus. *Korea.* New York: Charles Scribner's Sons, 1904.

Hane, Mikiso. *Modern Japan: A Historical Survey.* Boulder, CO: Westview Press, 1986.

———. *Peasants, Rebels, and Outcastes: The Underside of Modern Japan.* New York: Pantheon Books, 1982.

Hannam, June, and Karen Hunt, *Socialist Women: Britain, 1880s to 1920s.* New York: Routledge, 2002.

Haraway, Donna J. *Simians, Cyborgs, and Women: The Reinvention of Nature.* New York: Routledge, 1991.

Hartmann, Heidi. "The Unhappy Marriage of Marxism and Feminism: Toward a More Progressive Union." In *Women and Revolution,* edited by Lydia Sargent, 1–41. Boston: South End Press, 1981.

Harootunian, Harry. *Overcome by Modernity: History, Culture, and Community in Interwar Japan.* Princeton, NJ: Princeton University Press, 2000.

Harvey, David. *The Condition of Postmodernity.* Cambridge: Blackwell, 1990.

Hershatter, Gail. "The Subaltern Talks Back: Reflections on Subaltern Theory and Chinese History." *positions* 1, no. 1 (Spring 1993): 103–30.

Hirshbein, Laura Davidow. "The Flapper and the Fogy: Representations of Gender and Age in the 1920s." *Journal of Family History* 26, no. 1 (January 2001): 112–37.

Hollis, Patricia. *Women in Public: The Women's Movement 1850–1900.* London: George Allen and Unwin, 1981.

Holt, Alix. *Selected Writings of Alexandra Kollontai.* Westport, CT: Lawrence Hill and Company, 1977.

Horn, David. *Social Bodies: Science, Reproduction, and Italian Modernity.* Princeton, NJ: Princeton University Press, 1994.

———. "This Norm Which Is Not One: Reading the Female Body in Lombroso's Anthropology." In *Deviant Bodies: Critical Perspectives on Difference on Science and Popular Culture,* edited by Jennifer Terry and Jacqueline Urla, 109–28. Bloomington: Indiana University Press, 1995.

Hulbert, Homer B. *The Passing of Korea.* New York: Paragon Book Gallery, 1906.

Hunt, Everett Nichols, Jr. *Protestant Pioneers in Korea.* New York: Orbis Books, 1980.

Hutton, Marcelline J. *Russian and West European Women 1860–1939: Dreams, Struggles, and Nightmares.* Boston: Rowman and Littlefield Publishers, 2001.

Hwang, Kyung Moon. *Beyond Birth: Social Status in the Emergence of Modern Korea.* Cambridge. MA: Harvard University Asia Center, 2005.

Ibsen, Henrik. *A Doll's House.* New York: Dover Publications, 1992.

Jager, Sheila Miyoshi. "Women and the Promise of Modernity: Signs of Love for the Nation in Korea." *New Literary History* 29 (1998): 121–34.

Janelli, Roger L., and Dawnhee Yim Janelli. *Ancestor Worship and Korean Society.* Stanford, CA: Stanford University Press, 1982.

Johnson, Chalmers. *MITI and the Japanese Miracle: The Growth of Industrial Policy, 1925–1975.* Stanford, CA: Stanford University Press, 1982.

Johnstone, Bruce F. *Japanese Food Management in World War II.* Stanford, CA: Stanford University Press, 1953.

Joyce, Patrick, ed. *Class.* Oxford: Oxford University Press, 1995.

Kelly, Gail P., and Phillip G. Altbach. "The Four Faces of Colonialism." In *Education and the Colonial Experience,* edited by Gail P. Kelly and Phillip G. Altbach, 1–5. New Brunswick, NJ: Transaction, 1984.

Kelly, Joan. *Women, History, and Theory.* Chicago: University of Chicago Press, 1984.

Kelly, John D. *A Politics of Virtue: Hinduism, Sexuality and Countercolonial Discourse in Fiji.* Chicago: University of Chicago Press, 1991.

Kendall, Laurel. *Getting Married in Korea: Of Gender, Morality, and Modernity.* Berkeley: University of California Press, 1996.

———. *Shamans, Housewives, and Other Restless Spirits: Women in Korean Ritual Life.* Honolulu: University of Hawai'i Press, 1985.

Key, Ellen. *The Century of the Child.* New York: G. P. Putnam's Sons, 1909.

———. *Love and Marriage.* Translated by Arthur G. Chater. New York: G. P. Putnam's Sons, 1912.

———. *The Renaissance of Motherhood.* New York: G. P. Putnam's Sons, 1914.

Kim, Helen. "Rural Education for the Regeneration of Korea." Ph.D. dissertation, Columbia University, 1931.

Kim, Seung-kyung. *Class Struggle or Family Struggle? The Lives of Women Factory Workers in South Korea.* Cambridge: Cambridge University Press, 1997.

Kim, Yung-hee. "From Subservience to Autonomy: Kim Won'ju's Awakening." *Korean Studies* 21 (1997): 1–50.

Kim, Yung-Chung, ed. *Women of Korea: A History from Ancient Times to 1945.* Seoul: Ewha Womans University Press, 1976.

Ko, Dorothy. *Teachers of the Inner Chambers: Women and Culture in Seventeenth-Century China.* Stanford, CA: Stanford University Press, 1994.

Koh, Hesung-Chun. *Korean Family and Kinship Studies Guide.* New Haven, CT: Human Relations Area Files, 1980.

Knodel, John. *The Decline of Fertility in Germany, 1871–1939.* Princeton, NJ: Princeton University Press, 1974.

Koo, Hagen. *Korean Workers: The Culture and Politics of Class Formation.* Ithaca, NY: Cornell University Press, 2001.

Koo, Hagen, ed. *State and Society in Contemporary Korea.* Ithaca, NY: Cornell University Press, 1993.

Kwon, Insook. "The 'New Women's Movement' in 1920s Korea: Rethinking the Relationship between Imperialism and Women." *Gender and History* 10, no. 3 (Nov. 1998): 381–405.

Lee, Hoon K. *Land Utilization and Rural Economy in Korea.* Chicago: University of Chicago Press, 1936.

Lee, Hyo-chae. "Protestant Missionary Work and Enlightenment of Korean Women." *Korea Journal* 17, no. 11 (Nov. 1977): 33–50.

Lee, Ki-baik. *A New History of Korea.* Translated by Edward W. Wagner with Edward J. Shultz. Cambridge, MA: Harvard University Press.

Lee, Peter, ed. *Flowers of Fire: Twentieth-Century Korean Stories.* Honolulu: University of Hawai'i Press, 1974.

———. *Sourcebook of Korean Civilization.* Vol. 2. New York: Columbia University Press, 1996.

Lefebvre, Henri, *Critique of Everyday Life.* Translated by John Moore. London: Verso, 1991.

———. *The Production of Space.* Translated by Donald Nicholson-Smith. Oxford: Blackwell, 1993.

Lerner, Gerda. "Reconceptualizing Difference among Women." *Journal of Women's History* 3 (Winter 1990): 106–22.

Levi-Strauss, Claude. *The Savage Mind.* Chicago: University of Chicago Press, 1966.

Lew Young-ick. "The Kabo Reform Movement: Korean and Japanese Reform Efforts in Korea, 1894." Ph.D. dissertation, Harvard University, 1972.

Lockwood, William W., ed. *The State and Economic Enterprise in Japan: Essays in the Political Economy of Growth.* Princeton, NJ: Princeton University Press, 1965.

Lombroso, Ceseare, and Guglielmo Ferrero. *Criminal Woman, the Prostitute, and the Normal Woman.* Translated by Nicole Hahn Rafter and Mary Gibson. Durham, NC: Duke University Press, 2004.

Lowell, Percival. *Choson: The Land of the Morning Calm.* Boston: Ticknor, 1888.

Macherey, Pierre. *A Theory of Literary Production.* Translated by Geoffrey Wall. London: Routledge and Kegan Paul: 1978.

Marcus, Steven. *Engels, Manchester, and the Working Class.* New York: W. W. Norton, 1974.

Marx, Karl. *Capital: A Critique of Political Economy.* Vol. 1. New York: International Publishers, 1967.

Mass, William, and Andrew Robertson. "From Textile to Automobiles: Mechanical and Organizational Innovation in the Toyoda Enterprises, 1895–1933." *Business and Economic History* 35, no. 2 (Winter 1996): 1–37.

McLellan, David, ed. *Karl Marx: Selected Writings.* Oxford: Oxford University Press, 1977.

McNamara, Dennis L. *The Colonial Origins of Korean Enterprise, 1910–1945.* Cambridge: Cambridge University Press, 1990.

McNay, Lois. *Foucault: Feminism.* Boston: Northeastern University Press, 1993.

Memmi, Albert. *The Colonizer and Colonized.* Boston: Beacon Press, 1967.

Miln, Louise Jordan. *Quaint Korea.* New York: Charles Scribner's Sons, 1895.

Minichiello, Sharon A., ed. *Japan's Competing Modernities: Issues in Culture and Democracy 1900 1930.* Honolulu: University of Hawai'i Press, 1998.

Mitchell, Sally. *The New Girl: Girls' Culture in England, 1880–1915.* New York: Columbia University Press, 1995.

Mitchell, Timothy. *Colonizing Egypt.* Berkeley: University of California Press, 1991.

Mohammed, Jan. "The Economy of Manichean Allegory." In *The Post-colonial Studies Reader,* edited by Bill Ashcroft, Gareth Griffin, and Helen Tiffin, 18–23. New York: Routledge, 1995.

Mohanty, Chandra Talpade. "Under Western Eyes: Feminist Scholarship and Colonial Discourses." In *Third World Women and the Politics of Feminism,* edited by Chandra Mohanty, Ann Russo, and Lourdes Torres, 51–80. Indianapolis: Indiana University Press, 1991.

Molony, Barbara. *Technology and Investment: The Prewar Japanese Chemical Industry.* Cambridge, MA: Harvard University Press, 1990.

Moose, J. Robert. *Village Life in Korea.* Nashville: Publishing House of the M. E. Church, 1911.

Moskowitz, Karl. "The Creation of the Oriental Development Company: Japanese Illusions Meets Korean Reality." *Occasional Papers on Korea,* no. 2 (March 1974): 73–121.

Myers, Ramon H., and Mark R. Peattie, eds. *The Japanese Colonial Empire, 1895–1945.* Princeton, NJ: Princeton University Press, 1984.

Moore, Henrietta L. *A Passion for Difference*. Bloomington: Indiana University Press, 1994.

Nahm, Andrew. *Tradition and Transformation: A History of the Korean People*. Elizabeth City, NJ: Hollym, 1993.

Najita, Tetsuo. *Japan: The Intellectual Foundations of Modern Japanese Politics*. Chicago: University of Chicago Press, 1974.

———. "Japan's Industrial Revolution in Historical Perspective." In *Japan and the World*, edited by Masao Miyoshi and H. D. Harootunian, 13–30. Durham, NC: Duke University Press, 1993.

Najita, Tetsuo, and J. Victor Koschmann, eds. *Conflict in Modern Japanese History: The Neglected Tradition*. Princeton, NJ: Princeton University Press, 1982.

Nakamura, James I. *Agricultural Production and Economic Development of Japan 1873–1922*. Princeton, NJ: Princeton University Press, 1966.

National History Compilation Committee, ed. *Yun Ch'i-ho's Diary*. Vol. 2. Seoul, 1974.

Nisbet, Annabel Major. *Day In and Day Out in Korea*. Richmond, VA: Presbyterian Committee of Publications, 1919.

Ohnuki-Tierney, Emiko. *Culture through Time: Anthropological Approaches*. Stanford, CA: Stanford University Press, 1990.

Ohkawa, Kazushi, and Henry Rosovsky. "The Role of Agriculture in Modern Japanese Economic Development." *Economic Development and Cultural Change* 9, no. 1 (Oct. 1960): 43–69.

Ong, Aihwa. "Japanese Factories, Malay Workers: Class and Sexual Metaphors in West Malaysia." In *Power and Difference: Gender in Island Southeast Asia*, edited by J. M. Atkinson and S. Errington, 385–422. Stanford, CA: Stanford University Press, 1990.

———. "The Gender and Labor Politics of Postmodernity." *Annual Review of Anthropology* 20 (1991): 279–309.

———. *Spirits of Resistance and Capitalist Discipline: Factory Women in Malaysia*. New York: SUNY Press, 1987.

Oppert, Ernest. *A Forbidden Land: Voyages to the Corea*. New York: G. P. Putman's Sons, 1880.

Paik, George L. *The History of Protestant Missions in Korea 1832–1910*. P'yŏngyang: Union Christian College Press, 1929.

Paik, Nak-chung. "The Idea of a Korean National Literature Then and Now." *positions* 1, no. 3 (Winter 1993): 553–80.

Palais, James. *Confucian Statecraft and Korean Institutions: Yu Hyŏng-wŏn and the Late Chosŏn Dynasty*. Seattle: University of Washington Press, 1996.

———. *Politics and Policy in Traditional Korea*. Cambridge, MA: Harvard University Press, 1991.

Pak, Jihang. "Trailblazers in a Traditional World: Korea's First Women College Graduates, 1910–1945." *Social Science History* 14, no. 4 (Winter 1990): 533–58.

Park, Soon-won. *Colonial Industrialization and Labor in Korea*. Cambridge, MA: Harvard University Asia Center, 1999.

Pearse, Arno. *The Cotton Industry of Japan and China*. Manchester: International Cotton Federation, 1929.

Peis, Kathy. *Cheap Amusements: Working Women and Leisure in Turn-of-the-Century New York*. Philadelphia: Temple University Press, 1986.

Peterson, Mark A. *Korean Adoption and Inheritance: Case Studies in the Creation of a Classic Confucian Society*. Ithaca, NY: East Asia Program, Cornell University, 1996.

———. "Women without Sons: A Measure of Social Change in Yi Dynasty Korea." In *Korean Women: View from the Inner Room*, edited by Laurel Kendall and Mark Peterson, 34–38. New Haven, CT: East Rock Press, 1983.

Polanyi, Karl. *The Great Transformation: The Political and Economic Origins of Our Time*. Boston: Beacon Press, 1957.

Poovey, Mary. *Making a Social Body: British Cultural Formation, 1830–1864*. Chicago: University of Chicago Press, 1995.

———. *Uneven Developments: The Ideological Work of Gender in Mid-Victorian England*. Chicago: University of Chicago Press, 1988.

Poster, Mark. *Critical Theory of the Family*. New York: Seabury Press, 1978.

Prakash, Gyan. "Subaltern Studies as Postcolonial Criticism." *American Historical Review* 99 (Dec. 1994): 1475–90.

Pugh, Martin. *Women and the Women's Movement in Britain*. New York: St. Martin's Press, 2000.

Rabinow, Paul. *French Modern: Norms and Forms of the Social Environment*. Chicago: University of Chicago Press, 1989.

Rabinow, Paul, ed. *The Foucault Reader*. New York: Pantheon Books, 1984.

Rafael, Vicente L. *Contracting Colonialism: Translation and Christian Conversion in Tagalog Society under Early Spanish Rule*. Durham, NC: Duke University Press, 1993.

Randall, Jane. *The Origins of Modern Feminism: Women in Britain, France, and the United States*. New York: Schocken Books, 1984.

Rapp, Rayna. "Family and Class in Contemporary America: Notes toward an Understanding of Ideology." *Science and Society* 42 (Fall 1978): 257–55.

Research Center for Asian Women, Sookmyung Women's University. *Women of the Yi Dynasty*. Seoul: Cheon Poong Press, 1986.

Rhodes, Harry A. *History of the Korean Mission Presbyterian Church U.S.A., 1884–1934*. Seoul: Chosŏn Mission Presbyterian Church U.S.A., 1925.

Riley, Denise. *"Am I That Name?" Feminism and the Category of 'Women' in History*. Minneapolis: University of Minnesota Press, 1988.

Robinson, Michael E. *Cultural Nationalism in Colonial Korea, 1920–1925*. Seattle: University of Washington Press, 1988.

Rodd, Laura Rasplica. "Yosanao Akiko and the Taisho Debate over the 'New Woman.'" In *Recreating Japanese Women 1600–1945*," edited by Gail Lee Bernstein, 175–98. Berkeley: University of California Press, 1991.

Rodgers, Daniel T. *The Work Ethic in Industrial America 1850–1920*. Chicago: University of Chicago Press, 1978.

Rosaldo, Michelle Zimbalist. "The Uses and Abuse of Anthropology." *Signs* 5, no. 3 (1980): 389–417.

Rosaldo, Michelle Zimbalist, and Louise Lamphere, eds. *Women, Culture, and Society*. Stanford, CA: Stanford University Press, 1974.

Rose, Sonya. "Resuscitating Class." *Social Science History* 22, no. 1 (Spring 1998): 19–27.

Rosovosky, H., and K. Ohkawa. "A Century of Japanese Economic Growth." In *The State and Economic Enterprise in Japan*, edited by W. W. Lockwood, 47–92. Princeton, NJ: Princeton University Press, 1965.

Rousseau, Jean-Jacques. *Emile: Or, on Education*. Translated by Allan Bloom. New York: Basic Books, 1979.

Rutt, Richard. *Modern Transformation of Korea*. Seoul: Sejong Publishing Company, 1970.

Ryu, Dae Young. "Understanding Early American Missionaries in Korea 1884–1910: Capitalist Middle-Class Values and the Weber Thesis." *Archives de sciences sociales des religions* 113 (Jan.–Mar., 2001): 93–118.

Samuel, Raphael. "Mechanization and Hand Labour in Industrializing Britain." In *The Industrial Revolution and Work in Nineteenth Century Europe*, edited by Lenard R. Berlanstein, 26–40. London: Routledge, 1992.

Sangari, Kumkum, and Sudesh Vaid, eds. *Recasting Women: Essays in Indian Colonial History*. New Brunswick, NJ: Rutgers University Press, 1990.

Sanger, Margaret. *Pioneering Advocate for Birth Control: An Autobiography*. New York: Cooper Square Press, 1999.

———. *Woman and the New Race*. New York: Truth Publishing, 1920.

Sato, Barbara. *The New Japanese Woman: Modernity, Media, and Women in Interwar Japan*. Durham, NC: Duke University Press, 2003.

Sauer, Charles A., ed. *Within the Gate: Comprising the Addresses Delivered at the*

Fiftieth Anniversary of Korean Methodism First Church. Seoul: Korean Methodist News Service, 1934.

Savage, David W. "Missionaries and the Development of a Colonial Ideology of Female Education in India." *Gender and History* 9, no. 2 (Aug. 1997): 201–21.

Savage-Landor, Henry. *Corea or Cho-sen: The Land of the Morning Calm.* New York: MacMillan, 1895.

Scott, James. *Domination and the Arts of Resistance: Hidden Transcripts.* New Haven, CT: Yale University Press, 1990.

———. *Seeing Like a State.* New Haven, CT: Yale University Press, 1998.

Scott, Joan Wallach. "Gender: A Useful Category for Historical Analysis." *American Historical Review* 91, no. 5 (1996): 1052–75.

———. *Gender and the Politics of History.* New York: Columbia University Press, 1988.

———. *The Glassworkers of Carmaux: French Craftsmen and Political Action in a Nineteenth-Century City.* Cambridge, MA: Harvard University Press, 1974.

———. "On Language, Gender, and Working-Class History." *International Labor and Working Class History* 41 (Spring 1987): 1–14.

———. "The Woman Worker" In *A History of Women: Emerging Feminism from Revolution to World War,* edited by Genevieve Fraisse and Michelle Perrot, 399–426. Cambridge, MA: Harvard University Press, 1993.

Scott, Joan, and Louise Tilly. "Women's Work and the Family in Nineteenth-Century Europe." *Comparative Studies in Society and History* 18, no. 1 (1975): 36–64.

Scott, William. *Canadians in Korea: Brief Historical Sketches of Canadian Mission Work in Korea.* Toronto: Board of World Missions, United Church of Canada, 1975.

Sedgwick, Eve Kosofsky. *Epistemology of the Closet.* Berkeley: University of California Press, 1990.

Sen, Gita. "The Sexual Division of Labor and the Working Class: Towards a Conceptual Synthesis of Class Relations and the Subordination of Women." *Review of Radical Political Economics* 12, no. 2 (Summer 1980): 76–86.

Sewell, William H., Jr. "Artisans, Factory Workers, and the Formation of the French Working Class, 1789–1848." In *Working-Class Formation: Nineteenth Century Patterns in Western Europe and the United States,* edited by Ira Katznelson and Aristide R. Zolberg, 45–70. Princeton, NJ: Princeton University Press, 1986.

———. *Logics of History: Social Theory and Social Transformation.* Chicago: University of Chicago Press, 2005.

————. *Work and Revolution in France: The Language of Labor from the Old Regime to 1848*. Cambridge: Cambridge University Press, 1980.

Sharpe, Jenny. *Allegories of Empire: The Figure of Woman in the Colonial Text*. Minneapolis: University of Minnesota Press, 1993.

Sharpe, Pamela, ed. *Women's Work: The English Experience 1650–1914*. London: Arnold, 1998.

Shields, Robert. *Lefebvre, Love, and Struggle: Spatial Dialectics*. London: Routledge, 1999.

Shin, Gi-wook. *Peasant Protest and Social Change in Colonial Korea*. Seattle: University of Washington Press, 1996.

Shin, Gi-wook, and Michael Robinson, eds. *Colonial Modernity in Korea*. Cambridge, MA: Harvard University Asia Center, 1999.

Shin, Susan S. "Economic Development and Social Mobility in Pre-Modern Korea: 1600–1860." *Peasant Studies* 7, no. 3 (Summer 1978): 187–97.

Shorter, Edward. *The Making of the Modern Family*. New York: Basic Books, 1977.

Sievers, Sharon L. *Flowers in Salt: The Beginnings of Feminist Consciousness in Modern Japan*. Stanford, CA: Stanford University Press, 1983.

Silberman. Bernard S., and H. D. Harootunian, eds. *Japan in Crisis: Essays on Taishō Democracy*. Ann Arbor: Center for Japanese Studies, University of Michigan, 1999.

Silverberg, Miriam. "Remembering Pearl Harbor, Forgetting Charlie Chaplin, and the Case of the Disappearing Western Woman: A Picture Story." In *Formations of Colonial Modernity in East Asia*, edited by Tani Barlow, 249–94. Durham, NC: Duke University Press, 1997.

Sinha, Mrinalini. *Colonial Masculinity: The 'Manly Englishman' and the 'Effeminate Bengali' in the Late Nineteenth Century*. Manchester: Manchester University Press, 1995.

Smelser, Neil. *Social Change in the Industrial Revolution: An Application of Theory to the Lancashire Cotton Industry, 1770–1840*. London: Routledge & Kegan Paul, 1959.

Smith, T. R., ed. *The Woman Question*. New York: Boni and Liveright, 1918.

Smith, Thomas C. *Native Sources of Japanese Industrialization, 1750–1920*. Berkeley: University of California Press, 1988.

Søland, Brigitte. *Becoming Modern: Young Women and the Reconstruction of Womanhood in the 1920s*. Princeton, NJ: Princeton University Press, 2000.

Soltau, T. Stanley. *Korea: The Hermit Nation and Its Response to Christianity*. Toronto: World Dominion Press, 1932.

Spivak, Gayatri C. "Subaltern Studies: Deconstructing Historiography." In *Selected Subaltern Studies*, edited by Ranajit Guha and Gayatri C. Spivak, 3–32. New York: Oxford University Press, 1988.

Spurr, David. *The Rhetoric of Empire: Colonial Discourse in Journalism, Travel Writing, and Imperial Administration.* Durham, NC: Duke University Press, 1994.

Stansell, Christine. *City of Women: Sex and Class in New York 1789–1860.* Urbana: University of Illinois Press, 1987.

Steinmetz, George. "Workers and the Welfare State in Imperial Germany." *International Labor and Working-Class History* 40 (Fall 1991): 18–47.

Stone, G. P. "Appearance of Self." In *Human Behavior and Social Process: An Interactionist Approach*, edited by Arnold M. Rose, 86–116. Boston: Houghton Mifflin, 1962.

Stone, Lawrence. *The Family, Sex, and Marriage.* New York: Harper and Row, 1979.

Stoler, Ann Laura. *Race and the Education of Desire: Foucault's History of Sexuality and the Colonial Order of Things.* Durham, NC: Duke University Press, 1996.

Strange, Julie-Marie. "Menstrual Fictions: Language of Medicine and Menstruation, c. 1850–1930." *Women's History Review* 9, no. 3 (2000): 607–28

Suh, Sang-chul. *Growth and Structural Changes in the Korean Economy 1910–1940.* Cambridge, MA: Harvard University Press, 1978.

Ta Chen. "The Labor Situation in Korea." *U.S. Department of Labor Bureau of Labor Statistics* 31, no. 5 (Nov. 1930): 26–36.

Tilly, Louise A., and Joan Scott. *Women, Work, and Family.* New York: Routledge, 1987.

Thion'go, Ngugi Wa. *Decolonizing the Mind: The Politics of Language in African Literature.* Portsmith, NH: Heinemann, 1981.

Thompson, E. P. *The Making of the English Working Class.* New York: Vintage, 1996.

———. "Time, Work, and Industrial Capitalism." *Past and Present* 38 (1967): 56–97.

Trotsky, Leon. *Women and the Family.* New York: Pathfinder Press, 1970.

Tsurumi, E. Patricia. *Factory Girls: Women in the Thread Mills of Meiji Japan.* Princeton, NJ: Princeton University Press, 1990.

———. "Visions of Women and the New Society in Conflict: Yamakawa Kikue Versus Takamure Itsue." In *Japan's Competing Modernities: Issues in Culture and Democracy 1900–1930*, edited by Sharon Minichiello, 335–57. Honolulu: University of Hawai'i Press, 1998.

Tu, Wei-ming. "Probing the 'Three-Bonds' and the 'Five-Relationships in Confucian Humanism." In *Confucianism and the Family*, edited by Walter H. Slote and George A. DeVos, 121–36. Albany: SUNY Press, 1998.

Tucker, Robert, ed. *The Marx-Engels Reader*. New York: W. W. Norton, 1978.

Underwood, Horace. *Fifteen Years among the Top-Knots or Life in Korea*. Boston: American Tract Society, 1904.

———. *Modern Education in Korea*. New York: International Press, 1926.

Uno, Kathleen S. *Passages to Modernity: Motherhood, Childhood, and Social Reform in Early Twentieth Century Japan*. Honolulu: University of Hawai'i Press, 1999.

Viswanathan, Gauri. "Currying Favor: The Politics of British Educational and Cultural Policy in India, 1813–54." In *Dangerous Liaisons: Gender, Nation, and Postcolonial Perspectives*, edited by Anne McClintock, Aamir Mufti, and Ella Shohat, 85–104. Minneapolis: University of Minnesota Press, 1997.

———. *Outside the Fold: Conversion, Modernity, and Belief*. Princeton, NJ: Princeton University Press, 1998.

Voloshinov, V. N. *Marxism and the Philosophy of Language*. Translated by Ladislav Matejka and I. R. Titunik. Cambridge, MA: Harvard University Press, 1986.

von Ankum, Katharina. *Women in the Metropolis: Gender and Modernity in Weimar Culture*. Berkeley: University of California Press, 1997.

Wagner, Edward. "The Korean Chokp'o as a Historical Source" In *Papers in Asian Genealogy*, edited by Spencer J. Palmer, 23–32. Provo, UT: Brigham Young University, 1972.

Waley, Arthur. *The Analects of Confucius*. New York: Vintage Books, 1989.

Walkowitz, Judith R. *City of Dreadful Delight: Narratives of Sexual Danger in Late-Victorian London*. Chicago: University of Chicago Press, 1992.

Weber, Eugen. *Peasants into Frenchmen: The Modernization of Rural France, 1870–1914*. Stanford, CA: Stanford University Press, 1976.

Weedon, Chris. *Feminist Practice and Poststructuralist Theory*. Cambridge: Blackwell, 1997.

Weems, Benjamin B. *Reform, Rebellion, and the Heavenly Way*. Tucson: University of Arizona Press, 1964.

Williams, Raymond. *The Country and the City*. New York: Oxford University Press, 1973.

———. *Keywords: A Vocabulary of Culture and Society*. New York: Oxford University Press, 1983.

———. *Marxism and Literature*. Oxford: Oxford University Press, 1997.

Wolf, Eric R. *Peasant Wars of the Twentieth Century*. New York: Harper and Row, 1969.

Wolf, Margery. *Women and Family in Rural Taiwan.* Stanford, CA: Stanford University Press, 1972.

Wollstonecraft, Mary. *A Vindication of the Rights of Women.* Edited by Charles Hagelman. New York: W. W. Norton, 1967.

Woo, Jung-en. *Race to the Swift: State and Finance in Korean Industrialization.* New York: Columbia University Press, 1991.

Woo-Cumings, Meredith, ed. *The Developmental State.* Ithaca, NY: Cornell University Press, 1999.

Wood, Elizabeth. *The Baba and the Comrade: Gender and Politics in Revolutionary Russia.* Bloomington: Indiana University Press, 1997.

Woycke, James. *Birth Control in Germany, 1871–1933.* London: Routledge, 1988.

Yamamura, Kozo. "The Japanese Economy, 1911–1930: Concentration, Conflicts, and Crises." In *Japan in Crisis: Essays on Taishō Democracy,* edited by Bernard S. Silberman and H. D. Harootunian, 299–328. Ann Arbor: Center for Japanese Studies, University of Michigan, 1999.

Yang, Hyunnah. "Envisioning Feminist Jurisprudence in Korean Family Law at the Crossroads of Tradition and Modernity." Ph.D. dissertation, New School for Social Research, 1998.

Yoon, Soon-young. "Review Essay: Women's Studies in Korea." *Signs: Journal of Women in Culture and Society* 4, no. 4 (1979): 751–63.

Yoshimi, Yoshiaki. *Comfort Women: Sexual Slavery in the Japanese Military during World War II.* New York: Columbia University Press, 2000.

Young, Iris Marion. "Gender as Seriality: Thinking about Women as a Social Collective." *Signs: Journal of Women in Culture and Society* 19, no. 3 (1994): 713–38.

INDEX

Abe Isoo, 81
adoption, 23
advertisement, of erotic texts, 164–65.
    See also *ppalgan ch'aek* (red books)
aeho (love and protection), 90
agricultural crisis: colonial rural policy
    and, 101–3; collapse of handicraft
    industries, 108, 114; household
    expenditures and, 104; impact on
    rural women and the family, 106–10;
    impoverishment and out-migration,
    103–8; Japanese rice imports and,
    102–3; land tax and, 102; "starva-
    tion" exports, 105; tenancy and,
    103–4
ajinomoto (MSG), 87. *See also* domestic
    science
ajŏn (local civil functionaries), 211n7
Akiba Takashi, 170
Albertson, Millie M., 52
Allen, Horace N., 45–47
ancestor veneration: Confucianism and,
    12, 32; criticism of, 85; missionary
    views of, 47
anch'ae (inner quarters), 22
An Ch'ang-nam, 194
An Ki-yŏng, 83

An Myŏng-gǔn, 62. See also *paegoin*
    sakkŏn
An Yŏng-sŏn, 11
Appenzeller, Alice, 203
Appenzeller, Henry G., 45
Arishima Takeo, 2
asa tongmaeng (death by starvation
    strike), 149. *See also* labor; *yŏgong*

Bae, Hyŏng-sik, 2
Baltimore Women's Medical College,
    252n32
Bank of Chōsen, 169
Bank of Japan, 233n30
Baron, Ava, 159
Bebel, August, 166, 248n116
bi (female slave), 26
Big Push, The, 8. See also *minjung*
biopolitics. See population
birth control: advertisement and, 165;
    biopolitics and, 189; contraceptives,
    91, 167–68; curing social ills with,
    92; decay of public morality and,
    91–92; education and, 189–90;
    eugenics and, 89–90, 187; liberat-
    ing women and, 91; Malthusian
    politics and, 190–91; moratorium

nobi (slave), 25–26
No In-hwa, 11

obstetrics. *See* gynecology
Oda Fumio, 156
oegŏ nobi (outside resident slaves), 25
Ogino Kyūsaku, periodic abstinence
   and, 89
Oju yŏnmun chang jŏnsan'go (Random
   expatiations of Oju), 34–35
ŏnmun. See han'gŭl
Ōno Tamotsu, 109, 237n64
Oppert, Ernest, 17–18
Oriental Development Company (Tōyō
   takushoku kabushiki kaisha), 169,
   233n33
Ōta Tenrei, intrauterine device and,
   89
Ōtake Hirokichi, 226n101
Ōyama Chōyō, 129

Paehwa haktang, 59
paegoin sakkŏn, 62
paekchŏng (outcasts), 19
Paik, George L., 47
Pak, Ch'an-hŭi, 84
Pak Che-ga, 34
Pak Chi-wŏn, 34
Pak Esther, 252n32
Pak Ho-jin, 92, 176, 245n60
Pak Hwa-sŏng, 109, 138–39, 151
Pak, Jihang, 88
Pak Kyŏng-wŏn, 193–95, 198
Pak Sa-jik, 71
Pak, Sun-ha, 168
Pak Wŏn-hŭi, 154
Pak Yŏng-hŭi, 231n2
Pak Yong-ok, 7
Pal Pong-sanin, 187–88
pan ch'in-yŏng (bridegroom going to
   bride's home for marriage cere-
   mony), 22
Pang In-kŭn, 83
Pang Sŭng-bin, 77

Park Chung-hee, economic development and, 7
patriarchy, Chosŏn dynasty and, 16,
   19–20
Peace Preservation Law of 1925,
   246n86
pharmaceutical products: marketing
   of, 166–67
Pinghŏgak Yi, 35
Pogu yŏgwan (women's clinic), 45–46
Pokŏn undongsa (Sanitation Movement
   Society), 89
pŏlgŭm chedo (penalty-fine system), 122–
   23, 124
pongsahon (service to the bride's family
   as hired hands), 24
Poovey, Mary, 86, 161, 183, 185
population: biopower and, 5, 189;
   health and, 14; national strength
   and, 89; number of rural schools
   and, 67. *See also* birth control;
   governmentality
poststructuralism, gender analysis
   and, 10
ppalgan ch'aek (red books): as frivolous
   entertainment, 165–66
primogeniture, 20, 23
production: modern transformation
   of, 101; women as laborers, 110–16
proletariat: class difference and, 153;
   women and, 154, 168–69. *See also*
   socialism
proletarian literature, 137. *See also*
   KAPF; Kang Kyŏng-ae; Yu Chin-ho
pronatalist movement, 177–78; new
   roles for expectant fathers and, 180.
   See also childbirth
prostitution: debt and, 106; licensed,
   236n60; number of, 106–7, 236n59,
   unlicensed, 186–87. *See also* red-
   light district
public transcripts, 69, 222n49
puch'ae (debts), 105. *See also* agricultural
   crisis

Text: 10/15 Janson

Display: Janson

Compositor: Integrated Composition Systems

Printer and binder: Maple-Vail Manufacturing Group

Made in the USA
San Bernardino, CA
10 August 2020